Let My HANDMAID Speak

A History of Women in Ministry in the International Pentecostal Holiness Church from 1901–2011

Jeraldine T. Posey, D.Min.

WestBow
PRESS
A DIVISION OF THOMAS NELSON

Copyright © 2011 Jeraldine T. Posey, D.Min.

All rights reserved. No part of this book may be used or reproduced by any means, graphic, electronic, or mechanical, including photocopying, recording, taping or by any information storage retrieval system without the written permission of the publisher except in the case of brief quotations embodied in critical articles and reviews.

Good News Translation® (Today's English Version, Second Edition)
Copyright © 1992 American Bible Society. All rights reserved.

Scripture taken from the Holy Bible, New International Version®. Copyright © 1973, 1978, 1984, 2010 Biblica. Used by permission of Zondervan. All rights reserved.

Scripture taken from the King James Version of the Bible.

WestBow Press books may be ordered through booksellers or by contacting:

WestBow Press
A Division of Thomas Nelson
1663 Liberty Drive
Bloomington, IN 47403
www.westbowpress.com
1-(866) 928-1240

Because of the dynamic nature of the Internet, any web addresses or links contained in this book may have changed since publication and may no longer be valid. The views expressed in this work are solely those of the author and do not necessarily reflect the views of the publisher, and the publisher hereby disclaims any responsibility for them.

Any people depicted in stock imagery provided by Thinkstock are models, and such images are being used for illustrative purposes only.

Certain stock imagery © Thinkstock.

ISBN: 978-1-4497-2062-9 (sc)
ISBN: 978-1-4497-2063-6 (e)

Library of Congress Control Number: 2011933362

Printed in the United States of America

WestBow Press rev. date: 10/12/2011

DEDICATION

To the many "torch bearers" (lady ministers)
of the Truth for living by the principles
of the Word and preaching the same.
You have made a difference.

You heard the call of God to go forth into the world.
The path was not always a pleasant one in which to walk,
But you persevered in your service.
You stayed in the Truth of the Word;
You kept the faith in all things.
To be a woman at times seemed like a curse;
However, the Holy Spirit spoke through you
And made you something of worth.
Souls were blessed and added to the kingdom,
And your influence lives on today.
As handmaids of the Lord, you continue to speak.

Contents

Foreword vii

Preface viii

Introduction ix

Chapter 1   Women in Society 1

Chapter 2   She Works Vigorously 5

Chapter 3   Revive Us Again 42

Chapter 4   Her Works Bring Her Praise 60

Chapter 5   With His Stripes 67

Chapter 6   Bits and Pieces 75

Chapter 7   Deborah's Daughters 107

Chapter 8   Life Sketches 124

Chapter 9   In Memory of Her 176

Chapter 10 Write it Before Them 221

Chapter 11 God Has Spoken 346

Bibliography 350

Periodicals 352

Acknowledgement 359

About the Author 361

Foreword

The first woman to ever live provides a life story that depicts the impact of women across human history who have proclaimed to their world a Savior who would redeem all who would be redeemed. Eve, though a part of the tragedy, became the person whose seed would restore all that had been lost to mankind and the entire Universe. She became the instrument in God's hands that produced hope in the midst of chaos. You would think that she, who participated in the fall, would be the most undeserving person to have a part in providing good news to a human race whom, otherwise, had no good news to hear. God chose her who, through pain and heartache, produced the seed that would be the Savior of the world. What a story of grace to the broken!

This message of grace to those who are broken has flowed through womanhood in many ways throughout history. In my own life, I first heard the gospel story as a child through my godly mother and grandmothers. I heard it through lady evangelists that came through our community of churches. I was converted at age 15 in my mother's arms. I was sanctified and filled with the Holy Spirit while devout women prayed with me. As a teenage preacher, I was invited to minister by lady pastors such as Lynnette Mosley and Eva Belle Brown. I could go on with my personal journey of how lady evangelists, pastors, teachers, and missionaries have influenced my life.

This book, long overdue, penned by Sister Jeri Posey, is a tribute to the women of ministry in the International Pentecostal Holiness Church. I count it an honor to salute these heroines of faith.

We have 122 lady ministers in the North Carolina Conference whom we designate as "Deborah's Daughters." They are evangelists, teachers, pastors, pastors' wives who team with their husbands in ministry, and conference directors of ministries. They serve on conference level councils. They are working gallantly, honorably, and with great effectiveness. We salute all of them, and Dr. Posey who is reminding us of their great place in the work of the kingdom in the past and in the present, and who will continue to be great in their labors for our coming King. Thank you ladies of the cloth, and thank God for you.

Bishop Jim Whitfield
North Carolina Conference
International Pentecostal Holiness Church

Preface

Several conferences are not represented in this book, not through an oversight, but because they did not respond to the request to send the names and addresses of their women ministers. The same is true for many of the ladies who did not return the survey form asking for information about their ministry, so I have only their names to use. I regret this, as I wanted a large representation of the women so our denomination today would have a more complete record of what these dear ones have accomplished in the ministry, while caring for a family, getting an education, working full- or part-time, teaching Sunday school, singing in the choir, and engaging in a host of other activities yet being faithful in the proclamation of the Word of God.

Many of the lady ministers of the Pentecostal Holiness Church are unsung heroines because often they have not received the encouragement or recognition due them simply because they are a woman. Still they have continued to work alongside their husband as his assistant in the pastorate. Few of them have had the privilege to pastor a church on their own.

Others have worked in the field of evangelism, traveling to places far and near to share the gospel. One of my earliest memories as a teenager, recently converted, is of several lady evangelistic teams coming to our church in Hopewell, Virginia to hold revivals. I also can think of several other women who brought truth, enthusiasm, and fire with their preaching. The International Pentecostal Holiness Church (IPHC) owes each of them a great debt of gratitude.

Much of the information in this book is given in the words of the person who wrote the sermon or article. This was done so the reader could experience through them what they were feeling. Letting them speak in their own words was my way of introducing them to the reader. Their words live on.

(**Authors note:** Chalk all mistakes up to human error.)

Introduction

The purpose of this book is not intended to stir up strife or to dispute scriptural issues some may hold dear about the propriety of allowing women to preach. The debate on this point has existed all too long. Countless books have been written on the subject addressing both sides of the matter. Good folk have expressed their opinions (we all have one), but the argument has not, and probably will not, ever be resolved to the satisfaction of all concerned.

Despite the dissension, history shows us that many faithful, godly women have heard and answered the call of God to proclaim the truth of His Word. The International Pentecostal Holiness Church has recognized and accepted these precious ladies into the pulpits of its churches as pastors and evangelists, but some denominations and individuals have denied women of their true status as ministers of the gospel.

Quoting Harold Paul on this subject, in his book *From Printer's Devil to Bishop*, "In the Pentecostal Holiness Church, women are not only recognized as members but also admitted to the pulpit, and occasionally pastor churches. They have been elected to positions of official capacity on conference official boards. This is usually the exception to the rule and practiced only because of the lack of suitable men to fill the position. Some women have been outstanding in pulpit ability, and have been often acclaimed as evangelists rather than charged with administrative and judicial responsibilities." This statement speaks volumes about how lady ministers fared during the early part of the twentieth century.

We have but to look at the Bible to readily acknowledge that God has used women successfully to prophesy (foretell) and preach (tell forth). In the Old Testament we read of women like Miriam (Exodus 15:20), Deborah (Judges 4:4), Huldah (2 Kings 22:14), and Isaiah's wife (Isaiah 8:3) each of whom is referred to as a prophetess. Of course, we know this to be a female prophet: one blessed and called by God to expound His truth. Since the word *prophet* refers to a person who spoke for God and who communicated God's message without fear to the nation of Israel, God's chosen people, then *prophetess* certainly must apply to women who served in the same office doing similar work. We acccpt the fact that men like

Isaiah, Nahum, Habakkuk, Malachi and the host of others who ministered in Old Testament times were servants of God with a special calling. So, also, we accept the women.

Likewise, in the New Testament, we read about Anna (Luke 2:36-38) and Philip's four daughters (Acts 21: 8-9) who prophesied. Then we see the women associated with the Apostle Paul and what he had to say about them. In Romans 16, we have record of a number of women servants of the Lord in various churches: Phoebe (v. 1-2), Priscilla (vv. 3-4), Tryphena, Tryphosa, Mary, Junia, and Persis (vv. 6-15) are mentioned as laborers in the Lord. Euodias and Syntyche are referred to in Philippians 4:2 as being leaders of the church at Philippi. According to 1 Corinthians 11:4-5, women prophesied and prayed in church.

Priscilla, the wife of Aquila, first mentioned in Acts 18:2 merits a closer look. When Paul first arrived in Corinth, he met this wonderful couple. After about eighteen months there, Paul, Priscilla, and Aquila went to Ephesus. Later, a man by the name of Apollos, described in Acts 18:24 as *"an eloquent man and mighty in the Scriptures,"* came to Ephesus. He was speaking boldly in the synagogue, but it appears from the story recorded in Acts 18:24-26 that his theology was not complete. He knew only about the baptism of John. When the couple heard him speak, they took him aside and explained God's way to him more accurately. Here, we find Priscilla as a teacher. She was one who had been so well taught of God that she could instruct a man spiritually. In Romans 16:3, Paul called Priscilla and Aquila his *"fellow workers."* By using this term, the Apostle considered this couple official evangelists and teachers.

From early in the first century, women were active as representatives in the cause of Christ. The New Testament tells us of women who were involved in evangelism, hosting churches in their homes, prophesying and speaking in tongues, and serving as deaconesses. Church history confirms that the prominence of women in ministry continued into succeeding generations.

The Bible translator Jerome arrived in Rome in A. D. 392 to attend a church council and stayed in the home of a woman named Marcella. She persuaded him to hold Bible classes for some of Rome's most distinguished women. He, in turn, convinced the women that they should study Hebrew so they could read the Old Testament in the original language. Much came from this Bible study. Marcella's home became a center for prayer, study, and Christian charity; she established the first convent for women on the outskirts of the city of Rome; and other women were inspired to dedicate their lives to helping Jerome with his Bible translation.

In 410 A.D., when Rome was invaded by the Goths, Marcella was eighty-five years old. The Goths beat her with whips but finally let her go to the Bascilica of St. Paul, which was used as a refuge for the poor, where she died a few days later. Thus, she became one of a great cloud of witnesses who knew Jesus as her Lord and Savior and made the supreme sacrifice of her life in service for Him.[1] What dedication!

Historically, we know that women founded or reformed the orders that kept Christianity alive through the Middle Ages. During that period of time, women found the outlets for service they needed in the church. The greatest opportunities for women to minister came with the Wesleyan revival in England in the eighteenth century. Unlike the Reformation, which affected women in a negative way, the revivals in England and the Great Awakening in America brought a positive change in people's attitude about women preaching. John Wesley appointed women as local preachers and itinerant ministers. However, time after time, ground that had been gained was lost, and the same battles had to be fought over again with each new generation.[2]

During the early years of the nineteenth century, Charles Finney encouraged women to pray and testify in public. History tells that he had to fight for the privilege of conducting meetings that included both men and women and for letting women speak. Because of this man, the door remained open for women to use their gifts in some of the churches that were touched by the revivals of that era.[3]

Elizabeth Ford Atkinson, Charles Finney's second wife, held meetings that were so well attended that the ladies filled the room where she spoke and then stood about the door on the outside, as far as they could hear. In December of 1858, the Finneys went to England where Elizabeth had spoken ten years earlier, and once again large crowds attended all her meetings.[4]

Amanda Smith, a black woman who was born a slave, was used of God to break down prejudice on three levels: against blacks, against the doctrine of holiness, and against female evangelists. The holiness denominations that grew out of the revivals of her time (1868) continued to give women opportunities to preach. Many women quoted Joel's prophecy (2:28), "And it shall come to pass afterward, that I will pour out my spirit on all flesh; and your sons and your daughters shall prophesy," as the basis for women proclaiming God's Word.[5]

Since this work is not intended to be a rehashing of church history, suffice it to say that through the years, as noted, the issue has been debated, women have gained ground only to lose it again, and, even in our twenty-first century society, some still refuse to let God's handmaids speak. Why has the modern church neglected its responsibility to allow women, as well as men, to fulfill the Great Commission? As Kari Malcolm wrote in *Women at the Crossroads*, "The call to enter the kingdom through Jesus, the Way, needs to be proclaimed by both men and women. We have a world to win for Jesus Christ. The ship is sinking, and we are standing on the shore arguing about who should go to the rescue – men or women."[6]

(**Author's note:** The following will give us a glimpse at what some other folk have had to say about women preachers.)

"Women Preaching"
by
Rev. R. B. Hayes

"Women preaching seems to be the talk of today, so let's see what the Bible has to say about them preaching, or prophesying. These two words are synonymous.

"We notice back in Exodus 15:20, *'And Miriam the prophetess, the sister of Aaron, took a timbrel in her hand, and all the women went out after her with timbrels and with dances.'* In Judges 4:4-5 we read, *'And Deborah, a prophetess, the wife of Lapidoth, she judged Israel at that time. And she dwelt under the palm tree of Deborah, between Ramah and Bethel in Mount Ephraim, and the children of Israel came up to her for judgment.'* Then in Psalm 68:11-13, *'The Lord gave the word: great was the company of those (women) that published it. Kings of armies did flee apace: and she that tarried at home divided the spoil. Though ye have lain among the pots, yet shall ye be as the wings of a dove covered with silver, and her feathers with yellow gold.'* Again in Joel 2:28-30, *'And it shall come to pass afterwards that I will pour out My Spirit upon all flesh; and your sons and your daughters shall prophesy; your old men shall dream dreams, your young men shall see visions. And also upon the servants and upon the handmaids in those days will I pour out My Spirit.'*

"We come now to the New Testament. Luke 2:36-38 states: *'And there was one Anna, a prophetess, the daughter of Phanuel, of the tribe of*

Aser; she was of a great age, and had lived with an husband seven years from her virginity. And she was a widow of about fourscore and four years; which departed not from the temple, but served God with fastings and prayers night and day. And she coming in that instant gave thanks likewise unto the Lord, and spake of Him to all them that looked for redemption in Jerusalem."

"Again, in Luke 24:10, 11, and John 20:17, 18, where a woman preached the first sermon after Jesus rose from the dead. In Acts 2:16-19 we see where Peter on the Day of Pentecost quoted Joel 2:28-30. In Acts 21:8, 9 we read these words: *'And the next day we that were of Paul's company departed and came unto Cesarea, and we entered into the house of Philip the evangelist, and abode with him: and the same man had four daughters, virgins, which did prophesy.'* Also in Romans 16, we find twelve women preachers and workers in this chapter, and the first one Paul commends is *'Phebe our sister, which is a servant of the church which is in Cenchrea, and that ye receive her in the Lord as becometh saints, and that ye assist her in whatsoever business she hath need of you. For she hath been a succorer of many, and of myself also.'* And we see a servant in the church is a pastor of a church.

"We learn by all the above Scriptures that there have been women preachers throughout Bible history, and we notice in every holiness movement that women preachers were in the crowd. We are living in the Holy Ghost dispensation, when Joel said God's Spirit would fall upon all flesh, and your sons and daughters shall preach, or prophesy, which means to preach; and then when the Spirit fell on the day of Pentecost, Peter said, *'But this is that which was spoken of by the prophet Joel, And it shall come to pass in the last days, said God, I will pour out of My Spirit upon all flesh, and your sons and your daughters shall prophesy [or preach], and your young men shall see visions and your old men shall dream dreams.'* He did not stop there, but he says, *'And on My Servants and on My handmaidens will I pour out in those days of My Spirit, and they shall prophesy [or preach].'* Thank God, it takes in the colored women too.

"Then we notice when Jesus preached to the woman at the well, when she got saved she left her water pot and went into the city, and many of the Samaritans of that city believed on Him for the saying of the woman which testified, *'He told me all that ever I did'* (John 4:39). So we see the Bible is full all along with women preachers and helpers and workers for God. We notice in every great holiness movement when the saints are red hot for God and the burden of the lost is upon them, they lose sight of churchanity, sectarianism, the world, and the only burden of their hearts is to get souls saved and sanctified and filled with the Holy Ghost.

"There always were women preachers and helpers on hand then, but when we get our eyes on churches, creeds, and slack up, we elbow the women preachers off. Why do we do this? Because we cooled down. Women have been on the scene in every great movement for God. She was last at the cross and first at the sepulcher, preached the first resurrection sermon, for preaching is glad tidings, and that was what the woman told after Jesus had risen from the dead. Let her preach! God says they shall. Glory to our God and the Lamb forever. She has lain among the pots long enough. As a Pentecostal church let's turn her loose and give her the freedom and liberty that God gives her. Your brother in Jesus, saved, sanctified, baptized with the Holy Ghost, looking for Jesus to come and take us home, body healed, glory, glory, glory!"[7]

In his book *Questions and Answers on the Scriptures and Related Subjects*, Dr. Paul F. Beacham, President of Holmes Bible College, addresses this issue with his answers to three questions.

#460. Should a woman preach? Yes, if God calls a woman to preach she should do so just the same as anyone else. I think that the following Scriptures quite well show this: Acts 2:17, 18; 21:9; I Corinthians 11:5."

#461. What did Paul mean by, "Let your women keep silence in the church"? From the connection in which the statement in question appears, it seems that some of the women were asking for explanations of certain things which were said in the public services, and caused unnecessary interruption. Paul further shows that they could wait and ask about these things at home.

#462. Where does the Bible give authority for ordaining women as preachers? The prophecy that "Your daughters shall prophesy," might be understood to give authority to recognize them as preachers. If women are called and anointed by the Spirit to preach, there could not be any objection to their having the proper recognition of the Church in doing the work. However, a distinction may be recognized in speaking under the inspiration of the Spirit, and preaching as an ordained minister of the Gospel. Women had a large and important place in the work and ministry of the early church, but it can hardly be shown from the Scriptures that they were ordained as preachers, even though they must have served as deaconesses (Rom. 16:1; I Tim. 3:11). The reference in Timothy means literally, "Even so women in like manner must be grave, not slanderers, sober, faithful in all things." That is, a woman who is to be recognized as a deaconess must have this qualification.[8]

Lois Tripp wrote an article for *The Helping Hand*, January/February 1988 issue titled **"WOMEN** – Liberated to Minister" in which she states, "Women today are enjoying a liberty like no other time in history to proclaim the Word and to be leaders in their communities." She goes on to say that women are recognizing their gifts and area of ministry and are responding to God's call on their lives. She thinks that perhaps the right-to-vote, offered to women in 1920, laid the foundation for the acceptance of women's ordination.

"The Pentecostal Holiness Church," she writes, "has given women a prominent place within its ranks. Women here have been a vital part of our growth, from the home to the community to the church and even to the pulpit. Denominationally, we rank high in giving women an opportunity for ordination and ministry."

Lois believes that while many denominations are struggling with the place of women in the ministry, "charismatic and Pentecostal congregations are increasingly welcoming their ministry with open arms. Women are being sought out to teach Bible studies, minister healing and deliverance, and share from the Scriptures to the entire congregation, as well as to women's groups. Pastors are recognizing women's innate sensitivities and are encouraging them to express what they are sensing in the Spirit."

She concludes by saying, "As Christian women today, let us seek to achieve our highest potential under God and express it in ministry to people. We are marching, and will continue to march, across the close of this century proclaiming the good news of the Word through fulfilling the calls of ministry on our lives to people of all walks of life in the church, community, home, and the world."[9]

Some women, according to Shirley Spengler Rohde in an article she wrote for *Woman's Touch*, September/October 1987 and reprinted in *The Helping Hand*, January/February 1988, feel that freedom came to them in the feminist movement. What we need to keep in mind as we consider what all this means for women in ministry is that we are beginning to understand something that has been in effect for many centuries. Jesus was the liberating force for women, rather than the "liberation movement."

For centuries women have exerted efforts to initiate some sort of a feminist crusade. The first wave, which was about suffrage or the right to vote, began in the eighteenth century and continued until the twentieth century. The second stage of this movement began in the early 1960s and continued through the late 1980s. What triggered this second emphasis was a book written by Betty Friedan and published in 1963, *The Feminine Mystique*. This book was the beginning of the modern era's "women's lib" which sought to give women an equal standing with men in most every way.[10]

Again, what we have failed to see is that Jesus set women free and honored them during His ministry. He picked them for many responsibilities that elevated their status and placed them in key positions, which have already been discussed earlier in the Introduction.

An article titled "Some Leaders Are Born Women" that appeared in the *Issachar File*, March 1999, Dean Ridings, communications manager for Christian Camping International/USA, wrote about an event that occurred in the life of Susie Stanley, when a friend shared about her upcoming wedding. Susie, who was in seminary at the time, thought it would be a joy to perform the ceremony. However, Susie's friend asked if she could recommend a male pastor to conduct the wedding because she and her fiancé did not believe in women preachers. Stanley was quite shaken by the comment.

Because of this, Susie's passion has been to help women thrive in leadership positions. She has been able to do that as a professor of historical theology at Messiah College in Grantham, Pennsylvania, and through Wesleyan/Holiness Women Clergy International of which she is founder and executive director.

Mr. Ridings continues, "Certainly men and women do have their differences. However, when it comes to leadership, women leaders emphasize that they have more in common with their male counterparts than some might think."

He uses information from five women in his remaining comments to demonstrate how God uses women in leadership and offers practical ways that Christian leaders can encourage them to follow God's leading.

Ridings quotes Christina Accornero, director of advancement and recruitment at Indiana's Anderson University School of Theology, as saying "I don't think I bring anything special [to the ministry] because I'm a woman. I have unique personality traits and God-given gifts and talents." Apparently, she meant using those gifts and talents in ministry.

ReeAnne Hyde, associate pastor for community life at Bresee Church of the Nazarene in Pasadena, California states, "I know what it feels like to be overlooked, resented, and condescended, so I work hard at inclusion."

In answer to Ridings' question "How can pastors encourage women in their congregations to consider leadership opportunities and respond to a call of leadership?" Hyde responds, "When a woman is drawn to leadership, help her see there are many ways God elects for women to demonstrate His kingdom purposes. Don't limit them."

Sherry Conway, senior pastor of Okemos Church of the Nazarene in Okemos, Michigan, says, "Pastors and church leaders should encourage women they sense are called to preach."

Lucia Delamarter, senior pastor of Everett Free Methodist Church in Everett, Washington, responds this way: "Pastors shouldn't be afraid of the challenge. If a gifted woman is part of your congregation, bring her into ministry. Releasing her to do what the Holy Spirit has gifted her for will release your church to receive what the Spirit has for it."

Lastly, Ridings cites Accornero's response: "We must get away from this gender thing and find the best, most equipped, most talented leaders who are called by God to move our churches into the next century."[11]

Lest these responses appear too one-sided, because they are all from a female point of view, Bishop Leggett wrote an article in the same issue of *Issachar File*, titled "Affirming Women in Ministry." He stated, "In highlighting women in ministry, Paul challenges the church to recognize the vital part women have in the work of the kingdom. He is full of praise for their diligent labors. Women did 'great work for the Lord' in the first century. They held leading roles in shaping the church. The history of the church cannot be written without their names.

"Though the Pentecostal Holiness Church has always encouraged women in ministry, the numbers of women in ministry today do not reflect this. The church must be more open to women in every phase of leadership. Women helped launch the church in the first century. Their ministry is crucial to an effective church in the 21st century."[12]

Apparently, the admission of neglect in properly recognizing women in ministry led to the confession stated in the "Sin of Male Domination" at the Solemn Assembly held in Fayetteville, North Carolina, August 23-24, 1996: "Gender differences are never to become a platform for discrimination and division, but rather are attributes to enhance and complete Christ's body. We recognize the sin of male domination and acknowledge that we have withheld from women places of honor in the church. We have not affirmed the ministries of qualified women by releasing them to serve in places of leadership." The prayer of repentance states, "Create in us a new sensitivity to the God-given gifts of the women of the International

Pentecostal Holiness Church, that there may be unity and greater power in our worldwide ministry."

The affirmation in part reads, "We affirm that we are equal partners in the work of Your kingdom and commit ourselves to recognize Your gifts in all members of the body of Christ without regard to gender. We acknowledge that You have called women to definite ministries and gifted some for leadership roles in Your Church. We affirm them in their spiritual gifts and callings and will compensate them accordingly."

(**Author's note:** This material from the Solemn Assembly has no copyright.)

Thank God, this is a giant step forward in recognizing those godly women who have struggled for so many years in the background. Hopefully, the spirit of this confession will be fully accepted and implemented throughout the denomination.

---

[1] Kari Malcolm, *Women at the Crossroads*, pp. 97-99.
[2] Malcolm., pp. 111, 113.
[3] Malcolm, p. 121.
[4] Malcolm, p. 123.
[5] Malcolm, pp. 124-25.
[6] Malcolm, p. 132.
[7] Rev. R. B. Hayes, "Women Preaching," *The Advocate*, July 11, 1918. (The official organ of the IPHC had several different names through the years, but *The Advocate* is used throughout this book for consistency.)
[8] Paul F. Beacham, D.D., *Questions and Answers On the Scriptures and Related Subjects*, pp. 527-28.
[9] Lois Tripp, "**WOMEN** – Liberated to Minister," *The Helping Hand*, January/February 1988, p. 3.
[10] Shirley Spengler Rohde, *Woman's Touch,* reprinted in *The Helping Hand*, January/February 1988, pp.6-7.
[11] Dean Ridings, "Some Leaders Are Born Women," *Issachar File*, March 1999, pp. 1, 3-4.
[12] Bishop James Leggett, "Affirming Women in Ministry." *Issachar File*, March 1999, p. 2.

CHAPTER 1

Women in Society

Women have been an integral part of society since the dawn of creation. True, the Triune Godhead purposed to make man to inhabit the creation They had spoken into existence, so God said: *"Let Us make man in Our image, according to Our likeness . . ."* (Genesis 1:26-NKJV). The Genesis story later informs us *"And the Lord God formed man of the dust of the ground, and breathed into his nostrils the breath of life; and man became a living being. The Lord God planted a garden eastward in Eden and there He put the man whom He had formed"* (Genesis 2:7, 8-NKJV). However, we soon learn that *"the Lord God said, 'It is not good that man should be alone; I will make him a helper comparable to him'"* (Genesis 2:18-NKJV).

God formed every beast of the field and every bird of the air and gave them to Adam for him to name. The Bible tells us that Adam did indeed give names to the cattle, the birds, and the beasts, but no helper comparable to him was found (Genesis 2:19, 20). So God caused a deep sleep to come upon Adam, and He took one of Adam's ribs, and closed up the flesh. From that rib the Lord of all creation made a woman and presented her to Adam (Genesis 2:21-22).

Since that time, women have worn many hats. They have been wives, mothers, sisters, friends, doctors, nurses, educators, astronauts, pilots, truck drivers, police officers, military personnel, and the list can go on and on ad infinitum. Volumes have been written about their accomplishments in the field of literature, science, medicine, and engineering, among others. However, very little has been published to sing their praises as ministers of the gospel throughout the countries of the world.

This book, then, is an effort to put into words some of the accomplishments of the women ministers of the International Pentecostal Holiness Church and record for posterity that these ladies have served their God, their denomination, their families, their churches, and their communities as bright, shining lights of the Truth of our wonderful Lord.

They preached in tents, brush arbors, cottage prayer meetings, banquet halls, auditoriums, and churches. They served as evangelists and pastors leaving a mark on untold thousands who, in turn, have also become ministers, missionaries, Sunday school teachers, youth workers, and Women's Ministries leaders; they have carried the gospel to the ends of the earth. This movement has been something that the devil has not been able to stop. Along with their male counterparts, they have faced adversity and hardship, sometimes with very little financial support, but they have refused to give in or give up. Their voices still speak to us, although some have been silenced by death. Their words of wisdom and spiritual insight sound a clarion call for us today to run this race with patience and be faithful to the end.

Lord, let your handmaids continue to speak!

(Author's note: Agnes Robinson wrote an article that was printed in *The Helping Hand* for May/June 1986 about the influence women can have. Mrs. Robinson was a minister and a minister's wife, who knew first hand about the many roles a woman plays. The following is a reprint of that article.)

"Women Can Make a Difference In their Worlds"

"Throughout the pages of God's Word, there are great women whose lives shine with a radiance undimmed by the passing centuries. They are individuals whose characters were untarnished by the wickedness and moral decay of their own generation.

"Some are outstanding because of their faith, others their courage; still others are known for their unselfishness, their willingness to sacrifice.

"In Rebekah, it was her faith as she made her decision to leave her home and family and make that long trek across the burning desert wastes to become the bride of a man she had never seen. Through this act of faith, she became the mother of Jacob, who was in the lineage of faith.

"In Jochebed, the mother of Moses, we see an outstanding example of resourcefulness as she dared to defy the laws of Pharaoh. Fashioning a little ark of bulrushes, making it waterproof so that her little boy would be safe, she placed the ark in the flags by the river's bank and set her little girl, Miriam, to watch over it.

"Her faith was rewarded, for soon she had her son returned to her and she could care for him in her own home and teach him the ways of God. How well she must have done her job, for when he was of age, he became the mighty emancipator of his people, the great lawgiver – all because a little woman dared to do the impossible.

"Deborah is outstanding because of her courage. At a time when all Israel was oppressed by the Canaanites, she obeyed God's instructions to go out against the mighty hosts of Sisera in battle. The battle won, Deborah tuned her harp and sang a song of victory, won by faith and obedience to God's command.

"We all look with admiration upon Ruth, the little Moabitish widow, who so willingly left her home and kin to go with her mother-in-law into the land unknown to her. She gladly assumed the support of Naomi and labored unselfishly in the fields to supply their needs. The purity of her devotion and her eager acceptance of her mother-in-law's God led her to become the bride of the wealthy Boaz, and ultimately the grandmother of King David, through whose lineage Jesus Christ was born on earth.

"On and on we could go – from Genesis to Revelation – naming one after another: Miriam, Abigail, Esther, Hannah, the Shulamite woman, the widow of Zarephath, Anna, Mary, the mother of Jesus; Elisabeth, Mary and Martha, Lydia, Priscilla, Eunice, Lois, and countless other women whom Paul called 'helpers in the Gospel.' They were women who excelled, women who served, women who were faithful, women who were courageous, women who dared to do what was right when all was against them.

"How it thrills our hearts to read of their courage and faithfulness. It inspires us to strive to reach greater heights of achievement, to go to deeper depths with God and to widen our paths of service.

"Radical changes are taking place in our world today in every area of life; changes that stagger the minds of even the experts. Materialism, humanism, and the desire for instant gratification have undermined basic views and morals of [today's] generation.

"The inroads made upon the youth of our land by the drug cultures [are] surpassed only by the merciless effects of alcohol to which many are turning. With more than nine million know alcoholics in the United States, the average age of alcoholics has now dropped to include Junior Hi's and even grade school children.

"Illicit sex, illegitimate births, abortions, homosexuality, pornography are all being more readily accepted in today's society. The crime rate continues to spiral with thefts, rapes, kidnappings, murder, terrorism, mass murders, and senseless bombings by activists.

"We could go on painting a dark picture and hopeless picture of the multitude of problems that hover like a black cloud over all mankind. But we who know Christ know the solution. We know He is the answer to every problem of life, and that He came that man 'might have life and have it more abundantly.'

"How can we as Christian women relate to today's problems? Should we be concerned with the physical needs as well as spiritual needs of the world? Do we have a responsibility to help alleviate the pain of the lonely, the sick, those in hopeless poverty, those who have found the burdens of life too hard to bear? What is our responsibility to our youth who have lost direction in life? What is our civic duty as a Christian to help right the wrongs in our world?

"Sometimes in our church circles and in Christian homes we tend to live in a little secluded world of our own where many of these tragic problems are not evident. But we must wake to the needs around us as well as the problems of our nation and our world. Awareness of this world's needs also means awareness of the world's pain, starvation, poverty, hopelessness, and ignorance. To visit in some nations, and even in some of our major cities, is to see the terror, the hunger, the animal existence so many people experience.

"Awareness also means insight into the meaningless lives of many of today's people. With all of our progress, prosperity, and advanced technology, people still have a thirst for meaning in life. This is the frontier of greatest demand for every woman to become involved in witnessing to this world. The other part of involvement is to have a compassion for others – to truly care. You will find yourself searching for those you can lift. You will reach out with your heart to others, yearning to lend a helping hand, longing to ease their burden, praying that you might bring them to know Christ as the solution for their need.

"We listen to today's newscast with dismay and wonder what the future holds for our world. But you and I know the remedy for much of the heartache and suffering – we know our wonderful, compassionate [Savior].

Will we remain aloof, or will we become involved in sharing our Christ with others?"[1]

Some of the things that jump out in this article are words like *service, faith, resourcefulness, courage, obedience, unselfishness, purity*, and *devotion*. These are the characteristics of the lady ministers who have stepped to the front to make our world a better place in which to live. Mrs. Robinson also poses a number of questions. These questions have been a part of the challenge to countless women who have responded to the call of God to help change our society. They truly have made a difference.

May God bless the memory of those who have gone on to their heavenly reward and bless the efforts of those who continue to carry the torch of Truth.

---

[1] Agnes Robinson, *The Helping Hand*, May/June 1986, pp. 4-5.

CHAPTER 2

She Works Vigorously

"She sets about her work vigorously; her arms are strong for her tasks" – Proverbs 31:17-NIV.

Reading through the information that follows, you will see that these ladies are involved in ministries that are as varied and as beautiful as the colors in a kaleidoscope. They are creative, energetic, bright, enthusiastic, educated, and imminently equipped by God for the work to which He has called them. They are dedicated, consecrated, willing, and wanting to step up to be used in any way possible to reach the churched and unchurched. They are daughters, sisters, wives, mothers, grandmothers, and friends. Some of them pastor churches; others are evangelists; a few are involved in music ministry and working with youth. Several of them are involved in prison ministry, trying to salvage what is left of wasted lives. Others stand ready to fill a pulpit, teach a Sunday school class, work with the Women's Ministries locally, or do whatever else is needed. Often, they do not get the chance; they are not asked.

They give credit to others who have been their mentors, male and female. They express appreciation to parents who walked before them and set a good example. They are grateful for the formal education they were able to acquire at bachelor's, master's, and doctorate levels. Some have only elementary education, but that is no reflection on their character or ability. "God isn't looking for ability; He is looking for availability." What these women have accomplished is nothing short of a miracle.

Most of them have reared children, run households, served in many capacities in their local churches and conferences, worked full- or part-time, run their own businesses, and founded Christian organizations to further the cause of Christ. Paraphrasing Hebrews 11:32, 33, *"And what more shall I say? I do not have time to tell about Martha, Betty, Louise, Lois, Krista, Thelma, Janice, Kathy, Ruth, and hundreds of others, who through faith conquered kingdoms, administered justice, and gained what was promised."* In the pages that follow, they will speak for themselves.[1]

KRISTA ABBOTT
Sonshine Network (Florida) Ministries

She states she was called to ministry in 1993-94 while attending Southeastern University in Lakeland, Florida. After many significant encounters with God, she accepted her destiny. However, it wasn't until 2000 that she officially began to pursue her calling by seeking minister's license and, subsequently, ordination in 2002. In her pursuit of her ministry, she had many opportunities to develop the gifts that God gave her through creative art and writing. Opportunities to preach, teach, and minister from the pulpit were limited because of the policies of the churches she attended.

Krista says that the biggest obstacle she has had to overcome in the ministry was the effect that a previous pastor's words had on her confidence as a minister. At the beginning of the process for obtaining license, she attended a small country church with about one hundred members. The pastor at the church was an encouragement for her to use her gifts to assist him with all facets of the ministry there, except pulpit-based ministry. "This, I believe was the result of his personal beliefs about women ministers and their 'place' in the church. As I was discussing with him my dreams of ministry, he said to me 'You will never have a pulpit ministry; you are called to just help churches.' Those words had a profound impact on me for several years," she reports. She did continue in the ministry, but her confidence was squashed.

Later, she found another church – larger and more contemporary – where she found additional opportunities to fulfill her calling. "While attending this new church," she writes, "I learned about word curses and how to break them. I broke the power of the words my previous pastor had spoken over me and life was once again breathed into my dreams and visions." This new city and new church provided the opportunities she needed to expand her ministry. She was able to teach adult based Sunday school classes – using curriculum she developed. Through this, she formed a friendship with the music minister and was recruited to be the primary writer of the holiday musical productions for the next four years. While at that church, she wrote and produced four full-length Christmas programs and also served the Senior Pastor as a ghostwriter and publishing consultant for four manuscripts.

Most recently, she has begun doing consultant work for an international ministry based in Texas and hopes to expand this area of ministry. She is a consultant in the area of publishing, musical productions, plays/drama, and product and web development.

She concludes with, "While, I received little support and encouragement from the 'men in ministry,' I have always had the support and encouragement of my Father in heaven. I am already seeing signs of a new vision and plan for the next level of my destiny."

Deborah Adams
Pennsylvania Conference

Deborah is a licensed minister. She has co-pastored with her husband who, she says, has always been her greatest encourager. They became involved with the IPHC when their church, River of Life, merged with Liberty Christian Church. The two churches became Life Spring Christian Church, where her husband is now the senior pastor.

(**Author's note:** A story about this merger was in the *IPHC Experience*, October 2004.)

Patricia Aman
North Carolina Conference

Rev. Aman was saved in 1959 and dedicated her life in service to God at the First Baptist Church in Dothan, Alabama. She states that she was baptized with the Holy Spirit in 1986 in a weekly community Bible study in Newton Grove, North Carolina.

The ministries in which she has been involved are varied. She has pastored several churches and is the founder of Coffee with Pat Internet Ministries; in 2009 she was involved in planting a new church in her conference.

Her activities go beyond the realm of church with her involvement with the 4-H Club. In 1980, she was presented an award by Governor Jim Hunt of North Carolina honoring her as Volunteer of the Year.

Hobbies include reading, arts and crafts, boating, and collecting Civil War era items. She is writing a book on spiritual warfare and a children's book called *The Turtle and the Giraffe*.

Karen Atkins
Appalachian (Virginia) Conference

Karen grew up in a Pentecostal Church of Christ in Kentucky as a fourth generation Pentecostal. At an early age, a love for God was instilled in her heart by her mother. When she was fifteen, the family moved to West Virginia and started attending a Pentecostal Holiness church, which she has attended since 1966, except when she was away at school.

In 2003, God began dealing with her about applying for minister's license. After a brief wrestling match, she conceded and began the process. Her original goal was to get a local church minister's license, but she found she couldn't stop there. At age fifty-seven, she was in the last year of the ordination process. She indicates, "My question has never been 'Why?' but I was curious about 'Why now?' One day God gave me answer enough with this verse – Philippians 3:12b: *'Not that I have already attained, or am already perfected; but I press on, that I may lay hold of that for which Christ Jesus has also laid hold of me.'*-NKJV. This is where I am."

Her pastor has been very supportive. In conclusion she states, "I FEEL like I am preparing for an upcoming need for prepared leadership as my home church grows, but I am open to whatever God desires. I don't have any specific ambitions of my own. If God never uses me in any capacity, I am thankful for the reading, studying, and depth of learning this program required of me."

Eilish Ayento
New Horizons (East Oklahoma) Conference

Eilish was ordained in July of 1994 in the old West Oklahoma Conference. She has pastored and started several chapels in Kansas and co-pastored with her husband. Most recently she served an independent church, Christian Faith Fellowship, in Lincoln, Arkansas, but because of a stroke, she had to resign until her health improved.

Sister Ayento states that her father-in-law, by his example, taught her to be strong in the face of adversity and to live her life in such a way that people would know by her Christian walk that she is a daughter of God.

"I haven't encountered too many difficulties in being a woman minister. I personally believe that this is due to the fact that I have a strong personality and persevere when I know that God has called me to handle the situation or position. However, brother ministers have been asked to minister when I knew that I had the message for the service."

She believes that we as Christians have a mandate to lead as many souls to Christ as we can. "We are in spiritual warfare, and the spoils are far too valuable to lose the battle. We, as women, need to stand strong in our faith and become equipped to face this spiritual warfare in the power of the Holy Ghost and under the blood of Jesus Christ. We need not be fearful of any enemy that already has been defeated for we are warfare women and fully equipped for the battle. In the cross we always win."

Mary Baumgartner
Heartland Conference

This lady is a retired ordained minister, who spent fifty-nine years actively working as a servant of the Lord Jesus Christ. Three of those years she was pastor of the Butler Oklahoma Pentecostal Holiness Church.

Mary spent her entire adult life teaching groups, from children to adults. She also led the singing in the church that her brother, S. E. Roachell, pastored. Since he was blind, she assisted him in his ministry as needed. When he passed away, she pastored the church until she became disabled in 2006.

Juanita Bearry
Sonshine Conference

Juanita is now retired, having spent about fifty years in ministry, including twenty years co-pastoring with her husband. She states that she gave her heart to the Lord at age eleven and has lived for Him since then. During her full time of service for God, she did not encounter any difficulty because she was a woman. Sister Bearry's older sister greatly influenced her in her ministry.

Jane Bloss
Mid-Atlantic Conference

Jane says that she learned early in her ministry that it was "important to know who I am and what my gifting is. I needed to be at peace first with myself before trying to be accepted into the role of minister, evangelist, or pastor. When this happened, I stopped trying to make people accept our calling [as ministers] and us for just who we are in God." She further indicates that she doesn't defend who she is as an ordained minister; she just lets her ministry and anointing validate her calling. "If men stand in the way of God's purposes for my life, they will give an answer to Him – not me. Man didn't call me – God did; therefore, I don't have to prove anything to men – just obey my Father. When I function with this mindset, it lifts a heavy load off my shoulders so I can concentrate on what I am to be doing for Him."

She states further that the Scripture says in Proverbs 18:16 that our gift will make a way for us and bring us before great men. God has made a way for us women many times. She was shocked when she was asked to be the Conference CE Director. "My gift earned me respect with my peers as I functioned in this position."

Personally, she finds it distasteful when she hears a woman minister spending time just before preaching defending her calling and wasting precious time that could be better spent validating her calling by an anointed word or teaching.

She feels she had been blessed during her thirty-four good years of ministry serving as co-pastor in two different churches with her husband and now as an IPHC missionary in south Asia.

Ruth W. Brookshire
Alpha (Alabama) Conference

Rev. Effie C. Williams, Ruth's mother taught her by example to fear, honor, and obey God; to serve humbly, diligently, and joyfully, no matter how obscure the assignment; to trust God for direction and provision; to pray in all situations, casting all cares on the Lord; to ignore possible ridicule for responding to the call of God; to keep confidences and not to be a talebearer nor a faultfinder.

Her husband, Joseph W. Brookshire, now deceased, had a lasting influence on her life. He served as a Navy chaplain for seventeen years, ministering aboard ships and in chapel communities. Later, he was a pastor for eleven years. She says he taught her to be patient; to turn the other cheek; to look for esteem and acceptance from the Lord; to minister wherever God placed her; and to love those who are broken hearted, weak, lonely, fatherless, disillusioned, and bitter.

She served for almost five years in music ministry with Rev. Patricia Saxon Mann in Athens, Georgia. Patricia influenced Ruth greatly with her humility and her love for God expressed in outreach to the depressed, jobless, homeless, unwanted, and hopeless.

Ruth learned from Patricia to be constantly guided by the Spirit. She also learned through her that you cannot judge the worth of a man by his appearance or his countenance or his manner. Underneath the mask of the face, there is a person who has endured pain, misery, rejection, and disillusionment. God wants to work through us to love those who are hurting and to show that He has reconciled them to Himself. We are ambassadors of that reconciliation.

Greta Campbell
Upper South Carolina Conference

While she was still in high school, she traveled in the summer singing with her sister, Inez Campbell Hart, who spent many years in evangelistic ministry before her marriage to Pastor Phillip Hart. During this time, Greta received the call to ministry but did not yield to the call right away.

On October 13, 1951, she took a brave step and began a two-week revival preaching her first sermon from a text found in Isaiah 43:2. She was licensed by the Upper South Carolina Conference on June 28, 1952, and began a full-time evangelistic ministry.

Patsy Welch from Lake City, South Carolina joined her in 1953 as a singer and musician. They were later joined by Ramona Ready from Mobile, Alabama forming The Greta Campbell Trio. The trio ministered in revivals and camp meetings from the East to the West Coast and recorded eight albums.

In April 1970, while in a revival in Wagoner, Oklahoma, a lady (who was a visitor) gave a prophecy that Greta's ministry would be changed somewhat. A few days later, she returned home and learned that a Christian television station was being built in Greenville, South Carolina by Jimmy and Joanne Thompson. They contacted her and asked if she was interested in being a part of the television ministry. She had no problem knowing how to respond because the Holy Spirit already had answered.

The station came on the air October 27, 1972. The ladies sang the theme song "We've Come This Far by Faith." They were in the thirty-fifth year in 2007 of television ministry with a potential coverage of eight thousand homes. This figure does not include the coverage by dish and cable networks in other areas where the program was carried.

"The flag-ship program of WGGS TV 16 is called 'Nite Line.' This is a live ninety-minute program (two hours some nights) consisting of Christian music, interviews, and testimonies. We have prayer partners receiving prayer requests by phone throughout the program and this connects us directly with our viewing audience. Salvation reports are called in from night to night," Greta states. She was asked to host Nite Line on Thursday nights, and she feels blessed to be a part of this tremendous outreach for Christ.

Patsy Welch works with her as musician and producer of the program. At times they sing on the program with Greta's brother Willie. Along with the TV ministry, Sister Campbell continues to speak and sing as the Lord leads her.

Marie Cardenas
Rocky Mountain Conference

Marie's place of ministry for twenty-five-plus years has been Aglow International. Working with them was done during the years she was rearing her children. For her, Aglow was a place of learning what ministry was about and where she grew in the knowledge of God. She specified that her particular area of gifting is teaching.

While her youngest son was in high school, she returned to school and earned a B.A. in English with a minor in Spanish. In December 2008, she completed the work for a master's degree in religious studies with a specialization in Biblical Women's Studies.

Lillie Fae Creasy Dawson
Cornerstone (Western North Carolina) Conference

Rev. Dawson is an ordained minister who lives in Axton, Virginia. She obtained her formal education at Holmes Bible College* in Greenville, South Carolina and Bethany Theological Seminary in Dothan, Alabama receiving bachelor's, master's, and doctorate degrees in theology. In addition, she is also a nurse. Her ministry has extended over more than fifty years.

(**Author's note:** The school has been known by various names through the years, but Holmes Bible College is used in this publication. It began as Altamont Bible and Missionary Institute when it was located on Paris Mountain, outside Greenville, South Carolina. When Brother N. J. Holmes moved the school to Greenville, it was named Holmes Bible College of Theology and Missions. Later it became Holmes College of the Bible, Holmes Theological Seminary, then, Holmes Bible College.)

June Easter
Cornerstone Conference

"I feel God has called me to be a minister to the nursing homes," writes June. The staff and the elderly, even families of some of the residents, call her to be an intercessor. She started out ministering room-to-room to some who never leave their rooms and to some who are never visited by their families. She enjoys her ministry to them and especially praying with and for the residents. She states that she has been thrown out of atheists' rooms, only to be welcomed later. The nursing home residents have become her extended family. She feels that they are more of a blessing to her than she could ever be to them. Anointing and praying for them individually is a special treat that reaches straight down to their heart and does the work intended through Jesus Christ. In the services she conducts, they sing, pray, worship, serve communion, and do memorial services for the residents who have died.

Tina R. Foutty
Appalachian (Virginia) Conference

Tina reports, "As a leader of Overcomers for Tree of Life Ministries for four to five years, I believe in the blood of the cross and in the Word of God that if we confess our faults to one another and pray, we will be healed." Countless people have been set free as a result of the life changing work of this ministry. God uses her in street ministry as well.

She is a licensed minister in her conference, working as an evangelist and in other areas as the Lord provides the opportunities. This has been her ministry for about eight years.

Nina Franklin
Cornerstone Conference

Sister Franklin was eighty-four years old when she sent in the information form in 2008. Apparently she exerted quite an influence on her family, as her son and several grandsons are pastors. Her ministry spans more than fifty years serving as a pastor in Roanoke and Danville, Virginia and also as an evangelist.

Dr. Marysue Huffman Freeman
North Carolina Conference

"No individual is too young or too old to accomplish the work of the ministry" is the way Marysue puts it. "Do not underestimate the positive impact of a Godly home."

She believes that the primary education of utmost importance to all Christians and essential to every individual involved in the ministry is obtained from the Word of God, through praying, fasting, and allowing the Holy Spirit to use us. Dr. Freeman states, "We must be a willing and yielded individual to the Holy Spirit. Every minister should be filled to overflowing with the Spirit with the evidence of speaking in other tongues, thus allowing the gifts and manifestations of the Holy Spirit listed in Corinthians and in Ephesians for the help and perfecting of the saints to operate/flow through them."

Rev. Freeman has ministered in most states in this country and all of the military theaters in the world including more than forty-seven countries.

Aida Fuentes
Sonshine (Florida) Conference

Aida reports that she has never encountered difficulties being a woman minister and has been fully accepted. As an ordained minister, she has been working in Florida in men's prisons. Even though this ministry has been a challenge, she always has been respected and God's work through her appreciated. She also has served as a pastor.

Catherine Funkhouser
Mid-Atlantic (Maryland) Conference

Sister Funkhouser is now past ninety years old, so her activities have been curtailed because of her age. However, she was involved in the Lord's work in her conference for about sixty years, starting with her being licensed to preach in Washington, D. C. in 1948. She pastored on her own and also has co-pastored with her husband.

Nelle Burnette Goodman
Alpha (Alabama) Conference

Nelle was active in women's ministry as a means of serving the Lord. She was licensed as a minister in 1997 but spent forty years before that assisting her pastor husband until the time of his death. They pastored in Brewton, Anniston, and Flomaton, Alabama; Kreole, Mississippi; and Cantonment, Florida. She writes, "I've loved it all. I feel so rich knowing so many wonderful people and being of help along the way." Her conference superintendent encouraged her to get license so she could continue being a part of the conference – as he said, "Make it legal what you have been doing for years."

Her current position (at the time of her report) is Prayer Chairman and Senior Adult Director of the conference.

She attended Emmanuel College in Franklin Springs, Georgia.

One of her daughters is a Down's syndrome child. The following article, written by Sister Goodman and reprinted in its entirety, tells the story.

"JULIE"

Mothering or ministering to a Down's syndrome child is not always easy, but I am rewarded abundantly by my child's accomplishments and love.

Julie is nine years old and full of life. Mentally, she is graded at one and a half to two years old. To describe her requires many adjectives: loving, outgoing, happy, stubborn, rebellious, irritating and aggravating at different times. She has many moods and sometimes her unlovely qualities are very dominant. At these times it is difficult to minister to her with kindness and usually it takes the 'fly swatter' to get things under control.

When Julie was born into our home, I was 44 years old, and our children were grown. Rhetta was 22, Ronnie was in the third year of college, and Tim was 14. It was a time of anxiety, turmoil and frustration that came to Hale and me, and we were really puzzled when the doctor informed us that our expected child would be retarded. The prayers of many people brought the peace and marvelous grace of God's assurance that Romans 8:28 is true. We lived on that promise. The Holy Spirit brought comfort to us that He would be with us in a walk of faith.

Caring for Julie as an infant was simple. She was slow and sluggish, but we gave her as much love as parents and siblings could. We took her everywhere we went and never felt embarrassed or ashamed. We even took Julie to General Conference in Oklahoma City, in 1977, and she attended every session with us. Julie had to have heart surgery to repair a hole in her heart during the month of her first birthday. After this she seemed to be happier, stronger, and began to notice and enjoy things more. She even started going to school when she was 15 months old. This has been good for mother and child. Julie learns a lot, and I get free time.

When Julie started walking, our attention had to be fastened on her constantly. She is a destroyer of everything. We sometimes call her 'the tornado.'

Julie is perfectly happy. She has no sense of guilt or shame. I am the one who has these feelings. There are times when it is like a tempest raging within me. For example, when she opens the refrigerator and pours food or drink on the dining room carpet, or rakes her hand across a cake for a party, or reaches up and pulls pots off the stove with prepared food for a meal, I come apart. I have need of patience in a hurry. Tensions mount high, and I minister to Julie with screams and paddlings and then fall on my knees in prayer.

Getting dressed to go to church is frustrating. Shoes and socks are put on as many as three or four times. Many two-year-olds do this, but remember I've had a two-year-old for years.

We live in a parsonage across the road from the church. Sometimes Julie refuses to walk over, and sometimes she goes in a run, but she truly loves to go to church. All the people at church love Julie, and she goes around and greets each one with hugs and kisses. Her love has reached all of them, and she never meets a stranger. Praise God for understanding people.

Julie's greatest love is music. She asks for tapes and knows who and what she wants to hear. Her memory for songs is almost incredible. Many times she swings and sings loud enough for all the neighbors to enjoy.

We have our most difficult times at the table. It is not uncommon for her to overturn her plate of food or fling a spoon full just for attention. That is when she gets plenty of attention with a 'time out' period until she can return to the table and 'eat right.'

Julie is very sensitive to the moving of the Holy Spirit. She is taught the Word in a special Sunday school class and has learned several verses and Bible stories. On occasions she has requested certain songs during a service that has truly been inspired by the Lord as they seemed to be the key to the moving of God's Spirit. On one occasion she was attending the Women's Prayer Meeting. One of the women, who was being treated by chemotherapy for a malignancy, asked for prayer because that morning she had fear come upon her. Julie was sitting all by herself looking at a book, but immediately she spoke up and said, 'Sing, By His Word,' The words are, 'By His Word I have no fear in me. By His Word death cannot swallow me. By His Word I have prosperity. By His Word sickness cannot dwell in me. By His Word I walk in victory. By His Word I've been set free.' Needless to say as we sang, the Holy Spirit ministered to the woman in need and to all of us.

Julie prays often. She continually tells us to 'pray and agree.' Many times I've listened as she sits on the porch praying and singing and also praying in tongues. She ministers to us as much as we minister to her.

There is never a dull moment at our house when Julie is home. Nobody is free from servitude to her. One day she may want me to do everything, the next day it is another member of the family. There are not many things in self helps that she can manage yet. We do a lot of living!

Yes, sometimes I feel sorry for myself. The burden gets heavy and I shed tears, but God comes and ministers His love, grace and mercy and in turn I grow spiritually.

We know that Julie was put into our home for us to learn how to love and to receive love. For eight years I lived across the street from a man who was injured at birth. He was severely retarded and he would holler and flip rubber straps. I would pray, 'God, please don't ever let me have a retarded child.' I'm sure that God heard those prayers, but God knows what is best for us.

Having Julie in a parsonage has given lots of people opportunity to serve God by ministering to her and to us. We have been blessed so much that we could never repay the Lord.

'In everything give thanks for this is the will of God in Christ Jesus concerning you.'[2]

(**Author's note:** My heart goes out to and my hat goes off to Sister Goodman as she struggled with the challenges of a child with Down's syndrome but continued to labor faithfully as a pastor's wife, as a licensed minister, and as president of the Conference Women's Ministries. Mrs. Goodman wrote me on March 29, 2010 that Julie died in her sleep on March 9, 2009. May God bless Julie's memory to all who knew and loved her.)

Rhetta Jean Goodman
Alpha Conference

Rev. Goodman states that she has been in ministry of some kind all her life. She has served as church pianist, youth leader, and Women's Ministries Director and Christian Education Director in the Alpha Conference. Her work also has taken her out of the United States to Haiti as a missionary where she served two and a half years.

Dr. Brenda Grasty
Cornerstone Conference

Brenda serves as Director of the Conference Women's Ministries and sings in a gospel group called "One Voice Trio." She writes, "Recently [we] had a church that cancelled our group . . . because they read that I was an ordained minister in the IPHC. But praise God many have realized the calling God has placed on women. I pray all will be enlightened."

Louise Gschwend
Redemption Ministries (Eastern Virginia) Conference

Even though Louise was a missionary having served many years in Africa, she and her husband, Ronald, also pastored the Bethel Church in Virginia when he was in the Naval Reserve stationed in the Norfolk area. She filled in as preacher/teacher whenever he had duty and had to stay on base. She is now retired and lives with her husband in South Carolina. Their tenure in Africa is mentioned in *The Simultaneous Principle*, a history of IPHC world missions for the first one hundred years, written by Dr. Frank G. Tunstall.

Carrie Banks Hampton
Georgia, Texas, East Oklahoma Conferences

"Grandmother Carrie and my grandfather, Harry W. Hampton, were married in Atlanta, Georgia in 1906. When they both received the Baptism of the Holy Ghost they became affiliated with the Pentecostal Holiness Church and were soon both licensed ministers. Grandmother Carrie assisted my grandfather as he pastored churches in Georgia, North and South Carolina, and Florida. Moving West in 1927, they pastored churches in Oklahoma and Texas. In 1938, with her health failing, Grandad took her back to Georgia and they lived in Franklin Spring until her death. She is buried in the cemetery by the college [Emmanuel]. Grandmother Carrie died before I was born, but people – family members and many others – have told me of her ministry as she worked alongside Grandad in everything he did."

(**Author's note:** This information was sent in by Sister Hampton's granddaughter, Wanda Elliott.)

Inez Campbell Hart
Georgia Conference

Inez has devoted sixty-plus years to the ministry. Fifty of those years she was assisting her husband as pastor of the Flatwoods Pentecostal Holiness Church. Before her marriage, she was an evangelist for three years.

Sharon Hartman
Appalachian Conference

Sharon indicates that she was a shy girl that God called to minister. She wanted to go to the mission field, so the Missions Board told her husband he had to go to school before they went. He went to Holmes Bible College for four years and graduated in 1977. He was still not called to be a minister, but he was willing to go and work and be with her. The Board still would not send them since Mr. Hartman was not a minister. She worked as Christian Education Director for years and then several years as an associate pastor. Now, the Lord has favored her with a pastorate. She feels that she is blessed.

Myra Hastings
Cornerstone Conference

This lady came from a Baptist background, but age fifteen carried her into new horizons. She "saw the light" and was filled with the Holy Spirit. She tried to talk to her parents about it, but they said it was of the devil. At age nineteen, she was told to leave home because she continued to believe the Pentecostal way.

The Lord touched her dad's heart, and he let her stay at home while attending college. He allowed her to go to the church of her choice after reading a letter she wrote about wanting spiritual freedom.

At the time she wrote, she was forty-five years old, and her parents were still trying to change her beliefs. Even though they strongly disagree with her, they do respect her for her stand for Christ.

God has helped her through trying times and has made her strong in faith. He helps her daily through partial motor paralysis on her left side as the result of a birth defect. He saw her through the death of her firstborn child at full term, and then gave her a healthy daughter five years later.

Myra says that God's mandate to her is "Mend broken people."

Marie Haydock
Upper South Carolina Conference

Sister Haydock was raised in a poor home where her life was one of abuse and incest. She was denied her education. Through the Lord, she is where she is today. The Lord has set her free. He broke the bonds in which she felt she was being held captive.

All the hurt she carried for over forty years is gone, and she has been sharing her testimony with everyone she meets. She states that she is not afraid because God has been so good to her.

Cindy Hiott
South Carolina Conference

Cindy holds a bachelor of science degree from Charleston Southern University and has received other training through the Conference School of Ministry. She finds that keeping ministerial and family duties in the right order of priority has been difficult. "Being a minister, a wife, and mother can be hard when you are needed in all three areas at the same time," she writes. Her field of ministry is as a youth pastor.

Patricia Holden
South Carolina Conference

Sister Holden has been a licensed minister in her conference for thirteen years. During the time God was calling her, she had cancer, and while recovering from her sickness, the Lord dealt with her in such a way that she knew that the calling was to preach. She used a radio ministry as an outreach for about a year. After that, she filled in as pastor of the North Myrtle Beach Church for a short while and has been faithful to preach wherever a door is open.

Becki Hudson
South Carolina Conference

Becki began a women's Bible study for the community in 2005, as she felt that the Lord wanted her to minister to women to help them learn about God's Word. She is visiting shut-ins and nursing home residents. She says she had learned that God uses women in a mighty way. "They need to stand up and be counted."

Mae Ingram
New Horizons Conference

Mae pastored with her husband for forty-six of the sixty years she has been in the ministry as a licensed minister of New Horizons Conference. She helped to get the Youth Camp started when the conference was known as West Oklahoma, and she worked with the young people for nineteen years. Even though she has been involved in the work of the Kingdom in many ways, she says, "I can't say I ever accomplished anything worthy of mentioning." That is typical of a humble servant of the Master.

Mildred Jenkins
Appalachian Conference

Rev. Jenkins serves as associate pastor of Cornerstone Church in the Appalachian Conference. She has been a licensed minister for five years. Mildred holds a bachelor of science degree in interdisciplinary studies, pre-K through 6th education from Old Dominion University in Virginia. Mrs. Helen Harrison has been her mentor and mother in the Lord.

Dr. Betty Jo Jones
South Carolina Conference

The Lord called Dr. Jones into the ministry at the age of twenty-four. Very few women preached in her area of Florida in those days, but doors of opportunity started opening, mostly in her home church and very gradually those opportunities spread to Alabama, Georgia, Tennessee, and Louisiana. She received license in Florida in 1974 and was ordained in June 1990 in another organization. She had an evangelistic team for eight years, with a six piece band; worked for nine years as a volunteer minister and counselor for a correctional institute, and often filled in for pastors to take a much needed vacation.

The most enjoyable station of all, she indicates, was when she worked with Native Americans in Montana, which she did for more than three years. There were five different tribes with which she worked moving her motor home from reservation to reservation.

Loretha W. Jones
Redemption Ministries Conference

Loretha's philosophy is that it is vital to learn that God is more important than the ministry; our relationship with the Father should come first. God is still seeking true worshippers – people who can hear what the Spirit of the Lord is saying to His church and are willing to make necessary changes in their lives. Even though she has experienced ups and downs in ministry, she has found God to be faithful.

She believes that the church is about to experience an abundance of God's glory. Ministers, as well as the rest of the body of believers, should be in preparation by studying the Word and spending time in His presence. Her own experience has taught her not to despise small beginnings. God's light shining upon us will dispel all darkness. So, she finds, it does not matter if you are a woman in ministry. What is important is the relationship we have with God. Ministry calls for more time spent with Him. Be available. Since God's abundant light is about to shine, her advice is that we want to be ready.

Patsy Jones
North Carolina Conference

Patsy writes, "God promised when He called me to preach that I would never go alone, that He would always be with me as I ministered His Word. He has been faithful to His promise for almost thirty years." She is confident He will always keep His Word. She pastors the Stantonsburg Pentecostal Holiness Church in Stantonsburg, North Carolina.

Dr. Marja Lindqvist
Sonshine Conference

Dr. Lindqvist holds a doctor of philosophy degree in pastoral counseling, a degree from a business college in Finland, and a nursing degree. She is director of a nonprofit organization, Beraka International. In addition to her work in Florida her labors, along with her husband, have carried her to Finland, Russia, India, Sri Lanka, England, Haiti, and Eastern Europe.

Amy Adams Linkous
Georgia Conference

Amy was licensed in the Appalachian Conference in 1999, but she now belongs to the Georgia Conference. She attended Emmanuel College and Mercer University, earning associate and bachelor's degrees respectively. Both schools are in Georgia. She assists her husband in his pastorate at The Rock, Georgia.

Thursia Long
Alpha Conference

She is ordained in the conference having spent forty-eight years in ministry, primarily as a pastor. Myra Spence greatly influenced her career because of her pattern of a humble, yet strong Christian minister. She writes, "I answered God's call to preach His Word when I was fourteen years old. I was given Mission Worker's license in July 1942." Again quoting her, "No, the way has not always been easy. We women have occupied the lower seats of the church, but never has the Lord considered us to be any person of second class status."

Now, she is past eighty and feels she is nearing the end of her earthly journey.

Karen Lundquist
Pacific Western Conference

Since the time Karen was a young girl, she had a deep desire to know the Lord. Her religious roots reach back through generations of missionaries, preachers, Christian musicians, and songwriters. While she was growing up, her grandmother was her greatest inspiration, as she was a portrait of the strength and faith of a godly woman.

As a young girl, Karen preached to the angels and make-believe people from a pulpit she made from a cardboard box. Even then, the Lord had planted inside her a desire to share the gospel.

After straying from the Lord in her youth, the Holy Spirit began to draw her back. Today, she is sharing the Word and ministering as the Lord opens the doors of opportunity to her. She is answering the call God placed upon her life.

Rev. Lundquist is founder of Home Fire Fellowship and Embrace the Fire Ministry. The latter was birthed through the life-experiences of "embracing the Lord in the midst of the fiery trials" instead of running away from them. "The Lord is a pure holy fire that purges and cleanses our heart from fear and sin, and He desires His bride to experience and understand what it is to worship and embrace that purity and holy fire."

Wilma Jo Mahan
New Horizons Conference

Wilma Jo came into the Pentecostal Holiness Church in 1985 and began pastoring officially in April of that year. In 2008, she was pastoring the Quinton Pentecostal Holiness Church in Quinton, Oklahoma. She had been preaching for forty-four years when she was seventy years old. She says that she was saved when a woman evangelist was preaching and also received the Holy Spirit when a lady preacher was ministering where her mother-in-law was pastoring.

She reports that she is still asking God for a great harvest of souls. Her battle with cancer in 2001 was a real test for her, but she is grateful for God's healing power as she is now cancer free.

Janice Marshburn, Th. D.
North Carolina Conference

This lady is outstanding in her leadership ministry in her conference, as she is Director of Deborah's Daughters (lady clergy of the conference); a member of the Bishop's Strategic Advisory Council; Assistant Director of the Conference Women's Ministries; Director of Women's Ministries, music coordinator, and Sunday school teacher in her local church. She also serves as an evangelist. In 2010, she was elected Women's Ministries Director of the North Carolina Conference.

Reflecting on who has influenced her career or been a mentor to her, she said, "Rev. Dr. Vera Griffin has encouraged me to study the Scriptures and dig for a deeper meaning. To search for Truth and to get it right. She is also the one who encouraged me to get my degree. Although she currently resides in Texas, we spend countless hours on the phone discussing Biblical truths."

In her secular life, Dr. Marshburn worked for the federal government at Camp Lejeune for more than thirty-six years, retiring in 2010 to devote more time to her ministry.

Louise Paramore Mayhue
Appalachian Conference

Louise Mayhue at age eighty-five years had spent sixty years in ministry beginning as a licensed preacher in 1945 in the North Carolina Conference. She attended Holmes Bible College in South Carolina receiving a bachelor of sacred literature degree from that institution. In 1950, she married John R. Mayhue, who is also a minister. They are now retired.

Rev. Sylvia Sexton, with whom Sister Mayhue evangelized for a short time, was a positive force in her life. They were together working for the Lord for four months in 1947.

She indicated that she had been fully accepted as a lady minister, never feeling that it was difficult.

In *"The Mayhue Messenger,"* a newsletter, her husband wrote that they had been able to sell their mobile home and move to Roanoke, Virginia to be near their sons.

Adelita Suarez Mayo
Sonshine Conference

When God called Adelita into ministry, she did not really see the whole picture of her calling. She became a licensed minister in the IPHC in 2001. In 2002, she lost her husband in a tragic accident. Six months later, she started working as a volunteer at the women's and men's correctional institutions in Ocala, Florida where she teaches Hispanics and also preaches to all in the chapel at the compound.

After working as a volunteer for five years, the Lord really impressed upon her to become a chaplain in 2005. She graduated in Puerto Rico from the Association of Chaplains in Missionary Action, Inc.

She has been named to be Director of the Jail and Prison Ministry in Ocala being the first woman chosen for this position. She knows it had to be God Almighty.

As director of the ministry, she started visiting the Marion County Jail with other volunteers from her church. In 2007, she was nominated Volunteer of the Year at Lowell Correctional Institution in Ocala, Florida. To God be all the glory!

Marie McCarty
New Horizons Conference

Her daughter, Betty Lovelace, writes, "She is almost ninety-eight years old and is suffering from dementia. At the moment, I do not have exact dates, but I believe she started her pastoral duties under Rev. Leon Stewart who was in Tulsa, Oklahoma at the time. I believe the assignment was to be temporary, but she was there for several years. I'm thinking she started pastoring when she was about fifty or fifty-two years of age. I'm not sure what year she started pastoring the church in Oolagah, Oklahoma. She was there a number of years and led the congregation in building a beautiful little church building. She went from there to the Calvin, Oklahoma church and retired from there."

Jeannie "Kitty" Mears
Cornerstone Conference

"Many times, in a rural setting, a woman minister is seen as someone who is only good enough to lead either a children's or a women's group. They are accepted as pastors only if their husbands are the senior pastor. Most of the time, women have to seek employment in the secular field in order to make ends meet financially, especially if the church they are pastoring has no parsonage." This is the way Kitty describes her views on women ministers.

Loretta Meneley
New Horizons Conference

Loretta has been ordained since 1997. She was assistant pastor in Jay, Oklahoma for seven years. Her other work includes playing the piano and teaching young people. Pastors Tony and Patty Besmer gave her encouragement to reach out; however, she feels that no one at higher levels in the IPHC has listened to the cry of women to minister.

Dr. Marie Mewald
Appalachian Conference

Rev. Mewald received her Ph.D. from Christian Life School of Theology in Columbus, Georgia. She was assistant pastor at Christian Life International in Salem, Virginia for three years and has been in the ministry since 1977.

Juanita Long Mullins
Pennsylvania Conference

Juanita came into the world in Johnson County, Kentucky, near the town of Painesville, in the waning days of 1930. Music found a way into her life at a very early age, and she began getting attention for her singing when she was just seven years old.

Her parents later moved to Waverly, Ohio, and then to Richlands, Virginia where she graduated from high school in 1950 and worked in health care there. In 1948, she felt her calling into the ministry and has ministered the Word and songs most of her life.

She is an established writer and has written for most of the Pentecostal magazines, as well as other publications. She wrote gospel tracts for two publishers in Minnesota and Tennessee.

Radio and TV have been a part of her ministry from early years to now. Back in an early era, country music artists found themselves working with a sponsor, whether on the radio or for their personal appearances. In Juanita's case, her personal appearances included the music department of many Ben Franklin stores, as well as other similar places that back then were called "five and dime" stores. She made visits to many radio stations, all through the United States, tirelessly promoting her music.

A 1974 article mentions that Juanita had published a song book of more than 120 of her favorite hymns, and many other song books were published in her name. That same article mentions her recording a song she wrote, "Jesus Is Waiting for You," with background vocals by the Revelators.

She and her husband pastor the Pentecostal Holiness Church in Ashtabula, Ohio. On most Sunday mornings, Juanita leads the services. Even hip replacement surgery has not slowed her down one bit.

A case of memorabilia from her career, including song books, records, TV tapes and other mementos, is on dispay at her church.

Kaye Munoz
Cornerstone Conference

Kaye was called to preach and be a missionary when she was eighteen years old while at Holmes Bible College. She went on to other colleges and began teaching in Virginia in public schools. She was born in Eden, North Carolina and grew up in Mayodan, North Carolina and always attended Pentecostal Holiness churches.

In 1974, she left Heritage Bible College in Dunn, North Carolina, where she had been teaching and served the IPHC as a missionary in Costa Rica. She married Manuel Munoz from San Jose, Costa Rica in 1979, and later they served under the Evangelism Department of the IPHC in Hawaii for five years.

Kaye pastored two churches in Costa Rica, one that she pioneered. She assisted her husband in pastoring a Hispanic church attended by military people from Spanish-speaking countries. In addition, she helped found Redemption Bible College in Hawaii, with Dr. Adrian Yuen. The couple has served the Lord in the Rio Grande Valley, Mexico and Mission, Texas for almost twenty-four years.

She retired from teaching recently, but she and Manuel still evangelize. Her determination is to serve God as long as they have life in them, and she prays for a great revival to come.

Carol Watson Oglesby
Sonshine Conference

"At times it's very hard being a woman in what by most is considered to be a man's job or calling," writes Carol Oglesby. She says God did not consult her when He called her and did not need anyone else to okay it. She feels that women work doubly hard to not only minister but fill all the other capacities that they do. Any woman in the ministry must be sure of her calling and commitment to God.

She serves as a pastor, a wife, a mother, and a grandmother and has her own a business. She is grateful that God called her, and she tries every day to be the example He would have her be.

Sister Ethel Jordan was co-founding pastor of the church Carol now pastors, Jena Pentecostal Holiness Church.

Jennifer Oliver
North Carolina Conference

Jennifer was twenty-eight years old when she sent in this report in 2008. She had been a part of the IPHC's World Missions Ministries, pastored alongside her husband, and led music for Pentecostal Holiness churches. At the time she responded she was working with her husband as directors of Alternative to Abortion Ministries (ATAM), which is a place where young women who are pregnant and in need of refuge could go to have their babies rather than go through an abortion. They also pastored Plymouth and Harvest Fellowship Pentecostal Holiness Churches.

Many times she applied for jobs in churches, but the male pastors would rather not work with a female, even in music ministry. She knows the importance of guarding the heart and being careful how things appear. She often feels that the combination of being young and female greatly limits her opportunities. However, God has continually used her, and she states she serves Him with all of her heart because she knows her rewards are in heaven.

Carole Palmer
Golden West Conference

Carole holds a bachelor's and a master's degree from California State University. She is an ordained minister, involved in ministry for twenty-eight years. She indicates that she has received many opportunities to preach, teach, and share through the years – everything from preaching a Sunday service to performing leadership training at local, conference, and general denominational levels to speaking at several women's retreats. Her writing experience includes an eight-part Bible study for the on-line IPHC Women's Ministries (WM), which is still available, and she continues to write for the IPHC WM *Potpourri* on a quarterly basis. This publication is distributed to Conference WM Directors.

Diana V. Peel
Pacific Western Conference

Sister Peel, a licensed minister in her conference, has been a minister for twenty-one years. Her education includes training at Advantage College, Southwestern Christian University, and Fuller Theological Seminary. She writes, "I have learned to lean into God and follow the gifts He has bestowed upon me whether they are accepted by the church or not. More importantly, I have learned that battling with the church for acceptance is a tool of my enemy to keep me unfocused and my attention diverted rendering me unable to walk in my gifts."

Ruth Robinson Powell
South Carolina Conference

After Ruth joined the South Carolina Conference in 1952, she pastored two churches: Rhems, near Georgetown and Red Oak, near Cottageville. Her husband, Halley, joined the conference in 1960, and she assisted him in pastoring Cades, Savannah Bluff, and Laurel Hill churches.

In 1970, they were accepted by the World Missions Department as missionaries to Mexico. They worked in Hispanic churches along the United States-Mexico border while attending language school in Edinburg, Texas. In 1971, they moved to Monterrey, Mexico and worked briefly in Emmanuel Bible School. Later, they were assigned to Puebla, Mexico to plant and establish churches. After about seven years they had a church of sixty members and a smaller congregation near Mexico City. Today both the congregations average 475 each.

Around 1980, they returned to the United States, where she attended Pan American University and earned a B.A. degree in English and Spanish and a master's in education.

In 1992, they moved back to South Carolina and pastored the Zion Church in Conway for seven years. They retired in 2000 and moved back home to Hamlet, North Carolina.

Camellia Puffer
Pennsylvania Conference

Along with her husband, David, Camellia is associated with Exousia Ministries as part of Exousia Christian Assembly in Orlando, Florida. The ministry has been in existence since February 1997 and continues to serve the Lord in the areas of teaching, preaching, music ministry, sketch board evangelism, street outreach, and practical assistance to small churches.

Their vision is equipping, enabling, and encouraging the people of God through in-depth teaching of the Bible and practical help for congregations in need. Their hearts are also turned toward the start-up of smaller congregations. They are equipped to lead worship either inside or outdoors. They offer classes in evangelism, theology, and New Age deceptions.

Their Statement of Faith and Purpose indicates more about where they stand scripturally. "Exousia Ministries is dedicated to the teaching of God's Word in a way that will promote right worship through a correct understanding of the person and character of Christ Jesus. We accept, as irrefutably true, the divine inspiration of the Bible and the historical reality of the life, ministry, death, and resurrection of Jesus of Nazareth. We believe that it is the Father's will that salvation is granted only through receiving the finished work of the Lord Jesus as stated in the Scriptures. We believe in the ongoing ministry of the Holy Spirit and the reality of His gifts which He gives to each one as He wills, for the profit of all. We believe that Christian growth is essential to spiritual wellness and is an ongoing process fueled by right knowledge and holy affection for our heavenly Father and his manifestation as the King of kings and Lord of lords."

In 2002, the Puffers moved to Pennsylvania to assist aging family members, and as a result, moved the ministry to the Pittsburgh area. It was after the relocation that Camellia started the evangelistic street outreach, Art of the Covenant (AOTC). She is a graduate of International Seminary in Apopka, Florida with a bachelor's degree in biblical studies.

Julia Batson Purifoy
North Carolina Conference

Julia was a co-pastor with her husband, McElree Purifoy. Their first pastoral assignment was Grifton, North Carolina in an incomplete building of cinderblocks situated beside a ditch that sometimes served as a sewage drain. The building had no conventional floor, but rather wood shavings on the dirt, and a large homemade wood door for the front entrance. Within two years, the building was improved, and attendance increased from an average of ten to approximately seventy-five. She also served with her husband on the Navajo Indian Reservation at Greasewood Faith Mission, Ganado, Arizona. They planted a church there where they pastored for twenty-two years.

Julia received a bachelor's degree in theology from Holmes Bible College, Greenville, South Carolina.

(**Author's note:** The preceding information was furnished by Rev. McElree Purifoy, surviving spouse. Julia died on April 4, 1993.)

Deloris G. Rapp
Upper South Carolina Conference

"I have received excellent support from the IPHC as an African-American female," reports Deloris. She has pastored but currently serves as a chaplain. Her B.S. degree is from Lander University, and her master's of divinity is from Erskine Theological Seminary.

(**Author's note:** Erskine is located in Due West, South Carolina.)

Mary Alice Alderman Richardson
Georgia Conference

She held many week-long revivals in Kite, Georgia, with Rev. Sarah Perdy, another Georgia Conference woman minister who pastored. These were held mostly in the 1980s. She also filled the pulpit for her local pastor, Willis Fortson, then pastor of Mountain Gap Pentecostal Holiness Church.

Even in her elderly days, she maintained an elaborate letter writing ministry in which she encouraged many – especially women. She often "prayed through" for solutions to hard problems in the community, local church, and the wide body of Christ. She often received a word from the Holy Spirit increasing the faith of many, including those in the community with other denominational affiliations. Many of all faiths knew she heard clearly from the Lord and believed for healing and help as a result of her witness.

This lady is a prime example that education is not a necessary requirement to be a faithful and useful servant, as she completed only the third grade; yet God used her in ways that perhaps others could not have.

(**Author's note:** This information about Rev. Richardson was sent in by her granddaughter, Amy Linkous.)

Renee Ross
New Horizons Conference

Renee says that she has been a member of the IPHC in Wetumka, Oklahoma since 1974. She became the pastor there in 1994. This church has always been where her heart is.

According to her, the other areas of ministry are varied: female pastor representative on the General Board of Administration, IPHC; board member of Home Missions Conference; Evangelism USA board member on the general level; board member for New Horizons Conference; and conference Women's Ministries Director. She was ordained in 1986.

Her husband is a rancher and is a great support to her in her ministry.

Margaret E. Salas
Ephesians 4 Network

Margaret says, "Your personal experience is very important in ministry. It helps . . . because then you do so [minister] with compassion, understanding of situations, and love." She believes that when you know you are called, no matter what you experience, you learn not to take anything personally. Her advice is "trust God and strive to develop what He has placed in you."

Her father, Rev. Samuel Medrano, now deceased, taught her most of what she knows about pastoring.

The greatest difficulty she has encountered is her struggle to be accepted and taken seriously in ministry by many fellow male ministers.

Cathy Snyder
Mid-Atlantic Conference

Cathy says that loneliness is the greatest difficulty she has encountered as a woman minister. There are not many women ministers in the area in which she lives.

Her husband, who has been a true blessing, has been a wonderful mentor in her life. He also encourages her in her calling. She preaches, teaches, and holds other leadership positions in the church, but for the most part she mentors others. She says that can be quite draining at times, but believes that is 90 percent of the call.

"God called me as an evangelist first and that is what comes out in my preaching, but I also have a pastor's heart. There are no gray areas in this Christian walk."

Jewelle Edwards Stewart
South Carolina Conference

Mrs. Stewart ended her second term as Executive Director, IPHC Women's Ministries in July 2009. She states, "I was born into a pastor's home and married a minister who was pastoring at the time of our marriage. Consequently, I've been involved in 'the ministry' all my life, but did not pursue credentials until my early 50s."

She was involved in her husband's pastoral and administrative work in the Alabama (Alpha) Conference for thirty-six years and for three and a half years in the South Carolina Conference, before she was elected denominational leader of the Women's Ministries in 2001.

Her godly parents, Rev. C. B. and Lessie Edwards, as well as, Agnes Robinson and so many others had a positive influence on her career. She states, "I have gleaned from a host of wonderful people who were totally sold-out to God."

Jeannette A. Storms
Pacific Western Conference

Born on October 29, 1944, Jeannette Anne Storms grew up in Fort Madison, Iowa, in a home where her parents were committed Christians. As a child she was sensitive to the Holy Spirit, accepting Christ as her Savior and later experiencing Spirit baptism. After graduating from high school, she went to Holmes Bible College in Greenville, South Carolina, and then to Southern Nazarene University located in Bethany, Oklahoma. In 1965, she began her ministry in the California Conference, working with children and youth.

After graduating from college, she taught English to middle school students at Pan American College in Monterrey, Mexico for two years. At the same time, she learned Spanish and did a variety of ministries including jails, evangelism, children's ministry, and teaching at Emmanuel Bible College in Monterrey. She has traveled to Zambia, Central Africa, where she taught at the Bible Institute there for two years.

She ministered in Osaka, Japan and visited a number of countries in Asia including the Philippines, Hong Kong, and Thailand. Then she continued on to China, Mongolia, and Russia on a prayer journey. Afterward, she planted and pastored a church in Fernley, Nevada, outside Reno.

In 1990, she was appointed Dean of Pacific Coast Bible College in Sacramento, California, where the student body grew steadily under her administrative direction. She served as Missions Director and board member of the Pacific Western Conference for eight years. Her education continued with graduate classes at several schools before graduating from Regent University in Virginia Beach, Virginia receiving a doctor of ministry degree and the Award of Excellence.

Since 2001, Jeannette has served as a full-time Professor of Practical Ministry at The King's College and Seminary in Van Nuys, California. She travels to London twice a year to minister with Agape Christian Fellowship and other ministries. As time permits, she preaches and teaches at local churches, prayer seminars and women's conferences. She sees her present primary role as one of training and mentoring leaders in developing a new generation of ministers, pastors, and missionaries for global harvest.

Teresa Strickland
North Carolina Conference

Teresa Strickland is an ordained minister who is involved in hospice work. Her training was obtained through the School of Ministry at

Northwood Temple in Fayetteville, North Carolina. Pastor Randal Strickland was a mentor to her when she started attending the church he pastored in 1997. She states that he allowed her to function in the gifts God gave her. This action built her confidence in the Lord. The greatest difficulty she has encountered being a woman minister has been those who think God does not call women to preach.

Geraleen Talmage
Appalachian Conference

Much of Geraleen's fifty-seven years in ministry was spent in Africa as a missionary; however, since retiring she and her husband are still actively involved in their conference. They serve as advisors to the adult senior's program, The Golden Eagles, on the conference level.

She states, "There were times that I was nominated for various positions that had traditionally been held by men, immediately the conference was informed that this nominee should be a man."

Her degrees were earned at Holmes Bible College, Greenville, South Carolina (Th.B.) and Lynchburg College, Lynchburg, Virginia (B.A.).

(**Author's note**: Her illustrious missionary career is highlighted in *The Simultaneous Principle* by Frank Tunstall.)

Rebecca Tate
North Carolina Conference

Rebecca realized quickly that if she wanted to pastor, she must be prepared to pioneer a church. For three years, she refused simply because she is a woman and dreaded all that she knew she would have to face. The area in which she lived at that time was deeply and severely against women ministers. According to her, it still is except for a few denominations which are breaking through the prejudice. Despite this difficulty, the Holy Spirit led her, her husband, and their young son to begin a work. They started with nothing, except the knowledge that God was leading.

The members of the church and Sister Tate leaned upon God and sought Him continually for nineteen years, and He blessed. It was never easy, but God eventually blessed them financially and physically. They bought a 3000 square foot building that was eventually made into a lovely place of worship. They gave to missions and to charities, and their church was responsible for planting three churches in Romania. They reached out into the community with healing and deliverance.

Rebecca reports that her greatest honor was to begin the church built on prayer. They had prayer meeting every Wednesday night for the nineteen years she was there as pastor. They prayed together at least an hour. Within a few years this became the favorite meeting, attended by at least 80 percent of the congregation. They grew to love the presence of the Lord and the power of praying together.

She states that she has been in the ministry for approximately thirty years. The greatest difficulty is being a woman, which has been a hindrance in being accepted, and therefore, limited her worth in the Kingdom. The Word and prayer have not been limited, however.

Roberta Trujillo
Pacific Western Conference

Roberta is a licensed evangelist who believes it is important to rely on the Holy Spirit. She had learned to trust His leading and guidance and to be faithful to the call in spite of what she "thinks" or "feels." She has been in ministry fifteen years.

Vickie L. Viars
Appalachian Conference

Rev. Viars received her ministry training through Maranatha College in Dublin, Virginia, which is conference-sponsored, earning a bachelor of science degree in biblical studies. She thinks women are not being recognized in ministry and are not being given opportunities like men are.

Carolyn Wade
Appalachian Conference

Carolyn Wade currently serves as pastor of Rock Haven Ministries, which formerly was the Madison Heights Pentecostal Holiness Church. She has been in that position since 1992. She was born again on September 8, 1968, and called into the ministry in 1969; however, at the time of the call she did not recognize nor accept it.

Positions began to open for training, such as involvement in the women's auxiliary, and positions as assistant youth leader, teen Sunday school teacher, then assistant pastor, and ultimately pastor. She reports that "God has also moved her into other areas of labor conducting revivals and holding teaching sessions in various places."

In her secular job, she began working with the Lynchburg City Schools in 1970 starting as a food service worker, but God moved her through the ranks to the position of Coordinator for the School Nutrition Program. Through this she gained experience concerning administrative duties, dealing with the public, and problem solving.

After taking the necessary courses in the Pentecostal Holiness denomination, she received her license for ministry in 1992 and was ordained in 2006. Her goal has been to seek excellence in her life and be a living example of how God will move you up to higher positions as you prove yourself faithful and trustworthy.

She lives in Lynchburg with her husband Charles (Buddy), who has been a great supporter in her ministry. They have five children and seven grandchildren.

Betty Walling
South Carolina Conference

She writes that she began her music ministry at the age of nine having been saved at that age and immediately called to serve God. Three people who influenced her life include a Sunday school teacher, Bonnie Thurman, who went home to be with the Lord in May of 2008 at ninety-nine years of age; her paternal grandfather, and her husband, Rev. Robert Walling.

Her grandfather used the Bible as a teaching tool in administering discipline. He made her read a chapter or chapters depending on her offense then go to him and explain what the Scriptures were teaching. This began when she was only three years old, so her older sibling, usually the partner in crime, had to read the chapter to her and help her understand the significance.

Her husband showed to her and others around them the life of a true Christian. They pastored many churches; they used vacation time to go overseas for crusades or teach in one of the denomination's colleges. They also were involved in prison ministry for six years while pastoring. Often Robert preached in one section of the compound while she did so in another part.

Other aspects of her ministry include teaching seminars and serving as music director in five churches. Her husband plays twenty instruments, and she plays organ, piano, melodica, and accordion. Since Betty was ten, she traveled with evangelists using her musical ability. Later, she started doing puppetry.

She expresses that "The greatest difficulty [faced in ministry] was [not being accepted] here in my own country, yet overseas very accepted. When my husband had his home going on July 15, 2006, I was told to leave the church we were pastoring. (I was associate pastor). 'There is no church for you.' Had I been a male minister, I would have either stayed on or been given another church."

She was licensed by the South Carolina Conference in 1991 and ordained in 1993.

Debra F. Whiteside
South Carolina Conference

Debra writes, "I really have a testimony." She was married at the age of fifteen because her father signed for the marriage to keep from having to pay child support. She remained in that marriage for eleven years, which resulted in emotional, spiritual, and financial bankruptcy. Two years after the divorce, she met and married a man with three small children ages four, six, and eight.

During those years, she wandered around spiritually until she came to a church named Lighthouse. At every altar call, she would run to the front and cry out to God. Her life was not working, and she began to wonder where the abundant life described in the Bible was.

This second marriage ended when her husband left her. For two years she prayed for reconciliation, wondering how this could happen to a child of God. She did a lot of soul searching to try to determine why she had chosen two men so much like her own father.

Through all of this, however, God was good. He sustained; He administered grace to go on. Because of her experiences, she was able to start a class for those who were single again. All of the years of bad times had been a school of God's training.

She is currently pastoring [January 2008] Trinity Pentecostal Holiness Church in Lancaster, South Carolina. The next chapter in her life has just begun; the book is not finished yet.

Dr. Twila Wilczynski
Ephesians 4 Network

"I have a desire to press into the perfect things of God according to Hebrews 6:1a, 4-5. There is more to the things of God than the basic principles of repentance, faith, baptisms, resurrection, and judgment. Part of the mandate of my life is to help people learn to partake of the Holy Ghost, taste the Word of God and walk in power," she writes.

Twila has two associate degrees, a bachelor of fine arts and a doctorate in biblical studies. She and her husband founded Living Waters Christian Church in their conference. After ten years in the ministry, she indicates that not being received by men and women as a minister called by God has been her greatest difficulty. She feels that people sometimes unconsciously think adversely of women in the ministry and that it is a grassroots problem.

Myrtle Wood
Appalachian Conference

Sister Wood is a retired licensed minister having devoted sixty-five years of service to her Lord. She graduated from Holmes Bible College as valedictorian and from King's Business College in Charlotte, North Carolina. She assisted her husband in pastorates in the conference for forty years. Myrtle said the greatest difficulty she encountered being a woman minister was balancing church duties with family responsibilities.

(**Author's note:** Unfortunately, the response to my request for input was very small when compared to the number of forms sent out – more than six hundred. Only seventy-four forms were returned. The ladies who did return them represent eighteen of the twenty-seven conferences in the IPHC. My thanks to those who took the time to furnish the information. I have used their responses with permission.)

"Leave her alone," said Jesus. "Why are you bothering her? She has done a beautiful thing to me . . . She did what she could." – Mark 14:6-8a-NIV

While in Bethany in the home of Simon the Leper, Mary the sister of Martha came with an alabaster jar, anointed Jesus' head, poured the costly perfume on Jesus' feet, then wiped them with her hair. Some of the disciples voiced angry criticism of this apparent extravagance. Jesus rebuked Mary's critics and defended her action, calling it a beautiful thing. He saw it as an expression of love and devotion to Him.

Often in our efforts to serve God, skeptics and critics stand on the side line and voice their opinions that what we do is stupid, wasteful, and unreasonable; however, God looks into our hearts and sees either true love and devotion or hypocrisy. Only He understands our motives. If we serve Him in love, consecration, and sincerity, no matter how small and insignificant our actions, He will say "well done." The fact is that we should do what we can.

The previous accounts are representative of those who have done just that. They have given of themselves in the vineyard of the Lord. Life was not always good to them, and the circumstances were not always favorable, but we can see from their own stories and those written by others that they persevered in spite of the difficulties. These women are real life examples of those who did and are doing beautiful things for the Lord.

---

[1] The information in this chapter was obtained from forms respondents or a family member returned to me, but the entire text of their comments is not always included.

[2] Nelle Goodman, "Julie," *The Helping Hand*, July/August 1986, p. 5.

CHAPTER 3

Revive Us Again

"Will you not revive us again, that your people may rejoice in you?" – Psalm 85:6-NIV.

Never in the span of human history has man not needed revival. No matter how close we get to God, we can look up and see one more rung on the ladder we need to step up on. The Apostle Paul's philosophy was one of pressing onward, forward, and upward for Christ. The call of God to humankind has been to bring them to such an intimate relationship with Him that they can feel His heartbeat. He wants them pure and dedicated, not half-hearted in their devotion to Him. He wants His Church, the Bride, ready for His return. That requires a perpetual spirit of revival. God's words to Israel during the reign of Solomon at the completion of the temple are relevant for us in this generation: *"If my people, who are called by my name, will humble themselves and pray and seek my face and turn from their wicked ways, then will I hear from heaven and will forgive their sin and will heal their land."* – 2 Chronicles 7:14.

In this the twenty-first century, God's people are no less in need of a great spiritual awakening than were His people in Isaiah's time, 760 – 698 B.C. (ca.). Since God does not change, then His requirements are the same from one civilization to the next.

The cry of man repeatedly has been for the Divine Sustainer of Life to bring spiritual healing to his broken heart. After exercising every possible ability and scheme to aid himself, the individual has often waited until he hit rock bottom before calling upon the Lord.

Nehemiah, cup-bearer to King Artaxerxes, wrote about this condition when he felt led of the Lord to rebuild the walls of Jerusalem after the return of the Southern Kingdom of Judah from Babylonian captivity: *"Then I said to them, 'You see the trouble (distress-KJV) we are in: Jerusalem lies in ruins, and its gates have been burned with fire. Come, let us rebuild the wall of Jerusalem, and we will no longer be in disgrace'"* – Nehemiah 2:17-NIV.

What was the reason for that distress? The nation had become cold and indifferent toward God; they had violated His commandments; they had gone away from Jehovah; He had allowed a heathen power to exercise control over them taking them away from their beloved land. After seventy years they realized why they were where they were. Nehemiah made provision for the priests and the temple worship to resume; he reformed the abuses; he restored the sanctity of the Sabbath. Revival came after much prayer, repentance, and change.

Look at Ezra's plea later in the book of Nehemiah 9:36, 37: *"But see, we are slaves today, slaves in the land you gave our forefathers so they could eat its fruit and the other good things it produces. Because of our sins, its abundant harvest goes to the kings you have placed over us. They rule over our bodies and our cattle as they please. We are in great distress"*-NIV.

Jeremiah in Lamentations voices this same fervency of spirit in confession and seeking God for restoration on the part of the nation of Judah: *"See, O Lord, how distressed I am! I am in torment within and in my heart I am disturbed, for I have been most rebellious . . . ."* – 1:20-NIV.

Scripture after Scripture reminds us of the awfulness of drifting away from God because of weakness, arrogance, pride, sin, and neglect. These attitudes demand that we come to the Almighty in repentance, pleading with Him for revival as those in days gone by.

The following give accounts of God's moving in various revivals, all preached by lady evangelists, as reported in *The Evangel, The Co-Worker,* and *The Advocate* published by the IPHC from May 1949 to September 1979.

"Abbotsburg Reporting Best Revival in Church History"

Mrs. Moses Thomas reports that the Abbottsburg Pentecostal Holiness Church had just experienced one of the best revivals in the history of the church. It took a lot of praying and working together to bring the revival spirit their way. Some said the church had been dead for years, but this was not true.

They began prayer meetings New Year's night in the homes praying for a revival. This continued for five weeks. After this Sister Viola Benson was invited to come and conduct a meeting for them.

The fire was already burning when she arrived, and she helped fan the flame. Sixteen were saved, twelve sanctified and four received the baptism of the Holy Spirit. Thirteen joined the church; more are expected to join later. Sister Benson was with them eleven nights. Seekers would stop their work and come to the church to join in the prayer held each morning at ten o'clock. Three received their baptism during those morning prayers.

The evangelist left, but the revival continued. They are trusting God for a great gathering of souls as God does hear and answer prayer.[1]

(**Author's note:** The following is a revival schedule for Pearl Benz that appeared in *The Advocate*, November 16, 1950, covering the latter part of 1949 through July of the following year. This is followed by a report of one of her revivals in the East Oklahoma Conference that was published in the January 10, 1952, issue of *The Advocate*.)

"Old Time Revival"

A two weeks revival at the Bethel Pentecostal Holiness Church in the East Oklahoma Conference closed Sunday night November 25, 1950, with many in the altar. Rev. Pearl Benz of Ardmore was the invited evangelist. Sister Benz came with a message that stirred the church as well as sinners; her message was the type of preaching that Bishop Melton described in the *Advocate*, November 8, as being needed in our churches. It certainly had its effect in this revival: seven saved, seven sanctified, four received Pentecost – many were healed.

Sister Benz preached to the standard of holiness and Pentecost as the preachers did forty-two years ago. That type of preaching will produce the genuine. The folks came to the altar, gave up their tobacco, and prayed through in the old time way.[2]

"Thirty Experiences in Del City, Okla. Revival"

Rev. Pearl Benz of Ardmore, Oklahoma conducted a revival at the Del City Church in Oklahoma in which there were thirty experiences.

Of this number ten were saved, eleven sanctified, and nine received the baptism of the Holy Spirit.

Mrs. Benz was assisted in the services by Rev. and Mrs. James McAlister of Norman, singers; and Miss Helen Weston, pianist.[3]

"Lowland and Hobucken Have Great Revivals"

Pastor Viola Jarvis reported that she received four new members into the Lowland Church, two of whom did not have the Holy Spirit. While giving them the right hand of fellowship one of them received the baptism. The other lay under the power ten hours.

At the close of one of the Sunday services at Hobucken as she was shaking hands at the door, one of the regular visitors was saved and sanctified at the door and shouted up and down the aisle.

She expressed her thanks to God for real old time religion and requested prayer that the year will be the best in the history of these churches.[4]

"Revival Continues in Pulaski"

Rev. C. J. Peyton, pastor, made a report of the first three weeks of revival services with the Pentecostal Holiness Church in Pulaski, Virginia. Miss Helen Marie Parrish was the evangelist. The revival began with the morning service December 29, 1951, and Helen stayed with them three weeks. While there, she spoke to the freshman and sophomore grades in the high school. She is the first Pentecostal Holiness speaker to ever address any part of the high school in Pulaski. Helen also spoke to the fourth, fifth, and sixth grade students of the Jefferson Street School.

The report stated that the revival continued after Helen left, with Rev. A. D. Evans, an evangelist of the Western North Carolina Conference, doing the preaching. He was with the Pulaski church for two weeks.

During the five weeks of revival there were seventy-two experiences and thirty-eight members added to the church. The church attendance in general improved. On February 10 of that year, they had 253 present for Sunday school.

The pastor wrote: "The revival goes on, though the evangelist has gone."[5]

"Revival in Batesburg"

September 7th brought to a close the best revival the Batesburg [church in South Carolina] had experienced for years. Mrs. Mattie Smith of Jacksonville, Florida was used mightily of God in this tent revival to awaken and strengthen the three sponsoring Pentecostal Holiness Churches: Amick Grove, Double Branches, and Twin City.

Many messages were given and interpreted by the Holy Ghost. At least seven souls were saved. Church members and pastors were stirred and revived, and going back to their churches with a determination to seek God's will and do it.

Many sick bodies were healed. They expressed thanks to God for those three weeks of spiritual manna. Words cannot express appreciation for Mrs. Smith's anointed ministry. "Her consecration and obedience have been a great inspiration to us. We truly believe that God sent her our way."[6]

"From Sister Goff"

The revival at Pikeville, North Carolina closed October 26, 1952. Six received the Holy Spirit. Among them was the deacon of the church who had sought for the infilling for seven years. Quite a number were saved and sanctified and several joined the church. Sister Goff's daughter, Ada Lee, had the regular evangelistic services; Rev. Goff conducted the children's services.

The meeting was well attended. Sister Goff stated that the church was a live, spiritual one and an unusual number of young people have been baptized in the Holy Spirit. They had a real wide-awake Auxiliary and Sunday school.

"I'm still on the battlefield, will be seventy-two in December, but I've got the same mind to work I had when I was sanctified at fifteen years of age," writes Sister Goff.[7]

"Work in San Benito"
Rev. Henrietta Liles

On December 15, 1950, a little evangelistic party pulled out of a bank of snow in Benton Harbor, Michigan, tackled icy roads in sub-zero weather, and started for Texas between blizzards. The Liles' family had less than forty dollars to make the trip on. They had been told they would never make it. Their eighteen-year-old son had the responsibility of towing their thirty-three foot house-trailer. It was his first experience to tow anything, and he had only about three months of driving experience, but he believed he could make it. Like Christian in Pilgrim's Progress, they encountered a few difficulties, but God quickly supplied the need, and on December 21, just a week to the day, and almost to the hour, they pulled into Weslaco, Texas.

After conducting a revival there, the Liles, under the supervision of William J. Moore, established a little church in January 1951, in San Benito, Texas, which is about twenty-six miles from Weslaco. In a rented building they began with eight members and twenty in Sunday school. After a month they moved into a rented building, and then in the spring bought a lot on which they built a little church building. In June they started having services in it.

At a watch-night service at Weslaco, New Year's Eve 1952, two of the young people received definite calls to service. Jeanette Liles, Rev. Henrietta Liles' daughter-in-law, got her call to preach, and has been conducting services, and held one revival. Her daughter, Esther Liles, got her call to Africa, and was at that time a student at Southwestern Bible College in Oklahoma preparing to go to the mission field. A few months before, her son, William Thomas Liles, tarried unto three o'clock in the morning for the baptism of the Holy Spirit. Later, another daughter, Mary E. Bell, received her call to preach, and preached her first sermon at the monthly fellowship meeting at the church in San Benito the following week. Many others have been deeply moved, and people have been healed.[8]

Rev. Effie Roberson, Evangelist

Rev. Effie Roberson reported in *The Co-Worker* about a number of revivals that she conducted. She states, "When I arrived in South Boston to begin a revival I was happy to find a group of prayer-warriors. As the revival continued I was deeply impressed with the interest shown in prayer." As a result of this intense intercession they experienced God's mighty presence as "waves of glory swept over the congregation every night. It was a time of drawing near to God."

At the Shelby Pentecostal Holiness Church they "rejoiced in a great awakening as the mighty power of God swept over the congregation from time to time." Sister Roberson indicates that "there were times the Lord blessed so wonderfully that the midnight hours arrived and still people would not want to go home."

Three young men, whose wives were members of the church, went to the altar to seek God for deliverance from sin and were saved. There was "real joy in the camp" with shouting and praises lifted to glorify God.

Effie writes about the Siler City church, "On Easter Monday we began a meeting and the Lord wonderfully met with us." One man said, "This is the best revival we have had in fifteen years." God also stretched forth His hand as the Great Healer and many experienced His touch. This was described as an old time holiness revival and mentioned that holiness is the need of the twentieth century church.

The Lord also visited with the people of the Falls of Nuese Pentecostal Holiness Church. The people there were very discouraged because there were so few of them to carry on the work. They were lifted up above their shadows of despair and encouraged to move on for the Lord. The latter part of the week the Lord began to deal with the lost, and people began to seek God until they prayed through.

During the revival at the Bassett church the "spiritual tide seemed to rise higher and higher each night. God was in that place. The Lord began to save, sanctify, baptize with the Holy Ghost and heal."

At Pisgah View she reports, "There were not too many experiences, but there was a great moving toward God among the saints." It was a time when people made wrongs right and sought forgiveness, when negligent Christians renewed their covenant with God and saints again had a longing to be in the house of God.

"On the last night of this revival," Sister Roberson says, "the church was filled with approximately another church full outside." The power of God was so strong and so greatly filled the place that people were weeping and wanting to be saved even after the service had been dismissed.[9]

"Oildale Church Reports"

Mrs. Bessie Anderson, wife of Rev. W. J. Anderson, conference superintendent, recently held revival services at the Oildale Church in Bakersfield, California.

In the revival twelve were saved, four sanctified, and two received the baptism of the Holy Spirit.[10]

"Turner Conducts Revival in Carthage, N.C."

Carthage Pentecostal Holiness Church was blessed by the ministry of Rev. Grace Turner and her husband.

Mrs. Turner preached soul-stirring messages that brought souls to the altar seeking salvation and other definite experiences with God. Twelve were saved, eight sanctified, and six received the Holy Spirit.[11]

"Twenty-Five Experiences at Yadkinville"

The Yadkinville Pentecostal Holiness Church in the Western North Carolina Conference was richly blessed by the ministry of Miss Betty Baxter and Miss Faye Penland in a revival September 11-20, 1964. They preached, sang, and worked under the anointing of the Holy Spirit

There were twenty-five definite experiences: eight saved, twelve sanctified, and five received the baptism with the Holy Spirit. This revival resulted in eight new members in their church.[12]

"Twenty-Seven Experiences in Braggs Revival"

The Braggs, Oklahoma Pentecostal Holiness Church enjoyed a two weeks' revival with Freda Adams of Childers, Texas as the evangelist. She preached every night under the anointing of the Holy Spirit. Her father, who was with her, is a good altar worker and was a great help in the meeting. They were a great blessing to the church.

They had twenty-seven experiences: thirteen saved, seven sanctified, seven filled with the Holy Spirit, eleven baptized in water, and ten joined the church.[13]

"Revival at Greenwood Church"

God greatly blessed the Greenwood Pentecostal Holiness Church in Hampton, Virginia with a wonderful Holy Ghost revival in early January with Betty Baxter and Faye Penland from Maiden, North Carolina as the evangelists.

From the very first service God blessed and souls were saved, sanctified and filled with the Holy Spirit. It was a time when people ran to the altar seeking God and at times would pray late into the night.

In a little more than one week God saved thirty-two people, sanctified twenty-two, and filled twenty-one with His Spirit. Seventeen joined the church, and as a body moved closer to God with a greater desire than ever to proclaim the wonderful message of Christ.[14]

"Revival at Roanoke Rapids"

The Pentecostal Holiness Church in Roanoke Rapids, North Carolina closed on April 13 one of the best revivals the church had in some years.

Misses Betty Baxter and Faye Penland ministered under the anointing of the Holy Spirit every night. Along with the pastor, Rev. B. C. Horrell, the church body had been praying for a mighty revival. The burden Betty and Faye have for the lost just fit in, and God worked through them to meet the spiritual needs of the church.

Approximately sixty experiences were witnessed at the altar. This does not include the ones that received a definite healing in their bodies. God greatly used this evangelistic team in expounding the gospel to the lost and awakening the church. Many people who had been reluctant to do so before this revival sought deeper experiences with the Lord. A wonderful awakening of the Christians as well as the sinners and community was realized in Roanoke Rapids.[15]

"Old Fashioned Brush Arbor Revival"

God gave a vision of an old-fashioned brush arbor to members of the Pentecostal Holiness Church in Pea Ridge, Arkansas, a small town with a population of nine hundred in beautiful northwest Arkansas, in the Midwest Conference.

Plans were made, poles were erected, and then loads of brush were piled on top. The pews and altars were boards on blocks of wood. The pulpit was eye-catching. It was only a pole erected upward with a 12" by 12" board nailed onto it. The brush arbor was the talk of the town.

After two weeks of labor on the arbor, services got under way on July 6th with the church pastor, Rev. Bobby Schooley, preaching the first week. Evangelist Clymena Bowling, formerly from Springfield, Missouri, continued the meeting for an additional two and one-half weeks. She preached an old-fashioned gospel under the anointing of the Holy Spirit. People came from miles to be in the services, many who had never been to a brush arbor previously.

Souls were saved, sanctified, and baptized with the Holy Spirit. Short legs were lengthened, back conditions were corrected, and diseases and sicknesses were healed.[16]

"Greta Campbell Trio Conducts Revival at Langley"

During the first week-end in April 1973, the Greta Campbell Party from Greenville, South Carolina was in revival at the Langley Pentecostal Holiness Church, Langley, South Carolina.

The anointed messages brought by Sister Campbell, together with the beautiful and inspiring music by Miss Campbell and Miss Patsy Welch, were a great blessing to the church. A wonderful spirit prevailed in each service, and the congregation reaped the benefits from this outstanding ministry.[17]

"Sixty-Eight Experiences at Faith Church"

The Faith Pentecostal Holiness Church in Greenville, North Carolina recently closed a great Pentecostal revival. They experienced a number praying through to the Pentecostal Baptism for fourteen consecutive services. According to their testimony there were twenty-two saved, fourteen sanctified, thirty-two baptized in the Holy Spirit. Several were healed. The gifts of the Spirit were also manifested.

On the last day of the revival, July 8, 1973, the Faith Church joined with Grimesland and Hodges Chapel Churches for a water baptismal service, and the pastors baptized forty-two in water, twenty of these being from the Faith Church. They received nine members into the fellowship of Faith Church with others to join later. God is still moving in the land getting people ready for Christ's return.

The evangelist for this revival was Mrs. Shirley Jones of Selma, North Carolina. She came to America from Australia at the close of World War II and has been saved, sanctified, filled with the Spirit and called to preach since arriving in this country. She is a dynamic speaker with a Spirit-anointed message and a great altar worker, especially in praying with those seeking the baptism in the Spirit.[18]

"Husband-Wife Evangelistic Team to Have Retreat Here"

A Spiritual Retreat at Hodgesville Pentecostal Holiness Church began on Sunday, September 23, 1979, at 11:00 a.m. and continued nightly through Friday. Rev. and Mrs. S. J. Williams served as the evangelistic team.

The Rev. S. J. Williams has been a pastor and evangelist, and for nine years was a personal representative for Oral Roberts. Mrs. Williams is also an evangelist and a well known teacher on prayer. She has taught public school and has also been a professor at Oral Roberts University.

Katie Campbell
Evangelist
Virginia Conference

Mrs. Katie Campbell was a well known evangelist who traveled widely in the Pentecostal Holiness Church. She was much loved by those who knew her well and by those who knew her only through her ministry.

Rev. Wesley Peyton wrote this about her: "Aunt Katie was one of the most outstanding evangelists in the Virginia Conference. She and her daughter Libby Daniels used to sing together. Their premier song was "When I Wake up in Glory."

"She preached twenty-one revivals at the Pentecostal Holiness Church in White Sulphur Spring, West Virginia. She returned to many churches on an annual basis. Her ministry brought revival. She lived by faith, loved her hot tea, 'shouting,' and grapefruit.

"When I was a young pastor, she spoke for me in Greenville, North Carolina. I called and asked her how I should advertise her. She replied, 'Tell them the King's daughter is coming to town.' Indeed she was the king's daughter. She spoke with dignity and was one of the few women preachers that men seemed to enjoy hearing in that day and time."[19]

(**Author's note:** The following are excerpts from various articles appearing in the *Virginia Conference News* about revivals held by Sister Katie Campbell. When criticized about being a woman preacher, Sister Campbell would reply that women helped bring sin in the world, so they needed to help get it out. I knew her through the number of revivals she held in Hopewell, Virginia when Rev. L. C. Synan was pastor of the Pentecostal Holiness Church there. I was a teenager, but her ministry blessed me. Her son, Carl Lee Campbell, a pastor in the Eastern Virginia Conference, influenced me to attend Holmes Bible College.)

"Sister Campbell at White Sulphur"
1954

On January 24, 1954, Mrs. Katie Campbell of Shenandoah, Virginia went to the White Sulphur Springs Pentecostal Holiness Church in West Virginia to conduct its mid-winter revival for the fourth consecutive year. The attendance was good considering the amount of sickness in the church, which affected whole families. However, the same old-time Pentecostal preaching was enjoyed by old and young alike, and the church was uplifted.

As in the past, people from other denominations attended and enjoyed these services. Also, as in the past, Sister Campbell's ministry brought souls to a saving knowledge of Christ.

The revival closed February 7, with ten saved and two sanctified. One other person was saved after the revival services were over. They were expecting to receive some new members into the church that month.[20]

"Mrs. Campbell Conducts Revival at Redland, N. C."
November 1955

On October 2, the Redland Pentecostal Holiness Church began a revival with Evangelist Mrs. Katie Campbell as the invited speaker. God blessed her efforts in a great way. God gave definite experiences in almost every service. Her messages were fire-filled and the presence of God was felt by all.

There was conviction on sinners and Christians were drawn nearer to God.[21]

"Mrs. Campbell in Birmingham"
December 1955

Pastor O. N. Todd, Jr. reports a spirit of revival has been present in the North Birmingham Pentecostal Holiness Church for some months. On November 6, 1955, Sister Katie Campbell began a series of services delivering messages full of love and power from on high. They were used of God in bringing many sinners to Christ, to help those seeking to be sanctified, and to encourage others to pray through to the Baptism of the Holy Spirit. Sister Campbell's singing was also a source of real inspiration and blessing. A number of folk were healed by the mighty power of the Great Physician.[22]

"Mrs. Campbell in Richmond"
December 1955

The West End Pentecostal Holiness Chapel enjoyed a successful revival conducted by Sister Katie Campbell. Bernard Moss wrote that she inspired their souls in the Lord. Four people were saved during the week and many were drawn nearer to the Lord.[23]

"Mrs. Campbell in Revival at Bethel"
February 1956

The Bethel Pentecostal Holiness Church in the Western North Carolina Conference had a two weeks' revival with Mrs. Katie Campbell as evangelist. The Lord blessed the church in such a way that all the membership (with the exception of two elderly women) were present and shouting the victory the closing night.

Families came weeping to the altar, and on a Sunday a man, his wife and daughter were saved. Both husband and wife prayed through and received the baptism during the meeting.

There were sixteen experiences in all. Nine were saved, five were sanctified and two prayed through to Pentecost.[24]

"Mrs. Campbell Conducts Revival with the St. John P. H. Church"
March 1956

Rev. Carlton Eades, pastor of the St. John Pentecostal Holiness Church in the Western North Carolina Conference, reported that Mrs. Katie Campbell had recently closed a successful revival there. Several were saved in the services and four united with the church at the close of the revival.[25]

"Salem Enjoys Another Good Revival"
June 1956

Twenty-one definite experiences were recorded as a result of the revival conducted in the Pentecostal Holiness Church in Salem, Virginia. Evangelist Katie Campbell did the preaching. There was eager and enthusiastic interest in every service because of the inspiring and anointed preaching of God's Word. Souls were saved and reclaimed. Some prayed on through to the deeper experiences of sanctification and Pentecost. The hearts of the Christians were encouraged and many who had never done so before joined in a chain of prayer that ran from 6 a.m. until 7 p.m. each day.[26]

The story repeated itself time after time when Sister Campbell held revivals at the Hunter's Fork Pentecostal Holiness Church in the Eastern Virginia Conference; in Burlington, Winston Salem, Elizabeth City, Tyner, and at Howard Memorial Pentecostal Holiness Church in Greensboro, North Carolina; Richmond and Altavista, Virginia; and in Bloxham Heights, Florida. Many of these were repeat revivals for the location, with some churches having Sister Katie preach for them nine or more times.

These revivals mentioned above were held between February 1956 and December 1958 and resulted in more than one hundred, thirty experiences. Of course, this does not include all the revivals Sister Campbell held. All of the churches reported great success in the meetings. "Sister Campbell preaches old-time holiness," wrote Rev. L. T. Chappell, pastor at Tyner.

Other comments about her ministry speak of her anointing and how she blessed their church. "Sister Campbell has proven to us that an old fashioned gospel message will still get the job done." "When Mrs. Campbell brought her messages in her own wonderful way she was a great blessing to the church." "If this world had more Katie Campbells it would be a better world in which to live." "We were thoroughly blessed by her ministry." "We were inspired by our evangelist." "The church felt the impact of the revival spirit through the inspiring messages delivered by the evangelist."

What a wonderful legacy this dear saint of God has left for her family and friends, those to whom she ministered, and to the Pentecostal Holiness Church! Only eternity will reveal the good she has done. Her life was truly dedicated to her Master, and she was an amazing ambassador of the Lord Jesus Christ.

The Advocate, The Challenge, The Evangel, and other publications, often printed the availability of evangelists and/or their schedules for coming months. Some of those mentioned were the following:

EVANGELIST	FROM	YEAR
Johnson – Houser	Gastonia, NC	1950
Pearl Benz	Ardmore, OK	1950
Lacie Bass & Melba Littleton		1951
The Greta Campbell Trio	Greenville, NC	1964
Lou Spencer	Carey, NC	1981
Jeraldine Posey	Hopewell, VA	1981
Baxter-Penland	Maiden, NC	1986
Rita Boyette	Goldsboro, NC	1986
Dana Craig	Bangor, ME	1986
Jean Duncan	Lewisville, NC	1986
Vera Griffin	Goldsboro, NC	1986[27]

In the December 1961 issue of *The Challenge*, the official publication of the South Carolina Conference, a number of lady ministers' names were listed who were giving their full-time to evangelistic work: Mrs. Lula Mae Putnam, Miss Ann Chavis, Mrs. Ela Winn, Miss Natalie Carnes, Miss Dorothy Mae Welch, and Mrs. Lila Medlin. The same article states that other evangelists were available, but these were the only ones giving their full-time to this ministry. They were available for meetings anytime and anywhere in the conference.[28]

"Youth Camp Speakers"

Speakers for the 1969 Youth Camps are the Greta Campbell Party of Mobile, Alabama. Miss Greta Campbell has for a number of years been active in evangelistic work full-time. She and Miss Patsy Welch are excellent singers and musicians, having made several records. Their musical ministry is a tremendous complement to their success. Very few have met with such great acceptance across the denomination.[29]

These women evangelists were listed in *The Challenge*, Winter 1971: Natalie Carnes, Hazleen Graham, Hazel Griffith, and Mildred Osborne. Of these, Natalie Carnes is the only one mentioned who was also an evangelist in 1961.[30]

"Fires of Revival and Evangelism At Lancaster First Church"

The Lancaster First Pentecostal Holiness Church, Lancaster, South Carolina was blessed with a great revival led by Rev. Shirley Jones in November of 1988. Prior to her going, the church conducted a fervent prayer vigil seeking a true revival brought by the Holy Spirit, and God sent one their way by His servant and evangelist.

One could look into the face of this precious little lady from Australia and see Jesus. The fruit of the Spirit was evident; she made the Gospel come alive with her testimony, and the love of Christ was real.

The words spoken by the preacher were not lost on those who heard. This congregation was hungry for revival. The power of conviction was felt even by those who had become cold and indifferent. Twenty-two were saved, eleven sanctified, ten were baptized with the Holy Spirit, and eight new members were added to the church. As many as twenty church members who had lost their way were reclaimed.

The Spirit stayed alive after the evangelist was gone and the church was earnestly endeavoring to be faithful to God.[31]

"Greenville First in Spiritual Quest"

The Greenville First Pentecostal Holiness Church in Tennessee entered a spiritual quest for the move of God on March 1, 1955. An Intercessory

Prayer Power Release began the next day with fasting, an aggressive outreach, and giving toward revival.

Janetta Adams, of Ashland, Kentucky, an ordained minister in the Appalachian Conference, was scheduled to be in revival with them April 2-5. In 1989, she and her two sisters formed a country gospel singing group, Mountain Harmony. She began her solo ministry in 1993, making her first recording that same year. Janetta is assistant pastor to her father, Rev. Billy Adams, at Burning Bush Pentecostal Holiness Church in Flemingsburg, Kentucky.[32]

The following information appeared in the *Appalachian Conference Messenger* in 1998:

Lee McKenzie, a native of West Virginia, had transferred from the Sonshine (Florida) Conference to the Appalachian Conference after living in Florida and South Georgia for forty years. She is an ordained minister and a licensed practical nurse. Sister McKenzie is available for revivals, retreats, seminars, outdoor meetings and pulpit vacancies.

Vickie McLaughlin Viars, a licensed minister in the Appalachian Conference, was seeking opportunities to preach. At that time she was ministering at Evansham Manor Rest Home in Wytheville, Virginia, and had two radio broadcasts that aired the first Saturday of each month, alternating.

The "Blessed are the Broken" was heard over WCRR in Rural Retreat, and "The Broken but Blessed" was broadcast over WBLB in Pulaski.[33]

Two others appeared in the same publication in 2000.

The Rev. Kathy Sandlin, an ordained minister in the Upper South Carolina Conference, serves as the first full-time WIN Director of the Conference and of the IPHC.

A former pioneer pastor and church planter, Kathy resigned a full-time church to take the Ministry of Intercession to all who would receive it. She is preacher, teacher, singer, songwriter, musician, and has authored several books such as *School of Intercession: Volumes I, II and III; Altar Worker/Prayer Counselor Training Manual; Prayer Diary of a Mother's Heart; Handmaiden For Harvest* and others.

Kathy earned a bachelor of theology degree and at the time was working toward her master's in ministry degree.[34]

(**Author's note:** The information above was used to announce Kathy as the speaker at the June 2000 Women's Ministries Convention.)

Sharon Hartman, an ordained minister in the Appalachian Conference, announced her availability to fill in weekends for pastors or hold weekend revivals. Also she would help in holding Christian Education workshops in teacher training, children's ministry, Sunday school, and doctrine.

She has worked in Christian Education for twenty-five years serving as Christian Education director, Sunday school superintendent, youth minister, director of Vacation Bible School, teacher of many various classes from adult to children, and filling many other positions.

Sharon is a teacher in the public school system, holding B.S. and M.S. degrees in elementary education with an endorsement as an elementary principal.[35]

Another article that was published in *The Challenge*, Spring 2003 reported a revival at Wagener, South Carolina. where Gladys Capers served as pastor. She states: "Souls were saved, Spirit-filled, healed, and set free. Holy laughter was manifested, and some said they would never be the same following these services." Evangelist Sylvia Bowen preached this revival.[36]

Revivals in the IPHC conducted by women have not been limited to these cited, but this is characteristic of those taking place in the three decades referenced (1949-1979). Too, the emphasis in this book is on women in the ministry as pastors and evangelists. The point is to highlight their efforts and successes in the role to which God called them and opened doors of opportunity for them to be vessels through whom He could move and minister.

Some interesting observations about these reports of revival by different evangelists are they usually lasted from two to four weeks, sometimes longer. They resulted in a number of experiences: saved, sanctified, baptized in the Holy Spirit. People were healed. The evangelists' preaching was anointed by the Holy Spirit, and the churches grew with people who received these experiences joining the church. One thing of vital importance was prayer. Some of the churches had been praying for a while before the evangelists arrived. Others had prayer meeting all day every day during the revival, or one morning a week during the meetings. The key is that they prayed down revival. It will come again to us if we seek God.

Yes, revival fires burned. These great ladies mentioned and many others not named, studied the Word, prayed to God, and traveled extensively to preach the gospel to all who would hear. Many responded with tears of repentance, saint and sinner alike, as the Spirit moved upon them.

God grant that the day of revival will come upon us in this twenty-first century and the time will soon appear when the pulpits of all churches will be open to receive women to minister as God has called them. Release these ladies and allow the Holy Spirit to move through them to bless others. Let these vessels of honor speak, for the Lord has ordained them to give forth His Word. They too have rivers of living water gushing out of them to help restore the barren land of souls that has become dry from neglect. They have a message; they have the anointing; give them the opportunity.

Lord, let you handmaid speak!

---

[1] *The Evangel*, May 1949.
[2] *The Advocate*, January 10, 1952, p. 8.
[3] *The Advocate*, March 3, 1955.
[4] *The Evangel*, March 1951, p. 3.
[5] *The Advocate*, February 28, 1952, p. 12.
[6] *The Advocate*, October 2, 1952, p. 4.
[7] *The Advocate*, November 27, 1952, p. 13.
[8] *The Advocate*, December 4, 1952, pp. 11, 14.
[9] *The Co-Worker*, November 1954, pp. 3-4, 6.
[10] *The Advocate*, March 3, 1955.
[11] *The Advocate*, March 17, 1955.
[12] *The Advocate*, October, 31, 1964
[13] *The* Advocate, October 31, 1964
[14] *The Advocate*, April, 12, 1969.
[15] *The Advocate*, May 24, 1969.
[16] Lorene Fletcher, *The Advocate*, November 13, 1969, p. 15.
[17] *The Advocate*, June 29, 1973.
[18] *The Advocate*, November 8, 1973.
[19] Letter from Rev. Wesley Peyton.
[20-26] *Virginia Conference News*.
[27] *The Advocate*.
[28] *The Challenge*, December 1961.
[29] *The Evangel*, June 1969.
[30] *The Challenge*, Winter 1971.
[31] *The Challenge*, Spring 1989, p. 3.
[32] *Appalachian Conference Messenger*, March 1995.
[33] *Appalachian Conference Messenger*, 1998.
[34] *Appalachian Conference Messenger*, 2000.
[35] *Appalachian Conference Messenger*.
[36] *The Challenge*, Spring 2003, p. 4.

CHAPTER 4

Her Works Bring Her Praise

"Give her the reward she has earned, and let her works bring her praise at the city gate" – Proverbs 31:31-NIV.

The following women distinguished themselves as a "first" in their field. It took courage to go where their gender does not usually go; they were walking on paths that female feet had not trodden. Yet, they dared to move in that direction because God was leading them to break new ground; they succeeded and opened the door for others to follow. The clarion call goes forth to those who remain on the sidelines to take up the sword of the Spirit and the shield of faith, put on the breastplate of righteousness, shod your feet, and "Go ye"!

"First Woman Superintendent Appointed"

Rev. Mrs. Doyce Dunn

An historic milestone was reached in the Pentecostal Holiness Church with the appointment of the church's first woman superintendent [June (?)1984]. She is the Rev. Mrs. Doyce Dunn, superintendent of the Northwest Conference.

Rev. Dunn was pastoring and serving as assistant superintendent in her conference. With the resignation of Superintendent C. J. Reaves in December, the General Evangelism Board consulted with the Northwest Conference Board and reached the decision for Rev. Dunn to assume the role of superintendent. She was unanimously approved.

"The Board's decision appears to have been a wise one," says General Evangelism Director Vinson Synan. "We have received letters of support and commendation of her leadership thus far. She is a capable and talented person, well able to fulfill the requirements of the office."

Rev. Dunn was born and reared in Oklahoma and has been a minister of the Pentecostal Holiness Church since 1964. She has pastored in the California and Northwest Conferences since 1965. Her most recent pastorate was at Gospel Temple in Portland, Oregon. She has served on the Northwest Conference Board for twelve years. She and her husband have pioneered two new churches: one in Oroville, California, in 1970, and one in Springfield, Oregon, in 1980. She is the mother of five children.

"I love the people of this conference," says Dunn. "I have seen their sacrifices and discouragements. We share the same vision for the work of the Lord. It has seemed many times that our sacrifices were in vain. But God has a plan for us – a plan for growth . . . . I am praying and seeking His direction and asking Him for wisdom to know our priorities."

Under Rev. Dunn's leadership, the Northwest Conference has set a goal to have a total of ten churches by the end of this quadrennium and to become an intermediate conference with twenty churches by the end of next quadrennium.[1]

(**Author's note:** The following two articles are reprinted in their entirety. The first is presented in the words of Chaplain Christy Sorrow; the second is information about her written by Lt. Col. Bob C. Lynch.)

"Conversation with a Female Chaplain"

Christy Sorrow

You are the first female chaplain I have ever seen, is the response I hear often. Sometimes the phrase is accompanied by a snicker, a stunned look, a sigh of relief, and, occasionally, a declaration of why women should not be ministers.

Female ministers make up a small minority of the chaplaincy – approximately 22 of the 650 Air Force Chaplains. We are still pioneers of sorts, even though our "trailblazer" has served for more than 20 years.

On Acceptance

The question I hear most often is "How have you been accepted as a minister?"

Pioneers naturally encounter difficulties when breaking into new territories. A small fraction of the people we try to minister to stall at the gender issue and strongly express their conviction that a "woman's place" is not in the pulpit. Another small, yet shocking, minority, try to demean us with harassing remarks or gestures.

Still others – both men and women – show relief at discovering that there is a female chaplain on staff. These individuals seem more comfortable discussing their problems with a woman than with a man.

But, in my own experience, I find that a greater majority of the people to whom and with whom I minister accept me as an equal. They simply allow me to be myself and do the work to which I have been called.

On Calling

It is sometimes difficult for me to answer the question, "How did you decide to do this?" The simple truth is: this is where God wants me. I am here for no other reason.

If I were trying to prove that a woman's place is wherever she wants to be, surely I could have chosen work that didn't require me to wear combat boots. If breaking into a 'man's world' had been my goal, there are certainly more glamorous positions. In the beginning of this journey, God made it clear that this is where He wanted me, and He has confirmed my direction on several occasions over the past 14 years.

It has been a long trek. The struggles of surrendering my will to God's, seminary, chaplain candidacy, civilian pastoral experience, marriage, and finally, the call offering me a slot for active duty – consumed the first half of the journey. I have spent the past seven years seeking God daily for wisdom to minister to the men and women of the Air Force.

Some days that ministry happens in combat gear playing war games and wondering with my "flock," *What if this were real?* Other days find me on foreign soil – Saudi Arabia, Norway – experiencing home-sickness along with them, yet looking to God, and pointing the way to God, for strength to sustain us. Some 24-hour periods are spent making death notifications, comforting the bereaved, and weeping with spouses and children who have lost loved ones in fiery plane crashes. Other days are filled with counseling as I try to offer the hope that Jesus Christ is right for whatever is wrong.

Of course, there are also times when I rejoice in a hospital room, thanking God for His new and precious gift of life. Sometimes we celebrate a promotion or a holiday, or simply share conversation or a smile that says, "I care."

On the Future

"Do I plan to make a career of this?" I can only say my future depends on what the Lord has in mind. If His plan calls for 20 years or more on this mission field, then with His strength, grace and guidance, I will be here. If He directs my family elsewhere tomorrow, we are ready to face the challenge.

On Marriage

My higher calling is that of wife and mother. Rick and I have two children, Kyle (3) and Callie (nearly 2). [This was in 1996.]

Rick is a full-time, stay-at-home dad. Our life is different, but it works for us. I probably pray for more wisdom with this ministry (family) than for the one I do in the "blue suit." If I fail here, any other success is insignificant.

On Becoming a Military Chaplain

If I could counsel other men or women considering the military chaplaincy as their place of full-time ministry, I would ask, "Are you sure of God's direction?" If so, start walking in that direction, and let Him handle the details, both now and throughout your military career. There is a tremendous need for godly women and men with the heart for the members of the United States military and who want to bring the people to God and God to the people.

By Lt. Col. Bob C. Lynch

Christy Sorrow's ministry as a female military chaplain has been met with some resistance, but the acceptance has far outweighed those unwilling to receive her.

We are blessed to have a woman like Christy representing the PH Church in military uniform. She has never carried a chip on her shoulder or tried to prove that 'a woman can do it better.' She simply lets the Lord use her to minister to the needs of the men and women in the blue and camouflage uniforms.

Her ministry also touches the families assigned to her base, especially when the military member is on assignment for 45, 90, 179, or even 365 days away from home. Whether it be in the hospital at Elmendorf Air Force Base, Alaska, or in the sands of Saudi Arabia, wearing dress blues or desert camouflage, she is ready to share the good news of Jesus Christ and to reach out to those with personal needs.[2]

"Tarpley Commissioned as Second Female PH Air Force Chaplain"

The September 2005 issue of the *Experience* reported that Sarah Tarpley had been commissioned a first lieutenant in the Air Force Reserve as a chaplain representing the IPHC.

She is a graduate of Southwestern Christian University (SCU) in Bethany, Oklahoma and also of the Assemblies of God Theological Seminary in Springfield, Missouri, with a master of divinity degree. In May of 2005, Sarah became the pastor of First Love Pentecostal Holiness Church in Enid, Oklahoma. On June 29, of the same year she took the oath of office to become a chaplain, the second female to do so from this denomination.

According to Hugh H. Morgan, who was Sarah's endorser, "Sarah has been assigned to do her reserve training as an Individual Mobilization Augmentee at Vance Air Force Base, Enid, Oklahoma."

She is the first alumna from SCU to become a military chaplain.[3]

Intercultural Ministries

Charlene West
Heartland Conference

Charlene has served as pastor, evangelist, church planter, teacher, director of a Bible Institute, and secretary-treasurer of Missions and Conference funds. Also she has planted or been on the church planting team to begin at least ten churches and is founding pastor of Centro de Celebracion church in Oklahoma City.

Her father, Rev. C. H. North, taught her to love and study the Bible; he taught her the basics of Christian doctrine and led her to experience them. Another great influence in her life was her late husband, Rev. Russell West. It was by his side that she accepted the call to preach. They worked as a team, and he gave her opportunity to develop in her call.

Rev. Mrs. West, who at the time was Director of Intercultural Ministries for the IPHC, a position she held for almost seven years, wrote, "A major breakthrough for reaching our nation with an effective and sensitive cross-cultural ministry took place after the last General Conference when Evangelism USA's office of 'Hispanic Ministries' was broadened to become 'Intercultural Ministries.' Ethnic representatives were then appointed to form an Intercultural Advisory Council to chart new goals. The Council's initial meeting gave birth to our Intercultural Proclamation which recognizes that all Christians, regardless of race, color, language or national origin, are one in Christ. It declares that we must reach all people with the Gospel and plant churches within our cultural diversities."

Charlene has been called by some an apostle to Spanish-speaking people. She has been gifted by God to provide authoritative leadership and has been most effective in planting new churches, training, nurturing, and pastoring.

Through the Intercultural Ministries office she made available a manual on church planting, growth, and involvement for ethnic outreach, as well as other books and vital materials that were translated for use. She has also been interactive with conferences and churches to help establish the School of Ministry for training ethnic ministers. In May 1997, the Hispanic congregation of Tulsa, Oklahoma's Evangelistic Temple graduated its first nine students.

In 1998, Charlene planted Centro de Celebracion, and through that project has trained eight men and women to be ministers. She moved the growing congregation into a larger church facility, the old Muse Memorial Church, in Oklahoma City and continues the process of discipling Spanish-speaking leaders.[4]

Shirley G. Spencer
Heartland Conference

Shirley is probably best known to most Pentecostals as Executive Editor of Publications of the IPHC, a position in which she considers herself somewhat of a pioneer for women. In 1975, she accepted a job with Advocate Press as executive secretary to the editor in chief of publications, who resigned the position four years later. The Board of Publications then asked her to be interim executive editor until the summer of 1981 when a decision would be made about someone to fill the position permanently. She was appointed as the denomination's first female executive editor of publications. She held that position until her retirement in March 2010.

During that period of time, she oversaw the publication of the church's official journals, *The Pentecostal Holiness Advocate, IssacharFile,* and *IPHC Experience.* In her words, "I also edited numerous books as well as One

Accord Resources (a line of Sunday school curriculum used by a coalition of denominations). I also authored reams of articles, booklets, and leaders' guides based on texts recommended for study in the IPHC."

Over the past thirty-three years, God has opened the door for her to serve with four general superintendents, Bishops J. Floyd Williams, Leon Stewart, B. E. Underwood, and James D. Leggett. For twenty-nine years she served as secretary/treasurer of the International Pentecostal Press Association, and for nineteen years Shirley was a member of the Pentecostal-Charismatic Curriculum Commission. She was the first female to chair that commission, "which prepares the outlines for adult Sunday school curriculum produced and published by five major Pentecostal publishing houses." She has also served twice on the Conference Christian Education Board.

Her mentor was Lois Bunkley who encouraged her in her work as an editor and as a Christian educator. "Perhaps the most important thing she did for me was to recognize my potential and my calling as a teacher and gave me opportunities to grow" she says.

"As a result of my role as executive editor," Mrs. Spencer writes, "I have been blessed to travel to nearly every continent in the world and to many of the 50 US states. I have interviewed countless interesting leaders and laypersons and have been privileged to tell their stories." She reports that she has been privileged to attend eight Pentecostal World Conferences and other events that have broadened her worldview.[5]

---

[1] "First Woman Superintendent Appointed," *The Advocate,* June 1984, p. 15.
[2] Christy Sorrow, "Conversation with a Female Chaplain," *The Advocate,* May 1996, pp. 12-13.
[3] *IPHC Experience,* "Tarpley Commissioned as Second Female PH Chaplain," September 2005, p. 16.
[4] Charlene West, "Intercultural Ministries," *Evangelism USA,* August/September 1997, p. 6 and "Meet Charlene West," *IPHC Experience,* January 2004, p. 11.
[5] Respondent information form and e-mail dated April 27, 2010.

CHAPTER 5

With His Stripes

"But he was wounded for our transgressions, he was bruised for our iniquities: . . . and with his stripes we are healed" – Isaiah 53:5.

"A Soul Stirring Story of How God Healed A Girl Who Said
'IT COULDN'T HAPPEN TO ME'"
by
Pauline Caddell Knowles

In her own words, Pauline Knowles presented a word picture of herself as a young lady who had a very serious disease, tuberculosis, yet one who moved on to become a woman of faith. She went to the sanitorium a sick unbeliever, but she became a born again believer who continued to be ill.

Pauline wrote, "And yet, there was the doctor's solemn verdict given in words that spelled 'the end' for everything I had ever hoped for in this world. I was 19 years old, and I had dreams like other girls. This world was all I had at that time, and that was taken from me, snatched away by one brief sentence spoken by my doctor, after he had taken all the tests to prove it: 'You have tuberculosis in both lungs.'

"I had to go to the sanatorium – the doctor said for at least six months, maybe a year. Home never looked so sweet to me as it did at that time . . . . I must be separated from my mother and father, getting only brief glimpses of them on their occasional visits to me in the sanatorium. . . ."

After a two week wait before there was a place opened for her, Miss Caddell stayed in bed at home under the doctor's care. They were indescribable days – a kind of nightmare of waiting and suffering. Day and night she suffered from a fever that consistently ranged between 100 and 103 degrees. Pleurisy had her sick on her stomach. She could eat very little, and what she ate, she could not retain. Night sweats kept her in added misery through the hours of darkness. The searing pain in her lungs was like a knife plunged into her chest.

Her words continue: "I was almost in a daze that morning of March 16, 1949, when they took me to the sanatorium. I tried to evade the reality of my situation, tried not to think of what I was facing. When we arrived . . . , they gave me a bed in a room with a lot of other girls, but oh, how much I was alone. I cried night and day. I was so lonesome and afraid. I didn't realize then just how alone I was. I was alone without God. How lost I was! My lungs were not all that was diseased. My heart was sick; my soul was diseased with sin . . . . In the dead of night, I could hear the groans and moans of the suffering and dying around me. My nerves were gone. I lived in fear."

She relates how she would lie in her bed at night and tremble because her past had caught up with her; she feared dying and going to hell. She tried to pray and longed for someone to take her fears away. A lady came to the sanatorium and talked to the residents about religion and Christ; however, she did not present the plan of salvation, so Sister Pauline remained in her sins.

God had mercy on her and spared her life. Slowly she began to gain some strength. A good Christian woman in the bed next to hers had been praying for her, but Pauline was not aware of this at the time. The lady was so sure that God would save her roommate that before she went home, she asked Miss Caddell to write to her when she gave her heart to the Lord. Leaving her Bible with Pauline, she asked that she read it every day, which she did for months, until she discovered the truth that set her free.

She had no idea of the change that would take place in her life before she returned home. On November 25, 1950, in the sanatorium she heard guitar music and moved closer to hear more. Later a man took out his Bible and read Matthew 18:11, which is part of the parable of the lost sheep: *"For the Son of man is come to save that which was lost"*-KJV. She knew immediately that she was a lost sheep, and her life changed that night.

Even though she knew nothing about the Bible, not even John 3:16, she began to hunger and thirst after the Word. She began to read and study as often as possible. As she sat at the feet of Jesus, the Holy Spirit taught her what she needed to know. She was led into the experience of holiness as she prayed seeking the Lord for all of His blessings. While she was kneeling in front of the commode, she died to the world and the Lord sanctified her.

She wrote, "The thing just kept growing in my heart until I just had to tell someone else about it. At midnight, I got out of bed and started writing letters to friends. The first one I wrote went to the lady who had given me the Bible in the hospital. The next went to my family telling them of how I had been saved."

The story goes on to say, "My friends in the sanatorium seemed to think that my religion would wear off in a little while, but it didn't stop there. I kept on seeking God until He sanctified my soul. Everything was going so well that I was not prepared for the next blow that fell upon me."

After twenty-two months in the hospital, instead of getting better, she found she was growing worse. She was fully expecting to be released to go home after the next X-ray, but instead she heard from the doctor that the disease was spreading.

Of course, this was discouraging news, but Pauline turned to the Lord and believed things would work out for the best and for His glory, and they did. She had never thought of being healed by the power of God until the Christian lady who gave her the Bible, wrote her about the Rev. Oral Roberts who was going to be in High Point, North Carolina and wanted her to go be prayed for in that meeting. Sister Caddell had decided not to go until she received a letter from her mother telling her to go to a service to be prayed for, and God would heal her. "I started praying for God to show me what I should do," she says.

At the same time all of this was happening, Pauline's mother came to visit her and brought Brother Roberts book *If You Need Healing Do These Things*. The young lady felt God had answered her prayers and showed her His will. She knew it was God's will to heal her body immediately, so she made up her mind to go to High Point.

She was aware of the doctors' attitude toward faith healing and their opposition to others who had left the sanatorium to go to a healing campaign because they said the excitement was too much for the patients. Knowing this, she decided not to ask for permission to go.

In May 1951, she left so sure of her healing that she did not plan to go back to the sanatorium. Her parents took her to the healing campaign, arriving around ten o'clock in the morning to wait until service time that evening at seven-thirty, but she said the time seemed comparatively short compared to the number of months she had been waiting while enduring the illness. People who were already there prayed for her during the day, so by the time Brother Roberts prayed for her, she had forgotten the devil and all the doubts he tried to plant in her mind.

Her family pastor, the Rev. H. E. Johnson, was also present for the meeting that night, and he told Brother Roberts how long she had been sick, about her time in the hospital, and how she had suffered. Brother Roberts then laid hands on her to pray for her healing. She felt the power of God go through her body, knew she had felt the touch of the Master's hand, and accepted her healing.

She testified: "How real the power of God is today! Just think how long I had suffered when my healing had been paid for all the time, paid in the cruel stripes that were laid on the precious back of the Son of God. If we would only take God at His word and trust Him for deliverance, we would soon learn that all things are possible to him that believeth."

After her return home, she immediately started doing light work around the house. She was still very weak but was so happy to be home again after twenty-seven months. She did not continue her treatments, but her strength returned rapidly day by day. She conducted prayer meetings and told everyone what God had done for her.

This was not the end of the battle, however, because she was called into question by the Health Department because someone had registered a complaint about her. She was given two options: return to the sanatorium for tests to determine if she was healed or go to the State Hospital for two years. She agreed to go for a final check up. The doctor promised that if all the tests proved negative, she would be discharged, but he did not keep his promise and kept her there six months rather than eight weeks, even though the results were negative.

She used her time back in the sanatorium to testify to patients and tell them what God had done for her and could do for them. She prayed for the sick, talked to the unsaved, and God honored her efforts. Satan was ever present trying to break down her faith, but God was there too, and He was more than a match for the devil. Upon her discharge, she returned home and has been able to serve God ever since.

AN UPDATE FROM 1951-1986

"Today, I am still rejoicing in the love of God. I know He is the 'same yesterday, today, and forever.' He has given me a rich and full life since He saved me and healed my body of tuberculosis. God called me into the ministry, and I have been faithful to preach the Word. In 1961 the Lord gave me a wonderful husband to help me in the ministry. We have had a great life together. We have raised seven children – five [of his] by a previous marriage – mother killed in a car accident, and two of our own – ages 22 and 18. We have stayed active in evangelistic and pastoral work. Our desire is to be faithful and to declare all the counsel of God . . . ."

PASTOR CONFIRMS STORY

Rev. H. E. Johnson was the family pastor at the time of Miss Caddell's illness and healing. He gives the following information concerning her story:

"I have known Pauline Caddell for several years and can vouch for her story. Her healing was instant and the renewal of her strength was rapid and steady. I saw her previous hospital record which said little likelihood of recovery and after she was prayed for, I talked with the doctor who said she was well."[1]

Rita Knowles, Sister Pauline Knowles' daughter, writes that her mother was born to Colon and Nettie Caddell on October 18, 1929 in Rockingham, North Carolina. She was the third of eight girls born to the Caddells. When she was eight years old, the family moved to Castle Hayne, near Wilmington, North Carolina.

The family had no church connection when Pauline was growing up, but God was looking for a way to get their attention. She feels that her diagnosis of tuberculosis and subsequent healing related above, was what He used to move in her life and in the lives of her family members.

The Caddells had a friend who was a member of the Wilmington First Pentecostal Holiness Church who invited two of her younger sisters to attend. They enjoyed the services and continued going. Meanwhile, her mother went to the hospital for minor surgery. Rev. H. E. Johnson, the pastor of the Wilmington Church, went there to pray for her after Pauline's sisters requested prayer for their mother at church. He asked Mrs. Caddell if she would promise to come to church if God touched her. She kept that promise as the Lord continued to move to save the family. Pauline's mother, father, and some of her sisters were saved, joined the church and stayed there until they went to be with their Savior.

Rita continues, "Our mother was a proud servant of God and a walking tribute to Pentecostal Holiness truth.

"The devil tried to defeat Mama until her last breath, but on March 18, 2009, she finally met her Master that she had dedicated her whole life to.

"There will never be a replacement in the home, church, or our lives on earth, but we are sure that Heaven has a perfect angel at this time, and she is still working for her Master."

Pauline's daughter Rita states that her mother had battled breast cancer, fought and won, they thought, since she was cancer free for three years. Then she developed a kidney infection, and the doctor discovered she had cancer throughout her body. She was bed-ridden for twenty-four weeks before she died.

The tumors caused coma-like seizures after which she would sleep for three to four days. Her family stayed by her bed around the clock even though they knew there was nothing they could do except hold on to their faith. Mr. Knowles stayed in the Word during those trying times reading the Bible through several times drawing strength and comfort.

The daughter says, "Mama spoke of death quite often with a strong desire of seeing her mother and father, but the selfish part of her did not want to leave her family." There were seven children, eleven grandchildren, and two great grandchildren. She also left behind five sisters and a husband of forty-eight years.

After she died, her husband, Mr. Wil, went in the room, laid his hands on her and asked for God's blessings on the family. As he began speaking in tongues, the Holy Spirit filled the room. Even though that manifestation did not relieve the human hurt, the assurance that Sister Knowles was no longer suffering was a comfort to the family.

"Mama's testimony," Rita continues, "will live forever in every life that she ever touched. She was loved by many that knew her."

Day after day, the Knowles family saw Pauline's faith grow as she learned to trust God for healing again. At the time appointed, God did bring deliverance. Even though she lived to have another dreaded disease, she never lost her trust in her Savior. Her death may seem a defeat to some, but to her, it was the ultimate healing because now she rests in the arms of Jesus in a place where there is no pain or suffering.

Sister Knowles' ministry was anything she could do to witness for the Lord. She worked in the local church, held home prayer meetings, and passed out tracts. She taught Sunday school, worked with the youth and helped in daily Vacation Bible School.

During the time of these activities, she was still seeking God for His will for her life. She would pray until the spirit of weeping came upon her; she searched her life to see if there was anything that the Lord was not pleased with. She felt that she was as committed as she knew how to be, but did not want to admit she was called to preach. She held back because she knew how some people felt about women preachers; however, after a while, she accepted the call and felt peace in her heart about the decision.

She was licensed to preach in 1955 and ministered as an evangelist until 1958, when she was assigned to pastor the Penderlea Pentecostal Holiness Church. She was twenty-seven years old, single, and had no pastoral training. Even though she was young and scared, she trusted God all the way. Because she did not know how to drive, she had to depend on her sister and her nephew to drive her back and forth the seventy-mile round trip to the church.

When she first arrived at Penderlea, she found a small cement block building out in the country. The congregation was in debt to the conference for $1,000 it had borrowed to construct the church. She also found a congregation made up mostly of women and children. There were no indoor restrooms, and the only water supply was an outside pump that would lose its prime. All of the windows needed to be replaced. They did not have even a window fan for comfort.

Sister Pauline writes, "Even though I had a few to work with, I felt God had sent me. I accepted it as a challenge . . . and gave them all I had." In answer to their prayers, the Lord sent more people to the church. Willie Knowles and his wife were members, and their son Rodney and his family later joined.

One night, the Willie Knowles family was involved in a head-on collision in which his wife was killed. The children had minor cuts and bruises, but Willie had both legs broken. After his recovery and he was back in church, he and Pauline felt that God had a plan for them to have a future together. They both prayed about this relationship, as they did not want to make a mistake.

On July 28, 1961, they were married. She says, "I needed him in my ministry, and he needed me in his home. With him in my life, I have had greater opportunities as a pastor. My ministry was much stronger."

The moment she said "I do," he helped her to adjust to the five children that he brought into the marriage. They worked together in the home and in the church. The Lord also blessed their union with more children.

New people were added to the church, and a little more money was available to make the needed repairs to the building. Her husband, along with the other men, took the lead in building the Sunday school rooms they wanted to add. They replaced the old windows that were about to fall out with lovely stained glass windows. The men built a vestibule with two nice bathrooms on one side and also got water inside the church. They were on the move, so they put carpet in and replaced the wooden pews with padded one. They remodeled the walls of the sanctuary with paneling.

As time went by, her husband felt led of God to build a fellowship hall. They were so inspired about this project that they went out the night that the decision was made and laid out the plans in the glow of car lights. Every one worked: the men did the building; the women and children cleaned up behind them. Pauline stayed home and cooked chicken stew, field peas, and collards or turnip greens to feed them as they worked.

As the church grew in number, it also grew in size. They eventually made plans to build an education department by constructing six new

Sunday school rooms. God's blessings were apparent as He called three men from that church to preach the gospel: Rodney Knowles, Jerry Green, and Lloyd Harris.

Sister Knowles was active also as an evangelist, even while pastoring. She had a radio program on WPJC, Burgaw, for fourteen years. Of this ministry, she writes, "I had good success, and I feel that I did my best work as far as reaching people with the Pentecostal message."

The Rev. Hazel Wilson had a great impact on Pauline's life and ministry. Hazel taught Pauline many things through her preaching and her personal relationship as a friend. Sister Knowles attended her first Falcon Camp Meeting with Hazel in 1953 and was so moved by the fellowship, music, and preaching that she could hardly take it all in. The weather was hot; there were no conveniences and few bathrooms; the cafeteria was in the basement of the white dormitory. Just to be there was worth any sacrifice they had to make. People went there to worship the Lord and were "prayed up" when they arrived, so they were ready to receive what God had in store for them. "That was camp meeting at Falcon: a time of good preaching, singing, and testifying. It was a time of great spiritual blessing."

Pauline was thankful to God for the Pentecostal Holiness Church and the gospel it stands for. She was never ashamed of or afraid to preach its doctrine for "the Word of God backs it up." [2]

---

[1] Pauline sent me this information printed in a 16-page booklet along with the form I mailed to her to obtain personal data about her and her ministry. At the time, she was a retired ordained minister in the North Carolina Conference, having spent 56 years in the ministry. Her pastorate at Penderlea lasted forty years. She died March 18, 2009, at the age of seventy-nine, shortly after I received her story.
[2] A letter written by Rita Knowles, a daughter of Pauline and Willie Knowles.

CHAPTER 6

Bits and Pieces

"Do and do, do and do, rule on rule, rule on rule; <u>a little here, a little there</u>"
– Isaiah 28:10-NIV.

(**Author's note:** The information below is given under year headings, but it may not correspond with the date in the article. The date agrees with that of the publication cited.)

This chapter is made up of bits and pieces of information about women in the ministry in the International Pentecostal Holiness Church who have made an impact on the communities where they labored. They were beautiful flowers who bloomed where they were planted. They were voices crying in the wilderness to awaken a sin-sick people. They were loving hearts who reached out to those who were unloving and unlovable by the world's standards. However, we see in them the kind of *"agape"* love demonstrated first by God, then through His servants.

Perhaps what they did seemed small at the time. Maybe they received no applause or recognition for their efforts. Certainly they ministered in hardship, often facing the realization that they were not accepted simply because they were women. Still, they carried on as teachers, pastors, evangelist, and leaders. They have been women with a vision for the Lord, who have striven to make a difference.

1901

Berta Maxwell was ordained to preach by the **North Carolina Conference** at the **Second Annual Convention** held in Magnolia, North Carolina. She was a minister from 1901 until 1919, when she asked that her name be dropped from the conference roll. However, she continued her membership and ministry in the Pentecostal Holiness Church. Mrs. Maxwell was the first primary teacher at the Falcon Holiness School when it opened in 1902. She and her husband, Murdoch Maxwell, were the parents of six children.

In 1920, Sister Maxwell organized the Mizpah Prayer Band in Falcon, which was active past her lifetime, with Charity Sasser Autry being the last leader. Brother Oris Hubbard, a descendant of Mrs. Maxwell, writes, "As a boy, I remember the praying of great women of God in our home during those prayer meetings." He also states that he remembers seeing, when he was a child, Berta's name on a memorial sticker in their church hymnals. Her descendants still live in Falcon and remain active in lay ministry.[1]

(**Author's note:** In my research, I have seen Mrs. Maxwell's name spelled **Berta** and also **Bertha,** but Oris Hubbard informed me that her name was **Roberta** Royal Maxwell.)

1908

Rev. Berta Maxwell was appointed to serve on the Foreign Missions Board. This action was taken at the **Ninth Annual Convention** on November 16, 1908.[2]

1909

After receiving the Baptism of the Spirit in 1909, Lillie Bourland Smith along with her husband were used mightily of God as Pentecostal Holiness evangelists in eastern Oklahoma, western Arkansas, Florida, Georgia, and other sections in the East.[3]

1911

Mrs. Clark Eckert joined the **Florida Conference** in 1911 and co-pastored with her husband at a number of churches. They brought the Coconut Grove Church (Miami) into the Pentecostal Holiness Church. After her husband's death, she continued to pastor there. For years, she was a leader of the youth work in Florida.[4]

Rexie Gilbert Evans, wife of Rev. Dan Evans, was filled with the Holy Spirit in 1909; she moved to Oklahoma City in 1910. They were largely responsible for starting the Bethel Church near Seminole. They became members of the **Oklahoma Conference** in 1911.[5]

1919

The **Quarterly Conference** of District No. 1 convened at the Fairview **(Oklahoma)** church, May 31, 1919. Sisters Dolly York and Myrtle Stone were listed as being absent from that meeting.[6]

The **Fourth Quarterly Meeting** of the Franklin Springs District of the **Annual Conference of Georgia** met with the Nicholson Church on October 11, 1919. Mrs. S. J. Britton, a pastor, was present, as was Mrs. Dessie McCurley, an evangelist[7]

(**Author's note:** Mrs. S. J. Britton is also referred to elsewhere as Mrs. F. M. Britton.)

At the **First Quarterly Conference** of the Wagoner District held on November 1, 1919, in Wagoner, **Oklahoma**, the following ordained ministers are mentioned: Mrs. M. K. Shannon, no report; Mrs. M. A. Mann, reported.[8]

Later, on November 7, 1919, the **First Quarterly Conference** of the **Oklahoma District** convened at the Oklahoma City Church. Sister J. C. Williams, a pastor, sent in a good written report. General evangelists absent were Sisters Willard Short and Sallie Tolbert. Lula Skelton, a local evangelist, was also absent.[9]

A report of the Stationing Committee of the **North Carolina Conference,** Wilson District, December 18, 1919, listed the names of three women ministers who were classified as local evangelists: Mrs. Dovie Dunn, Mrs. R. D. Nobles, and Mrs. Cassie Sigwalt.[10]

1920

The **Georgia Conference** minutes showed that Mrs. F. M. Britton, an assistant pastor, and Mrs. W. H. McCurley, an evangelist, were present for the conference.[11]

The **Second Quarterly Conference** of the **Oklahoma District** met February 7, 1920. Enrolled as a general evangelist was Rev. Sallie Tolbert and as a local evangelist was Lula Skelton[12]

Listed as members present for the **Second Quarterly Conference** of the Mountain Park District, **Oklahoma**, which convened on February 13, 1920, were Mrs. Adelaide (Dan) Muse and Annie Brott. Absent, but with a written report submitted, was evangelist Annie Comack.[13]

The Anderson District of the **Upper South Carolina Conference** met for their **Second Quarterly Conference** on April 10, 1920. Rev. Mrs. Avie Dunn was present.[14]

Mrs. O. N. Todd, an evangelist, was present for the **Second Quarterly Conference** of the Griffin District in the **Georgia Conference**. The conference was held on April 9-11, 1920.[15]

Among the pastors present for the **Third Quarterly Conference** for the Wagoner District of the **Oklahoma Conference** May 7-9, 1920, was Rev. Mrs. M. K. Shannon.[16]

1921

No women ministers were appointed to any committee according to the *Minutes of the Fourth General Conference of the Pentecostal Holiness Church* which met in Roanoke, Virginia May 3-11, 1921.[17]

1925

The **Baltimore Conference** (later called Eastern Virginia, now Redemption Ministries) met at Richmond, Virginia, November 12, 1925. Mrs. Hattie Edge and Mrs. J. W. Everheart were listed as evangelists in the Norfolk District.

Lady evangelists in the Anderson District of the **Upper South Carolina Conference** were Mrs. J. R. Jones, Mrs. Avie Dunn, and Lula Ferguson.

The **Georgia Conference** reported Mrs. S. T. E. Dudley, Mrs. J. D. Parker, and Mrs. Nolie Goolsby as local evangelists.[18]

1932

The Committee on Missions for the Annual Conference of the **Lower South Carolina Conference** (now known as the South Carolina Conference) was made up of three women, two of whom were ministers: Mrs. J. L. Wall and Mrs. S. J. Britton.[19]

1933

The report of the Committee on Examination of the **Lower South Carolina Conference** recommended for ordination Mrs. M. L. Canady and for license Lessie Polston.[20]

1935

Miss Mary Sue Britton was recommended for ordination; Lila V. Medlin, Pearl Fagen, and Natalie Carnes received license to preach. This was part of the report of the "Committee on Examination of Applicants for Credentials" for the **Lower South Carolina Conference**.

The report of the "Committee on Missions" also appearing in the conference minutes of this same year was signed by three women, all ministers: Miss Emma Britton, Mrs. J. L. Wall, and Mrs. S. J. Britton.

(**Author's note:** The number of women whose names appear on the conference register represents about 12 percent of all ordained ministers and 38 percent of all those licensed.)[21]

1936

A committee report on "Examination of Applicants for Credentials" for the **Lower South Carolina Conference** showed that Mrs. J. T. Warren was accepted from the Congregational Holiness Church to receive local minister's license. Mrs. Minnie Calder and Mrs. Lessie Polston were approved for ordination.[22]

1937

The report of the "Stationing Committee" for the twenty-seventh annual session of the **Lower South Carolina Conference** specified that the following ladies were appointed as pastors: Rev. Mrs. Lessie Polston, Cheraw and Haystown; Rev. Miss Minnie Calder, Wadesboro and Ellerby; Rev. Mrs. F. B. Graham, Little Star; Rev. Mrs. Pearl Fagen, Gum Springs. As evangelists, Laura Graham, Mary Sue Britton, Mrs. M. L. Canaday, Miss Natalie Carnes, Nita Alexander, Mrs. S. J. Britton, Mrs. Ethel Moore, Mrs. Lila Medlin, and Alma Graham, were named. Nita Alexander and Alma Graham were also licensed to preach at this conference.[23]

1938

Lucille Swails was recommended by the "Committee on Examination" to be licensed by the **Lower South Carolina Conference**.[24]

1939

The conferences usually publishes the amount of tithes paid annually into the conference by each minister. The report from the Fourteenth Session of the **Tri-State Conference** shows that these ladies paid the following amounts:

Dovie McKanue	Licensed evangelist	$3.75
Eldeen Gambill	Licensed evangelist	20.00
Millie Futrell		8.13
Mrs. D. R. Hammond		4.25
Ruth Helms	Licensed evangelist	1.00
Janie Holland	Ordained evangelist	20.74

Mrs. Janie Holland was appointed as pastor in Mayfield, Kentucky, and Mrs. D. R. Hammonds in Cardwell, Missouri. The latter lady was an ordained minister. Mrs. Effie Cope was recommended for ordination at that conference.

The **North Carolina Conference** reported these tithes paid into the conference in 1939.

Ethel Strickland	$3.15
Eva Bell Holland Brown	4.20
Victoria Moore	1.25
Beadie Noble	5.00
Mrs. W. V. Shepherd	2.38
Effie Poland	2.00
Martha Williams	2.00

(**Author's note:** These figures indicate the limited funds these ladies received from their ministry since this presumably represents 10 percent of their income.)

Another record of women pastors and the churches that they served appears in the **Lower South Carolina Conference** Yearbook showing in a listing the value of some of the church property.

Minnie Calder	Wadesboro	$2,500
Lessie Polston	Cheraw	1,800
Mrs. S. T. Britton	Pisgah	500
Alma Graham	Bolton's Chapel	800

The following "Report of Committee on Public Morals" was written by three ordained women ministers in the **Oklahoma Conference** in 1939.

"We, your Committee on Public Morals, recommend that we preach the Word, and we feel that if this is done, men and women will find Christ. When we find Christ our moral problems will be solved.

"We urge our pastors and evangelists to stay in the middle of the road and lift up Christ. We encourage our people to conduct themselves as becometh Holiness. We are sure that our outward conduct manifests that which is within.

"That we read good wholesome literature. We desire that our young people especially be encouraged and instructed in the reading of wholesome literature. That our pastors try to help put such literature in their hands.

"That God will give us wisdom to encourage our children to attend church and Sunday School with us, as they need the great doctrine of Holiness instilled into their hearts."

Mrs. Jessie Campbell, Chairman
Mrs. Martha R. Rose
Myrtle Stone"

That same year the "Committee on Memoirs" was made up of three ordained lady ministers: Annie E. Carmack, Chairman; Gertrude Adair; and Margaret Howard, a missionary. The Missionary Committee at the twenty-ninth annual session of the **Lower South Carolina Conference** was made up of five lady ministers: Mrs. J. L. Wall, Mrs. Lessie Polston, Mrs. Laura Graham, Miss Minnie Calder, and Mrs. Lila Medlin.

Marie Maloy, Mamie McDonald, Evelyn Reid, Mrs. G. Sigwalt, and Mrs. C. M. Wheeler were listed as evangelists in the **Florida Conference** in the 1939 Yearbook.

Evangelists in the **Georgia Conference**, according to its 1939 Yearbook, were Daisy Jones (L), Mrs. C. A. Jordan (L), Mrs. W. H. McCurley (O), Mrs. S. T. E. Dudley (O), Neelie Goolsby (L), Mrs. L. V. Little (L), and Mrs. W. B. Bishop (L). (L = Licensed; O= ordained)

The following women ministers in the **Kansas Conference** served on committees at the annual session of the conference: P.Y.P.S. (Pentecostal Young People's Society) Committee – Beulah Taylor, Eulah Taylor, and Mary Ford; Resolutions Committee – Mary Ford, and Nettie Wedeking.

Mrs. A. N. Goodwin, in her annual report, stated she preached seventeen times, led prayer meeting one time, prayed for the sick several times, assisted in four nights of service at a school house. She also paid $3.55 into the conference treasury. Her report made at the annual meeting of the **Missouri Conference** was accepted, and her character was passed.

The **Oklahoma Conference** reported the following lady ministers transferred into the conference at this annual meeting: Stella Buchanan and Tinnie Shockley from East Oklahoma, and Mary Ford from Kansas. Mrs. Hal Spence transferred out to the Florida Conference. One minister, Grace Andrews, was dropped from membership in the conference for not reporting as required. Mrs. N. C. Brandstatt and Ella Lou Wedel withdrew from the conference.

The Stationing Committee report from the **Ontario Conference** in its tenth annual session showed a number of women who were named as being ministers: Mrs. M. Brook, Miss Miller, Mrs. McCready, Mrs. M. E. Hutchinson, Miss Ensom, Mrs. Mack, Mrs. Martin, Mrs. Mentz, and Mrs. M. Scott.

The **Panhandle Conference** at its fifth annual session reported Mrs. Irene Wilson, Mrs. H. O. Byerly, Mrs. Eska Galvin, and Mrs. Opal Manning as ordained ministers; Clara Coffman and Vessie King as licensed. New lady ministers received were Lucile King and Wanda Keller. (A small group of people had met in session August 27, 1934, at Carnegie, Oklahoma, for the purpose of organizing an Annual Conference in the Panhandle. Rev. Mrs. H. O. Byerly, an ordained minister in the **Panhandle Conference** served as Secretary-Treasurer.)

Evelyn Egger, Mrs. F. D. Haag, Velma Smail, Inez Wasmund and Mrs. B. D. Landon were listed as women ministers in the sixth annual session report for the **Pennsylvania Conference**.[25]

1940

Mrs. Dorothy Donithan became a minister in the **California Conference** this year. She later served the Woman's Auxiliary as Missions Corresponding Secretary and Regional Director.[26]

1941

Mrs. C. H. Linn, an ordained general evangelist, reported $11.00 tithe for the year July 1941 – July 1942, at the **Maryland Conference**.[27]

1942

Rev. Natalie Carnes served as a member of the Committee on Evangelism, and Lucile Barns, Mary Sue Evans, Nita Alexander, and Lila V. Medlin were among those on the Committee on Publication for the **Lower South Carolina Conference**.[28]

1944

The Minutes of the Thirty-fourth Annual Session of the **South Carolina Conference**, formerly called the Lower South Carolina Conference, showed that a number of women were assigned to pastor churches that year. Mrs. B. B. Sellers was assistant pastor with her husband at Wadesboro; Mrs. J. L. Wall assisted her husband at Scranton and Lake City; Mary Sue Evans was placed at Cook Chapel and Little Star; Mrs. H. C. Alexander went to Floyd's Chapel; Natalie Carnes pastored Georgetown; Mrs. Carl Thurman was assistant to her husband at Charleston and Red Oak; Mrs. J. L. Frazier assisted her husband at Oak Grove and Bethany; Mrs. F. B. Graham pastored Antioch and Bonneau; Lila Medlin and Ruth Kirby were co-pastors at Holly Hill and Riverside; Mrs. J. Paul Jones served with her husband at Sumter; and Mrs. Ethel Moore pastored Rock Hill.

Listed as evangelists were Alma Graham, Lucile Barnes, Laura Graham, and Mrs. J. T. Warren.

The **Mississippi Conference** had no women ministers.[29]

1945

The Woman's Auxiliary of the **North Carolina Conference** became a church-wide organization at the suggestion of Bishop Muse, then General Superintendent of the Pentecostal Holiness Church. He proposed that the ladies "break it down to Annual Conferences, and thence to local churches." Mrs. Lila Berry was largely responsible for the organization of this women's group on May 10, 1944, in Falcon, North Carolina. She was "an effective evangelist, pastor's wife, mother of eight, community leader, and became the first General President of the Woman's Auxiliary." Mrs. Dan Muse was the first vice president and Mrs. J. H. King, secretary-treasurer. Mrs. Berry traveled more than 32,000 miles in her Woman's

Auxiliary work, receiving less that $700 after her expenses. She also helped her husband in his pastorate.[30]

(**Author's note:** Mrs. Berry, Mrs. Muse, and Mrs. J. H. King were all ministers.)

1946

In the report of the Committee on Division of Labor for the **Alabama Conference**, the only names of women that appeared as pastor or assistant pastor were Mrs. O. N. Todd at North Birmingham and Mrs. H. H. Morgan at Faith Tabernacle, both of whom served along with their husbands. Several lady evangelists were mentioned in the same report: Miss Eleanor Cato, Miss Lavella Ezell, Mrs. Lou Eria Ealum, and Miss Rachel McGraw.

Four women ministers were listed as assistant pastors in the **British Columbia Conference** Stationing Committee Report: Mrs. M. E. Botting, Port Moody; Mrs. G. A Byus, Tacoma, Washington; Mrs. D. Stewart, Chilliwack; and Mrs. M. Robinson, Bergen. Also, four lady evangelists were named in that same report: Miss Myrtle Milley, Mrs. Georgia MacAuley, Miss Ruth Wiese, and Mrs. Mary Wilson.

Those listed as retired or inactive were Miss Alice Ridley, Mrs. Juliette Soule, and Miss Frances Kinley.

The **Georgia Conference** appointed two women ministers as general evangelists: Mrs. J. M. Turner, and Mrs. Frank McLendon, and one as a local evangelist, Mrs. W. E. Poole.

Rev. Mrs. Nellie Hood and Rev. Mrs. Ora Hibbert were assigned as co-pastors with their husbands in the **Kansas Conference**.

The report of the Committee on Division of Labor for the **Maryland Conference** reported Mrs. J. G. Lalor as an ordained evangelist; Mrs. Dallas Tarkenton and Lila Respass as licensed evangelists.

Rev. Mildred Loudy was assigned to pastor Pleasant Ridge church by the **Mississippi Conference**. She was the only woman to be appointed as a pastor in the conference in 1946.

Likewise, the **Missouri Conference** assigned one lady minister to pastor: Rev. Mrs. Bessie Palmer at Rose Lawn in Sadalia, Missouri.

Sarah Honeywell and Elizabeth Todd were assigned to pastor the Amarillo church; Mrs. A. J. Brice, Garfield; Mrs. Carl Flippin, Guymon; and Mrs. C. C. Howard, Turpin.
These ladies were members of the **Panhandle Conference**.

The **Tri-State Conference** appointed Mrs. V. A. Henry to pastor Emmanuel and Mrs. Elsie Jones, Lynville, Kentucky.

The following women ministers were appointed evangelists in the **West Oklahoma Conference**: Alma Hatchett, Sybil Wells, Gladys Myrick, Callie Winders, Pearl Miller, Kathrine Barger, Bernece Merkey, Laura Thornton, Maude Ward, Sybil Gresham, Mrs. Loweta Chesser, and Vera Hutcherson.[31]

1947

In the 1947 Yearbook, the **South Carolina Conference** reported 126 ministers; ninety-three ordained; thirty-three licensed. Of this number, eighteen were women, making them 14 percent of the total number.[32]

1948

In the 1948 *Yearbook,* the **Tri-State Conference** reported a ministerial membership of thirty-six. Of that number, eight were ladies, which represent 22 percent of the total.

The **Upper South Carolina Conference** had ninety-eight ministers in 1948 – eleven were women. This number of women is about 1 percent of the total ministers in the conference.

A seldom heard of conference, **Texas-Mexican**, reported its number of ministers as forty-four. Only three of those were women, representing almost 7 percent.

Fifteen percent of the 108 ministers were female in the **Virginia Conference** as reported in the 1948 *Yearbook*.[33]

Mrs. Clara Louise Peel Williams assisted her husband as co-pastor of the Scotland Neck, North Carolina Pentecostal Holiness Church. When they went there in 1948, the membership was only thirty-six, and services were held in a rented building. In 1950, the membership had grown to sixty-eight, and they led in the building of a brick church located in a desirable section of town. Clara was a licensed minister at the time and a graduate of Holmes Bible College, Greenville, South Carolina.

1952

The **Central Carolina Conference** had no women ministers in 1952.[34]

1953

Based on the report of the Stationing Committee for the **South Carolina Conference**, the number of women assigned to pastor churches was increasing gradually through the years.[35]

In the spring of 1950, a family of three, Brother Ray and Sister Elsie Inman and their son, Keith, walked into the service of a small Pentecostal Holiness Church in South Whittier, California. They were searching for a place to worship where there was a spirit of unity and the presence and power of the Holy Spirit. They found the place, accepted the doctrine of the church, and became members. Sister Inman was elected church secretary, her husband became a deacon, and Keith played the steel guitar.

A year later, the Conference Committee on Division of Labor assigned Sister Elsie Inman, a good Spirit-filled preacher, as pastor of the church. Immediately, she saw the need for a bigger and better building, but they were not financially able to construct a new building. However, God gave the good folk there a vision and determination to start a building program by faith.

The spirit of love, labor, service, sacrifice, unity, and understanding characterized the work there. The men, under the supervision of Brother Inman, did the carpentry work mostly in the evening hours and on Saturdays. The women cleaned, painted, helped with the framing, stucco, wiring, trimming, and many other carpentry chores.

Elsie bought most of the materials and ran the many necessary errands, in addition to the hours of untiring labor she spent at the church. The job was an immense one, and there were many difficulties, but God had spoken to His servant and assured her that He would help and support the work.

On Sunday, March 8, 1953, they moved into the new church building which was dedicated as a place that had been set apart as a monument of prayer and unity. It was to be an emblem of faith, courage, and determination of the congregation.

Tuesday evening following the dedication service, they began a revival conducted by Evangelists Edwyn and Vera Rupert, and the Lord marvelously poured out His Spirit upon them.

After the revival, Sister Inman resigned as pastor of the church to become an evangelist.[36]

1954

Rev. Mary Haag served as a board member of the **Pennsylvania Conference** at the time of this report printed in *The Helping Hand*. She was responsible for organizing a Women's Auxiliary in Truxall and writes, "These women are faithful and willing workers whose hearts are stirred with a great desire to do things for God and the church, and to bless humanity."[37]

From "The Gospel Travelette" comes the report of some of the work done by Rev. Clara Hicks with her husband, Rev. Robert Hicks. This publication was a newsletter printed by this evangelistic team to inform their readers about what they were doing for the Lord. During their meetings, they were raising funds to buy a washing machine for the Falcon Orphanage. God so wonderfully blessed their efforts, and the people cooperated so well, that they were able to send two machines and to do so earlier than expected.

They also describe their revival at Scotland Neck, North Carolina with Rev. T. O. Todd. Among the fourteen experiences was the salvation of the pastor's daughter. While there, they held two brief services at the sock mill where a number of the church members worked. On the last Sunday of the revival, the Sunday school attendance record was broken with 150 in attendance.

They left Scotland Neck on Monday, June 21, 1954, and held one-night services in several locations on the way home. The first one was at Fayetteville, North Carolina, where they had an overflow crowd. There were six experiences in that one service. The next night they were in Bladenboro, where a young mother prayed through to salvation. They were delighted to see a couple who had been saved in a previous revival in September 1949. They were still going strong for the Lord.

On Wednesday night, they were in Tabor City, North Carolina where God gave them a spirit of revival. Two people prayed through in the service. They were pleased to notice that the congregation had made improvements in their church.

On Thursday, they were at Matthew's Tabernacle near Lake City, South Carolina. God gave four definite experiences that night.

Saturday night and Sunday morning found them at Amick Grove, near Saluda, South Carolina. Several years earlier Clara had done some of her first preaching there. Both services had five or six experiences.

They closed out their one-week tour on Sunday night with a service at Abbeville, South Carolina, Sister Hick's home church, where they had a crowded auditorium. Five people were saved. The Hicks were members of the South Carolina Conference.[38]

The first annual session of the **Great Lakes Conference** reported no women ministers.[39]

1955

The *Advocate* published an article to recognize Rev. and Mrs. L. B. Edge on the observance of thirty-five years in the ministry. They were noted as one of the most successful husband-wife pastoral teams upon their retirement from the ministry. Sister Hattie Edge was graciously used of God in evangelism and anticipated continuing to be available for revival work. She was a licensed minister in the **Eastern Virginia Conference.**[40]

1956

According to the minutes of the Forty-Sixth Annual Session of the **South Carolina Conference,** 7 percent of the ordained ministers were women and 28 percent of licensed ministers were women.[41]

1957

The *Pentecostal Holiness Advocate*, August 3, 1957, reported that Rev. Alice Wilson, pastor of the First Pentecostal Holiness Church in Okmulgee, Oklahoma resigned to move to Oklahoma City, where her twin daughters would be attending Southwestern Bible College. She preached her farewell sermon Sunday, June 30.[42]

The **Georgia Conference** Woman's Auxiliary hosted the General W.A. Convention this year. Mrs. Dallas Tarkenton, a minister in the conference, served as the Conference W. A. President. Rev. Dorothy Donithan conducted a workshop on "The Standard" for the Convention.

Mrs. J. L. Russell, Sr., **North Carolina Conference** W. A. President and a minister, wrote a regular column called "Program Aids" for *The Helping Hand*.[43]

1958

Ada Lee Thurman served on the Resolutions Committee; two other lady ministers, Mrs. J. L. Wall and Mrs. David McKenzie, were appointed to be on the Committee on Memoirs at the forty-eighth annual session of the **South Carolina Conference**.[44]

1961

The Helping Hand reported, in the January 1961 issue, the death of Mrs. Haddock in a car accident on November 16, 1960. She and her husband were en route to Oklahoma City for the Feast of Ingathering when the accident occurred. Five days before leaving on this trip, Sister Haddock wrote Mrs. Blanche King a letter from which Mrs. King quoted in her article, "Conference President In Fatal Accident." She stated that, "a few sentences from that letter speak of her devotion to duty better than anything I might write about her: 'These have really been full days for me. I have finished my round of district conferences and am getting ready for the Feast of Ingathering and Harvest Train next week. I organized two new Auxiliaries[:] one at Perrytown, Okla[homa], a new church[;] and one at Socorro, N. Mex[ico], where we have a mission church . . . I had dreaded the trip to Socorro so much. I felt I just couldn't hold out to drive so far, as I didn't feel well at all in my body. I really prayed, and before time to go I felt calm and resigned . . . Sister King, if we really obey the Lord and do His will we are going to have to make a sacrifice. It is wonderful how the Lord gave me strength for the trip and sent with me.'" Mrs. Haddock was an ordained minister in the **Great Plains Conference**.[45]

1962

Two women, Miss Dollie Mae Bowen and Mrs. Bessie Watts, were licensed to preach at the fifty-second annual session of the **South Carolina Conference**. Lacy Drew received ordination. The Committee on Memoirs recognized Rev. Ethel Moore, who had died in 1962 after serving faithfully as a minister for thirty years.

The same report records the ministers' tithes paid for that year. Generally speaking, the ladies' totals are much less that those sent in by the male preachers.

Mrs. H. C. Alexander	$37.00
Neta Byrd	11.00
Natalie Carnes	83.50
Flossie Cooper	25.00
Josephine Cox	39.60
Lacy Drew	260.00
Lila Medlin	23.00
Josephine McDaniels	32.00
Thelma Player	84.23

The names of 153 ordained ministers appeared in the minutes, twelve of those being women. This represents only 7 percent of the total number ordained. The number licensed ministers listed were sixty-two, sixteen of them being women, representing 25 percent of the total.[46]

1965

"REPORT ACCEPTED AND CHARACTER PASSED"
Compiled by
Marilyn A. Hudson with Alicia Hutson
Southwestern Christian University
April 2006

(**Author's note:** This article is reprinted, with permission, as written.)

Introduction

"The year was 1965 in Wellington, Kansas, in the home of the pastor of the local Pentecostal Holiness Church. The guest evangelist, Mary E. Ford, was a woman just easing out of middle age wearing a cream colored chiffon blouse, a sturdy brown woolen skirt, with fading hair escaping from its once tidy bun. Her wide pleasant face was a roller coaster of expressions from intense concentration to hearty laughter.

"Sitting at the parsonage piano, a sturdy black upright, she is surrounded by the daughters of the pastor and a friend of theirs who often came to visit. The visitor [Mary Ford] entertains them playing snappy standards from the forties and crooning tunes from the fifties. She responded to the news that the oldest girl was taking business courses by encouraging her to keep her chin up and not let the men bully her . . . .

"To all of those gathered around the piano that afternoon she shared her love of God, her courage, her experience, and sense of fun. To each and every one there she encouraged them to 'press on' in their faith and to get a good education." ([1] The first pastor of the author was the Rev. Sallie Mae Flippin, Wellington Pentecostal Holiness Church, Kansas (1960). Her second pastors were Evelyn and Bill Thompson, Wellington. As a teenager she had the opportunity to spend time with Mary E. Ford . . . when she was a guest in the home of Rev. Hoyle Baker.)[47]

(**Author's note:** Later in the book, the reader will find a sermon written by Mary E. Ford. She was an ordained minister in the Oklahoma Conference, transferring there in 1939.)

1967

The report from the Saltsburg Church in the **Pennsylvania Conference**, which was pastored by Rev. Sophia Fordyce, indicated that the Sunday school attendance was on the increase. They just began a new class for another age group and welcomed two new teachers to the staff during March. The church started having evening service on Easter.[48]

1968

Rev. Valla Cleta Bland wrote in the *East Oklahoma Conference News* that she felt led to write to the most "blessed people in the world. I want to encourage everyone – pastors, evangelists, lay members and all – to keep your eyes on Jesus; the end is so near!"
She was told by a specialist in Tulsa on September 10, 1968, that she would never get well and never be able to preach again. Her faith was in the Lord for healing, if not in this life, then in the one to come.[49]

1969

The Greta Campbell Trio from the **Upper South Carolina Conference** announced in the *Advocate* the availability of a new record, "Lead Me Saviour," which could be ordered from Advocate Press for $4 for a mono and $5 for a stereo. "One does not live by bread alone" was the theme of the new album that contained twelve great songs, "superbly sung and blended to the soft tones of the organ, piano, and violin."[50]

Mrs. Blanche Leon King, a licensed minister in the **Georgia Conference,** delivered the 1969 commencement address at Emmanuel College on the occasion of its fiftieth anniversary.

Mable Crouser and Catherine Monhollen were the only two women ministers whose names appeared in the Minutes of the **Great Lakes Conference** at its fifteenth annual session.

The **British Columbia Conference** [Canada] reports only three licensed women ministers: Mrs. M. Thomas, Miss M. R. Webley, and Miss I. Anstice.[51]

1971

Sarah Honeywell, Mrs. A. C. Kersey, and Mrs. J. H. Miller were mentioned in the **Great Plains Conference** Minutes as ordained ministers. Mrs. B. A. King, Mrs. M. L. Lunsford, and Mrs. F. M. Mathis were listed as licensed ministers.[52]

1972

From the *News Monthly* comes the report of ministers recently transferred into the **Oklahoma Conference**. Clara Guinn, an ordained lady minister returned her membership to Oklahoma from Southern California. Irene Morrison, a licensed minister from the Kansas Conference was assisting Rev. George Payne in the work at Airline Church. Maggie Woodruff, an ordained minister from the Ozarks Conference, transferred to West Oklahoma to pastor the Frederick Church with her husband.[53]

1973

Ladies appointed to pastor churches in the **South Carolina Conference** at their annual meeting June 29-July 1, 1973, were as follows:

Broad Swamp	Mrs. W. R. McCutcheon
Freemont Mission	Sally Stone
Green Branch	Edna Yon
Orangeburg	Mary Sue Evans
By-Way	Thelma Player

Hickory Grove	Lacy Drew
New Zion	Josephine Cox
Pioneer	Helon Phillips

Kathleen Taylor was approved for ordination.[54]

Two evangelists, Rev. Miss Linda R. Faber, a minister in the **Western North Carolina**, and Rev. Miss Shelby Jeffcoat, a minister in the **South Carolina Conference**, announced their availability for revivals in *The Challenge*, Winter 1973. Linda attended Holmes Bible College, Greenville, South Carolina, and Shelby went to Emmanuel College in Franklin Springs, Georgia. They call themselves "The King's Children."[55]

1974

Rev. Opal Plowman, pastor of Palmdale Church, received the Pastor of the Year Award for 1973 in the **Southern California Conference**.[56]

1978

Mrs. Frances Tarkenton was one of the featured speakers for the King Memorial Lectures held at Emmanuel College annually. She was a graduate of Georgia College at Milledgeville and Holmes Bible College in Greenville, South Carolina. A former school teacher, Mrs. Tarkenton was named one of the Outstanding Elementary Teachers in the nation in 1974. Further, "she is a minister in the Pentecostal Holiness Church and is currently serving as pastor of the Trinity Temple Church in Smyrna in the **Georgia Conference**.[57]

The Committee of Examination for the **Alabama Conference** in the fifty-fourth annual session recommended Mrs. Genene Baggett for license. The Division of Labor Committee appointed two female pastors: Thursia Long at Pleasant Plains and Genene Baggett at Century.[58]

1980

According to information in the archives of the South Carolina Conference, the Trinity Pentecostal Holiness Church, formerly known as the Sunset Pentecostal Holiness Church, was founded September 1968 by Rev. Flossie Cooper in a house provided by one of the charter members, Mrs. Lula Sheppard. The church was organized in November 1968, with five members.

The Zion Church, located seven miles north of Conway, South Carolina on Highway 701, was founded by Rev. Laura Graham.

Rev. Doris Shull and her husband Clinton felt the call to go to Williston, South Carolina to begin a new work. Their first meeting was held June 8, 1975, and the church was organized on August 4 of the same year. Doris was called to preach in 1969 and was ordained by the South Carolina Conference in 1974.

The Wadesboro Church was born out of a tent meeting held in 1928. Sister Minnie Calder was pastor when the first church building was constructed.

Rev. Helon Phillips was founder of the Pioneer Pentecostal Holiness Church located in Moncks Corner, South Carolina.

The Rock Hill First Pentecostal Holiness Church was organized as a result of a tent meeting held in 1942. Rev. Mrs. Ethel Moore was the first pastor of the church, where she served for three years. During her time there the church purchased a lot that was later the site of a new sanctuary which was built in 1946 under the leadership of another pastor. In the late-1940s, a young lady, Miss Dorothy Mae Welch, was called by the Lord to preach His word. She felt led to go to the old home of her grandparents in the eastern part of Clarendon to preach to her relatives. From this endeavor, with help from other ministers in the community and the Superintendent of the South Carolina Conference, the Pine Dale Church was organized in 1948.

Bonneau Church was constructed by Rev. T. O. Evans, Superintendent of the South Carolina Conference and evangelist R. E. Powers. Mrs. Josephine Warren was the first pastor.

Park Street Pentecostal Holiness Church was organized as Riverside Pentecostal Holiness Church by Rev. Mrs. Lila Medlin on Gist Street in Columbia, February 4, 1943.

The Friendfield Pentecostal Holiness Church had its beginning in 1942. It was conceived in the heart of a humble woman in the community that loved the Lord, her neighbors, and wanted to see them saved, and she set out to do something about it. She started by having services in the homes in the community. People began to get saved, and soon revival was born. This servant of the Lord was Rev. Nina Alexander.

On December 2, 1962, Rev. Flossie Cooper began the Gibson Church as a mission. They secured an old house in which to conduct services; later they purchased land and another old house to use for their services. The church was organized on May 31, 1963, with eight members.

By-Way Church was founded in March 1960 by Rev. Thelma Player. The church was formally organized with eight charter members on May 22, 1960, in a portable tabernacle supplied by the South Carolina Conference.

In the spring of 1925, Gospel Mission was organized by Rev. M. L. Canady and his wife, Lula Mae. The church later became the Great Falls Pentecostal Holiness Church.

In 1949, Rev. Sue Evans became the pastor of the Mt. Beulah Pentecostal Holiness Church. During her pastorate, the education building was added.

Mary Sue Evans pastored the Orangeburg church for three years. She was the second minister to lead this church.[59]

1981

At the 1981 Inspirational Conference of the **Southern California Conference**, Opal Rouse was appointed World Missions Director. Ordained women ministers listed were Violet Curlee, Minnie Davidson, Suda Faulkner, Murel Jones, Norva Moore, Rosie Shifflet, Inez Weed, and Mary Velma Williams. Those women who were named as licensed ministers were Lillie Rae Moore, Essie Petty, and Opal Rouse.[60]

1983

The culmination of many years' struggle as a congregation was realized recently as the people of the Century Church in Century, Florida shared in a dedication service of their new building. This took place on April 24, 1983, under the pastoral leadership of Sister Fannie Wright, who went there in 1981. This church was located in the **Alabama Conference**[61]

1985

In the 1985 **South Carolina Conference** Minutes, they report having 185 churches. Eleven were pastored by lady ministers,[62] which is 6 percent of the total number of ministers.

1992

The following information about Deborah Williams was published in the February 1992 issue of *The Evangel*, the official organ of the North Carolina Conference. While working as the Evangelism Director at the church her father pastored, Deborah earned her B.S. degree in biblical studies from Lee College, Cleveland, Tennessee in 1986. During her years as a student, she preached in prisons, jails, and nursing homes. She also ministered in the local coffee house to troubled young people. Her call led her to evangelize the Indians on reservations in Arizona, as well as being a well-known speaker and leader in Women's Aglow.

In 1986, her horizons expanded when she moved to San Diego, California to work for Morris Cerullo. Through the next year, she traveled across North America as Testimony Director with his team as an interviewer and writer, and she trained thousands of crusade workers.

In 1988, she found worldwide evangelism opportunities with a three month tour alone to Kenya, East Africa. Since that initial trip, she has returned to Africa several times and worked closely with Pentecostal Holiness missionaries there, especially Rev. and Mrs. Philip List.

She joined the **North Carolina Conference** as an ordained minister in 1991. Rev. Chris Thompson, Evangelism Director at that time, wrote "Deborah is a revivalist, with a mighty message of heartfelt repentance always resulting in VICTORY! She comes full of love and faith for His people, with a fiery zeal that is contagious."[63]

This is a brief history of the years of service in ministry of Rev. Lila McCutcheon in the **South Carolina Conference** from 1952-1992.

  1952 licensed as an evangelist
  1953 pastored Scranton with her husband and evangelized
  1954 pastored Scranton and Barrineau with her husband and evangelized
  1955 pastored Scranton and Barrineau with her husband and evangelized
  1956 pastored Barrineau with her husband and evangelized
  1957 Sandy Bay and Willow Creek – assistant pastor
  1958-1959 Willow Creek – assistant pastor
  1960-1973 pastored Broad Swamp
  1971 ordained

>   1974-1983 Oak Grove – assistant pastor
>   1984 – retired
>   1989-1992 – Community – assistant pastor[64]

Rev. Leona Coker was pastor of a new ministry, The Potter's House, near the Fort Jackson Army base in Columbia, South Carolina. For some time Sister Coker felt God speaking to her and leading her in this area of ministry, which was committed to the preaching of God's Word for the whole person – body, mind, and spirit.[65]

On Sunday, October 25, 1992, the Bread of Life Pentecostal Holiness Church was organized. That morning, twenty-seven were present for Sunday school and the worship service. Twenty of that number joined to form the new church only eight weeks after they held their first service. Rev. Edna Sorrells pastored the new work. This was the first church organized by the **Appalachian Conference** after changing its name from the Virginia Conference.[66]

1995

Deborah Williams, international evangelist, from Fayetteville, North Carolina, conducted some meetings at the Draper Valley Pentecostal Holiness Church in the Appalachian Conference. She was available for other services in the conference. After earning her college degree in 1986, she traveled with a world-wide crusade ministry training thousands of workers. Since 1988, she has traveled full time in an evangelistic ministry that has taken her to Africa, the Philippines, and Russia.[67]

1996

The Living Springs Pentecostal Holiness Church in North Tazewell, Virginia, pastored by Mary Frances Begley was praying for success and prosperity in its new work. In the morning worship service on August 4, two visitors received the Lord as their Savior and were among those baptized in the service on August 11, 1996.[68]

1997

"In June 1990," Rev. Kathy Sandlin writes, "God called me to plant a church, and I responded by gathering a core group of 12 people and pursuing that call. God blessed our efforts and gave us steady growth. Soon we were able to purchase three acres of land with two existing buildings. This allowed us to open a soup kitchen, a community food bank, and a community clothes closet. We began conducting sidewalk Sunday schools and doing everything we could to build the kingdom of God. The church grew from twelve members to 175 and was thriving. But after pastoring this church five years, God began dealing with me about taking a new direction in my ministry."

While she was pastoring that church, she was also serving as part-time WIN Director for the Upper South Carolina. She states that she enjoyed the pastoral ministry, but felt God was directing her to serve full-time as the WIN Director in a ministry of prayer and evangelism. Almost immediately, she began to get calls from churches and conferences asking her "to conduct prayer conferences on intercession, spiritual warfare, praise and worship, and other related subjects."

She reported of several successful conferences in 1996 and 1997: November 1996 – Baton Rouge, Louisiana – a four-day prayer conference extended to a ten-day event – thirty-two saved, fifteen baptized in the Holy Spirit, many healed – The church received twenty-four new members.

February 1997 – North Augusta, South Carolina Bible Pentecostal Holiness Church – a three-day conference – seventy saved, sixty-four baptized in the Holy Spirit – The church experienced a tremendous prayer revival.

March 1997 – Falcon, North Carolina – This was a time of personal ministry and intercession for more than 125 people.

April 1997 – Clinton, North Carolina – three-day prayer conference, which lasted eight days – "The spirit of the church was liberated, and the members saw 15 saved and 10 baptized in the Holy Spirit." Twenty eight people joined the church.

"God is still sowing, filling, healing, delivering, and setting captives free," Kathy reports.[69]

1998

Evangelist and teacher Sonia Oliphant from Radford, Virginia announced her availability for revival services and women's meetings. She has served with her husband, Rev. Tom Oliphant, in full-time Christian ministry. For twenty-five years, she had conducted women's meetings and shared the pulpit with her husband. Her ministry emphasis is to bring light and hope to those in darkness and despair and to encourage believers to know what they are in Christ.[70]

2000

The *Appalachian Conference Messenger* reported in its May 2000 issue that Rev. Kathy Sandlin was to speak at the Conference Women's Ministries convention on June 3. She was described as a preacher, teacher, singer, songwriter, musician, and an author of several books on intercession/prayer and counselor training.[71]

Rev. Susan Wells, Conference WIN Director wrote an article title "A Passion for God" in *The Challenge*, Spring 2000 in which she indicates that the Lord had been speaking to her about a passion that He desires His people to have for Him. She wrote that she looked up *"passion"* in Webster's Dictionary, and that it revealed a Latin origin which means *"to suffer."* Of course, that word speaks of the sufferings of Jesus during the last week of His life, especially the crucifixion. She said her belief is that when the Spirit of the Lord moves upon us, He wants us to respond to Him like the Shulamite does to her beloved in the Song of Solomon. She says in chapter 1, verse 2, *"Let him kiss me with the kisses of his mouth: for thy love is better than wine."* The Hebrew word for *kiss* indicates the meaning to be *"to equip with weapons; armed men."* The idea is to allow God to equip us like armed men with weapons as the Bride of Christ. Her emphasis is that the next time the Spirit of the Lord touches one of His own, they should not be a passive recipient but should choose rather to respond with a passionate love for Him.[72]

2001

Kristie Howell was licensed as a minister by the **South Carolina Conference** on June 27, 1999. She was described in *Evangelism USA*, "As a music evangelist, she has a unique ministry of music and Word to people of all ages. Her desire is to see people come to know Christ in all that He is and to take our relationships with Jesus to the next level." She is a graduate of Emmanuel College, Franklin Springs, Georgia with an associate of arts applied music degree and a bachelor of science in religious education.

Deborah Williams Riley is a full-time evangelist, who for a number of years has been featured in women's conferences, retreats, and local church revivals. She is ordained in the **New Horizons Conference.** "Deborah speaks with a strong prophetic voice and is used powerfully in altar ministry. Many miracles have been experienced in her services and individuals have reported definite direction from the Lord for their lives as they sat under her preaching."[73]

Elizabeth Lynne Gilliam, a licensed minister in the **Appalachian Conference**, was available as a guest speaker or to fill in for pastors. She holds a bachelor's degree from American University's School of International Service in Washington, D. C. Elizabeth also studied French at the University of Paris, where she evangelized on the streets of Paris and the beaches of Biarritz.[74]

Rev. Vela Sizemore, a retired minister who lives in Austinville, Virginia, was mentioned in the *Messenger* to honor her birthday on January 27.[75]

2002

Pastor Ann Kreighbaum announced that the church family at My Father's House in Cottageville, South Carolina, had the vision to establish a Christian academy, K4-5th grade. The name of the school was to be Majestic Dove Christian Academy. They were preparing a handbook for students and staff and getting the church updated to building code compliance for a school. Also, they needed chalkboards, corkboards, and student desks.[76]

The Tazwell Pentecostal Holiness Church was experiencing miracles under the leadership of Pastor Nora Bishop and associate pastor Dana Truckenmiller. God told the church He would get them out of debt if they would obey Him. As the congregation sought the Lord, they were able to pay off the loan for the church van thirteen months ahead of time. About the same time, they had to go in debt again for a new roof. The Lord showed Himself faithful in helping them pay off this debt in seven months, rather than the original thirty-six months for which it was financed. At that time, the church was debt free.[77]

2004

The Appalachian Women's Ministries announced the annual Fall Retreat with guest speaker Rev. Peggy Eby from Houston, Texas. She works alongside her husband, Jim, through Mission Catalyst International (MCI), an organization they founded in 2001. The theme of the retreat was "A Night of Destiny" and was to be held at the Music Road Hotel in Pigeon Forge, Tennessee. Peggy, an ordained minister and anointed speaker, travels throughout the United States and in other countries for teaching and training leadership workshops. She also served on the World Intercession Network (WIN) Prayer Committee for the denomination. Jim and Peggy have been church planters, missionaries, and pastors in the **New Horizons Conference**.[78]

2005

This information appeared in the *Appalachian Conference Messenger* in January 2005. In June 2004, Bonnie Sue Cericola was ordained as a minister by the IPHC leadership team. She was a founding member of New Visions Church in Bluefield, West Virginia. Bonnie was born again in her early teenage years and has been a member of the denomination for more than thirty years. She served God in prison and women's ministries, as co-pastor, evangelist, revivalist, and church planter.[79]

"CELEBRATING FAITHFULNESS!" This is a brief review of the ministry of Rev. Thelma Player, a licensed minister in the **South Carolina Conference**.

1940   She began her ministry at the country jail with the chain gang. She also preached on street corners and in homes.

1948   Thelma received mission worker's license in the Pentecostal Holiness Church. She later went to Ellerbe, North Carolina and began a church in the home of Mr. and Mrs. Scott. From the house church, the Ellerbe Church was formed, where Rev. Player was pastor for twelve years.

1959   She began a mission in Outside Community and from this mission work the By-Way Church was founded, where she served as pastor for twenty-seven years until she retired. She had been retired for five years when she was called to go to the Cordova Church in 1990. Rev. Player remained there as pastor until November 2003.[80]

Margie Tanner is an ordained minister in the **South Carolina Conference** who is involved in ministry with her husband, Roger; her daughter, Robin; and grandson, Joshua. The daughter and grandson join with Margie in the singing ministry. In 2004, they were blessed to minister in twelve states and saw a great harvest of souls and many miracles of healing. Margie is an anointed preacher of the Word.[81]

Jeraldine T. Posey, D. Min., a longtime resident of Hopewell, Virginia recently published her second book, *God Is . . . In the Psalms*. She has spent much of her life as a minister and teacher sharing her understanding of God's influence with those around her. Dr. Posey says, "I think the Psalms speak specifically to what God is and His eternal presence in this world. If we could fully realize that He is ever before us revealing the many aspects of His nature, what joy and strength would come to our souls." About 20 years ago, she published her first book, *Gleanings for Private Devotion*.[82] Dr. Posey was the first woman to be ordained in the Eastern Virginia Conference. She and her husband, Francis, also served as missionaries to Africa in 1960-61. Both have pastored churches in the conference.

2006

The Prince of Peace Spanish Church in Charleston South Carolina was pastored by Ana Garcia. "This elderly, vivacious and loving lady continues to lead many to the Lord."[83]

As reported in the January 2006 issue of the *Appalachian Conference Messenger*, the Roderfield Pentecostal Holiness Church honored its pastor, Brenda Blankenship, on October 9, 2005. She became pastor of the church in 1996 when the congregation was made up of only six people. God gave her a vision to build, and since that time, many improvements have been made to the church property, and they were able to purchase some land next to them. A paved parking lot was also added. Pastor Blankenship then began to feel the call of God to return to evangelizing again. Her church will miss her.[84]

2007

Rev. Mrs. Thelma Player was honored for her service to God and the **South Carolina Conference** at the annual luncheon meeting of the Royal Elders, the retired ministers and their spouses.[85]

2008

The Challenge reports that the Sparks Afire Kids' Church of Cheraw Family Worship Center, Cheraw, South Carolina is experiencing the transforming power of God in the hearts of the younger youth. They have become passionate intercessors desiring their families and friends to know the love of God. The children lay hands on each other and pray for God to pour out His Spirit on them. When someone goes to the altar during the regular church services, it is the children who surround them in prayer. Seventeen of their students returned to the Lord, seven received Him for the first time, and four received the Baptism of the Holy Spirit. All of them are less than twelve years old. Kristen Sander, pastor of the church writes, "Three years ago I began ministering to 3 children on Wednesday evenings for thirty minutes after praise and worship. Now I work with fourteen rotating adult and teen volunteers who minister with me to twenty-five to thirty or more children for 1-1/2 hours on a weekly basis."[86]

2009

Cana of Galilee Pentecostal Holiness Church in the Canaan Community of Orangeburg County, South Carolina celebrated its 47th annual homecoming on Sunday, November 8, 2009. Rev. Eileen Gunnells was the pastor. The church was established on June 17, 1962.[87]

These tidbits have been gleaned from various sources covering the years 1901 to 2009. They form a chain of events that shows how these women fit into the work of the conferences of which they were members. Even though they have always been in the minority, they have not cried "discrimination," but have labored wherever they had the opportunity.

When the denomination was very young, women were allowed to share in the responsibility to spread the gospel. Whether they received the recognition due them is not known, but at least they did have some standing throughout the denomination.

No matter the conclusion drawn, some necessary observations are appropriate here. Most married women ministers appear on the rosters by their husband's name or initials. In some cases, even single women were listed only by an initial rather than their given names. A few conferences had no lady ministers at all. However, some of the ladies were appointed to committees on the conference level, they founded and organized churches, and they led successful building programs where they were pastoring.

They labored as writers, evangelists (nationally and internationally), pastors, teachers, conference speakers and musicians; they were active in jail ministries, in nursing homes, in children's ministries, and in Women's Ministries (as officials and leaders on the local, conference, and general levels); they preached revivals; they served as WIN Directors; they led prayer conferences. Notably, some were engaged in ministry for sixty-plus years. One of those with longevity in the ministry was Rev. Mrs. Hattie Edge, through whose ministry two young men were converted and later became Bishops of the Pentecostal Holiness Church: Rev. J. A. Synan, Sr. and Rev. J. Floyd Williams.

Their names go down in history of this denomination, not as famous individuals, but as humble wives, mothers, sisters, and friends, who vigorously strove to be at their best in a life totally dedicated to one thing and one thing only: to hear the Master say "Well, done."

Only God knows what good they accomplished.

---

[1] Dr. Harold Hunter, "Centennial Notes," July 20, 2010, www.iphc.org.; Oris Hubbard, e-mails dated August 5 & 6, 2010; Joseph Campbell, *The Pentecostal Holiness Church 1898-1948*, pp. 233-334.

[2] Minutes of the 9th Annual Convention, November 16, 1908, p. 7.

[3] Campbell, p. 337.

[4] Campbell, pp. 332-333.

[5] Campbell, p. 336.

[6] N. T. Morgan, District Secretary, "Quarterly Conference," *The Advocate*, July 3, 1919, p. 7.

[7] J. L. Barnett, Secretary, reporting for the Fourth Quarterly Conference of the Franklin Springs District of the Annual Conference of Georgia on October 11, 1919, *The Advocate*, October 30, 1919, p. 4.

[8] Arthur Smith, Secretary, reporting for the First Quarterly Conference of the Wagoner District, Oklahoma on November 1, 1919, *The Advocate*, November 20, 1919, p. 14.

[9] N. T. Morgan, reporting for the First Quarterly Conference of the Oklahoma District on November 7, 1919, *The Advocate*, November 27 and December 4, 1919, p. 6.

[10] Report of Stationing Committee, North Carolina Conference, *The Advocate*, December 18, 1919, p. 6.

[11] Georgia Conference Minutes, *The Advocate*, February 5, 1920, p. 14.

[12] Minutes of the Second Quarterly Conference of the Oklahoma District on February 7, 1920, *The Advocate*, March 4, 1920, p. 20.

[13] Minutes of the Second Quarterly Conference of the Mountain Park District, Oklahoma on February 13, 1920, *The Advocate*, March 25, 1920, p. 6.

[14] Minutes of the Anderson District of the Upper South Carolina Conference, April 10, 1920, *The Advocate*, May 13, 1920, p. 6.

[15] Minutes of the Second Quarterly Conference of the Griffin District of the Georgia Conference, April 9-11, *The Advocate*, May 20, 1920, pp. 2-3.

[16] Minutes of the Third Quarterly Conference of the Wagoner District, Oklahoma Conference, May 7-9, *The Advocate*, June 3, 1920, p. 4.

[17] Minutes of the Fourth General Conference of the Pentecostal Holiness Church, May 1921.

[18] 1925 Yearbook of the Pentecostal Holiness Church, Georgia Conference.

[19] 1932 Yearbook, Minutes of the Twenty-Second Annual Session of the Lower South Carolina Conference, p. 5.

[20] 1933 Yearbook, Lower South Carolina Conference Minutes, p. 6.

[21] "Report of Committee on Examination of Applicants for Credentials" and "Report of Committee on Missions," 1935 Yearbook, Lower South Carolina Conference Minutes, pp. 6, 8.

[22] "Report of Committee on Examination of Applicants for Credentials," 1936 Yearbook, Lower South Carolina Conference Minutes, p. 8.

[23] "Report of Stationing Committee," 1937 Yearbook, Lower South Carolina Conference Minutes, pp. 8-9.

[24] "Committee on Examination," 1938 Yearbook, Lower South Carolina Conference Minutes, p. 12.

[25] 1939 Yearbook, pp. 12, 24.

[26] 1940 Yearbook.

[27] 1941 Yearbook, Minutes of the Maryland Conference.

[28] "Report of Committee on Evangelism," 1942 Yearbook, Lower South Carolina Conference Minutes, p. 8.

[29] "Report of Stationing Committee," 1944 Yearbook, South Carolina Conference, pp. 7-8.

[30] Harold Paul, *From Printer's Devil to Bishop*, pp.131-136.

[31] "Reports of Committees on Division of Labor," 1946 Yearbook, pp. 69-71, 78-79, 83, 86, 89-90.

[32] 1947 Yearbook, South Carolina Conference, p. 46.

[33] 1948 Yearbook.

[34] 1952 Yearbook.

[35] "Report of Stationing Committee, 1953 Yearbook, pp. 8-10.

[36] Rev. Elsie Inman, "Southern California 'This is God's House,'" *The Advocate*, May 14, 1953, p.17.

[37] Rev. Mary Haag, "Truxall Auxiliary," *The Helping Hand*, June 1954, p. 10.

[38] Rev. Robert Hicks, "The Gospel Travelette," July 15, 1954.

[39] 1954 Yearbook

[40] "Rev. and Mrs. L. B. Edge Observe 35 Years in the Ministry," *The Advocate*, August 25, 1955, p. 2.

[41] "Conference Register," 1956 Yearbook.

[42] Mrs. Lorene Casey, "Pastor Resigns at Okmulgee, Oklahoma, *The Advocate*, August 3, 1957, p. 8.

[43] *The Helping Hand*, June 1957.

[44] "Committee Report on Resolutions,"1958 Yearbook, pp. 64-65.

[45] Blanche L. King, "Conference President in Fatal Accident," *The Helping Hand*, January 1961, p. 6.

[46] "Biennial Conference Minutes," 1962 Yearbook, pp. 3, 19, 21, 24-25, 31-34.

[47] Marilyn Hudson with Alicia Hutson, "Pentecostal Footnotes," Southwestern Christian University Library, Bethany, Oklahoma, April 2006.

[48] "The Northern Star," Pennsylvania Conference Newsletter, April 1, 1967.

[49] "East Oklahoma Conference News,"1968, front page.

[50] *The Advocate*, January 4, 1969, p. 5.
[51] 1969 Yearbook, Minutes of the Great Lakes and British Columbia Conferences.
[52] 1971 Yearbook, Minutes of the Great Plains Conference.
[53] "Oklahoma Conference News Monthly," September 1972.
[54] 1973 Yearbook, South Carolina Conference Minutes.
[55] *The Challenge*, Winter 1973, p. 13.
[56] "Southern California Conference News," February 1974.
[57] "1978 King Memorial Lectures," *The Advocate*, September 10, 1978, p. 20.
[58] "Report of the Committee of Examination," and "The Report of the Division of Labor Committee,"1978 Alabama Conference Minutes.
[59] South Carolina Conference historical records in the archives at Lake City.
[60] Southern California Inspirational Conference Minutes, 1981.
[61] *Alabama Conference News,* June 1983, front page.
[62] "Conference Register," 1985 Yearbook, pp. 38-41.
[63] *The Evangel*, February 1992, p. 4.
[64] South Carolina Conference historical records in the archives at Lake City.
[65] "The Potter's House," *The Challenge*, Spring 1992, p. 9.
[66] "New Church in Staunton Organized," *Appalachian Conference Messenger*, December 1991, p. 7.
[67] "International Evangelist Available," *Appalachian Conference Messenger*, May 1995, p. 5.
[68] "New Sanctuary in Tazwell," *Appalachian Conference Messenger*, September 1996, p. 2.
[69] "Prayer and Prophetic Evangelism," *Evangelism USA*, November/December 1997, p. 4.
[70] "Available for Revivals, Women's Meetings," *Appalachian Conference Messenger*, March 1998, p. 3.
[71] "Rev. Kathy Sandlin to Speak at June 3 WM Convention," *Appalachian Conference Messenger*, May 2000, p. 5.
[72] "A Passion for God," *The Challenge*, Spring, 2000.
[73] *Evangelism USA*, Spring 2001, back page.
[74] *Appalachian Conference Messenger*, August 2001, p. 3.
[75] *Appalachian Conference Messenger*, January 2001.
[76] *The Challenge*, Winter 2002.
[77] *Appalachian Conference Messenger*, July 2002, p. 8.
[78] Wanda Myers, "Women's Ministries," *Appalachian Conference Messenger*, October 2004, p. 6.
[79] "The Cericolas Ready to Serve," *Appalachian Conference Messenger*, January 2005.
[80] *The Challenge*, Winter 2005, p. 4.
[81] "Celebrating Faithfulness!," *The Challenge*, Summer 2005, back page.
[82] Mandana Marsh, "Minister and Teacher Pens Devotional Book," *The Hopewell News*, February 8, 2005, p. 5.
[83] "Hispanic Church News," *The Challenge*, Fall 2006, p. 18.
[84] "Roderfield Honors Pastor," *Appalachian Conference Messenger*, January 2006, back page.
[85] *The Challenge*, Fall 2007.
[86] Rev. Kristen L. Sanders, "Spotlight on Children's Ministry," *The Challenge*, Fall 2008.
[87] *The Challenge*, Spring/Summer, 2010.

CHAPTER 7

Deborah's Daughters

"Deborah, a prophetess, the wife of Lappidoth, was leading Israel at that time" – Judges 4:4-NIV.

(**Author's note:** The following is a brief historical sketch of the organization and function of Deborah's Daughters, in the North Carolina Conference, written by Dr. Janice Marshburn. To my knowledge, no other conference in the denomination has such a group.)

"Deborah's Daughters, originally referred to as Women Ministers, originated in 2002 under the leadership of Bishop Chris Thompson, of the North Carolina Conference of the International Pentecostal Holiness Church. At that time there were ninety-one women ministers. The organization was established with the intent of encouraging, training, and empowering women to fulfill their destiny in ministry; and to see women rise to their full potential working side by side with men in ministry.

"From the very beginning, there was a concern that the name 'Women Ministers' would be confused with 'Women's Ministries.' We gradually evolved to the name Lady Ministers. Later it was agreed upon that the term Lady Clergy was more appropriate since the organization was to be made up of women with credentials or those in the credentialing process. Alternative names were offered and discussed. One of the first names suggested was 'Deborah's Daughters.' Some were concerned that everyone would not be familiar with the biblical reference to Deborah. However, the desire/need for a name change became a topic of discussion at each meeting. The term 'Deborah's Daughters' kept resurfacing.

"On March 21, 2007, Bishop Chris Thompson approved the adoption of the biblical name 'Deborah's Daughters' as the official name of the Lady Ministers/Clergy of the North Carolina Conference of the International Pentecostal Holiness Church. Deborah's Daughters speaks of all lady clergy who are God's chosen mouthpiece for a time when His children need deliverance. She works not above or before, but alongside her male counterparts in building God's Kingdom. Deborah had the faith and Barak had the battle knowledge. She needed him as much as he needed her. Together they stood against the enemy destined for victory! This truly reflects the heart's desire of The Lady Clergy of the North Carolina Conference of the International Pentecostal Holiness Church – to work together to fulfill our God-given destinies and accomplish more for the Kingdom of God. TEAM – Together Everyone Accomplishes MORE!

"The current Advisory Council members of this organization according to their January 2010 newsletter are Janice Marshburn, Director; Patsy Vaughan, Assistant Director; Cindy Midyette, Historian/Secretary; Wilda Faircloth; Lydia Figueroa, Betty Rogers, and Louise Thompson, Council Members.

"On March 20, 2008, the group declared their mission and vision statements: 'MISSION STATEMENT: To encourage, support, train and empower women clergy to fulfill their destiny in ministry. VISION STATEMENT: See women clergy rise to their full potential.'"[1]

One of the reasons for the success of this organization in training and promoting lady clergy in the North Carolina Conference is that the previous bishop, Chris Thompson, and the current bishop, Jim Whitfield has been very supportive of their ministry. The following article written by Patsy Vaughan and a letter from Rev. Whitfield, expressing his appreciate for their work, show how each one of these men has promoted Deborah's Daughters.

Out-of-the Box Thinking for Women Ministers
Patsy Vaughan

Many people in ministry *talk* about thinking outside the box. Bishop Chris Thompson, Superintendent [Bishop] of the North Carolina Conference, does it.

With less than a year in office, Thompson discovered a need and planned a training event designed specifically for women ministers, who make up over 20 percent of the conference's total ministerial census. At a historical event in November 2002, he appointed an advisory council consisting of seven ordained women. His plan was to meet with the council annually to discuss the unique needs and interest of lady clergy and to plan training events accordingly.

Rev. Vaughan writes, "The ministry has been evolving and expanding and continues to evolve and expand. The annual spring training event is now designed to include ministry to Hispanic lady clergy. Regional mini-training events are also offered in the fall.

"The lady clergy of the North Carolina Conference are now experiencing new excitement, camaraderie, and networking, which was an essential focus of the Vision of Deborah's Daughters from its inception . . . .

"As the North Carolina Conference of the IPHC plunges ahead with a fresh vision to see lady clergy encouraged, trained, and empowered to fulfill their destiny and rise to their full potential in ministry, we see that vision actually materializing before our eyes. And we recall how that vision began – in the heart of a Spirit-led leader, willing to think outside the box, willing to recognize that the anointing knows neither gender nor race.

"May the vision continue."[2]

April 22, 2010

"Dear Deborah's Daughters,

Heaven alone knows the full impact women in ministry have made upon the world on behalf of the Kingdom of God. Regenia and I both have felt the influence of Deborah's daughters from our teenage Christian experience up to this very hour. Other ladies have set the stage for you to have opportunities that will far exceed their opportunities to minister the gospel in the power of the Holy Spirit.

We in the North Carolina Conference honor you in your calling from God. I salute you as front-line ministers of the gospel. Your role as ministers of God is the highest honor God could have put upon you. I am delighted to have such a group of committed handmaidens of the Lord on our ministerial rolls and in the North Carolina Conference ministry.

God bless you. I pray that you will have a great retreat and a blessed time together.

Your grateful Bishop,

Signed: *Jim Whitfield*

Jim Whitfield
Bishop
North Carolina Conference of the
International Pentecostal Holiness Church"[3]

Deborah's Daughters publishes a newsletter at least twice a year. It contains personal sketches and articles, some of which are quoted or paraphrased on the following pages.

In a message from the Director of the Lady Ministers dated August 2006, Rev. Dr. Janice Marshburn writes, "I would like to say it is a privilege to serve you in this capacity. It is the desire of the entire Advisory Council to be available to you for mentoring, encouragement, nurturing, prayer, and a source of information." This demonstrates again something more about the purpose of Deborah's Daughters and their desire to carry out in deed what they have written in their mission and vision statements. It is rather easy to come up with a group of words that may sound good on paper, but it is certainly another thing to put them into practice. This is clear in these excerpts.

Janice makes reference to something she recently had read from the book *Women in Leadership – One Minute Bible*. This book gives ninety leadership principles and devotions, one of which she cites: Principle number 83 – "Leaders never stop learning." She uses that as a basis to motivate the lady clergy in the conference to continue learning as they minister. Dr. Marshburn recognizes her responsibility as a leader to teach, to motivate, and to inform those under her influence.

She further challenges them with these words: "Are our priorities in order? Do we have a passion for learning? Gien Karssen wrote 'You can't live on borrowed knowledge. Reading and firsthand observation will make wisdom yours.' Ladies, fill yourself up so you will always have something to give out. Solomon said it this way, *'Wisdom is the principal thing; therefore get wisdom: and with all thy getting get understanding'* – Proverbs 4:7"[4]

Another word of encouragement from Janice was printed in the December 2006 issue of the *Newsletter* in which she recommends the book, *10 Lies the Church Tells Women* by J. Lee Grady. "The Bible has been misused to keep women in spiritual bondage. In his book, Mr. Grady reminds us that the gospel was never intended to restrain women from pursuing God or to prevent them from fulfilling their divine destiny. Read the book and learn how cultural bias, male pride, and misinterpretation of the Bible have paralyzed women who are called to do the work of Christ. However, be encouraged that God is rallying an army of Esthers who are willing to risk their lives, and break traditions in order to rescue a generation that has been marked for death."[5]

At the time that "Deborah's Daughters" officially became the name for the lady ministers in the North Carolina Conference, Janice writes in the

Newsletter for August 2007, "Have you heard? We now have the Biblical name 'Deborah's Daughters.'" She goes on to describe that the name indicates that the lady clergy work alongside their male counterparts.

Sister Marshburn tries to inspire those under her mentorship to stay the course, stand in her place, and do the work God has given her to do in His strength and by His guidance. The Holy Spirit, who was initially given on the Day of Pentecost, is still the source of power for us today. By His anointing men and women can still begin in Jerusalem, our home town; and then spread out into Judea, Samaria, and to the uttermost parts of the world. As we approach the second coming of Jesus let us purpose to do all we can, in all the places we can, with all the strength we can muster. God help us!

On a regular basis, in April and October of each year, these ladies meet together for fellowship, training, and renewal. In a report on such a gathering, Janice describes their Training Seminar on April 27-28, 2007, as "fantastic!" Eighty-two ladies were in attendance. Seven of those were from the Rise Up and Walk Deliverance Ministry in Spring Valley, New York also a part of the North Carolina Conference. "It was a great time of bonding," Dr. Marshburn writes. "Lives were changed! Rev. Dr. Lynn Lucas, Rev. Dr. Lydia Figueroa, Rev. Patsy Vaughan, and Rev. Martha Bedoya delivered a mighty word from God." They received $958 to purchase Bibles for the lady ministers in South Africa who are involved in the WIN ministry.[6]

Another retreat was held in Falcon, North Carolina on April 23-24, 2010, with the theme "Pulling Down Strongholds." Rev. Dr. Lynn Lucas from East Northport, New York was the guest speaker. She is the co-founder and senior pastor of the first church established in Elwood, New York. Lynn earned a doctor of theology and ministry degree from Christian Life School of Theology in Columbus, Georgia. She also graduated from Friends University, Wichita, Kansas, with degrees in psychology and sociology.

The report from Janice about this retreat was simple: "It was absolutely wonderful. We had approximately seventy-five in attendance. Women were delivered!" In her e-mail she explained one of the functions of Deborah's Daughters. Also, before every training session, each lady is contacted to offer her a special invitation to attend. This is their way of networking to keep in touch with the ladies to try to understand their needs and minister to them with prayer and encouragement.[7]

(**Author's note:** A feature in the *Newsletter*, "In the Spotlight," gives a brief biographical sketch of some of the ministers and their work. Several of them are featured below.)

Rev. Vera Griffin

She preached her first sermon from the pulpit sixty-four years ago in 1942. She was the first lady to be ordained in the North Carolina Conference and the first lady to have the title North Carolina Conference Evangelist. She filled that position for thirty years and was later one of three women ministers who pastored the Warsaw Pentecostal Holiness Church between the years 1964-1970. The congregation was able to construct a new sanctuary while she was serving as the senior pastor there. In 2006, she received a Ph.D. in philosophy and religion from the North Carolina College of Theology, Carolina Beach, North Carolina.

Rev. Cindy Midyette

Cindy states that her calling has been to *"Be watchful, and strengthen the things which remain, that are ready to die" – Revelation* 3:2. She was a member of a church that was nearly dead when she decided to vote "no" to closing it. The average attendance was about ten, and there was no money to pay a pastor. At this time she contacted Bishop Chris Thompson to inform him that she wanted to apply for local church ministers' license and do all she could to save the church. She did receive her license in 2002 and served the local congregation at Goose Creek Pentecostal Holiness Church in Grantsboro, North Carolina. In December of 2006, she reported that thirty-three people had been saved, the average Sunday morning attendance was fifty and at least twenty-two children were going to take part in the Christmas play that year.

Cindy received regular ministry license to preach in 2003 and was ordained in 2005. She is a lady on a mission.

Rev. Teresa Strickland

"On Tuesday night in November of 1994," Teresa says, "at a Women's Ministry meeting God confirmed the call, which I had sensed for some time in my spirit, to preach His Word. At that time I had really never heard the word HOSPICE." She indicates that she had been active in her local church since she was saved in 1991, taking part in evangelism, Missionettes [girls' group], prayer, and visitation in the hospitals and among the shut-ins. In 2002, she became aware of an opening at Cape Fear Valley Hospital for a Hospice Chaplain.

Teresa states that she had never sensed the call to pastor a church, but had no doubt of God's calling to preach. She was waiting for His will and direction, so when she filled out the application for the position of chaplain she felt encouraged because she saw God's hand preparing her for that position of ministry.

She had the opportunity to minister to those with terminal illnesses who were in hospice care. That ministry was to the whole person for body, mind, and spirit. She was able to read Scripture and pray for those who were literally on their deathbed, seeing some of them saved by God's grace.

Her comments are worth pondering: "God's love has become so real and so far- reaching to me. This may be hard to understand but I could not be any happier than when I am holding the hand of a dying person moments before they enter into eternity . . . I guess you could say that God has called me to pastor a church, 'His church' that is located in many homes across Cumberland and surrounding counties, where dying people are waiting to join Him in paradise."[8]

Rev. Donna Hawkins

Donna was a licensed evangelist in the Ambassadors for Christ Deliverance Ministry in Spring Valley, New York before she became a pastor. After feeling a definite call, she became the spiritual leader of Rise Up and Walk Deliverance Ministry also in Spring Valley. The church is still part of the North Carolina Conference even though it is located in New York. Sister Hawkins believes in kingdom building and grabbing souls from the clutches of the enemy so they will have hope. Through her ministry, she has learned how to get to know people by the Spirit.

Rev. Shelia Stewart

Even though Shelia was raised in the Baptist church, she had her first Pentecostal experience at a young age when she accepted Christ as her personal Savior during a gospel tent revival.

Evangelist Stewart has a heart for ministry, desiring to see that all women, especially young ones, realize their importance to God. No matter who they are, or where they have been, or what they might have experienced, God has called them for His purpose.

She lives in Fayetteville, North Carolina with her husband, with whom she has four children. In addition to being assistant pastor of Seed of Faith Ministries, she is also an entrepreneur and business owner.[9]

Rev. Cyrena McNally

Rev. McNally brought the congregation of Calvary Temple in Southport into the North Carolina Conference in 2008. This lady, from New Brunswick, Canada, has been in the ministry for twenty-five years, having evangelized throughout Canada and the United States. She has a master's degree in theology and Christian counseling and is a licensed Clinical Christian Counselor. Helping Hands Christian Counseling is an outreach of this same church she continues to pastor, which is known now by the name The Potter's House.

Rev. Betty Pope

Perhaps the ministry of Rev. Betty Pope is a bit unconventional, but she and her husband prayed and sought God's direction for their lives and became bikers for Jesus, in a motorcycle ministry. She states, "Many bikers never go through a church door; therefore, we go to them, wherever that might be. It could be a poker run, toy run, bike rallies, bars, or [a] hospital." They also minister at coffee stops along the interstates as the bikers stop off for a break. Their mission is to show compassion and love and to lend a listening ear. This motorcycle ministry is part of Mission M25 which "exists to network those who reach out to the Matthew 25 people groups," according to their website information. Further, "Mission M25 provides identity and connectivity for those ministers and ministries of the International Pentecostal Holiness Church" that are involved in reaching the neglected people of the world who do not know what to do. The organization "provides short seminars, one-week classes, 30-90 day training sessions, and a one-year (hands-on) course."

The headquarters of Mission M25 is in Amarillo, Texas. It is led by Rev. Gary Burd, Director.

Rev. Vanessa Polk

"I am a Strategic Church Education Consultant specializing in strategic vision development. I work with pastors, church leaders, congregations, educational institutions, and community organizations to craft strategic plans and training modules to clarify vision and build capacity. In addition, I have worked with Women's Ministry for the past fifteen years to help them recognize their ministry gifts, empower them to embrace their calling, and equip them to serve with confidence and humility," voices Vanessa Polk about her ministry.

In 2009, she was working as a consultant and educator for AJAMM Ministries International in Houston, Texas. The organization "seeks to help women in ministry sharpen their leadership skills and prepare them to engage in local, national, and international social change." It is all about igniting gifts to serve the community and expand God's kingdom.[10]

(**Author's note:** AJAMM is a Christian ministry and leadership development organization that guides, trains, and equips African/American women in and for ministry. The roots of AJAMM spring from the social justice/philanthropic ministry of the late Reverend Myrtle Magee and from the empowerment ministry of Reverend Audrey Johnson. These two women persevered in ministry in the 1970s and 1980s in a faith culture that was not always accepting of women.

As a way to memorialize the late Reverend Magee and to honor Reverend Johnson, Mary E. Washington and the organization's leaders coined the name AJAMM, which is an acrostic of the names <u>A</u>udrey <u>J</u>ohnson <u>a</u>nd <u>M</u>yrtle <u>M</u>agee. AJAMM views itself as "a community of women in the pulpit, the pew, and public places.")[11]

Rev. Iris Rodriguez

Rev. Rodriguez is a church planter. This is her story. "I was born in Hartford, Connecticut and grew up in Puerto Rico. I was saved in 1988 and was called to minister at the age of sixteen in Springfield, MA. My first sermon was preached from a radio station at the age of seventeen. I moved to Fayetteville, NC and married Roberto, a military service man, and had three beautiful children. We deployed to Honolulu, HI in 1995." In November 1969 she felt God's leading to plant the first Spanish Church in Honolulu, and the Sinai Church of God (Mission Board) was founded the next year.

When her husband retired from the army, they moved to Florida, where she served as an evangelist for more than six years. She participated in the evangelism and missions congress in the Dominican Republic and Puerto Rico and conducted revivals in Germany, Italy, and Portugal.

Iris planted another church in Jacksonville, North Carolina. This Hispanic church opened with a service on Mother's Day, May 11, 2008. As they grew, they moved their services to the Jacksonville High School cafeteria.

After a month, the Lord opened the door for them to be a part of the North Carolina Conference of the Pentecostal Holiness Church. That year she received her minister's license in the conference.

On February 2, 2009, their church was organized with thirty-three members. At that time, their attendance was about forty. Iris states that their mission for the Hispanic community in Jacksonville "is to **reach** many souls for the Kingdom of God, **making** disciples, and **training** the believers to fulfill the Great Commission."

Iris received training in church administration and theology from Lee College, Cleveland, Tennessee and Global University, based in Springfield, Missouri.

Rev. Sandy Nowiski

Sandy is another church planter, having founded Potter's Vessel in 2007. The group started services in Sandy's home, moved to a leased building for a short time, and then moved back to her home again.

Rev. Nowiski states that her "journey began with a burning passion for humanity that wasn't mine. I didn't know them, yet they took front stage in my mind. There was no reason for the love and compassion I felt."

She expresses that she was unaware that God could use an ordinary person like her to accomplish His purposes until she read a book titled *The Dream Giver* by Bruce Wilkinson. She started to get out of her comfort zone and allowed God to deal with her about her hang-ups about being a woman preacher/pastor. Her biggest problems were herself and her fear that her husband would leave her if she pursued her calling.

For at least two years, she experienced some hurtful things, but over and over the love of God was poured out over His people. The passion to plant a church is still burning, and Sandy is waiting for God's perfect timing as she rests in His hands.

Her advice is this: "If the Dream Giver has given you a dream I challenge you to let it happen. When you stand alone before Him remember He will not see your sex or what degree you hold in your hand but He'll search your heart to see what you had faith enough to allow Him to do through you."

Rev. Donna Hendrix

Donna, along with her husband, Tommy, works with senior pastor Gary Strickland at Kingdom Place Pentecostal Holiness Church in Lumberton, North Carolina. She is the Care Ministry Pastor there and has also been involved in jail and prison ministry. Both she and her husband work at Cape Fear Valley Hospital and are joint directors of Mission M25 for the North Carolina Conference.

She believes that God has given her "a heart for ministering to women whose lives have been damaged and broken. Along with ministering to women, God has allowed me the pleasure of leading hundreds of young teenage girls to the Lord resulting in healing and restoration through and by Him."[12]

Rev. Susie Weaver

This lady is described as the "Chainsaw Carving Preacher." She's unique! Her user name for e-mail, "sawdust preacher," indicates that she is serious about this ministry. According to her biographical information, she was ordained in the Congregational Holiness Church in Florida, where she evangelized and worked in jail and street ministry. She was also involved in the Women's Ministries as director in the Sonshine (Florida) Conference; however, in 2009, she joined the North Carolina Conference after marrying Rev. Kenneth Weaver, a minister in that conference.

She believes the Lord has given her a unique gift in that she is a chainsaw carver, a profession she has enjoyed for about thirty years. Her carvings vary in size from a peach seed to a twenty-two foot long log. When she is asked about formal training for what she does, she tells them "No, the Lord Jesus Christ gave me the gift." This work has opened many doors outside the pulpit for her to witness to the tremendous love and power of God.

Susie's sense of humor is apparent from a statement she made: "If you ever see a little short woman coming down the road with a chainsaw in one hand and a Bible in the other, FEAR NOT, IT IS I."

Rev. Loraine Thorne

"I was born to sharecroppers in 1941," writes Loraine. "Our resources were limited but my Daddy taught me the rich value of honesty, respect, and hard work. I grew up in church and gave my heart to Jesus at age twelve."

By the time she was thirteen, she felt the call of the Holy Spirit to preach, but it was not until she was an adult that that she really knew how to respond. In 1998, she was licensed to preach in the North Carolina Conference.

Her first pastorate was at Vicks Chapel (Faith Family Worship) in Rocky Mount, North Carolina, and she also served Calvary Temple as their pastor. The Lord opened other doors for her to minister through a radio and a television program. She was led to begin 4 Him Ministries which airs each Saturday morning on WHIG TV, Rocky Mount, giving her a forum in which to preach and pray for the sick.

On the local level, she leads the Adult Young at Heart class and is a substitute teacher in the public school system. She states that "God is truly blessing and has opened many doors for me outside the pulpit."

Rev. Myrisha Goodson

Myrisha feels that God has called her to serve in "pulpits that are not pulpits." This is because her profession as a nurse "has influenced and intertwined itself" with her ministry. She has held the hands of those who slipped away into eternity, stood by as a young mother found out she had cancer, and witnessed the first cry of newborn babies. Her work has carried her to Latin America where she was involved in setting up make-shift medical clinics and treating hundreds of patients.

When she realized what the Lord had in mind for her, her purpose in life became clear. She says, "My life was no longer compartmentalized into neat little boxes labeled wife, mother, nurse, minister . . . the gift and calling of God was the big box that held all the smaller boxes in place! Everything about me personally, professionally, and spiritually had a purpose: to build the kingdom of God!"[13]

What a wealth of versatility, accomplishments, and talent these ladies possess! Certainly, they are handmaidens that God has chosen for this time to be used of Him. How amazing that they function in so many different capacities and are able to maintain balance in their lives between families, jobs, pastorates, evangelism, and so many other activities. They have to be empowered for service through the ministry of the Holy Spirit in their lives. There is a dedication and commitment not often seen in these last days. So few, comparatively speaking, will give of themselves as these women appear to do.

(**Author's note:** The following articles that appeared in the Deborah's Daughter's *Newsletter* are reprinted with permission of the writers.)

"Step By Step"
Rev. Wilda Faircloth

"OK God, what's next?" I have been asking God that question for quite some time now. After God called me to preach the Gospel, I began taking steps to prepare for the ministry. He kept saying, "step by step." He said it after I received my local church minister's license. So, I kept studying and received a Minister's License. Again, He repeated it so I kept studying and I was ordained. He continues to reinforce it to me – "step by step." What a God we serve! He knows us so well. I'm a planner. If I knew God's plan in detail, prior to the manifestation of His plan for my life, I would impulsively slip in a detail or two of my own! Occasionally, He will shine the light on my future by way of a dream, a vision, or a prophetic word. These are the times I really get excited because He reassures me of His plan and His attention to my life. When others ask where I'm going in ministry, I just say "I'm waiting for God to open the doors." God knows us better than we know ourselves. That's why we can be so sure that every little detail in our lives is worked into something good.

Has He opened doors already? Of course He has. God is faithful! He has opened doors of opportunity for me to preach the Gospel at churches inside and outside of our Conference. He opened an in-home Bible study door for me. Teaching others in my home every week was a genuine delight! After several years, He closed that door and opened a Youth Ministry door when I least expected it. Getting to know and understand teenagers was a real opportunity. To love and be loved by them is truly an amazing and exciting experience. After a couple of years behind that door, He closed it and opened a prayer ministry and Sunday school teaching opportunity. Now, I get to preach every Sunday morning!

There are doors of ministry opportunities all around us but we must remember that God is not behind <u>every</u> door. Remember the television game show 'Let's Make a Deal.'? Well, the contestant would sometimes choose a door with stuff of no value behind it. They would be disappointed and downhearted. But, there would always be a door with a valuable prize behind it and the contestant would be ecstatic! The leadership of the Holy Spirit helps you and me to choose the right doors. Sometimes a door may appear to have little value but the Word of God says, *"Now He who searches the hearts knows what the mind of the Spirit is, because He makes intercession for the saints according to the will of God. And we know that all things work together for good to those who love God, to those who are the called according to His purpose"* (Romans 8:27-28-NKJV).

Let's continue to follow the leadership of the Holy Spirit as He opens doors and we continue to minister – "Step by Step."[14]

"For the HUSBANDS of Lady Ministers"
Pauline Knowles & Wil [her husband]

In the Old and New Testaments God called a few women such as Miriam, Deborah, Huldah, Anna, and the daughters of Philip, and anointed them as prophets. This was before the Day of Pentecost when Peter quoted the Prophet Joel saying, *"In the last days I will pour out of My Spirit upon all flesh: and your sons and daughters shall prophesy."* We know without a doubt that in these last days God IS pouring out His Spirit, anointing women, and calling them into the ministry.

The question is, where does the husband of the lady minister fit in, and what role does he play in her ministry? Let us look at the example Joseph, the husband of Mary. I feel sure he did not know what was expected of him. When he found out Mary was with Child, he did some serious thinking. Should he make her a public example, or put her away [privately]? When he was thinking about what was best for him to do, an angel of the Lord appeared to him and told him not to be afraid. She [Mary] was just obeying the call of God. Joseph had no more problems as to what his duty was. He was going to stand by his wife. No doubt there were questions asked and many remarks made, but Joseph had heard from God. Therefore, he was willing to bear the reproach with her and assist her in all her needs.

You men that find yourselves married to a lady minister, don't forget, when you married her the two of you became one. What a beautiful thing to see husband and wife working together. You have been called to work along with her. If you pray and seek God, He will speak to your heart, as he did to Joseph, and tell you not to fear.

God is in full authority in His Kingdom work. He tells us, *"You have not chosen Me, but I have chosen you and ordained you."* [John 15:16]

Satan might try to humiliate you and make you feel that you are in the background and not accepted or needed, but the real truth is you really don't know how much your wife does need you.

It grieves my heart that our husbands are not recognized more than they are. Many of them are hard working men in the church and have made countless sacrifices along with their wives.

I can speak for my husband, Willie Knowles. When he married me, he married my ministry. He has never had a problem with the fact I am a lady minister. He was the one that encouraged me to be ordained.

The Bible tells us we are laborers together in the Lord. We pray and read our Bible together, go to church, visit, and even go to conference together. He never tells me how or what to preach. He knows the Spirit is in charge of that, however, he does assist me in anything I need him for.

People may pass by and shake hands with your wife and not ask who you are. You may not be in the lime light as much as she is, but when God rewards her for reaching lost souls, you will also receive your reward.

Husband, stand by your wife. Pray God's blessings on her.[15]

"Even Jesus Needed 'Down Time' "
Patsy Vaughan

Do you ever feel guilty because you <u>need</u> time just for you? I recall a specific occasion when I was to meet a fellow minister for lunch. This lady has been a dear friend for years and we seldom got together. I was really looking forward to it when my friend graciously suggested that a couple from my church join us.

My reply was not so gracious. Please understand, I love this couple dearly; I enjoy spending time with them. It's just that I was anticipating the rare opportunity to fellowship with another minister without having to be in "ministry mode."

I knew she understood. Yet, the guilt set in immediately. How selfish I was being!

A few days later, I was still mulling it over when the Holy Spirit spoke to me: even Jesus needed down time.

Matthew 14:23 reads, *"And when he had sent the multitudes away, he went up into a mountain apart to pray: and when the evening was come, he was there alone."*

I began to meditate on not only specific scriptures, but the life of Jesus as a whole. The Holy Spirit pointed out four things to me:

* Jesus spent a lot of time alone with God.

He is the Son of God. He is God. Yet He placed significant priority on spending time alone with God. I personally think that He knew how essential that time was. It refreshed Him. It renewed Him. It rejuvenated Him. It helped Him stay focused. How could He have ministered or fulfilled His mission without it? How can we?

* Jesus spent considerable time alone with three very special friends: Peter, James, and John.

He also placed significant priority on spending time with Peter, James, and John. Yes, Jesus wanted to pour all He could into these three men. Yes, He knew that they would lead the Early Church. It was essential that they be taught and trained. But, I also think that He felt relaxed around them, that He enjoyed their fellowship, that their companionship may have actually ministered to Him at times.

*Jesus spent a lot of time alone with other friends: the disciples, the 70, those who supported His ministry.

This was the core group of the Early Church. The faithful: the Sunday morning, Sunday night, Wednesday night and revival attendees, the tithe payers, the ones who would get the job done. Spending time with them was of utmost importance.

*Jesus still had plenty of time to minister to the multitudes.

As women, we carry too much guilt! Don't ever feel guilty because you need time alone with God, or alone with a precious friend, or alone with a group of friends. That time is essential. It refreshes, renews, rejuvenates, and enables us to better minister to the multitudes.[16]

Lady ministers who are called Deborah's Daughters. What a unique idea! The analogy used to show the cooperation between Deborah and Barak in the book of Judges is a fascinating concept. Deborah first functioned alone as a judge, deciding disputes at her court, but when the time came for the nation to go to war to fend off its oppressor, the Canaanites, she summoned Barak to join her. He was to muster ten thousand men from the tribes of Naphtali and Zebulun and take them to Mount Tabor, at the command of the Lord. The general seemed to be reluctant, even in the face of a direct order from the Commander-in-Chief. *"If you go with me, I will go; but if you don't go with me, I won't go"* – Judges 4:8 - NIV, Barak says to Deborah. She agrees, but states in verse 9, *"[B]ecause of the way you are going about this, the honor will not be yours, for the Lord will hand Sisera over to a woman."* No doubt, Barak thought Deborah was referring to herself, but as the story progresses, we see God using Jael, the wife of Heber, to nail Sisera to the tent floor. In verses 23, 24 of the same chapter in Judges, we read these words, *"On that day God subdued Jabin, the Canaanite king, before the Israelites. And the hand of the Israelites grew stronger and stronger against Jabin . . . until they destroyed him."* That is the kind of cooperation needed between men and women engaged in the battle to destroy our common enemy: our Sisera, the devil. We must work side-by-side to do the will of God.

---

[1] Dr. Janice Marshburn, Conference Director, Deborah's Daughters, e-mail dated February 4, 2010.
[2] *IPHC Experience*, October 2008, pp 20-21.
[3] Letter from Bishop Jim Whitfield.
[4] Deborah's Daughters *Newsletter*, August 2006.
[5] *Newsletter*, December 2006.
[6] *Newsletter*, August 2007.
[7] *Newsletter*, January 2009.
[8] *Newsletter*, December 2006.
[9] *Newsletter*, August 2007.
[10] *Newsletter*, January 2009.
[11] Rev. Dr. Maxine Waddell, Chair, Board of Directors, AJAMM Ministries International, Inc., e-mail dated February 10, 2011.
[12] *Newsletter*, August 2009.
[13] *Newsletter*, January 2010.
[14] *Newsletter*, December 2006.
[15] *Newsletter*, December 2006.
[16] *Newsletter*, August 2007.

CHAPTER 8

Life Sketches

"The Lord is the strength of my life . . ." – Psalms 27:1b-NKJV.

James, in his New Testament letter, poses the question, *"What is your life?"* He then answers with the words, *"You are a mist that appears for a little while and then vanishes"* – 4:14c-NIV. This, of course, speaks of the transitory nature of life. All of us are aware that our time on earth is limited; our days are numbered, and that number is known only by God. However, we are not to sit idly by, waiting for our life to come to an end and walk off this stage of action having accomplished nothing. God breathed the breath of life into our being as a wondrous gift. The expanded definition of *"wondrous"* is filled with volumes of meaning when we look at words like *"remarkable, unusual, extraordinary, miraculous, fascinating, awe-full, marvelous, amazing, and astounding"* [1] Each one describes a new significance of the existence with which the Almighty has endowed us.

The Bible states that *"the Lord God formed the man from the dust of the ground and breathed into his nostrils the breath of life, and the man became a living being"* – Genesis 2:7-NIV. This makes it clear that God is the originator and giver of physical life with which we have been blessed, and He continues to be the source of all life to this day.

The New Testament expands on the idea of life. Through the pages of the Gospels and Epistles we can see it taking on a strong spiritual meaning, referring to the result of man's relationship with God. This spiritual life is also a gift from God, but differs from the physical life. It is called "eternal life," which is the highest quality of life. Eternal life comes through faith in Jesus Christ. He taught, *"He who believes in Me has everlasting life"* – John 6:47-NKJV. John wrote of Jesus earlier in his gospel, *"In Him was life and the life was the light of men"* – John 1:4-NKJV. Because the Light has shined into our lives, we have life eternal.

Our responsibility is to let the Light shine through us so others can see Him and experience this newness of life. We have been placed on this planet to bring glory to our Creator. We can do that through obedience to God. Our callings are different. Even those who have been called to the ministry aren't commissioned to do the same thing. The one thing that is clear, however, is that we are going to be held accountable for the things we do with the gifts He has given us. The life we live here and now will continue to speak, for good or bad, to someone in succeeding generations.

Shakespeare's Macbeth had a totally different view of life when he said "Life's but a walking shadow, a poor player that struts and frets his hour upon the stage and then is heard no more: it is a tale told by an idiot, full of sound and fury, signifying nothing"[2] He claims that people are like actors on a stage. It does not matter what they do because life is just a play, and no one's actions will truly affect anything.

The life sketches that follow show how meaningfully one's devotion and service to God **do** continue to speak. These faithful ones were more than players on a stage. Life in Christ had intrinsic value for them, and they set out on a journey that took them to the front lines of the enemy to preach the gospel of the Kingdom of God. They made a difference. What a challenge they leave for those of us who remain!

"Tribute To: Rev. Nita Alexander..."
South Carolina Conference

Rev. Alexander is affectionately known as "Aunt Nita" by many who know her. She is a retired minister in the South Carolina Conference and holds membership in the Friendfield Church.

As a young girl she didn't date many boys, but there were two special ones in her life. One was a young Pentecostal preacher; the other was Henry Clemmons Alexander her beloved late husband who was faithful in his support of her ministry. She states that she could never have done the things that she has done for God if it had not been for his support. She never learned to drive, but he took her anywhere she felt led to carry the gospel.

On September 27, 1921, she married Henry Alexander, and they made their home in Scranton, South Carolina. Six months afterward, both of them gave their hearts to the Lord. Rita was saved, sanctified, and received the baptism of the Holy Spirit in an hour's time.

Her ministry began with her preaching in houses and brush arbors in Florence, Lee and Lamar Counties, and in Georgetown, South Carolina.

In some of her house prayer meetings, the children complained of not being able to sleep because Sister Alexander's voice rang out all through the place. They would lie in their beds listening to Nita preach and shout the praises of God.

She experienced open ridicule from children in the neighborhood walking home from school who mocked her because of the tongues-speaking and the emotional display in worship. While attempting to organize a church at Willow Creek, she was threatened in various ways by those who fought holiness. One tried to run her down with his car as she and others walked to church. Later someone threatened to throw dynamite under the family's house where she was staying.

In 1938, she received her license to preach, and the following year she was assigned to the Red Hill Church near Georgetown. The year 1940 saw her pastoring not only that church but also the Thompson Church in Hemingway. She pastored both churches until 1941 when she went back into the evangelistic field.

"Because of the fact that she was a lady preacher, very few churches would accept her ministry even though she was known as a dynamic Holy Ghost filled preacher," the report from *The Challenge* states.

"Times were hard," she says, "but it was a good life. Our love for each other and for God smoothed out the rough roads."

Aunt Nita was in a rest home near Florence, South Carolina in 1989, but her light was still shining and her testimony had not diminished.[3]

Rev. Mrs. Mary Hayes Blake
Upper South Carolina Conference

Mary Hayes was born June 9, 1885, in Seneca, South Carolina. Her seventy-eight years of Christian service began at the age of nine when she started playing the old-fashioned pump organ for her father's evangelistic services that were held in churches, tents, school houses, open-air, and brush arbors throughout the Southeast with a concentration in Georgia and North and South Carolina.

Many people were saved, sanctified and filled with the Holy Spirit in those fiery evangelistic services. Mary not only played the organ, but she sang, testified, and worked around the altar. She and her brother went early and held services for the children.

During the days of these trail-blazing experiences when holiness and Pentecost were little known, the hardships, trials and adversities did not weaken her faith.

In 1907, Rev. G. B. Cashwell returned from California where he had gone to investigate the outpouring of the Holy Spirit at Azusa Street in Los Angeles, California, and where he received Pentecost. He held a revival in Toccoa, Georgia, where Mary was among the first to receive the baptism herself.

She became a licensed evangelist in the Georgia Conference in 1924 and transferred her membership to the Upper South Carolina Conference in 1929 when she and her family moved from Franklin Springs, Georgia to Greer, South Carolina.

During her years of ministry, she never neglected her family. In all her activities, whether preaching, witnessing, praying, singing, playing the organ, teaching a Sunday school class, or working with children, her heartbeat was winning souls. As late as 1973, churches existed because she obeyed the Lord in starting cottage prayer meetings.

Illness curtailed her active ministry, yet she still shared Christ through personal testimony, song, and hours of travailing prayer. Her daughter writes, "Her vibrant spirit, dauntless faith, and positive testimony took precedence over illness, old age, and infirmity. She had faith to live every moment of her life, and when she came to the end, that same faith took her into the eternal presence of her Lord."

Her Conference Superintendent, Rev. Zeb Smith, made the statement that "She will live on . . . in the lives of hundreds of preachers she knew, influenced and prayed for. She will live on . . . in the lives of thousands of laymen who came in contact with her and were influenced by her godly life. She will live on . . . in the victories she won in her prayer life. She will live on . . . in the battles of faith she won through struggles. She will live on . . . in the lives of her family and the contributions the Blake family has and is making in the ministry, in Christian Education, and in the professional and business world." [4]

(**Author's note:** She had eight children: five daughters, at least two of whom were also ministers; and three sons, one of whom was a minister.)

Miss Natalie Carnes
South Carolina Conference

Sister Karnes writes that she was raised in a Baptist church and was baptized when she was about thirteen years old. At a young age, she had a desire for the things of God, even though she had not been born again.

Her family moved to Miami some time later; she was saved there during a tent meeting sponsored by the Christian Missionary Alliance. One night at the meeting, the testimonies of the people sparked a real interest in the great peace and joy they were experiencing. She continued to go until one night she found herself responding to the invitation at the close of the service. She seemed to sense that Jesus paid for all her sins and her burden rolled away. Driving home that night, she says, "I looked up into the heavens, and they seemed to be saying 'Glory to God.'" Her experience of salvation was so great and wonderful that she stopped her friends on the street to tell them about Jesus and what He could do.

At the church she was attending, Calvary Baptist, she taught Sunday school and also was involved with a youth group that went to the county prison on Sunday afternoons to hold services. She preached her first sermon to convicts.

Soon after her conversion, she felt the call of God on her life and began to make plans to go to the Christian Missionary Alliance Bible School in Nyack, New York to prepare for the mission field. She was a student there for three years. She was sanctified and baptized in the Holy Spirit at school during a great outpouring of the Spirit of God. Natalie indicates that she had never heard a sermon on Acts 2 and did not know there was a Pentecostal movement.

As for her ministry, she worked in the Kentucky mountains when she first graduated from Bible school. She and another young lady went to Breathitt County, near Jackson, and spent the summer preaching in a school while living in a mining camp. They taught Sunday school, preached, sang, and held Daily Vacation Bible School for the people of that area.

They would preach on Sunday morning in one schoolhouse; in the afternoon they walked nearly two miles down the railroad track, crossed an old muddy Kentucky river in a boat, taught the same Sunday school lesson and preached again. The people in the area were very ignorant and called these two ladies foreigners. Sister Carnes states that they went through some real persecution and trials, but God was with them and worked miracles to supply their needs.

She and her co-worker went from there to do pioneer evangelistic work in New York. They preached in a number of places and started a new church in Lancaster, New York. At that time, she was a licensed minister with the Assemblies of God.

In 1933, she and her mother went south, where they were engaged in evangelistic work. She held her first meeting at Matthews Tabernacle near Lake City, South Carolina in 1934. Other churches in the area welcomed them in their ministry. One of their biggest revivals was at the Free Will Baptist Holiness Church in Turbeville, South Carolina. Whole families were saved, sanctified, and filled with the Holy Spirit during the five-week meeting. People burned their tobacco and threw away pipes and cigarettes. The congregation soon outgrew the church building there because of the revival and built a new one.

About the same time she met Rev. Tom Evans, Superintendent of the South Carolina Conference, who encouraged her to become a member of the conference; in 1935 she was licensed to preach. After that, she did evangelistic work in her own conference, in Upper South Carolina, Maryland, West Virginia, Western North Carolina, Florida, Pennsylvania, Texas, Canada, and Mexico. She was ordained in 1937.

In 1942, the conference sent her to pastor in Georgetown in the South Carolina Conference. While there God enabled them to get a church built during the war years, and the building was still in use at the time she wrote this information. The Sunday school attendance was fifty-four when she went there and was running about 140 when she left. The property was worth $3,500 when she was first assigned to Georgetown, but when she left in 1947, it had increased in value to $40,000.

In addition to Georgetown, she pastored Mount Pleasant, Galilee, Awendaw, and Ashley Heights. After her mother was called to glory to receive her reward in 1960, Sister Carnes again entered the field of evangelism.

The year 1962 is significant as Natalie ventured out by faith to get involved in mission work. She was joined by a friend, Nellie Watts, who went with her to Africa. They held meetings in Nigeria with Brother and Sister Noel Brooks. Then, in South Africa, under the supervision of Brother L. M. Duncan, Natalie and Nellie preached in different sections of the country. In the Krugersdorp area, they held meetings with Brother Jimmy Gardner. In Southern Rhodesia, they joined Brother and Sister

Lamar Pate in the work. Then they went to Northern Rhodesia to assist Brother and Sister John Guthrie.

Her travels took her to Argentina with a tent in 1964 and 1965. Because of the weather, they couldn't use the tent year round, so they raised money for a lot and built a church in Chajari, where there was no Protestant church at all.

On her way home, she did evangelistic work in Brazil for about four weeks. Then, she helped some other Pentecostal Holiness missionaries in Costa Rica, preaching in practically all the churches in the denomination there.

As reported in the Spring 1970 issue of *The Challenge,* the official conference publication, the Georgetown church honored her in the Sunday morning service on March 22, 1970. She preached an inspiring message, which was heavily freighted with a plea for biblical holiness. The pastor and his congregation gave her a liberal offering. She was in the field of evangelism for twenty-two years, and served five churches during her thirteen years of pastoring.[5]

Violet Meek Curlee
Golden West Conference

Violet was born on January 17, 1923, in Chickasha, Oklahoma into a Christian home. She was a third generation Pentecostal. In 1951, she was licensed to preach by the Southern California Conference and the next year was ordained. During her ministry, she planted at least one church, Trinity Life Chapel in Bakersfield, California, with her husband, Calvin Hedge, and co-pastored several others with him. From 1964-1986, she served as Conference Woman's Auxiliary Director and, in 1986, she became Director of World Intercessory Network (WIN), a position she held for thirteen years. Sister Curlee was also a member of the board of the Golden West Conference for two years.

While she was pastoring, she pursued a long-time desire for advanced education, and her first degree was conferred in 1973. She later (1999) earned a Th.D. from Phoenix Bible College and Seminary.[6]

Her sister, Ann McCraw, wrote a tribute to Violet titled "The Hands of a Shepherdess" in *The Helping Hand,* November/December 1995, which gives a more personal look at Violet's life and ministry.

"Disappointment etched its way across the face of the shepherdess, permeating her eyes with sadness. 'I have such ugly hands,' she moaned, scrutinizing every detail of her outstretched fingers. Then, thrusting her hands toward me as if to rid herself of them, she urged, 'Look at them! They're not dainty and beautiful. They look old, worn and weather-beaten. They . . . look like a man's hands.'

"In an attempt to shield the hated hands from view, she clasped them tightly together and placed them in her lap; a common practice due to her embarrassment. Then the story of her lifelong yearning to have beautiful, feminine hands – complete with long, tapered fingers and perfectly manicured nails – spilled forth.

"As her story ended, she lifted her head with an air of authority, and her voice took on the majestic tone of a divine edict. 'When it comes my time to go,' she announced, 'I want you to make sure they put white gloves on my hands before my funeral. I don't want people to see these ugly hands folded across my chest.'

"I mumbled something reassuring and the conversation ended. Since that day, however, I have given much thought to the strange request made by the shepherdess. And, at this point, I am unwilling to comply with her request. My reasons are varied.

"The shepherdess is my sister. She was only a ten-year-old child when our mother died. I was eight months old. Hers were the loving hands that held me, caressed me and comforted me during those lonely, empty years. To me, her hands are beautiful.

"Her hands worked the various harvest fields of California (including grapes, potatoes, peaches, prunes, berries, cherries, and cotton) so her three children could have a better life. They appreciated her valiant efforts, but had there been no such sacrifice, her loving hands would still be beautiful in their sight.

"Her hands helped in the construction of Trinity Life Chapel, which she and her late husband pioneered. She still pastors that same church, hence the term shepherdess. Over the years her hands have often cuddled the lambs and assured the sheep of her flock. Her hands are beautiful to all those she has touched, helped and lifted during her pastorate.

"The hands of the shepherdess have been laid upon the heads of countless brides and grooms as they were united in holy wedlock. Those hands have lifted babies up before the Lord in dedication. Those hands have been wet with the waters of baptism. Those hands have brought a healing touch to the sick.

"During a lifetime of ministry, the hands of the shepherdess have been blessed and anointed. Her hands have done the work of the Lord. Her hands have been healing hands, helping hands, loving hands, busy hands, ministering hands; they are beautiful in the sight of the Lord.

"Many fruitful years lie ahead for the shepherdess. Meanwhile, we, her friends, family and church have reached a unanimous decision; we refuse to put gloves on her hands when it's her 'time to go.' Those hands mean too much to each of us. In our time of need, joy or sorrow, those beautiful hands have reached out and touched our lives.

"So, in some far distant future, when it's time to bid the shepherdess a final farewell, her bare hands will lie folded across her chest. One by one we will march by and consider it an honor to look upon those beautiful hands one last time."[7]

(**Author's note:** Ann was a board member of the Pacific Coast Bible College and the director of the Phoenix Campus when she wrote this tribute to her sister. She and her mother-in-law, Ruby McCraw, are also ministers.)

Hattie Edge
Baltimore (Maryland)/Eastern Virginia Conference

In March 1977, *The Helping Hand* printed an article titled "Women in our Heritage" which featured Rev. Mrs. Hattie Edge. The writers, Mark and Judy Kamleiter, wrote about the arrival of some fiery evangelists in Raleigh, North Carolina, who were preaching an unfamiliar doctrine that they called the baptism of the Holy Spirit. This happened shortly after the turn of the twentieth century.

Hattie Spence, then fourteen years old, could watch from the window of her house across the street as the people from miles around came to hear about this strange power being preached. She was not allowed to attend the services in the big tent, however, as her parents did not understand about the speaking in tongues because it was strange to them, even though they were devout Christians.

The Spences, fearing this was a false doctrine, forbid their children to go until they had the chance to pray about this new teaching. One night after much prayer, Hattie's mother told her daughter to close the Bible, then open it and begin to read at that place. Hattie did as she was told and began to read from Acts 2:1, *"And when the day of Pentecost was fully come they were all with one accord in one place…and they…began to speak with other tongues, as the Spirit gave them utterance."*

Mrs. Spence was then convinced this blessing was from God, and, as she began to praise the Lord, she was filled with the Holy Spirit. Word of this experience spread quickly in the community, and the next morning, the house filled with people wanting to hear of what happened.

What occurred in her mother's life deeply changed Hattie's life as well. She hungered for this deeper experience and soon received the Holy Spirit herself. At this same time came her call to the ministry, "a ministry which would have far reaching and dramatic results."

Hattie began to fulfill her call even before she finished her schooling. During the summer, she traveled with Rev. and Mrs. J. H. King, conducting revivals. Before each nightly service, Hattie had services with the young people, leading many of them to the Lord. During the evangelistic services, she played the accordion.

When she was eighteen, she was playing her accordion at a street meeting in Fayetteville, North Carolina and met a man, Lon Edge, who later became her husband. After she and Lon were married, she took a short break from her ministry. After the birth of their only child, Naomi, the Lord urged her to return to His work. As Lon also felt a call, he sold his furniture business, bought a Model T, and they set out to labor in God's vineyard.

They met with much opposition in the first year of their ministry as they worked to establish a church in Elizabeth City, North Carolina. "By faith, they converted an old dance hall into a church and began to preach the full gospel." The church prospered in spite of the hard times and hostilities.

After six years, when the church was well established, Lon felt the call to move on to plant other churches. Hattie packed their belongings, and they once again moved out trusting God to direct their ministry. "They traveled from Florida to Maryland establishing Pentecostal Holiness Churches." In fact, they started more than 26 of them, most in the bounds of the Eastern Virginia Conference now Redemption Ministries.

The Lord brought the Edges to Norfolk, Virginia, after many years of almost continual traveling. There, they established the First Pentecostal Holiness Church and remained there as pastors for twenty-one years.

In addition to assisting Lon in his ministry, Hattie taught Sunday school and served as the first president of the Conference Woman's Auxiliary. This ministry required travel to visit the auxiliaries of the various churches. Their "meetings were deeply spiritual times of prayer, and many women received deep experiences with the Lord."

In 1955, Rev. and Rev. Mrs. L. B. Edge officially retired; however, they continued to minister as they had opportunity. Lon died in 1968, and even though Hattie was lonely after his departure to be with the Lord, she never wavered in her faith and continued to evangelize until her health started to fail. She then went into a senior citizen's home, where she ministered to the other residents and led several to the Lord.

"Those who visit her bedside cannot help but be inspired and moved by the tremendous spiritual power radiating from her. To visit with this precious saint of God is to touch for an instant the very roots of our heritage."[8]

Acts 9:36 – "This woman was full of good works and almsdeeds which she did."

These comments written by Mark and Judy Kamleiter certainly give us insight into the dedication and commitment in Hattie's life until the very end. She followed God regardless of the fierce opposition to the doctrines she preached. She married, had a child, and continued to do the Lord's bidding, no matter what happened. The sanctified ambition and determination can be seen in the number of churches she and Lon planted and in their ministry given to the First Pentecostal Holiness Church in Norfolk. Virginia.

She gave her life in ministry to God first, then to the Eastern Virginia Conference.

(**Author's note:** As a teenager I remember hearing Sister Edge preach in revivals that she held at the Pentecostal Holiness Church in Hopewell, Virginia where Rev. L. C. Synan was pastor. Time after time, she ministered wonderfully as she sang, "Elijah's God." Never did the Holy Spirit fail to send His glorious presence to authenticate He was in the service.)

Rev. Hazleen Graham
South Carolina Conference

Hazel Parsons was born in Williamsburg, South Carolina, the oldest of ten children. She grew up in a little Free Will Baptist Church with a childhood filled with her dad, brothers, and sisters singing and playing gospel music. Her father sang and played the gospel music, even though he never went to church and was not saved until late in his life.

As a child, she was sickly, but God healed her body, and she knew He had great things in store for her. To fulfill her calling, she became a minister and joined the South Carolina Conference, where she was a successful pastor and evangelist. She planted the Galilee Church at Cross and also served at Olanta and Willow Creek in Cades, South Carolina. She indicates it is harder for women to get approval to be a minister than it is for men.

Prior to her retirement because of physical disabilities brought on by a stroke, she worked as Executive Secretary to three Conference Superintendents (Bishops): Rev. Mark Potter, Rev. Jesse Simmons, and Rev. W. Terry Fowler, at the headquarters of the South Carolina in Lake City. She also worked for them before they became Bishop in their positions as Assistant Superintendent, World Missions Director, and Evangelism Director.

In 2003, the conference honored Sister Graham for her years of service. She was presented with a dozen roses, a plaque, a praying hands paperweight, and a monetary love gift.

The stroke affected her body, but her mind is sharp and alert.[9]

Rev. Ruth Heath
North Carolina Conference

Miss Heath became a member of the North Carolina Conference on August 28, 1948, even though her ministry began in 1940 at Holmes Bible College in Greenville, South Carolina. She was there for twelve years – first as a student and then as a teacher, also serving as Dean of Girls. She continued her education at Pembroke College, Pembroke, North Carolina and Furman University, Greenville, South Carolina.

When she joined the conference, she immediately began work as an evangelist. Her fields of labor led her into the pastorate where she served several churches: Warsaw, Hollands Chapel, Mt. Olive, Stedman, and Tyndall Grove Pentecostal Holiness Churches, in the North Carolina Conference. Ruth states that she helped physically in the building at the Warsaw, Garland, and Stedman churches.

To help support herself and the churches she pastored, she was a teacher in the public school system of Cumberland County for a number of years. For twelve years, she was principal of an elementary school and, for eighteen years, was liaison teacher and school social worker. In 1984, she was living in Roseboro, North Carolina and was still working to advance the cause of Christ.[10]

(**Author's note:** Read more about Miss Heath in Chapter 9.)

"Woman Minister is Active"
Mrs. I. Huggins
North Carolina Conference

"The woman pastor of one of Fayetteville's churches says she finds considerable biblical background to support pastoral activities for women. She is the Mrs. I. Huggins, pastor of the Lyon Memorial Pentecostal Holiness Church. In addition to being the only pastor for the 160-member church, Mrs. Huggins finds time to devote to extensive work involving agriculture extension.

"Asked about scriptural authority for women pastors, Mrs. Huggins pointed to the prophetess Huldah and judge Deborah in the Old Testament.

"She said the apostle Paul mentioned on one occasion that Phillip had four daughters who were evangelists. She said Paul once took Phoebe to a church and told the brethren 'to assist her in the business . . . apparently she went there to pastor or preach.'

"'The greatest example to me,' Mrs. Huggins said, 'is that it was Jesus who first lifted the woman to the status of equal with men in His sight or in carrying on His work.

"'It was Mary who tarried at the tomb and was sent by Jesus to carry the message directed by Him to the disciples that He would see them in Jerusalem.'

"Mrs. Huggins said, 'I think my congregation accepts me as well as a man.'

"The woman pastor said she performs all pastoral functions except the physical act of water baptism, for which she receives aid from area men pastors.

"In her sermons, Mrs. Huggins said, 'My one motive in life is to win a person to the Lord.

"'A man can't live right until he is born of the Spirit. It is my whole conviction if you can get a man really converted, born of the Spirit, it will automatically change his life.'

"This woman pastor said she is attempting to prepare her congregation for the Second Coming of the Lord.

"'Under the conditions we live under now, with so much sin in the world and with the signs shaping everywhere, we know that something is about to take place.'"

"In her personal worship, Mrs. Huggins said, she finds Jesus 'to be a wonderful friend. He has been my lifelong friend, one I could always count on.

"'Being a minister, you sort of live in a shelter, you are very set apart. You don't share a lot of things you would like to but you always take it to the Lord in prayer.'

"In 50 years of ministry, Mrs. Huggins finds her Pentecostal Holiness denomination different 'perhaps in our method of worship.

"'We worship freely. A lot of people look upon us as being very emotional but that really isn't true.

"'We do believe in glorifying the Lord. If a person feels like he would like to praise the Lord or like he would like to raise his hands, many times you will see tears flow.

"'Basically we all have one faith – we all are serving one God.'

"Mrs. Huggins said a Pentecostal Holiness doctrine is 'sanctification as a second definite instantaneous work of grace. We believe in living a separated life from the world.'

"Recently returned from the denomination's General Conference in Oklahoma City, Mrs. Huggins said her Westarea congregation moved into the Lyon Memorial building on Easter.

"A Cumberland County native, Mrs. Huggins attended the University of Tennessee and received an A. B. degree from Southwestern College in Oklahoma City.

"She was licensed to preach by the Cape Fear Conference of the Free Will Baptist Church in December 1929 and by the North Carolina Conference of the Pentecostal Holiness Church in 1950. She became the first woman pastor ordained by the North Carolina Conference in 1963.

"She has been active on various conference boards involving education and children's work.

"In agriculture extension, Mrs. Huggins was county council president four years, Southeastern District president involving 17 counties and served as delegate to various extension conferences.

"She served as chairman of the Cumberland County Memorial Park on the Raeford Road from 1967-77.

"Originally an Episcopalian, Mrs. Huggins said the early influence of Mrs. Lila Berry on her life brought her in the Pentecostal Holiness organization."[11]

Lila Isaac
Tri-State Conference

Mrs. Lila Isaac was active in the Woman's Auxiliary for many years. Even before they were organized on a national level, Lila started a local women's group at her church. Later, she became vice president of the Tri-State Conference where her husband was conference superintendent. After that, she became conference Woman's Auxiliary president.[12]

For eight years, she also served on the general level as Missions Corresponding Secretary. She made many contributions to *The Helping Hand* in her column "From the Field," writing articles about the work of the missionaries of the Pentecostal Holiness Church, and keeping its membership informed about the work of the kingdom of God abroad.[13]

Mrs. Isaac wrote of the projects the Woman's Auxiliary undertook to assist missionaries in an article published in *The Helping Hand*, September 1959: "For the past several years much cheer has been brought into the lives of our missionary families because the auxiliaries of our church have remembered them with packages and money gifts at the Christmas season. Each missionary family has been assigned to a conference auxiliary to be thus remembered. This we call our 'Sponsor Plan.'"[14]

In 1961, Mrs. Isaac became the fourth General President of the Woman's Auxiliary. This took place at the sixteenth General Convention of that organization October 16-18, at the First Pentecostal Holiness Church in Richmond, Virginia.

The Convention accepted with reluctance the resignation of Mrs. Blanche King, who had served as General President so faithfully and competently for eight years. However, Mrs. Isaac was well qualified to pick up the reins of the former president.[15]

"This place where I stand is sacred," were the first words she spoke after the election. She further said, "My fears are many, but my confidence bold in the talented, able leaders of our General, Conference, and local Auxiliaries. I will need your forbearance, and understanding; and I trust I can give back to you love and prayers."

She was described as bringing to her new position a "broad understanding of the work, gleaned through years of service – as a local W. A. president, as a Conference President, and as a Regional Director."

Lila was a resident of Memphis, Tennessee at the time.

Other accomplishments to her credit are the following:

> 3 years as secretary of the Pentecostal Fellowship of North America (P.F.N.A.)
> 4 terms as its president
> 1st vice president of the Woman's Fellowship of the National Association of Evangelicals (N.A.E.) for three years
> N.A.E. Woman's Fellowship President
> General Board of Education (Pentecostal Holiness Church)
> Children's Convalescent Board
> Church Ministries Board[16]

Mrs. Isaac was an outstanding leader; she became this kind of person because of her sensitivity to God's direction. Agnes Robinson, Editor of *The Helping Hand*, wrote these words about Lila:

"It has been a rewarding experience for me to work with Mrs. Lila Isaac during the past twelve years. Actually, our close association goes back further than that, for in 1961, shortly after her election as General Woman's Auxiliary President, she and I spent about ten days together at Franklin Springs in one of the Missions apartments revising the W. A. Manual.

"From the first we seemed to think in the same channel. One of us would start a sentence and the other would finish it. Our minds seemed to flow together. This was also true in our work on the Girl's Auxiliary programs.

"Mrs. Isaac has made a tremendous contribution to the expansion of the Woman's Auxiliary work. Starting where her predecessor left off, she built on the treasuring of all that had gone before. Like a skilled architect, she laid brick upon brick, expanding the programming, extending the ministries, and enlarging the scope of the work.

"Her keen insight and broad vision have enabled her to discern the needs of groups large and small at home and abroad. Her innovative ability has enabled her to plan new programs, or modify the old to meet the current needs.

"Her visits to the mission fields were far more than mere visits. Discussing the W. A. program in depth with missionaries, her perceptive mind was quick to pinpoint ways to adapt and implement the W. A. program on the level of the people. Study courses were developed. Translations of W. A. material were printed. And the work has expanded and grown.

"General church officials visiting the various mission fields have expressed amazement at the unity of the W. A. program around the world. Much of the credit is due this little bundle of energy.

"Neither did she neglect the W. A. in the homeland. Wherever you saw her she was ready for an enthusiastic discussion on the latest developments of the W. A. program. Her alert mind was always thinking ahead, planning how the ministries of the W. A. could be made more effective and how the W. A. leaders could receive a renewed challenge.

"Her hurried handwritten notes were always warm, yet right to the point. Her quarterly news letters – sometimes sent more often – were full of information never leaving the W. A. leaders wondering what should be done next. She seemed to anticipate questions before they were asked.

"If she had any fault as a leader, it was [that] she bore too much of the load herself instead of letting others share in the heavy responsibility.

"Lila Isaac is a great lady, with the rare combination of dignity and personal warmth. Her unfailing enthusiasm has been a real inspiration to me.

"I count it a privilege to have served at her side for twelve years. I love her dearly and shall greatly miss working with her on the Board. I'm glad she will be close enough for me to call on her when I need help.

"I have a feeling that, after a brief rest, she will be actively involved in some other endeavor for the Lord she loves.

"That's our Lila."[17]

(**Author's note:** An article titled "Focus on Prayer," written by Mrs. Isaac, appears in this book in Chapter 10.)

Mrs. Mae Grier Johndrow

Mae Grier was born in Texas in a two-room log cabin located eighteen miles north of Waco. Her parents were Christians who tried to direct her in the ways of God. She attended church and Sunday school regularly from the very beginning of her life. Among her earliest recollections are the family prayers, which took place three times a day.

She was saved at age six and sanctified when she was fifteen. Early in life, she felt a definite call into the work of the Lord and had a burning desire to tell others about Christ.

Sister Johndrow attended Holmes Bible College in Greenville, South Carolina, where she remained for a while as teacher, study hall supervisor, matron, and dietician where she oversaw the canning of foods to be used by the school. She also helped with Vacation Bible School work.

During her time at Holmes, she exhibited an unusual ability to organize, to discipline, and to operate the kitchen and girls' dormitory with order and precision. She was responsible for establishing many customs and plans at the school that lasted long after she left. Her influence was far reaching as she left an indelible impression on many girls who attended Holmes. By example she showed them the path of duty, sacrifice, and service.

She did mission work around Greenville, taught Sunday school, was involved in youth work, served as a pastor, and conducted evangelistic services. Her labors did not end when she became the wife of Mr. Johndrow who was at that time a faithful member of the Lamar Avenue Pentecostal Holiness Church in Memphis, Tennessee.

Mrs. Johndrow served as General Vice-President of the Woman's Auxiliary from 1949-1953.[18]

Blanche Leon Moore King
Georgia Conference

Blanche was born on the fourth of July into a family that lived in extreme poverty. Her father was a farmer and the owner of a gin and mill, but he suffered great loss because of a fire, when she was a small girl. The conditions in which the family was forced to live made Mrs. King appreciative of the things that God let come her way.

She went to a one-room school in their neighborhood through as many grades as were offered, then attended the State Normal School in Athens, Georgia. Later, she returned to the same one-room school as a teacher.

One night when Blanche was visiting one of her students, she found out the family believed in the doctrine of holiness. They told her the joys of salvation, and the father of the home informed her that they were praying for her. She was soon saved.

Rev. G. F. Taylor was making plans to open a church school in Franklin Springs, Georgia and needed trained Christian teachers. He asked Rev. Joseph King, General Superintendent of the Pentecostal Holiness Church, to help him secure them. He contacted Blanche Moore, who had been recommended by a mutual friend, and she became the first teacher hired at Franklin Springs Institute, now known as Emmanuel College.

In July 1919, Rev. King offered Miss Moore another position. She delayed her answer until September of that year, and the following June she became the wife of the General Superintendent.

The next few years were filled with the normal activities of making a home for her husband and taking care of the four children born to this couple. She spent much of her time in loneliness as Brother King was away from home for months at a time because he traveled around the country doing church work.

At the General Woman's Auxiliary Convention in 1945, she was elected General Secretary-Treasurer of that organization. In 1953, she was elected General President. Blanche also edited several departments of the Sunday school literature and was assistant editor of the *Advocate* for many years.

She was a profound thinker, a prolific writer, and a talented speaker who was much in demand. She held credentials as a licensed minister in the Georgia Conference.[19]

In the Foreword of the book *Yet Speaketh*, written by her husband, she wrote, "The burden of my heart since the passing of my husband has been that I might do something to perpetuate his memory and extend the influence of his consecrated life. In preparing his manuscript for publication and writing about the latter years of his earthly sojourn – the unfinished part of his autobiography, covering the years from 1933 to 1946 – this desire has been fulfilled to some extent. I have written simply and sincerely from my heart about his life and labors as I observed them.

"If as a result of reading this volume you are inspired to greater devotion to the Savior, then will have been fulfilled the statement which the Psalmist made, and which Bishop King repeated a few hours before his departure – 'I shall not die, but live, and declare the works of the Lord;' and throughout eternity with you we shall rejoice and praise God for His marvelous love that made us *'heirs together of the grace of life.'*"[20]

"Among the Women"
Viola Marley
Western N. C. Auxiliary President

Mrs. Viola Marley, daughter of Rev. G. W. Stanley, was born in Chatham County, N. C. She was born in a Pentecostal home, rocked in a Pentecostal cradle, and later became a member of the Pentecostal Holiness Church. Early in life she accepted Christ and felt the call to preach. In preparation for this calling, she attended Emmanuel College (then Franklin Springs Institute) in Franklin Springs, Georgia, and Holmes Bible College in Greenville, South Carolina. After graduating from Holmes, she assisted her father in revivals; later she entered full-time evangelistic work. For nine years, she evangelized in several conferences. Into the picture came Rev. H. J. Marley, and they were married September 9, 1943.

Mrs. Marley was elected president of the Woman's Auxiliary of the Western North Carolina Conference in 1948. Under her leadership, the auxiliary grew. She gave her untiring efforts to the growth of God's kingdom.

The subject of this sketch is widely known in the Pentecostal Holiness denomination for her consecrated life. Her ministry has blessed many in the past, and her life of usefulness continued as she served her conference as President of the Woman's Auxiliary. The membership of the Woman's Auxiliary in her conference was seven hundred in 1950. Their conference project for that year was to raise $1,000 for their cafeteria on the conference assembly grounds, and almost half of it had been raised by the first of September. They were expecting the tithes from the local auxiliaries to meet their obligation, according to the note from Mrs. F. V. Ellenberg, the Secretary-Treasurer of the Conference Woman's Auxiliary.

"From the reports coming to us, Mrs. Marley preached an excellent sermon to the ladies (and men) at the South Carolina Auxiliary Convention. May the Lord bless and use her as she continues to serve our church and her Master."[21]

"A Mother's Day Tribute To"
Eugenia McCartney
North Carolina Conference

Eugenia McCartney was born April 30, 1908, in Newkirk, Oklahoma. Her family was of pioneer stock and sterling character, and from early childhood these traits began to manifest themselves in her life. Eugenia could hardly have know that in later years she would be led by the Divine Hand and that her praises would be sung by many far from the community of her birth and childhood surroundings.

She married Mr. L. A. Ashburn at an early age, and one child, Bonnie Jean, was born to this union. Through her husband's family, Eugenia became acquainted with the Pentecostal Holiness Church. Not long thereafter, at a mission altar where Rev. Harry P. Lott was pastoring, she came face to face with her Savior and made Him Lord of her life. Mr. Ashburn passed away at age thirty-two.

Having felt the call to preach, Mrs. McCartney endeavored to prepare herself at both Emmanuel College in Franklin Springs, Georgia and Central State University in Edmond, Oklahoma. She earned the bachelor of science degree and, in later years, her master's degree from East Carolina University in Greenville, North Carolina.

Mrs. McCartney ministered in the early days of her calling in the Indian villages and towns of Oklahoma and in the Ozark mountains of Arkansas.

It began in Arkansas City near the close of an open-air meeting. Mrs. McCartney was seeking God's direction as to where He wanted her to go next. After several days of prayer, she had no leading, so at last she spread out a map and asked God to show her where to go. Her eyes fell on Fayetteville, Arkansas. An inward witness made her know this was the place, but with this awareness came an awful dread and fear. She knew no one in that town; however, she told the Lord she would start toward Fayetteville by buying a bus ticket for her and her daughter, Bonnie Jean, to Bartlesville, Arkansas. She knew a Pentecostal Holiness family there; then, she'd trust His leading from that point on.

As she rode toward Bartlesville, she was in prayer and a great peace enveloped her. When the bus stopped at Pawhuska for her to make connections with a Bartlesville bus, she discovered that the other bus was leaving before she could board it. The driver was very sympathetic and suggested she ride down to Skiatook on his bus and catch a later bus up to Barltesville. She did as he suggested, except for catching the later bus. When she arrived in Skiatook, she checked into a hotel for she intended to stay there until she could get clearer direction from God.

Upon inquiry, she learned there was a Pentecostal Church within walking distance, so she and Bonnie Jean walked to the church. To her wonderment, she also learned the pastor and his wife were leaving to go to

Fayetteville, Arkansas. Though the pastor had never met Mrs. McCartney, after prayer he told her he felt God wanted her to stay there a while. He asked her to stay in their home and to carry on his services in Skiatook, while he and his wife went to Fayetteville to try out for a pastorate there.

After two or three weeks, he returned. The church in Fayetteville called him to come as pastor, so it was agreed that Mrs. McCartney would go with them to help with the moving and to meet a young girl who had been praying all summer for God to send her a co-worker to carry the gospel to the neglected people of the Ozarks. Together, Mrs. McCartney and the young lady searched out schoolhouses where they could preach the Word. They found many hungry hearts. In one community, two women had met together and prayed for five years for God to send a preacher. In another area, a husband and wife had prayed seven years for a minister.

Mrs. McCartney traveled often on foot, sometimes with the mail truck, ministering to those who had little or no money and hardly enough food for themselves. She shared in their poverty, receiving what the people could afford – from a cup of sugar to a can of goat's meat. Eugenia's burning desire to preach the gospel and win the lost to Christ never diminished because of these circumstances.

In 1942, Rev. C. R. McCartney courted and married this lovely lady. She shared with him in his ministry – the pastorates of two Oklahoma churches, McLoud and Spencer.

Bonnie Jean married a young minister from the North Carolina Conference, J. Floyd Williams, who later became Bishop of the Pentecostal Holiness Church. In 1946, the McCartneys acquiesced to the wishes of her daughter and young husband and became members of the North Carolina Conference, but not until both of them had tarried long before God to determine His will concerning this matter.

In 1947, the McCartneys were assigned the Benson and Sharon churches in the North Carolina Conference. Later, she worked with her husband in the pastorates of Millennium, Oak Ridge, Elizabethtown, Rayford, Fuquay Springs, and Johnson Memorial in the same conference. While they were serving the Millennium Church, the chairman of the Falcon Children's Home Board contacted them about coming to the children's home. Mrs. McCartney was somewhat averse to the invitation but was reminded that God had spoken to her years earlier about working at Falcon. From 1950-1955, she stood by the side of her husband and rendered invaluable service to some eighty children by sharing their pains, sorrows, heartaches, and joys.

Following her husband's retirement from the Falcon Children's Home, Mrs. McCartney returned to her earlier profession, a teacher in the public school. She was employed by the state of North Carolina until her own retirement in 1974. She also returned to the Falcon Children's Home as a social worker and remedial reading specialist.

Mrs. McCartney was the North Carolina Conference Woman's Auxiliary president from 1947-1950 and wrote the General Woman's Auxiliary Manual with the assistance of Mrs. Ada Lee Thurman. In 1949, she presented it to the General Conference in Jacksonville, Florida, and it was adopted. That document has stood the test of time; after all these years, it is still the basic standard of the W. A. of the Pentecostal Holiness Church.

She has left many blessings behind. Among the greatest is the life of her faithful daughter, Bonnie Jean Williams, and her grandsons, Jay Floyd, James Ashley, and Jonathan. [22]

Emma Dora Miller
Virginia Conference

On May 18, 1872, in Augusta County, Virginia, a daughter was born in the home of Mr. and Mrs. R. S. Coffman. Emma Dora was one of four daughters God gave to this couple. Little information is available about her childhood, but what is known is that little girl was keenly interested in religion at a very early age. In fact, she was interested enough to join a Lutheran church even before she was converted.

Miss Coffman became the bride of George Thomas Miller on November 4, 1896, in Roanoke, Virginia. Shortly after their marriage, both she and her husband joined the United Brethren Church. Less than two years after her marriage, Mrs. Miller was converted in the Park Street Mission in Roanoke, Virginia under the ministry of Revs. Oakey and Hypes. In June of the same year, she was sanctified as a second definite work of grace and lived the holy, separated life for more than fifty years. Emma Dora and George were married for fifty-three years until her death separated them on September 10, 1950.

She had a unique ability to grasp the deep truths presented in the Bible. When Pentecost was first preached in Roanoke, she accepted the doctrine and was baptized with the Holy Spirit. Concerning this, Sister Miller gave the following testimony: "I had never seen anyone receive the

Baptism. I was the second one in Roanoke to receive the experience, and I came through about 11:00 p.m. speaking in other tongues." After receiving the Holy Spirit, Emma Dora became a charter member of the Pentecostal Holiness Church in Roanoke and remained a faithful member until the time of her death.

Knowing that the Lord had a work for her beyond the local church, Mrs. Miller was granted license to preach by the Virginia Conference. About a month after receiving the Holy Spirit, Sister Miller states she felt a definite call to teach the Word and promised the Lord she would do so. She observed, from a close study of the New Testament scriptures, that *"pastor"* and *"teacher"* were used almost synonymously, and since she was being appointed to pastoral work, she decided to be ordained in order to be better qualified for this sacred work.

Emma was an ardent Sunday school worker and served as a teacher for more than fifty years. She began this ministry in the Lutheran Church, teaching a class of twenty-five small children.

When the Roanoke Pentecostal Holiness Church was organized, she was made Superintendent of the Sunday school. While filling this position, she furnished the kindling and built the fire in the church and then taught a class.

Her husband, Georgie to her, was always supportive of her ministry. He stood by her in the work she did. She said, "Georgie never wanted me to receive anything for my service. Although he was a member of another church, he never opposed me in any way."

She was continually helping those in need and in destitute circumstances. It was impossible to tell all she did for the poor. Mrs. Miller was a true Dorcas. Her own words express it better than what anyone else could say. "My name is Dora, which means Dorcas. I have truly been a Dorcas worker for the Lord. For all that the Lord has enabled me to do, I give Him praise and glory."

When the time came when Sister Miller could no longer engage in active ministry, she was reluctant to retire, but she finally accepted the inevitable. Her testimony reveals something of her character. "I feel that the Holy Ghost abides today, and still leads and guides me. He has recently given me great assurance of Heaven by saying *'Thou shalt guide me with thy counsel, and afterward receive me to glory'"* –Psalm 73:24.

She knew in her heart, along with the Apostle Paul, that she had fought a good fight; she was about to finish her course, and a crown was awaiting her in Glory.[23]

"Women in our Heritage"
Daisy Morris
North Carolina Conference

Mrs. Daisy Grace Jones Morris, a Georgia native and eldest daughter of a family of eight children, became associated with the Pentecostal Holiness Church at the age of fifteen. Later, in adverse circumstances, church friends opened their homes to the Jones family. It was during this close relationship with the Newnan, Georgia congregation that she received the experience of sanctification and baptism in the same service.

The Newnan Church was a great source of help to Daisy in her Christian struggles of living in a home that had no knowledge of holiness. They helped her establish her faith. Often her Bible and religious literature was hidden in a nearby woods under a big rock for protection from destruction. It was such experiences as these that led her to pray for a constant renewal of strength.

An eventual launch of faith and the encouragement from the Newnan folks also led her to Holmes Bible College in Greenville, South Carolina, where she spent five years. From there she branched out wherever a door for Christian service was opened.

The first summer from Holmes was spent in the Falcon, North Carolina area with the Henry Goff family. Ada Lee Goff took Daisy under her wing. It was this summer the Ada Lee Goff – Daisy Jones Evangelistic Team preached its first sermons in Henry Goff's tent.

Her desire to attend Emmanuel College in Franklin Springs, Georgia was another venture by faith.

She was licensed to preach in the Georgia Conference in 1937. Bishop King singled her out in the conference and said "God has His hands on this little girl; we are going to pray especially that God will not let anything interfere with her work for Him." Her first pastorate was at the Goldmine Church in Georgia. While there, her means of transportation was by wagon or with whoever was going the five miles to the Goldmine community.

In the summer of 1944, Sister Daisy was requested to go to the Wilmington, North Carolina church and work as a Christian Education Director. This was the first church to promote that type ministry. She transferred her membership to the North Carolina Conference in 1945. Two years, later she was elected as the Youth Director for the conference and began to work among the youth.

Simultaneously with those four years of service, she taught school and initiated the youth camp program for the conference. During these years this program progressed to the point that it required a full-time director. It was during this time that the Vacation Bible School, Sword Drill, and recreation at youth camp were initiated into the conference program.

After her marriage to Reverend W. E. Morris, Conference Superintendent of the North Carolina Conference, she continued to extend her Christian ministries to great depths. While raising a family of four lovely children (Ronnie, Sandra Byrum, Susan Caddell, and Sylvia) she conducted a summer door-to-door campaign. The Airboro Church was organized from this special ministry. She pastored this church in its infancy. Rev. W. G. Batten was later assigned to the church, and she continued to work with the pastor. It was a warm and gracious ministry.

In 1977, she had served for twelve years as secretary-treasurer of the Falcon Children's Home where her husband, Eddie, was superintendent.

"While reaching out into the church, the school, the community, and the Children's Home, she has discovered over and over – when you love people, you love God. Her careful preparation and counseling, guidance and love have extended the ministry of Falcon Children's Home." These are just a few events in the life of this great "Woman in Our Heritage."[24]

Rev. Daisy Morris was described in the 1982 *North Carolina Conference Minutes* as "one of the great women of the Pentecostal Holiness Church. Like Dorcas in the New Testament, her life and influence is typical of those who are full of good works and almsdeeds, which she has done."[25]

She literally went beyond her strength in serving unselfishly her God, her church, Falcon Children's Homes, her husband, her conference and her children without concern for herself. The Pentecostal Holiness Church and the North Carolina Conference owe her a debt of gratitude, but only the Lord whom she loves supremely can give her a proper reward.

A Work of Grace
Daisy Morris
by
Sylvia Morris

"I will share information about my mother but I must preface it by saying her life is a work of grace. It's a story of God providing a way where there was no way. To know her is to see the hand of God weaved into every facet, going before her and making the way clear. Her life is like a good book you don't want to put down."

She continues, "Now, my mother did encounter discriminations just like others, but those discriminations were no obstacle to God paving the way for his will for her life. Truly, to me, it seemed she walked on air and slipped miraculously and gracefully around any discrimination she may have encountered.

"The first church she pastored was the Gold Mine Church located in Georgia. She pastored this church while she was attending Emmanuel College Georgia. But earlier, in her teens, she got her first preaching experiences under the loving care of Henry and Florence Goff. The Goffs traveled everywhere holding revivals. They took my mother in as a teenage with no place to go and began to nurture her new found Christian faith. Their daughter, Ada Lee Goff Thurman, was my mother's roommate at Holmes Bible School and my mother's best friend. When the Goffs set out to preach a revival, they took Ada Lee and my mother with them to do some preaching and they would have my mother share her testimony.

"When my mother married my dad, she felt her role was to support him and be a helpmate. However, my dad had no difficulty using women and he continued to use my mother in ministry. Whenever a church was having division and strife, my dad loved to send my mother to deal with the people because of her wonderful ability to defuse tensions and bring people back together. He continued to send her to preach whenever she would go. She began to do it less and less but only because she felt pulled in different directions. She was turning down daddy's request so her withdrawal from ministry was her choice and not because my dad didn't want to use her. He loved her church involvement. During her ministry, she fostered two missions (Airboro and Johnson Memorial) that are now firmly established churches of the Pentecostal Holiness Church."[26]

Ruth Hampton Morris
East Oklahoma (New Horizons) Conference

Wanda Elliott, daughter of Sister Ruth Morris, relates that her "mother was born in Atlanta, Georgia to Rev. Harry and Rev. Carrie Banks Hampton. Her father pastored the Franklin Springs PH Church, and she and her brothers and sisters attended school at Emmanuel at a time when they had Elementary, High School and College. Her family moved West in 1927, and her father pastored churches in Texas and Oklahoma. While pastoring at Westville, Oklahoma, she met my father, J. C. Morris. After their marriage, she received her call to preach. Mother and Daddy made the decision that she should attend Emmanuel College for further Bible training. He took Mother and me to Franklin Springs and returned to Oklahoma to operate his business. Looking back, it amazes me that in 1944 they would make this decision. Also they were willing to be separated when Mother was asked to pastor a church which had an unexpected need – Daddy would move us – me, my sister and brother with Mother so she could pastor, and he would commute, sometimes by bus to be with us on the weekend. I never remember him mentioning the inconvenience. It was always exciting when he arrived to be with us in church on Sunday. He totally supported Mother in her ministry. In 1950 my dad's business moved us to Stilwell, Oklahoma, where there was no PH church. Within a few months, Mother started services in our house. She pastored, sometime in our home, sometimes in rented buildings until a beautiful building was constructed in 1954. This is still a strong flourishing church today."[27]

Mrs. Adelaide Scott Muse

Mrs. Muse was born Adelaide Margaret Scott in Shawnee, Oklahoma. Her parents were pioneers and were among the first to settle in that territory. She showed an early desire to work for the Lord by teaching a Sunday school class for boys for years in a Baptist church.

In 1906, she met Daniel Muse whose mind was filled with adventure. This characteristic later led them both into service in the Master's kingdom. When the great Pentecostal revival swept the West in 1913, the Muses prayerfully and earnestly sought the fullness of the Pentecostal blessing until they received the baptism of the Holy Spirit. When Dan applied for license to preach, Adelaide applied for mission worker's license, and they received them from the Pentecostal Holiness Church.

She stated that "God did not call me to preach, but that my husband had enough work for two, and I worked with him." At times, when he was away from home because of his work, she preached in schools, brush arbors and in churches. She drove a Model T with patched tires and carried the gospel in all conditions.

Sister Muse continued her work for God by serving as the first General Vice-President of the Woman's Auxiliary for four years. After that she was elected General President in 1949, a position she held until 1953 when she resigned because of poor health.

"Mrs. Muse will never grow old. The spirit of the pioneers will always keep her youthful and enthusiastic; and her vision of the work of God keeps her ever ready to do or die. Within the hearts of all who know her, she holds a place of warm affection and admiration."[28]

Thelma Jacobs Player
South Carolina Conference

Thelma Jacobs was born in Chesterfield County, South Carolina at Pumpkin Center on July 28, 1911. Her parents were Lewis Jacobs and Daisy Dell Lisenby Jacobs. She was the oldest of eight children. She had three brothers and four sisters.

Her parents farmed, and Thelma's job was to care for the younger children and also help in the fields. However, she did attend Womber School for six years. At the age of twelve, she went to work in a meat market with her daddy.

In 1929, she met Henry Player who later became her husband. They had two children, Lucille Player Cannon, born in 1930, and Eugene, who was born in 1943.

She was diagnosed with cancer in 1940 but continued to work in the cotton mill. She was scheduled to have surgery for the condition when the doctor told her and her husband that she would be an invalid. She decided not to have the surgery but to trust the Lord for her healing. Thelma became desperate in prayer about her condition and felt led by the Holy Spirit to seek out Rev. Walter Patterson, who was then the pastor of the East Rockingham Pentecostal Holiness Church in South Carolina. He anointed her with oil and, along with his wife and daughter, they prayed for Thelma. From that day on her condition improved, and she accepted the call to preach.

She preached the gospel in county homes and jails and held Sunday school for children under the trees. She also held street services. Ruth Robinson Powell assisted Rev. Player in this ministry.

She received her minister's license and joined the South Carolina Conference in 1959. Before she received her ministerial credentials, she went to Ellerbe, North Carolina and started a work in a home. She built a church there and pastored it until 1959, when she went to the Outside Community in South Carolina, rented an old service station, cleaned it out, and started a work there by holding Sunday school on Sunday afternoons. This was the beginning of the By Way Pentecostal Holiness Church (now Living Waters). She built a church and fellowship hall there and pastored the church for twenty-six years.

She always has been a lady with great faith. Being one never to be satisfied to sit in church, she rented a house on Highway 74 in Hamlet, North Carolina and began to hold services. From there, she rented a building at Five Points in Rockingham, North Carolina and moved the work there.

At the time of her death in 2007, she was ninety-six years old and the oldest minister still pastoring in the entire IPHC.[29]

Lula Mae Putnam
South Carolina Conference

Before her conversion, Lula Mae was a professional wrestler. After God saved her, she became a pastor and an outstanding evangelist in the South Carolina Conference and the IPHC. The year she was licensed, she was appointed pastor at Friendfield. That was in 1954; then, in 1971 she was ordained.

Her preaching and ministry were truly anointed. The churches enjoyed some of their greatest revivals under her dynamic ministry. God gave her a special way with people. Her personality and preaching were tools that God used in His hand to bring people to repentance of sin and acceptance of the gospel.

The South Carolina Conference newsletter, *The Challenge*, published a list of the top ministers, based on the number of experiences recorded in their ministry. For several years, noted below, Sister Putnam was number one in these figures:

August through December 1970

Saved	Sanctified	Baptized in Holy Spirit
137	90	53

October 22, 1971 through February 1972

139	70	79

Top Ten Ministers for 1977

360	213	208

Top Ten Experiences for 1981

366	284	319

Can we see the anointing of the Holy Spirit by the fruit of her labors? The evidence is spelled out clearly. This was a real woman of God who had an abundance of sheaves to place at the Master's feet.

Sister Putnam died April 26, 1993, after some time in declining health. Her body was laid to rest in Charlotte, North Carolina, but her soul rests securely in the arms of Jesus her Savior.[30]

"THE ADVOCATE Salutes Martha Roberta Rose"
Oklahoma Conference

Martha Roberta Walker was born on Thursday, June 26, 1902, into a family of three brothers and four sisters. She had a loving mother and a stern invalid father, Gary Walker, one of Oklahoma City's first judges. She was saved, sanctified and received the Holy Spirit in 1909, at the age of six. She taught a Sunday school class at age ten and served as Sunday school secretary for the First Pentecostal Holiness Church in Oklahoma City.

Martha Walker preached her first sermon in that church, when she was twelve years old. She received her mission worker's license in 1920 at eighteen. That same year, she married Sterling C. Rose of Kentucky.

In 1931, Bishop Dan T. Muse asked her if it wasn't about time that she apply for minister's license. She agreed and received license the same year, when she was twenty-nine. She pastored both the Hinton and Lookeba churches in Oklahoma that first six months, alternating between Sunday morning and evening services. She was ordained in 1933. After pastoring Lookeba for three years, Martha Rose served a number of other churches in Oklahoma: Apache, Clothier, Union Grove, Spencer, and Norman.

Sterling and Martha Rose moved to California, where, with her husband, she and four other women built the church in Fresno. She later moved back to the Midwest where she pastored churches in Sarcoxie, Missouri and Pittsburg, Kansas.

Over the years, Martha Rose has served her Lord in many capacities. She has taught juniors in Sunday school for over fifty years and helped introduce the Daily Vacation Bible School in many of the Pentecostal Holiness churches. Martha Rose was instrumental in establishing the Woman's Auxiliary in the California Conference and served as its first president. She also served for a number of years as the superintendent of the Contra Costa County Sunday School division for Juvenile Hall in Martinez, California, and she wrote a program for the intermediate Bible Explorers of the Antioch Church in California.

Sterling and Martha Rose have three children who live in Oklahoma, eleven grandchildren, and ten great grandchildren.

At age seventy-six, after fifty-eight years of marriage, Sterling and Martha were still active in the Antioch Church. She was teaching a class of juniors and was working in the Woman's Auxiliary. Her first love is studying and sharing the teachings of Jesus – and looking forward to the Rapture.[31]

Renee Ross
East Oklahoma Conference

"A Woman With a Mandate from God"

Shirley Spencer writes, "Renee Ross is a woman who takes seriously her calling and commission from God. She believes she has a mandate to reach her community for Christ.

"As Renee's tenures as conference Women's Ministries president and member of the General Women's Ministries Board expired, she was content to support the ministries of the local church . . . Then, early in 1994, she sensed a strange uneasiness deep inside."

She had been a member of the Pentecostal Holiness Church in Wetumka, Oklahoma for twenty years. Mrs. Ross put her many talents to use as she played the piano, led praise and worship, taught classes, and occasionally filled in for the pastor, but a series of events led her to believe that God had a special work for her to do. Her spirit was troubled about what she was feeling and she began to experience insomnia and weight loss. She tried to repress what she felt, but it would not go away.

In response to an invitation that was made at the local Baptist Church where she was attending a concert, the pastor told her, "All hindrances and obstacles have been removed for you to follow God's will."

About a week later, Renee's pastor asked her if God was calling her to pastor the church. She told him how the Lord had been dealing with her, and he responded that God had shown him the previous week that she was sensing what God was trying to do in her. He indicated that he was willing to resign the church, so she could follow the leading of Holy Spirit.

While she was attending a Women's Ministries Retreat several weeks later, the congregation voted to accept her as its pastor. This came with the full support of Rev. Harris and the East Oklahoma Conference Board.

"Since Renee was chosen as pastor nearly five years ago [1994], the congregation has experienced an average annual increase of 27 percent." They were expecting to break ground soon for a new worship center.

The only obstacles Renee has faced as a woman pastor have been those limitations that she placed upon herself. She realized she had become introverted in her ministry when God led her to reach out to her own community and town.

In June 1995, the congregation adopted a new name, Living Water, for the church. Through the ministry of this pastor, the community is being impacted with God's grace and lives are being transformed.[32]

Rev. Jewelle Stewart
South Carolina Conference

Sister Stewart was "born into a life of ministry and grew up under the influence of godly parents and grandparents" who served as Pentecostal

Holiness ministers in the South Carolina Conference. First-hand, she observed the blessings that come from serving God.

After graduating from Holmes Bible College in Greenville, South Carolina, she married Rabon Stewart and, for more than thirty years, they pastored in the Alabama Conference where her husband served two terms as Superintendent. During that time, she worked in a variety of local and conference ministries.

"From 2001 to 2009, Jewelle served as Executive Director of IPHC Women's Ministries and was a member of the Board of Directors for the International Pentecostal Holiness Church and Falcon Children's Home Board. She also served on the 2006-2009 Structural Task Force for the denomination." Sister Stewart also spent several years on the Board of Directors and the Executive Committee of the National Association of Evangelicals (NAE) and is President Emeritus of its women's commission, the Evangelical Women Leaders of the NAE. She is an ordained minister in the South Carolina Conference.[33]

Janice Strickland
South Carolina Conference

Janice was saved at the age of nine. She was sanctified during a revival at the age of ten. Two nights later, she was baptized in the Holy Spirit. On July 31, 1966, at the age of twelve, she dedicated her whole life to God's service. She told a newspaper reporter, who interviewed her for an article, that she was not ashamed to serve the Lord after her conversion.

The Lord called her to preach when she was eighteen, and she was assured of His work in her. No one could convince her otherwise, because God's calling was definite. She says she has no regrets as a Christian.

She was licensed to preach by the South Carolina Conference on June 26, 1998. Besides preaching in many churches, she has devoted a lot of time to working in Youth Camp at Lake City, South Carolina and filling many positions in churches in the conference. She taught Sunday school, conducted children's church, played the piano, led the singing, sang in the choir, participated in and directed Christmas programs, and even cleaned the church.

Sister Strickland attended Holmes Bible College in Greenville, South Carolina from 1971-1975 and graduated with a bachelor of sacred literature degree. She says her stay there had a distinct spiritual impact on her life.

Mrs. Annie Odell Casper Taylor
North Carolina Conference

As the new bride of Isaac Samuel Taylor, (Ike), Annie moved with her husband from Kinston, North Carolina to Goldsboro, North Carolina, where he was employed by Carolina Power & Light Company. She quickly became acquainted with a neighbor who invited her to a Ladies Prayer Meeting and then to a revival. After attending, she soon accepted Jesus Christ as Lord and Savior and experienced the glorious gift of salvation. Soon, Ike also accepted the Lord, and they became affiliated with Oak Street Pentecostal Holiness (PH) Church, known later as the First Church in Goldsboro, North Carolina.

In the mid 1930s, they moved to Kenly, North Carolina with their growing family. By the early 1940s, she had begun to feel urgency in her spirit for special ministry for the Lord. Upon yielding to this calling, she was licensed by the North Carolina Conference. She began to conduct revivals and also pastored Niagra PH Church. After conducting a revival at the Bear Creek PH Church, later named Hood Memorial in Onslow County, she realized a real need in the Coastal Plains for full-gospel ministry. After a lot of prayerful consideration, she and her husband with their seven children made a dramatic move in December 1944 from Kenly to Swansboro, both in North Carolina. There, she pastored Bear Creek Church and Verona PH Church for several years.

In the 1950s, she and her family were very involved with the organization of other churches in Onslow County. Then, she pastored Graham Memorial PH church and Swansboro PH Church for at least two different assignments each going into the 1960s.

Because of her love for the Indian people, she visited Cherokee, North Carolina through her lifetime. In the mid-1960s, after becoming acquainted with the pastor of the Cherokee PH Church, she and her husband spent several summers there. They camped in the remote area of Big Cove, as they ministered to many personal needs – transportation for food and/or doctor visits, providing clothing for children – as well as the people's spiritual needs.

After her retirement, a small church group in the community of Belgrade, near Maysville, North Carolina contacted her because they needed a preacher. She went. She helped them organize a Sunday school; she played their piano and preached. That is where she was ministering for the Lord at the time of her death, July 18, 1969, at age sixty-three.

Many Scriptures in her Bible were highlighted and underlined, but one favorite she quoted frequently was Psalm 121:1: *"I will lift up mine eyes unto the hills, from whence cometh my help."* This sustained her on the many fronts of her life as wife, mother, employee, employer, and in her greatest passion – serving her Lord. [34]

Ada Lee Goff Thurman
South Carolina Conference
by
Charlotte Thurman Iaquinta

"My mother was born in Falcon, North Carolina on February 7, 1914. She was the 11th of 15 children born to Rev. and Mrs. H. H. Goff. She completely surrendered her life to the Lord at the Falcon Camp Meeting in the summer of 1937 when she was 23 years old. She went to Holmes Bible and Missionary Institute that fall 'by faith' and for the next 3 years learned to walk by faith to trust the Lord for EVERYTHING. She said she had told her daddy that she was going by faith, and he let her! During those years she preached in the summers often accompanying her parents in tent revivals, and she and her sisters also held 'Street Meetings' on Saturdays in North Carolina towns like Dunn and Fayetteville. After graduating from Holmes, she attended Emmanuel College for one year and Newberry College for one year. She married Carl W. Thurman on July 18, 1942. They were married in the Gospel Tabernacle in Dunn, North Carolina."

They started their married life pastoring Bethany Pentecostal Holiness Church in Shulerville, South Carolina and planting a church in North Charleston. There are many stories about that church planting experience that are extremely colorful, including their tent being burned and Brother Thurman being put in jail when their daughter, Charlotte, was a baby. They were in North Charleston for five years, and then sent to Columbia. "The next year my father evangelized and Mother pastored a rural church in New Holland, South Carolina." While there, they built a parsonage under her leadership and their daughter, Charlotte, was saved at the age of five. From there they went to Georgetown, South Carolina, where they were to stay for nine years. During those years she was Woman's Auxiliary Conference President (eleven years in office), edited the Women's Page of *The Advocate*. She held four to six revivals a year and co-pastored a vital and growing church. The church at Georgetown grew from fewer than one hundred in Sunday school to six hundred-plus. "My mother was a great Christian educator and motivator. Her influence was equally important to my father's in growth and stability of the church there. She was always active in the community as well as in the church and recognized as a woman of the year in the city."

Lancaster, South Carolina was the next pastorate. "While there, Mother completed her BA degree at Winthrop. Her degree was in Sociology, and she was certified to teach Language Arts and Social Studies, also. After that year, I started to college and Mother started teaching in the public schools. My father died in 1965, while pastoring the East Rockingham PH Church. She completed his term there as interim pastor and moved from there to Fayetteville, NC to be nearer to her family."

She worked at the Northwood Pentecostal Holiness Church as a volunteer for many years and went on staff in 1976, having taken early retirement to do so. She was Associate Pastor there for twenty-two years until her death in 1998. She was a preacher for sixty-one years and an ordained minister in the Pentecostal Holiness Church for fifty-eight years. She was still working and on staff at Northwood at the time of her death. It can be said of Ada Lee that she truly did "finish well."

Scores of ministers in the Carolinas were saved, sanctified or filled with the Holy Spirit under Ada Lee's ministry. Countless other fine laymen and laywomen all over this nation and around the world are her spiritual children. [35]

An article titled "Our President" about Mrs. Thurman was printed in *The Helping Hand*, November, 1953. Mrs. J. R. Cohn wrote about Mrs. Ada Lee Thurman's years of service as president of the South Carolina Conference Woman's Auxiliary. Ten years before this, when the Woman's Auxiliary was in its infancy, she was elected to that position.

From the time of her election, she was a rallying point for those who merely dreamed but lacked the faith to do. She was God's chosen leader for the ladies of the South Carolina Conference. Her enterprising spirit inspired others to join with her in the task of building the women's work in that conference.

"To accomplish the great task at hand, she did not hold back her strength, energy, and efforts just because we were not able at that time to pay her any salary. She worked right on for a number of years receiving nothing except her traveling expenses." The ladies heard that Ada Lee went as far as eighty miles on a bus, with two small children accompanying her, to attend some of the rallies. Later, her husband bought a car for her to use for her auxiliary work.

Even though she was involved locally with the auxiliaries, that did not keep her from also working at the conference and general levels. She was editor of the conference paper, *The Handmaiden*, for six years; she helped prepare the General Woman's Auxiliary manual, record books, and report blanks. She was chairman of the General Program Committee and contributing editor for *The Helping Hand* and the *South Carolina Conference News*.

She cooperated with the College Caravans and Falcon Orphanage's Harvest Trains. During one round of conference rallies, preceding the Harvest Train, she raised $1,000 for the Orphanage Scholarship Fund.

She was a minister who worked as a successful evangelist and was the wife of Carl Thurman, who pastored the Georgetown church in 1953 at the time this article was written. She was appointed a Sunday School District Booster, taught the Young Ladies Bible Class of the local church, and was a board member of their Woman's Auxiliary.[36]

Martha Edna Brown Virden
Georgia and North Carolina Conferences
by
Dr. James Adams

"Martha (Mattie) Edna Brown was born March 10, 1876, in Pike County, Georgia, into a Southland still suffering the ravages of a bloody Civil War. She was the oldest of four daughters and the fifth of eight children of Confederate veteran Dr. Allen Wilburn Brown and Susan Shuptrine Brown. Her parents were devout Methodists, attending the local Fincher Methodist Church where she was converted in a revival at the age of eighteen.

"Her conversion was for her a profound personal experience, markedly changing the focus of her life, which was manifested in a zeal for ministry and service. This zeal remained undimmed even after she assumed the duties of a housewife upon her marriage to Charles Edwin Virden on February 10, 1901, and the birth of a daughter, Annie Sue, November 10, 1902. With tireless energy and a real sense of mission, she continued her community outreach efforts of visiting the sick, supporting prayer meetings and distributing Christian literature.

"Ever seeking and searching for a fuller and richer Christian walk, she found fulfillment in the early holiness revival which came to her community, led primarily by several Methodist ministers around the turn of the twentieth century. She joined a number of her contemporaries in responding to the preaching of a renewal of the Wesleyan doctrine of entire sanctification and wholeheartedly sought and testified to receiving this experience. When her local Methodist church was reluctant to accommodate this renewal movement, she along with a contingent of friends of a similar persuasion, identified with a new congregation which was organized under the auspices of the Middle Georgia Holiness Association. This congregation affiliated with the Pentecostal Holiness Church in 1913, she being a founding member of what continues today as the Mountain Gap Pentecostal Church in the Georgia Conference.

"Shortly thereafter, in May, 1904, she was widowed. Bereft and grieved, but undaunted, she continue her Christian ministry efforts with renewed zeal. Thus, when she first heard the doctrine of Pentecostal baptism preached in her home community in 1907, she readily sought and received this experience. From this point on, she gave herself unreservedly to Christian ministry, becoming an ordained minister of the Pentecostal Holiness Church in November 1911, shortly after its organization earlier that year. At this juncture, she began to range farther [afield] with her ministry, conducting meetings and revival services farther from home.

"Feeling God's call for a broader ministry and the need for more preparation, in July 1913, she enrolled in Holmes Missionary and Bible Institute at Paris Mountain, Altamont, South Carolina, where she studied under its founders, the Reverend and Mrs. N. J. Holmes. She continued, alternating between missionary work in the North Carolina mountains and her studies at Holmes in summer until 1915. In the meantime, she transferred her ministerial credentials to the North Carolina Conference of the Pentecostal Holiness Church. She then felt God calling her as a missionary to China and began itinerating with Miss E. May Law who, then home on furlough, was preparing to return to her missionary work in China.

"Upon traveling and ministering together with Miss Law among Pentecostal groups over much of the United States, Mrs. Virden gained commitments for support from churches in Arizona, California, Washington, Oregon, and New Jersey. She and her daughter, together with Miss Law, sailed from San Francisco on October 17, 1917, on the *S. S. China* . . . .

"In March of 1920, her missionary stint ended, and on March 20 she and her daughter sailed from Hong Kong . . . arriving in San Francisco on

April 15, 1920. Never one to rest on past accomplishments, she immediately launched a ministry of promoting foreign missions, especially to China, which extended over the remainder of her life. She began this effort in Atlanta, Georgia in September 1920, and from there continued to plan her schedule to visit churches as they invited her." The General Conference of the Pentecostal Holiness Church, meeting in Roanoke, Virginia, May 3-10, 1921, recognized her missionary service and effectiveness with an unprecedented measure. She was appointed 'Missionary Evangelist' for the entire Church throughout all of its conferences. She was the first and, perhaps, the only one to be given this distinction. As one might expect, this gesture substantially enhanced her efforts to promote the cause of foreign missions and the support of missionaries throughout the Church.

"As she traveled among the churches, she pioneered the establishment of missionary societies in local churches, with the organization of both youth and adult societies. These missionary societies were designed to increase the awareness and the visibility of foreign missions and to promote its support in local churches. She was invited by those of other denominations and organizations as well to tell about her missionary experience and to present the cause of foreign missions.

"The invitations increasingly came, and her passion for reaching China's unreached masses with the gospel of Christ continued unabated for some fifteen years following her return from active service in the China mission field. Over this period, she was constantly engaged, tirelessly criss-crossing the country from south to north and from east to west informing and inspiring all those who gave her opportunity with her passionate concern for those souls who could only be reached through missionary outreach. Not only did she speak for missions in churches and religious groups, but civic organizations and radio stations also invited her to speak.

"Such fervency and intensity in the pursuit of her ministry took a heavy toll on her health and vigor in her mature years. Toward the end of these fifteen years of missionary evangelism, her health began to deteriorate rapidly, often requiring periods of convalescence between her travels. However, her zeal to tell the story of missions continued to drive her until, while enroute from Detroit, Michigan, to Oakland, California, she was forced to stop with friends in Phoenix, Arizona, to rest. While there, she grew worse, requiring hospitalization. She passed away on December 1, 1936, and was carried back to her native Georgia for her funeral at Fincher Methodist Church and burial in the Brown family burial plot in that church's cemetery."

(**Author's note:** Dr. James Adams sent this information about his great aunt, Martha Virden. The detailed comments about her missionary work are not included here, as I'm dealing primarily with ministry in the United States. Her work as a missionary is cited in *The Simultaneous Principle*, written by Dr. Frank G. Tunstall.)

Mrs. Virden's daughter, Annie Sue Virden, described her mother as "an ardent and zealous worker for God and the church." She believed that God gave Martha a patient love that endured no matter the wrong she suffered or the trials she bore. She had a love to seek the lost, a desire to intercede for their salvation. She knew that the Great Physician could heal, the Holy Spirit could comfort, and the Lord could give victory instead of defeat. She found God worthy of her trust.

Once while holding a revival at the Methodist church in Hope Mills, South Carolina, she experienced an attack by a group of boys who threw rocks against the outside walls. Some members of the congregation left the building because of their fear, but Mrs. Virden remained calm as if nothing had happened.

After this meeting, she went to Saint Pauls. The superintendent of the mill there was unfavorable towards the services, especially after he heard Martha was holiness and was teaching that people could be saved from sin. He sent a message to her to stop the meeting. Since it was being held in a home, Mrs. Virden asked if any of the household worked at the mill. When she found out that one of the sons worked there, she did move the services to another home not associated with the mill. She organized a Sunday school there with sixty members. Later, a chapel was built in that part of the town.

In the early days of her ministry in North Carolina, she wrote a letter about one of her meetings stating, "Many times rocks were thrown against the church, windows were crashed. Someone fired a pistol as we came out the door at close of service. The shot went over our heads. God took care of us. Our trust was in Him; we were not hurt."

One example of Mrs. Virden's faith in God's never failing power was told by Mrs. H. H. Goff in the book *Laid Up Treasures*: "Our son had spinal meningitis with terrible convulsions for twenty hours. He suffered all night, one convulsion after another. Next morning when we were praying for him, the spirit of God rested upon Sister Virden; she rebuked the enemy. The child was healed. Sister Virden prayed for the sick and they were healed. God used her to cheer the faint, help the fallen, and encourage those in despair."

Annie further depicted her mother as having "a spirit of forgiveness, humility, meekness and forbearance that caused her to endure much for Christ's sake. She faced life with her head up, developed a power, an endurance, a confident life; loving vitality that carried her energetically through life and made her work a blessing to humanity. Thrust out to learn the will of God in persecutions and hardships, she accepted her afflictions with gentleness and submissiveness, with a promise of a glorious tomorrow. Love for her King continually drew her heavenward and made her less of this world."

From the moment of her conversion, she experienced a complete spiritual transition. Her daily prayer was that self would die out and Christ would be seen. Annie Sue continued, "There was a clear consciousness of the Holy Spirit in her every movement; a spontaneous force for Christ, marked by an experience which lifted her up and compelled her out of herself; caused her to attain the highest and best that life offered, a steadfast apostolic spirituality and faith. Without this definite faith her life would have been empty and the world would not have been as greatly blessed and enriched."

The Pentecostal Holiness Church lost one of its most courageous and worthy members when she died after forty-five year of enduring strenuous difficulties in her work for the Lord. Her place could never be filled.

Churches in the mountains, valleys, towns, and cities of North and South Carolina were opened under her ministry. Many heard the gospel she preached before going to their heavenly reward. Others still living remember her prayers and sermons. Had she not gone into places where others feared to go, some would have not heard of God's redeeming love.

In the words of her daughter, "The world sounded no trumpets, nor rung any bells for her, but I am sure there is a shining record in The Book of Life. If crowns are worn there [heaven], one of purest gold [is] adorning her brow. Many souls for whom she had given her best gladly welcomed her. Others will follow bearing testimony. She has left her loving spirit in her stead."[37]

Gladys Watson
Alpha (Alabama) Conference
by
Donald Everett Watson, II

Gladys' grandson wrote, "My grandmother was saved when my father was 14 months old. She said that she had not been to church in about 2 years, but fell under conviction at home. After her salvation, she felt pressured to join the East Brewton Church of God in East Brewton, AL. Although they were good people, she did not feel that this was what God wanted her to do. It was about the same time that the Alco Pentecostal Holiness Church was organized in 1946 and was building its first building.

"Somewhere around 1985, the Lord led my grandmother into a new ministry outside of and in addition to her pastor ministry. This work involved writing monthly gospel literature in the form of tri-folds, quad-fold, and other pamphlets. I was just a teenager when she began this ministry.

"Recently [It isn't clear from the report who gave Donald the box.] gave me a box of her old writings that she had saved through the years. In one of these tri-folds entitled, *'Women in God's Vineyard,'* she recounted a good part of her early conversion and calling. (Although some of this may be somewhat repetitive of what I have told you, some of these sentiments are in her own words.)

> Please let me give a personal testimony in regard to the Christian woman and her relationship to the Church. I was not reared in Church. I missed out on a very important influence upon my life. My parents were good moral people, who knew that there was a God and that Jesus was a Savior. They were good law-abiding people, but they were not Church people. There was no church in our community near enough to attend, so I knew nothing about the Church.
>
> When I was twelve, there was a revival held in a home in our community. I attended and was saved. It was a wonderful, joyous experience for me. But having no Church to attend and no Biblical knowledge or training, I soon fell away from God. But I knew that salvation was real. God always dealt with me – always! So one day, at the age of twenty-two, God began to move in my life very forcefully. I was still in the same community, no Church nearby, no one to consult with about getting back to Jesus. But I began to read the Bible. I really didn't know how to pray but I began to pray. So really, I have learned all that I know and have been led in every detail of my life through God's mercy and my complete dependence upon God Himself.

It took about two weeks of desperate misery to bring my-self to a place that I was willing for God's will to be accomplished in me. You may have heard someone speak of 'old-time conviction.' Well, old time conviction came down upon me and remained with me until I made an unconditional surrender to Almighty God. I have in Him everything. He gave me eternal life.

I began to go to Church. I would hear others testify of wha God had done for them. They were saved, sanctified, and baptized with the Holy Ghost. I began to study my Bible to find out what these experiences were. I found them provided in God's Word and I began to seek God for these experiences in my life. God dealt with me to go to some people to straighten out some things I had said and the attitude that I had had. As soon as I obeyed Him He wonderfully sanctified me, set me apart wholly unto the Lord Jesus Christ to be used in His service and for His cause.

About a year later, after much prayer and dedication, and the study of the Word, God began to deal with my heart about the ministry. I would be in the altar every service asking for the Holy Spirit baptism. Every time I prayed, I would say, 'Lord, I will do anything you want me to do.' But deep down within my heart there was a thought, 'But preach.' I was not quite willing to do what I knew in my heart God was leading me to do. But I was so hungry to receive the Baptism of the Holy Spirit that I continued to ask until one night I got willing. I said, 'Lord, <u>I will do anything</u> you want me to do,' and I meant it – anything! . . .that was the night Heaven came down and filled my soul. I surrendered and He gave me the gift of the Holy Ghost confirmed with a heavenly language I had never spoken before . . . When God called me into the ministry, I did not know that some Churches do not allow their women to preach. I did not know that some Churches do not license women or ordain them. I just followed the leadership of the Lord and He has led me all the way.

"My grandmother was given her first opportunity in a revival by Brother and Sister Eby, two Mennonite area pastors who later went to the Cuban mission-field. Granddaddy said that my grandmother was opposed in this first revival by several of the Free-Holiness women in the area because her toes were showing through the tips of her shoes. However, it seemed that this revival was given Divine sanction when 4 souls were saved on the first night of the meeting!

"Of the different churches that she pastored during her lifetime, these included Century Pentecostal Holiness Church, Century, Forida; Phillipsville Pentecostal Holiness, Bay Minette, AL; Alco Pentecostal Holiness Church, Brewton, Alabama; East Brewton Pentecostal Holiness Church (now Faith Community Fellowship), East Brewton, Aabama. And although she was faithful to fulfill her mission wherever she was give the opportunity, her burden was in East Brewton, where she pioneered in 1967 and pastored for over 30 years."

(**Author's note:** Donald Everett Watson II wrote this about his grandmother, Gladys Watson. My thanks to him for such detailed information on her life and ministry and for providing the tri-fold pamphlet which is quoted above.)

Deborah Whipple
Heartland Conference

An article appeared in *Evangelism USA* in 1999 titled "Taking Control of the Air Before Sending in the Ground Troops," written by Debbie Whipple, an ordained minister in the Heartland Conference. The emphasis was on Prayer Walk Strategy, which was designed to prepare for revival based on a prophetic utterance by Chuck Pierce who said, "There will be revival through the church planting system where there will be great knowledge in how to church plant and how to come into increase in the future."

The first Prayer Walk was held October 2-4, 1998, in Denver, Colorado for the River Rock Church. Seven intercessors traveled to Denver from various parts of the United States to take part. Debbie led this intercessory team with help from Bane and Barbara James, Francis Pike, and Paul Brafford.

Many meaningful words of prophecy were given to Bronson Howell, pastor of River Rock Church, and his church planting team. All agreed that "prayer is the most vital part of any new work we do for the Lord."

The second Prayer Walk was in Lexington, Kentucky for Living Hope Christian Center, where Mark and Keeli McCallister pastored. God did marvelous things for the church by giving them a worship leader and three new families who made a commitment to God.

Evangelism USA closed out the year of 1998 with a Prayer Walk held in Oklahoma City, specifically for Centro de Celebracion, a church founded and pastored by Rev. Charlene West. She sensed a strong leading to pray over the city which led to many prophetic words and direction for the new church plant.[43]

In another article, "Don't Treat Me Like I'm Dying," that Deborah wrote for the IPHC *Experience,* and was published posthumously in March 2006, we get a closer personal look at who she was. She was administrative assistant in Evangelism USA at the Pentecostal Holiness Resource and Development Center in Oklahoma City, Oklahoma. She felt that was the best place one could work while fighting cancer.

In 2003, she was diagnosed with colon cancer and underwent the usual treatment: surgery, chemotherapy, and radiation. Things went well for a while; everyone thinking she was finished with the ordeal. However, in a routine checkup, the doctor found spots on her lungs and one in her liver, all of which were inoperable. Debbie wrote, "His [doctor's] prognosis was that I had six months to a year to live without chemotherapy and five years with the treatments."

Even with an overwhelming display of compassion and kindness from people around her, she began to notice that they were treating her differently. She soon realized that they were looking at her as if she were dying and that each interaction might be the last time they would see her.

Further commenting on having to battle this kind of attitude from others, she said, "I would climb the mountain of faith and belief; then one look of sorrow – reminding me what I was up against – would send me tumbling into the pit of despair."

She felt she had been given the tools to fight the enemy, but seeing a lack of faith in others' eyes was worse than a death blow. She had to force herself not to agree with them. She thought she needed them to agree with her in faith and prayer.

Using her words from the article, "As I see it, the only position I am given in the Word is to *believe* that He is my healer and there is none other. I have come to that place of peace and trust in the One who holds the keys to death, hell, and the grave. I am convinced that I will not leave this earth until my Lord says it is time. My earthly father has always told me that the greatest gift God has given us, besides our salvation, is that of not knowing when we are going to die. For that reason, no one has the right to speak death over us. We belong to the King, and He is the *giver* and *taker* of life . . . if I could speak one word to my brothers and sisters, it would be this: Don't treat me like I'm dying."[38]

(**Author's note:** Debbie ended a valiant three-year battle with cancer on January 5, 2006, when she went to be with the Lord.)

Effie Collier Williams
North Carolina Conference
by
Ruth Brookshire

"Mama was the daughter of a tenant farmer/carpenter/well-digger near Micro, NC. Her parents were members of a Pentecostal Holiness Church. Mama learned to trust God from their demonstration of faith in God to provide for them and their 11 children in financially hard times, especially during the depression. In 1934 she married Leon M. Williams and lived on a small farm. When my parents committed their lives to God in a revival at Bizzell Grove PH Church, Princeton, NC in 1940, she was called to preach. At that time, there were three children.

"She was an industrious woman and made many of the children's clothes, quilts, brooms, raised chickens, milked the cow, picked cotton, cooked, made butter, cleaned, swept yards, helped gather produce, dairy products and meat from the farm on Fridays, spending the next day in a distant town marketing the goods through residential neighborhoods. She helped build the new house next door for the growing family, soon to be six children.

"She was busy in church activities: she taught adult Sunday school classes, organized and served as president of the first Woman's Auxiliary at her local church, played the piano, led singing, researched and wrote the church history, and organized and directed the first Vacation Bible School. For a couple of years while Daddy was working in a job requiring him to be away all week, she took on the responsibility of the farm, driving the tractor, plowing the corn, cotton, beans, etc. in addition to her regular household duties and overseeing the four children still at home.

"She studied faithfully to meet the requirements of the conference to receive minister's license. Many days we returned from school and found her studying and writing, her Bible and other books piled on the ironing board which she used for a desk. After becoming a pastor, she served faithfully in the churches assigned to her, driving approximately 45 minutes each way to the first two churches for Sunday and for mid-week services.

"While pastoring, she also managed her own business, Johnston County Pecan Market, which was open for business six days a week. Somehow, she managed to do some cooking, sewing, and quilting during the hours which were not busy. (She made and sold innumerable pecan pies to cover renovations to the Selma PH Church, her last pastorate.) After resting for an hour or so on Sunday afternoons, she would drive to visit some of the members of the congregation. Her life was so full. She died at age 52, just a few weeks after resigning her pastorate due to ill health."

(**Author's note:** Ruth Brookshire, daughter of Effie Williams, sent in this information about her mother. Sister Williams pastored the Warsaw Pentecostal Holiness Church, Warsaw, North Carolina; Vicks Chapel PH Church, Rocky Mount, North Carolina; Selma PH Church, Selma, North Carolina during her twenty-five years of ministry. Ruth is an ordained minister in the Alpha Conference. Her biographical sketch is also included in this chapter.)

"My Grandmother, Dollie York, Was a P. H. Pioneer"
East Oklahoma Conference
by
Thurnace York

"Another name joined the list of valiant, deceased Pentecostal Holiness pioneers with the passing of Dollie York. Very aged and infirm, she was desirous to go to her long home. In death, as in life, she was ready for the higher orders of the big General up above. A few weeks ago she laid down her armor and, passing through death, entered into life eternal.

"There are those who might believe she laid down some things years ago with the silencing of her voice in sermon and song, and so far as the usefulness of her ministry was concerned. I think upon the humble cottage where her last years were spent, with few visitors and small recognition for the years of hardship in blazing a gospel trail for the infant Midwest Pentecostal Holiness Church. Hers was not a death that received world coverage. She died humbly and semi-forgotten. As often is the case with older persons, those who once flocked to hear Dan and Dollie York had passed away or were far removed. People sped by on the highway near her home and seldom glanced to notice or care that couple lived there who made a mark for Christ and blazed a trail that others might follow; here lived a man and wife who gave everything they had to God and were never sorry one day for the sacrifices they made or the hardships they endured.

"But I am sure grandmother's entrance into heaven was a royal one," Thurnace relates. "God keeps books, and he never forgets a life lived for His glory. He remembers long after churches cease to call for meetings, and stationing committees fail to call a name to mind. *For God is not unrighteous to forget your work and labour of love, which ye have shewed toward his name in that ye have ministered to the saints, and do minister.*" (Heb. 5:10) He watches over His own tenderly, not only in the night, but in the closing hours of life when failing strength precludes a more active service than worshipping God with strong and simple adoration.

"Grandmother was a remarkable woman. Once grandfather, Dan York, wrote a booklet of their life events. In it he says that his wife fit the description of the good woman in Proverbs 31. He quoted the entire chapter as an apt description of grandmother, Dollie York.

"She knew what it was to be put to severe tests, to be subjected to hardship and privation, to be called upon to make extreme sacrifice and to be unselfish far beyond normal expectation. She ministered in the days when holiness people were whipped, sandbagged, spit upon, drenched with slop water, egged, thrown at with snakes, and otherwise subject to gross indignities. She and Dan endured all these things and even faced the threat of hanging for the gospel they preached. They were shot at and slandered. Indeed, their record would well remind one of the latter part of Hebrews 11 which describes the sufferings of countless unnamed heroes of faith.

"Through all this grandmother and grandfather preached with joy and with power, their triumphant theme being: 'Zion marches on when under the blood.' With grandfather at a portable organ and with tambourine in grandmother's hand, they lifted magnificent voices in melodies of praise and power. They were known as the 'singing Yorks,' and they had a message of fire too. Sister Dollie was not a mild-tempered woman when it came to fighting the devil. Her eyes would snap and she would take to the battle like an entire platoon wrapped up in one. When she and the Lord let loose on the devil, he had a fight on his hands for sure. They dug thousands out of the pits of sin, reaching them from countless street corners, in prisons and out-of-the way places, as well as from the pulpit. Their pulpits were anywhere there was a sinner to be reached or a Christian to be spurred on. No place was too rugged for them to set their hands at digging out a church, and many churches in the mid-west stand as memorials of the early efforts of Dan and Dollie York." [39]

Some of these ladies mentioned are still living but are not actively involved in the ministry due to infirmities brought on by age. After reading about them, we know something of their fervency of spirit, their extraordinary determination, their profound perseverance, and their unquestionable devotion to their heavenly Father. They have left behind "footprints in the sand," so those who follow them can know, without doubt, that the path in which they walked will lead them home. Where He is, there we shall also be.

Their stories may have inspired you, and, perhaps, have made you weep at what these women have had to endure – yes**, endure** – for the sake of extending the gospel to the ends of the earth. They have not been discouraged; they have not let down in their zeal; they have refused to allow difficult circumstances to thwart the Kingdom work. People of lesser courage and stamina may have said it could not be done, but the power of the Holy Spirit working in the life of a person dedicated to the cause cannot be stopped by any force of the enemy. Let the naysayers and those with a negative vote be silenced in the presence of Him who is able to do whatever He wills.

In spite of persecution, poverty, loneliness, tragedy, loss, deprivation, and countless other obstacles, these ladies of faith and determination moved forward with only one goal in mind: reach the lost at any cost. Their desire was simply to exalt Jesus, to lift Him up for others to see, to point the sinner to the cross, and to encourage the saint to plod onward and upward toward the prize. This earth is a better place because of them, but *"the world was not worthy of them."* – Hebrews 11:38a-NIV.

Many of these ladies distinguished themselves in those things which were their responsibility in the Women's Ministries of the denomination. Although they may not have always been preaching, that was their field of ministry, and God took note of everything they did. We may never know all the good they accomplished, but that really is not important. What is important is that they followed His leading and devoted themselves to the work to which they were called.

TO GOD BE THE GLORY!

---

[1] Charlton Laird, *Webster's New World Thesaurus*, p. 669.
[2] William Shakespeare, "Macbeth," Act 5, Scene 5.
[3] *The Challenge*, Summer 1989, p. 3.
[4] Gertrude Blake Dillard, *The Advocate*, August 11, 1973, p. 7. (Gertrude is Rev. Mary Blake's daughter.)
[5] "Reverend Natalie Carnes Honored," *The Challenge*, Spring 1970, p. 4; biographical information sent in by her and used with permission.
[6] Respondent information form.
[7] Ann McGraw, "The Hands of a Shepherdess," *The Helping Hand*, November/December 1995, p. 13. (Ann is Rev. Violet Curlee's sister.)
[8] Mark and Judy Kamleiter, "Women in our Heritage," *The Helping Hand*, March 1977, p. 4.
[9] South Carolina Conference Minutes 2003; e-mails from Paula Leake dated May 27, 2010.
[10] "Appreciation Committee Report," North Carolina Conference Minutes 1984, pp. 37-38.
[11] Jim Pharr, *The Fayetteville Observer*, copyright 1977. Reprinted with permission.
[12] Alfreda Flowers, "General W. A. President, Mrs. Lila Isaac," *The Helping Hand*, July 1977, p. 5.
[13] "Mrs. C. F. Isaac Elected General President," *The Helping Hand*, November 1961, p. 4.
[14] Mrs. C. F. Isaac, "From the Field," *The Helping Hand*, September 1959, p. 4.
[15] Mrs. H. W. Brown, "W. A. Convention Elections," *The Helping Hand*, November 1961, p. 5.
[16] Alfreda Flowers, *The Helping Hand*, July 1977, p. 5.
[17] Agnes Robinson, "A Great Lady," *The Helping Hand*, September 1977, p. 5.
[18] "The First General Vice-President," *The Helping Hand*, September 1961, p. 13.
[19] "Our W. A. Officials," *The Helping Hand*, October 1961, p. 4.
[20] Mrs. Blanche Leon King, "Foreword," J. H. King, *Yet Speaketh*.
[21] Blanche Leon King, *The Advocate*, September 5, 1950, p. 10.
[22] Rev. W. Eddie Morris, "A Mother's Day Tribute to," *The Advocate*, May 14, 1978, pp. 9, 15.
[23] Rev. W. W. Carter, "Late Flower," *The Advocate*, November 30, 1950, pp. 4-5.
[24] Mrs. J. L. Russell, Sr., "Women in our Heritage," *The Helping Hand*, April 1977, pp. 3-4.
[25] 1982 North Carolina Conference Minutes, pp. 59-60.
[26] E-mail dated February 20, 2009 from Sylvia Morris, daughter of Daisy Morris.

[27] Information was sent in by Sister Hampton's daughter, Wanda Elliott.
[28] "The First Gen. V. Pres.," *The Helping Hand*, September 1961, p. 12.
[29] Archive files of the South Carolina Conference.
[30] This information was gleaned from several editions of *The Challenge*: Winter 1970, p. 5; Winter 1971, p. 3; Spring 1972, pp. 6, 9; Spring 1978, p. 7; Summer 1982, p. 8; Summer 1993; e-mail to Joel from Mike Coble found on internet April 17, 2009.
[31] Rev. Marvin Brown, "The Advocate Salutes Martha Roberta Rose," *The Advocate*, May 13, 1979, p. 11.
[32] Shirley Spencer, "A Woman with a Mandate from God," *Issachar File*, March 4, 1999, p. 4.
[33] This information comes from a colorful brochure, "100th Camp Meeting 1910-2010 – Centennial Celebration, South Carolina Conference, International Pentecostal Holiness Church," designed by The Welby Company and printed by the South Carolina Conference announcing the Centennial Celebration that took place June 17 – July 2, 2010 at Lake City, South Carolina.
[34] This sketch was presented by Dr. Janice Marshburn, Director of Deborah's Daughters, North Carolina Conference.
[35] This bio was sent in by Ada Lee Thurman's daughter, Charlotte Thurman Iaquinta.
[36] Mrs. J. R. Cohn, "Our President," *The Helping Hand*, November 1953, pp. 10-11.
[37] Annie Sue Virden, *Laid Up Treasures: The Life of Mrs. M. E. Virden*, pp. 21, 25-27, 30, 109-110, 146.
[38] Debbie Whipple, "Taking Control Of The Air, Before Sending In The Ground Troops," *Evangelism USA*, January/February 1999, p. 2; "Don't Treat Me Like I'm Dying," *IPHC Experience*, March 2006, pp. 6-7.
[39] Thurnace York, "My Grandmother, Dollie York, Was a P. H. Pioneer," *The Advocate*, November 6, 1958, p. 12.

CHAPTER 9

In Memory of Her

"I tell you the truth, wherever the gospel is preached throughout the world, what she has done will also be told, in memory of her" – Mark 14:9-NIV.

These obituaries speak clearly that the dear ladies mentioned breathed their last breath with praise on their lips and joy in their hearts. The words written about them pay tribute to them for their devoted service in the vineyard of the Lord. Each in her own way ministered as a pastor, evangelist, Sunday school teacher, Women's Ministries official, or in some other capacity. They were faithful; they were energetic; they were compassionate; they made a lasting impression for good.

Mrs. Agnes Robinson
South Carolina Conference
by
Lois Tripp

"On March 11, 1986, Agnes Robinson heard the hum of awakening spring in another world. The hum was so faint that no one else heard it but it was audible to her as she gazed at the western horizon into the eyes of her Saviour.

"The seasons of her life are over here. Standing at the river, no wind rustled the leaves; there was no lapping of the water. The only sound that Agnes heard was the gentle calling of Jesus as He led her across to the glorious world without sunset because there is no need for the sun. HE is the light of that city. Her roses have no thorns and her green plants need no water.

"Agnes was a lovely, vivacious lady who served her Lord and her church with all her strength. She had been the wife of a very successful pastor [the late Rev. H. P. Robinson], local Woman's Auxiliary president, South Carolina Conference WA Board for sixteen years; and was International WA President from 1977-1985. She had served as Editor of the WA magazine *The Helping Hand* 28 years; editor of *Reach* magazine 8 years; and Editor of the *Teen Teacher* [Sunday school] magazine 6 years. She also represented her denomination as secretary-treasurer of the Pentecostal Fellowship of North America Woman's Auxiliary and vice president of the Women's Fellowship of the National Association of Evangelicals.

"Since August, 1985, she had been a friend and confidant to me. I respected her vast experience in Women's Ministries. She had prayed and labored vigorously for the transition from Woman's Auxiliary to Women's Ministries and she saw that dream realized. On Monday afternoon, March 10, just hours before she made her transition, we talked extensively about the potential of women ministering and the GA [Girls' Auxiliary] program. Her influence will continue to be felt and experienced.

"As I stood beside the grave and watched them lower her earthly body into the ground, I realized that winter was over and spring was awakening for Agnes, the earth, and Women's Ministries.

"We will miss you, Agnes, but rejoice with you because your winter is over and eternal spring has begun!"[1]

"My Friend . . . My Spiritual Mother"
by
Doris Moore

"Who can find a virtuous woman? I did! Agnes Robinson was a virtuous woman.

"She was always giving to others and she had so much to give: love to those who felt no one cared; hope to those who felt defeated; encouragement to those who were depressed; strength to those who were weak; companionship to those who were lonely; patience with everyone she met.

"Mrs. Robinson loved missions and was truly a missionary at heart. When a need was presented by a missionary, she listened and responded by doing everything in her power to meet that need. She loved the missionaries and was never too busy to listen to their problems or experiences of joy. One of the highlights of her life was visiting the mission fields and sharing the love of God. She commented many times of her gratitude to the women of the Pentecostal Holiness Church for making those trips possible.

"Mrs. Robinson always had a smile for everyone she met and her favorite words were 'I love you – you are special.' She was special to me and everyone who met her.

"So many things I remember about you, Mrs. Robinson! I remember when you worked long hours preparing for a workshop or editing the *Helping Hand*. Also your working day and night to put together the new manual for the Women's Ministries Department, and always making everyone who came into your office feel as if they were the most important person on earth.

"I remember sharing your times of loneliness – when you longed to see your dear husband, with whom you now walk hand in hand through the streets of heaven. I have heard you wish you could spend more time with your three beautiful girls and their families, you wanted to be near those precious grandchildren.

"I remember seeing your face radiant with God's love as we shared God's Word and prayed – Oh! How you could open the Scriptures.

"I remember hearing your voice ring with laughter as we put the Christmas tree together – upside down!

"I remember most of all your quiet and gentle spirit. You never got angry with anyone or even raised your voice – I never saw you lose your temper. You were the picture.

"Ms. Agnes, death has taken you from us, but nothing can take away the wonderful memories I have of the years we shared together. Today I am a better person because you touched my life. I loved you in life – I love you now – you will always be my special friend. Thank you for letting me serve you and for being my Spiritual Mother!"[2]

Mrs. Lila Marguerite Green Isaac

A eulogy, written by Jewelle Stewart, was printed in the *IPHC Experience*, September 2006. The entire text of this article appears below.

"Lila Marguerite Greene Isaac, former general Woman's Auxiliary president, passed away at her daughter's home in Virginia Beach, Virginia, after several months of declining health. Her body was laid to rest beside that of her husband in the historic Lakewood Cemetery near Jackson, Mississippi. She was 94. Until her final hours, her mind remained sharp and her wit lively. She enjoyed life and lived every moment to the fullest.

"Mrs. Isaac spent her early years in Texas, where she graduated from Waco High School and attended college, studying public speaking – a subject she drew from over and over throughout her life. She married Carl F. Isaac in 1929, and together they entered full-time Christian ministry as evangelists, pastors, and administrator, roles they continued to fill until his retirement in 1972 and her retirement in 1977. At that time, she stepped down from a 16-year tenure as general president of the Woman's Auxiliary of the Pentecostal Holiness Church. She served in that capacity longer than any other leader.

"As general WA president, Mrs. Isaac traveled extensively throughout the United States as well as to Canada, Mexico, South America, Europe, Asia, and Africa. During those years, she also served as president of the Women's Auxiliary of the Pentecostal Fellowship of North America and as president of the Women's Fellowship of the National Association of Evangelicals.

"Mrs. Isaac was fully engaged in living life with excellence. As a lifelong learner, by example she challenged those she led to emulate her. Upon her 1961 election as the general WA president, Mrs. Isaac became the first in that role to serve on the General Board of Administration (GBA), the highest governing body of the Pentecostal Holiness Church. She broke ground for women in leadership and did so with her characteristic excellence, superb articulation, and true humility. Mrs. Isaac initiated and developed the annual WM Day and the first regional training retreats, which evolved into the quadrennial leadership training for conference WM Boards and Girls' Ministries teams now know as LIFT – Lila Isaac Fellowship and Training Summits.

"Her sparkling eyes and vibrant spirit drew people to her, and they were never disappointed. She was not only intelligent; she was interesting and inspiring. In her late 80s, Mrs. Isaac was the guest speaker at the LIFT retreat in Virginia Beach [Virginia] with the theme, 'You Are a Star!' Everyone present was in awe at her articulate message about the stars and how each one was in her own way, formed to be a 'star' for God.

"Every facet of Lila Isaac's life was polished to perfection. Her writing, speaking, conversing, training, and leadership gifts all displayed the flawless qualities that marked this rare stone, a precious gem of a woman who loved Christ and His work more than life itself.

"Mrs. Lila G. Isaac was the epitome of the Proverbs 31 woman. On behalf of her spiritual heirs and daughters, all those she served by example and continues to serve through programs she founded, I call her 'Blessed.'"[3]

She was a member of the Tri-State Conference.

Mary B. McKeehan
by
Rev. A. E. Robinson

Sister Mary McKeehan was born in Appanoose County, Iowa, February 23, 1872, and died May 12, 1917, at age forty-five. Brother Robinson states that his first meeting with her was when they were running the little paper, *Live Coals,* in Mercer, Missouri. Being in need of help, he interview Mary, and a few month later she joined them. That was in the early spring of 1902, and she was there almost continuously until they left Mercer in May 1904.

During that time she and Sarah Payne slept on a homemade bunk, in the Robinson's little two-roomed house, and worked together unselfishly and tirelessly as a team. Whether it was to work in the garden, set type, sew or visit the sick, anything that needed to be done – they were "on the job."

When the printing outfit was moved to Royston, Georgia, Mary again went to Mr. Robinson and worked with her usual energy, in spite of the fact that she had health problems that many times hindered her working; however, she possessed the rare quality of "stickability" that is so necessary.

In those days, Mrs. McKeehan was a member of the Fire Baptized Holiness Church. [That was the denomination that merged with the Pentecostal Holiness Church in 1911.] She was an ordained evangelist in that body and loved to preach the Word in its fullness. When she entered into evangelistic work in the early part of 1907, she came in contact with the teaching of Pentecost. After a careful and deliberate study of the subject, she became a seeker for the baptism of the Holy Spirit. In a meeting conducted by Brother J. H. King, who was Bishop of the Pentecostal Holiness denomination even before the merger in 1911 with the Fire Baptized Holiness Church, she did receive the same baptism that Peter and the early apostles received. From that time on, she never wavered in her belief or teaching of this Bible truth.

In 1908, at the Falcon Camp Meeting, she offered her services as representative of the Falcon Orphanage, now the Falcon Children's Home and, in that capacity, visited around leaving a good influence everywhere she went. She went to her home early in 1909, thinking she would return to the work in Royston again, but rather had to stay to care for her aged parents.

Brother Robinson writes, "Sister Mary kept free from the wildness that floated around in the name of Pentecost, without on the other hand compromising a hair's breadth with the errors that grew like weeds around them. All accounts given by our evangelists who visited there were favorable as touching her life and steadfastness, and even those who differed with her were obliged to admit the holiness of her life."

She left this world triumphantly, shouting and praising God until the last. With her departure, the Pentecostal Holiness Church lost one of its faithful members.[4]

The 1946 Yearbook paid tribute to a number of ministers who are referred to as "Our Sainted Dead."

CONFERENCE

Alabama	Mrs. I. H. Presley	1944
California	Rev. Mrs. Urchie Hallam, Evangelist	1940
	Rev. Mrs. Era Weese, Pastor	1943
East Oklahoma	Emma Revell	1937
	Mrs. C. L. Smith	1946
Eastern Virginia	Mrs. I. N. Spence	1929
Florida	Mrs. Millie Cannon	
	Mrs. Maude Harris Pitts	
Georgia	Mrs. J. D. Park	1935
	Mrs. Neelie Goolsby	1941

	Mrs. S. T. E. Dudley	1943
	Mrs. C. A. Jordan, Sr.	1944
North Carolina	Mrs. Annie Cotton Burnette	
Oklahoma	Grace Cook	1917
	Nancy Bond	1919
	Margaret Jones	1934
	Mrs. Jessie O. Campbell	1942
Ontario	Mrs. L. Martin	
Tri-State	Mrs. Janie Holland	1943
Upper South Carolina	Mrs. Avie Dunn	1940
	Mrs. J. R. Jones	1931
	Mrs. Bertha Pace	1940
	Mrs. F. A. Sullivan	1926
Virginia	Mrs. Alice Kelly	1926
	Mrs. Lucy Weis	1918
Western North Carolina	Miss Pearl Loftin [5]	

Rev. Beadie Noble

Sister Noble had been a Christian for forty-two years. In 1907, she heard the truth of the baptism of the Holy Spirit under the ministry of Rev. A. H. Butler. Upon hearing the doctrine, she accepted the truth and lived and preached it for years. She and her husband, Rev. R. D. Noble, joined the North Carolina Conference in 1912. Beadie was a faithful member, always standing up for the doctrines of the Pentecostal Holiness Church, which she loved so much until the time of her death.

Her funeral was conducted at the Kinston Pentecostal Holiness Church (her home church) by Rev. W. Eddie Morris, Conference Superintendent. He was assisted by Rev. A. H. Butler, a former pastor and superintendent, and by her pastor, Rev. L. E. Peyton. Her body was laid to rest in the Kinston cemetery, there to await the morning of the resurrection of the righteous dead.[6]

Rev. Edith Sutton

"It is written, 'Precious in the sight of the Lord is the death of His saints.'" Since last conference, the Lord promoted Sister Edith Sutton to her place in glory. She was faithful to her Christ and her conference since 1924. Using the words of the Master, "She is not dead, but sleepeth." May we who remain look forward in readiness to that great day of reunion.[7]

Rev. Venia Rodgers

Mrs. Rodgers and her husband, Rev. J. H. Rodgers, were involved in a head on car collision that fatally injured both of them. He was killed instantly and Sister Rodgers died about an hour later in a hospital as a result of the injuries received in the crash.

The accident occurred about 10 p.m., August 2, 1960, near Stoneville, North Carolina as the couple was returning to their home in Martinsville, Virginia after attending services at the Western North Carolina Conference Camp Meeting in Greensboro. Funeral services were held at the Martinsville Church. Bishop J. A. Synan and Conference Superintendent Rev. G. D. Yeatts preached the sermons and gave a final tribute to them as faithful ministers whose labors were ended and the final victory won.

Both of them were members of the Western North Carolina Conference. Mrs. Rodgers held Mission Workers License for several years and was given license to preach in 1954.

Some time in the early 1930s James Rodgers and his wife, Venia, attended a revival meeting near Martinsville when conviction seized their hearts. They went to the altar, repented of their sins, and believed on Jesus for salvation. Soon afterward, the young couple united with the Pentecostal Holiness Church in Martinsville and became active in the local church.

In 1956, Brother Rodgers became a General Evangelist and was active in evangelistic work. Sister Rodgers and two of their daughters traveled with him for about a year as a Family Evangelistic Party. She also conducted services elsewhere when she had the opportunity.[8]

Rev. Effie Poland

Mrs. Effie Poland, a minister in the North Carolina Conference for more that twenty-five years, passed to her reward Friday, December 13, 1963, in Parkview Hospital in Rocky Mount, North Carolina. Sister Poland had undergone surgery and was apparently getting better when a liver condition developed that sapped her strength beyond recovery.

Her funeral was held in her home church, Vaughn's Chapel. Rev. Jerome Hodges, Rev. Melvin Narron, and Rev. Eddie Morris conducted the funeral. Each spoke words befitting the life of this faithful saint of God who lived what she preached.[9]

Rev. Deborah Ellis

Rev. Deborah Ellis, long time member of the Ontario Conference, passed away at the age of seventy-five. She was faithful to her Lord and to her commitments as a minister in the Pentecostal Holiness Church. Her funeral was held in Ontario, on September 2, 1967.[10]

Rev. Effie Williams

Funeral services were conducted for Mrs. Effie Williams, Friday, March 7, 1969, at the Selma North Carolina Pentecostal Holiness Church of which she was pastor. She was a licensed minister in the North Carolina Conference having joined in 1955 and served faithfully for fourteen years. She was assistant pastor of Jones Grove and the Smithfield church and also pastored the Warsaw church and Vicks Chapel. For six years she was an evangelist.

Poor health caused her to give the church up for a short time, but she later resumed her duties as pastor. Her greatest desire was to please God, serve her church, and be a good wife and mother. In all these, she did a wonderful job. She continued to pastor until about two weeks before her death. She was faithful to the end; she fought a good fight; she finished her course. Now she is with her Lord and Savior.[11]

Rev. Mrs. L. A. Phillips

Mrs. Phillips joined the North Carolina Conference in 1966. She served as pastor of the Raeford Church most of the time, and even though she was in poor health, she worked untiringly to help build this church.

Rev. J. Doner Lee relates that "Her last words to me when she last visited the Conference Office about 10 days ago were, 'Brother Lee, I love my church and its people. I want to do God's will and to be found faithful in His service.'" She was faithful until the end.

Burial was in Westview Cemetery in Easley, South Carolina.[12]

Rev. Annie Odell Casper Taylor

Sister Taylor joined the North Carolina Conference in 1942 and served faithfully and well in a number of pastorates. She was dependable and loyal to the end. Her willingness to serve in any capacity, her devotion to the Lord and His cause, and her love for her family will long be remembered.[13]

Rev. Josephine Hartzell

Mrs. Hartzell was saved in 1926 and united with the First Pentecostal Holiness Church of Oklahoma City. She was sanctified shortly thereafter and later became a licensed minister in the Oklahoma Conference. Along with her husband, Rev. Howard Hartzell, she pastored the Sheridan Church. For a number of years, they also pastored several churches in the West Oklahoma Conference. She was a faithful follower of her Lord.

Her funeral was conducted by Rev. S. N. Greene and Rev. Paul Finchum on August 25, 1970. Burial was in Memorial Park Cemetery in Oklahoma City.[14]

Rev. Lila Medlin
Rev. Josephine Lane Warren McDaniels

"Whereas death invaded our ranks and removed from the walks of life our beloved Rev. Mrs. Lila Medlin and Rev. Mrs. Josephine Lane Warren McDaniels, (Big Mama), their souls having departed to dwell in 'The Undiscovered Country' from whose born no traveler returns.

"Their bodies were committed to the grave and their souls commended to God in the confident hope of the soon return of our Lord and Saviour, Jesus Christ, and the great resurrection day when we can be reunited in a world without end. These great handmaidens of God served well and their works will follow them.

"Expressions of sympathy to the families, but thanksgiving to God because [two] more have fought a good fight, finished their course, kept the faith, and now await the Crown. This conference is a better conference because they worshipped and served here. May our Lord bless the families of these Christian ladies, and may we ever hold their memory precious."[15]

Rev. Violet Mae Wall

Sister Wall was a native of Burke County, North Carolina born February 28, 1898. She became a Christian at an early age. After her education in the local schools, she spent one and half years at Falcon, after which she went to Holmes Bible College from 1918-1937.

She and her husband worked together in evangelistic and pastoral responsibilities for almost forty-two years. No job was too hard or too small for her; she could sweep the floor or fill the pulpit; teach a class or supervise Children's Church. Her service on the Conference Missions Committee was longer than any other minister in the history of the conference.

A church will be erected in Monterrey, Mexico in memory of this great woman, who served God, her conference, her church, and her people in a great way.

She was buried in Lake City Memorial Park to await the sound of the trumpet.[16]

Rev. Nellie Hoos Eckert Lee

Mrs. Lee was born April 20, 1881, in New Madison, Ohio. She was saved at the age of nine and served as secretary of the Sunday school in a Methodist Church from the age of ten until she was fourteen, when she became teacher of a class of beginners.

Nellie married Rev. Clark Eckert, a Methodist minister in 1899. While attending a camp meeting in Indiana, they both entered into the experience of sanctification. Because of his new ministry on holiness and sanctification, her husband was asked to leave the Methodist denomination.

After receiving the Holy Spirit in 1907, they joined the Fire-Baptized Holiness Church in 1908. Nellie was ordained to the ministry by Bishop J. H. King that same year. When that church merged with the Pentecostal Holiness Church in 1911, the Eckerts automatically became charter members of the new organization.

Following her husband's death in 1931, Mrs. Eckert went into full time service for the Lord. She was elected president of the Pentecostal Holiness Youth Society in the Florida Conference and served in that leadership capacity for fourteen years. God gave her a special burden for young people as she traveled throughout the states of Florida, North and South Carolina, Georgia and Kentucky holding youth revivals. Many youths came to know Christ through her ministry. When she retired as youth director in 1945, she was elected President Emeritus.

In 1946, she married the second time to Robert E. Lee of Toccoa, Georgia. The two of them continued in the work of the Lord with her preaching and him singing until his death in 1954.

Rev. Lee passed on to her reward January 9, 1973, at the hospital in Dunn, North Carolina and was laid to rest in the Falcon Children's Home Cemetery in Falcon, North Carolina.[17]

Rev. Natalie Carnes

Miss Natalie H. Carnes, age seventy-four, was a Pentecostal Holiness minister, evangelist, and missionary. She died February 2, 1974, in the Georgetown County Memorial Hospital after a lingering illness. Funeral services were in the Georgetown Pentecostal Holiness Church with Rev. David McKenzie, Conference Superintendent; Rev. Mark Potter and Rev. Elvio Canavesio officiating.

She was born in Bishopville, South Carolina on August 9, 1899, attended Lee County and Charleston Schools, and the Christian and Missionary Alliance Bible College in Nyack, New York.

Her ministry began in the mountains of Kentucky, but she returned to South Carolina in 1933 and became a minister in the South Carolina Conference. She did evangelist work in that conference as well as the

Upper South Carolina, Maryland, West Virginia, Western North Carolina, Florida, and Pennsylvania Conferences.

In 1942, Natalie was assigned to pastor the Georgetown church, and later she did pastoral work in the Charleston District. However, in 1942, Miss Carnes fulfilled a life long dream of doing missionary work. She and a friend, Miss Nellie Watts went to Africa and worked in Nigeria, Southern Rhodesia, Zambia, and South Africa. She made several missionary trips to Argentina and one to Costa Rica and Brazil. In all these places, her energy and dynamic personality were instrumental in reaching many people as she ministered to the churched as well as to the unchurched during forty years of ministry.

Sister Carnes was a dedicated, consecrated, and loyal minister who served her conference well. She will be greatly missed.[18]

Rev. Viola Sullivan Jarvis

Mrs. Jarvis was born October 12, 1909, and died June 21, 1975. She joined the North Carolina Conference in 1946 and retired in 1970. During the twenty-four years of her active ministry, she served as pastor and evangelist. Viola was known as a woman of great faith, with a message of holiness and power. Many people were blessed where she preached, and some of those attending here funeral were saved as a result of her ministry.

Rev. J. Doner Lee, the Conference Superintendent, states, "Several times I would call her to supply a small church for a given period. She never asked if they could pay, or how much. Her reply was always, 'Brother Lee, I will do my best. I am always happiest when I am preaching the Gospel.'"

Rev. Clayton Guthrie writes, "She has now joined the ranks of those who have heard a voice saying, 'Come up higher.' She, like Paul, has fought a good fight and kept the faith. The world did little note her passing, but up in heaven the welcome mat was displayed, a voice was heard in the halls of glory saying another soldier of the cross has come home."

Her pastor, Rev. W. H. Lewis notes, "Her works and labors told us very plainly, 'For me to live is Christ, and to die is gain,' as Paul stated in Philippians 1:21, for she traveled many miles, preaching, praying, and rejoicing in His vineyard." Her work was finished, and it was her time to go home.[19]

Rev. Dorothy Wedeking Plager

Dorothy Plager departed this life August 18, 1975, following heart surgery. She formerly traveled with the Copenhaver Trio. She preached and sang in several churches in the East Oklahoma Conference. She maintained her Christian integrity to the last; she loved people, and taught the Bible as long as she was physically able. Burial was in Salem Cemetery [20]

Rev. Katie Campbell

"Katie Campbell – Awake in Glory"
"In Memoriam"
by
Rev. A. M. Long

For more than thirty-five years "Aunt Katie" was a vital part of the evangelistic ministry of the Virginia Conference. It is no exaggeration to say that hundreds of thousands of people have thrilled to her singing of "When I Wake Up in Glory." Often she'd stop singing abruptly and deliver a powerful message or testimony and then pick up on exactly the right note and continue her song.

She was a great soul winner, and some years she would win almost as many souls as all the other ministers put together in her conference.

"On August 21, 'Aunt Katie' – as she was lovingly called by so many whose hearts she had blessed – went to be forever with the Lord. I'm certain that she's 'right at home' in that glory world because throughout her entire life she carried a part of heaven in her soul. On a moment's notice she was ready to share Jesus with anyone."

She was a modest woman – always underestimating herself, but to illustrate how popular she really was several pastors kept her booked annually. For more than twenty years she never missed a year conducting a revival at Elizabeth City, North Carolina. She went annually to White Sulphur Springs, West Virginia and to Buffalo Ridge, Virginia, just to name some of perennial appointments.

Brother A. M. Long continues, "Personally, I never left her presence without feeling I'd had a spiritual 'shot in the arm.' Even while she was in the hospital (and I talked to her via long distance telephone), she transmitted a contagious enthusiasm of triumphant Christian living."[21]

(**Author's note:** Mrs. Campbell was born in 1889; died 1975. She joined the Virginia Conference as a minister in 1940.)

Rev. Neta Byrd

Sister Byrd lived a full, rich, and dedicated life as a Christian and a minister in the South Carolina Conference. Since she joined the conference in 1948, her works praise her as a loyal, faithful, dedicated soldier of the cross. She left a vacancy in her home, her church, her conference and her denomination that can only be soothed by the balm of her godly influence.[22]

(**Author's note:** This obituary was printed in the South Carolina conference magazine in the fall of 1975.)

Rev. Louise Thomas

The ministry of Sister Thomas was short, but her influence will live on because of the godly principles she stood for. She carried with her an unquenchable desire to win the lost to Christ. Louise was loyal, faithful, and dedicated. Her life was a living witness to the saving grace and sanctifying power of Christ, and she was a channel through which the Holy Spirit could operate to demonstrate the power of God.[23]

(**Author's note:** This information about Louise was printed in the South Carolina Conference magazine in the fall of 1975.)

Rev. Hattie Edge
Rev. Annie Butler

"Sister Hattie Edge was admitted to the Conference at Falcon, North Carolina in 1920. She was a pioneer minister who assisted in founding several churches and was active in pastoral and evangelistic ministry during her 56 years of faithful service."

"Sister Annie Pearson Butler joined the conference in Hopewell, Virginia in 1935 and served as evangelist and assistant pastor of several churches. She distinguished herself as President of the Woman's Auxiliary of the Easter Virginia Conference."[24]

(**Author's note:** These two deaths occurred in 1978.)

Rev. Eugenia McCartney

Mrs. McCartney came to the North Carolina Conference from Oklahoma in 1946 and retired in 1973. During this time she pastored several churches and also was treasurer of Falcon Children's Home. Even after her retirement she continued as preacher, teacher, friend, and lover of the homeless. This she demonstrated by serving later in life as Liaison Teacher at the Home. She went to be with the Lord on January 23, 1978.[25]

Rev. Marie Houser
By
Blonnie Johnson

"On June 30, 1977, God took to heaven by dearest friend and co-worker, Marie Houser. For 38 years Marie and I traveled all over the United States as the Johnson-Houser Evangelistic Party. God gave us many souls, among whom are four ministers. Marie joined the Western North Carolina Conference in 1939, the year she and Blonnie began their work together. Later she became a member of the North Carolina Conference and remained there for seven years. She attended Emmanuel College in Franklin Springs, Georgia and later earned her B.S. and M.A. degrees at East Carolina University in Greenville, North Carolina. Marie taught in the Winston Salem City Schools and was a skilled artist."

The funeral service was conducted at the First Pentecostal Holiness Church in Winston Salem, North Carolina. She was buried in Hollybrook Cemetery in Lincolnton, North Carolina.[26]

DECEASED MINISTERS

	DATE JOINED	DIED
Mrs. Hilary Baldwin	1938	1948
Lucille Barnes	1938	1967
Mrs. F. M. Britton	1907	1955
Neta Byrd	1948	1975
Natalie Carnes	1935	1974
Josephine Cox	1947	1977
Alma Graham	1937	1980
Laura Graham	1934	1963
Rosa Johnston	1976	1980
Lila Medlin	1933	1971
Ethel Moore	1932	1962
Josephine McDaniels	1935	1971
Mrs. L. L. Wall	1930	1971[27]

Rev. Doris Lassiter Jones

Funeral services were conducted for Mrs. Jones on October 12, 1983, in the Millennium Pentecostal Holiness Church in Aulander, North Carolina. Doris was converted as a teenager, fifty years ago.

In 1958, feeling a definite call to Christian service, she applied for minister's license. On two different occasions, she was assigned by the conference to serve the Wakelon Church, which she did with faithfulness and love.

Even after her retirement, she continued to teach Sunday school and to assist her pastor in any way she could. In 1982, her church honored her by electing her to serve as president of the local Woman's Auxiliary. She led this phase of the work of the Kingdom until her death.

On Sunday, October 9, she was at all the services in her church. During the morning service, as a couple was singing a duet, the lady's voice gave way, and she left her husband to sing alone, but he sang only a few words until the Holy Spirit moved on Sister Doris. From where she was sitting, she joined in as though she were a part of the duet. The Spirit of

God came in such waves of glory that at one time more than seventy-five people were rejoicing in the Spirit.

That night when the pastor finished his message and the congregation stood, he asked that Doris stand beside him and lift them up before the throne of God. She prayed with such compassion and unction. The next morning about two thirty, she was rushed to the hospital and placed in the Intensive Care Unit. She never recovered in this life but was made whole in the presence of the Lamb. Her body was laid to rest in the Job Cemetery.[28]

Rev. Pearl Whichard Evans
by
Rev. James O. Evans and Rev. Thad White

Shortly after Sam and Ella Mae Whichard were blessed with the birth of a daughter, they took their newborn baby girl, Pearl, to the Williamston, North Carolina Pentecostal Holiness Church. That was the first place she visited outside the home following her birth, so from the beginning she was a child of the church. Under the influence of her father's preaching and her mother's godly life and teaching, she felt the call to preach and found her own place in the service of Christ.

She excelled in college and graduate school, where she was listed in "Who's Who in American Colleges and Universities." More than one of her professors at Duke Divinity School marveled at the depth of her gifts in preaching, teaching, and counseling.

Brothers Evans and White write, "The more she listened to God, the greater was her ability to identify with the deepest needs of those who sought her counsel. Pearl attributed her insight and discernment to the work of the Holy Spirit. Because of this belief, she saw the possibility of growth and hope for all whom she knew. She had the capacity to make the most of what she had to work with, whether in herself or others. Our family has been moved since her death by the many persons with whom she worked who have said, 'She touched my life.'"

She is described as courageous. While receiving chemotherapy for cancer, she pursued a second master's degree, which involved a daily trip to Baton Rouge for two years.

Although she was raised in a Pentecostal Holiness home as the daughter of a preacher, she served in the United Methodist Church having been ordained as an elder in that denomination. This position is the highest honor bestowed by the church other than that of District Superintendent or election to the office of Bishop. She was granted mission workers' license on the district level in the North Carolina Conference of the Pentecostal Holiness Church.

Her credentials are impressive:

Bachelor of Arts	Pembroke State University
Master of Divinity	Duke University
Master of Social Work	Louisiana State University
Certificate of Training (Association for Clinical Pastoral Education)	Duke Hospital & Georgia Health Institute

Pearl was co-pastor and Pastor Counselor of Davidson Memorial United Methodist Church in Lafayette, Louisiana and also the Lydia Church. Much of her later years were spent in intercessory prayer.

The tribute published in *The Evangel*, the official organ of the North Carolina Conference, goes on to address the love she shared with her family and churches. "She was close to her parents, siblings, husband, and children. She wished most to meet needs in their lives. Her unfulfilled desire was to continue to provide nurture and support to them."

On the day of her funeral, one of the ministers said, "Today, joined by her husband Wayne, members of the family, and a host of friends, and 'witnessed by a great cloud of witnesses in heaven rejoicing with Pearl,' the tabernacle of clay in which Pearl Whichard Evans resided for these short but effective thirty-six plus years, Sam and Ella Mae again bring her to the first place she visited as a baby, for her last visit upon this earth. Thus she has gone full cycle, having lived and died, and now returns to the place of her beginning."[29] (April 17, 1948 – July 2, 1984)

Rev. Henrietta Turpin

The funeral service for Mrs. Henrietta Premrose Turpin was conducted at the Joyner Funeral Home in Wilson, North Carolina on August 20, 1985. She was the daughter of George and Inez Premrose, born on October 22, 1911. Inez attended Paul's Valley School in Oklahoma.

She married L. E. Turpin when she was eighteen. In their early years, they were both saved and began to attend holiness meetings, which led them to a deep dedication to God. They were both called into the ministry and were licensed in the East Oklahoma Conference where they evangelized and pastored churches.

The Turpins felt the need for more knowledge of God's Word, so in 1936 they loaded everything into the old car and began the long journey from Oklahoma to Holmes Bible College in Greenville, South Carolina. After five years, they went back home to resume their ministry. They were later led to Mississippi, where they organized several churches.

In 1959, they moved their membership to the North Carolina Conference, where they labored together until Brother Turpin's death in 1976. Mrs. Turpin was a mother to their children, but also she was an associate pastor and helped in revivals when needed. The couple were a team in all the pursuits of life.

She passed away in the Wilson Memorial Hospital on August 18, 1985. She lived a long and useful life as a minister's wife and minister. Brother Eddie Morris writes, "Eternity alone will reveal the good Sister Henrietta Turpin did during her lifetime in rendering service to God and her church. It had to be a glorious day when she stepped from the pedestal of time into eternity"[30]

Rev. Margaret Smith Bell

On July 23, 1914, Margaret was born into the home of Leonard and Belvia Smith. The family lived near Clayton, North Carolina, where Margaret grew up and attended school. In her early years, she would play church with the other children, and she was always the preacher. Her life was given to Christ a long time ago.

When she was fourteen, she became very ill. She requested a saintly layman, Mr. Richard Johnson, to pray for her, and she was healed. Immediately, she told her mother that God had called her to preach. From that day on, her life was changed. She began reading the Bible to learn all she could about God.

She said "Yes" to the call to carry the Gospel when she was a young girl and entered the ministry when women were not accepted in many churches. In spite of objections, she followed her calling to become an evangelist. Barriers were broken down, and churches called her when they realized God's calling upon her ministry.

When she was nineteen, she attended Holmes Bible College in Greenville, South Carolina to further her education. She joined the North Carolina Conference in 1945 and, for five years, was a very successful evangelist. Several years later, she pastored the Saint John Church and married Mr. J. O. Bell that same year (1951). She also pastored Holland's Chapel in 1956-1957 and Peniel for 1958-1959.

Margaret was a good minister and prayer warrior. Her brother, Marvin, said that she prayed him through World War II on the battlefield in Normandy, and he came back home safely. She spent hours in prayer and supplication concerning people of whom she had personal knowledge that were going through trials. The Lord often revealed a specific message for her to give that individual to encourage them.

Sister Bell's last sermon was preached on October 2, 1985, at Tyndall Grove, where she was a member. The topic of her message was "Lying to the Holy Ghost," which dealt with the dangers of trying to deceive the Holy Spirit and the consequences of doing that.

Rev. W. M. Watkins, who was her pastor, states, "I personally feel that Sister Bell's experience with the Lord was up-to-date right to the very moment the Lord called her home." Her funeral was held on November 13, 1985, at the Tyndall Grove church.[31]

Rev. Mrs. Martha Williams

Sister Williams was born October 1, 1912, saved in her late teens, and soon entered the ministry as a mission's worker. She joined the conference as a licensed minister in 1945 and served as pastor of nine churches and also as an evangelist.

Rev. Warwick, who assisted with the funeral, writes, "Sister Williams had time to be a good wife and the best mother in the world. She walked with God and fulfilled her calling from heaven . . . She served twenty-nine years as a faithful servant of the Lord. No doubt, much of the time, she was not even receiving expenses for her travel."

In Rev. Henry's funeral message he mentions that he met Martha before he became a minister. He was impressed that she was a person who loved God with all her heart and was one who had a desire to please Him. She was a helper in the local church and would fill the pulpit when the pastor was away. She was described as being "dependable, capable, and ready to do any service for Christ's Kingdom . . . Martha was the expression of sobriety, Godliness, faith, honesty, purity." She showed her disdain for that which is evil and clung to that which is good.

Funeral services were held on Thursday, June 12, 1986, at the First Pentecostal Holiness Church in Williamston, North Carolina. Burial was in the Memorial Gardens Cemetery.[32]

Rev. Lula Mae Canady

God, in His sovereign will, called Sister Lula Mae Canady to her eternal reward in the early evening of Thursday, December 23, 1987. Even though she was in declining health for several years, she continued in ministry as long as possible. She was an ordained minister in the South Carolina Conference, who served alongside her husband in pastoring a number of churches. She also served as an effective evangelist.

"Several distinct qualities marked Sister Canady's ministry. She was **KNOWLEDGEABLE** in [the] Word and spoke with **Authority**. Her intense **Faithfulness** to God, her family and church will be a source of inspiration to those who knew her for many years to come."

She was eighty-six years old, having been born October 6, 1901. Her funeral service was held at the South Aiken, South Carolina Pentecostal Holiness Church on December 26, 1987. Ministers participating in the service were Rev. Gloria Rush, Rev. Marcus Rhodes, Rev. D. A. McKenzie, and Rev. M. Donald Duncan.[33]

Rev. Reatha Mae Clark

The Rev. Reatha Mae Simpson was born in Tarboro, North Carolina on August 14, 1923, to Rev. and Mrs. Horace M. Simpson. At the time of her birth, the Simpsons were evangelizing and had temporarily moved to the state. Soon, the family moved back to Florida where Reatha attended public school and graduated. She felt the Lord leading her to Holmes Bible College, Greenville, South Carolina, where she enrolled in 1945 and earned a Th.B. degree in 1947. Feeling a call to preach, she joined the Florida Conference the same year.

Reatha was a faithful minister of the Gospel as she served with her husband in pastoring about twelve churches over a period of forty-two years. She possessed extraordinary culinary skills, using them also in service to God. For years, the Clarks ministered to the physical needs at the Falcon Camp Meeting, youth camps, Harvest Train, and on many other special occasions.

"Reatha Mae Clark knew what it was to serve God, to give unsparingly of herself to every worthy cause that lifted up the name of her blessed Savior. Yet, more times than not – especially in her later years – she worked under great strain and pain. She knew what it was to have 'a thorn in the flesh.'"

The home going celebration service for Reatha was conducted in the sanctuary of the Lumberton, North Carolina First Pentecostal Holiness Church on May 12, 1990. The service was concluded in Falcon, North Carolina at the Children's Home Cemetery.[34]

Rev. Vertie Scott

Rev. Scott of Norfolk, Virginia, a retired minister of the Eastern Virginia Conference, went to her eternal reward on August 29, 1990. She became a minister of that conference in 1950. She served two pastorates: Bethel in Virginia Beach, Virginia, and one in Salisbury, Maryland. However, most of her ministry was in evangelism, in which she was most effective. Consistency and faithfulness marked her life. She was a lady with deep convictions who lived by those principles. Her testimony was, "I was saved at the age of eleven and gave my heart to Jesus. I was called bad names, made fun of, etc., but I stayed true to God."

She was saved at home in Chowan County, North Carolina, in the fall of 1914 and joined the Happy Home Pentecostal Holiness Church that year. After moving to Norfolk, Virginia, she was invited by Rev. O. E. Sproull in 1932 to be pianist for a new church starting in Norfolk. That church was known by several names – Lens Avenue, Norfolk First, and now Parkway Temple. When the church was organized, she was one of nine ladies who joined initially. At her death, she was the last charter member. In the local church she was a Sunday school teacher, did special singing, was active in Woman's Auxiliary, and was an effective altar worker.

Sister Vertie's later years were filled with physical disabilities; nevertheless, anytime that God, prayer, or church was mentioned, she tuned in with joyous response. The success of her life was found in God's amazing grace that guided her and ushered her into His presence.[35]

"MEMOIRS AND MEMORIALS COMMITTEE REPORT"

"Their presence is no longer with us, they will no more be here to shout and dance in the Spirit in response to the Gospel message being preached. Their voices will no more join in camp meeting singing . . . but they are now shouting and rejoicing on the streets of gold and uniting their voices in that heavenly choir, singing the Song of the Redeemed . . . They all have been delivered from the infirmities of this life and been made new.

Rev. Lacy Drew	Ordained - September 11, 1990
Rev. Mrs. Shelly Brinson	Ordained - October 19, 1990
Rev. Mrs. Bessie Cribb	Licensed - May 3, 1991"[36]

Rev. Mae Thomas

Mae was born in Johnston County, North Carolina to J. A. and Pearcy Ann Davis Jordan on May 22, 1911. She was converted to Christ in a cottage prayer meeting in Clayton, North Carolina in 1937. As a licensed minister, she assisted her husband in pastorates at Selma, Roper, Pinetown, Moores Chapel, Wallace, Penderlea, Jacksonville, Bizzell Grove, Pikes Crossroads, Vanceboro, Thomas Chapel, Scotland Neck, and Kenly.

Some of the remarks made by Rev. Wiley Vick, Interim Pastor at the Kenly Pentecostal Holiness Church, summarize a life well lived. "The life of Sister Thomas was a portrait of a devoted Christian." That is the highest honor and the greatest compliment one could have given her.

"Sister Thomas was a Christian wife." She worked diligently by her husband's side until the time of his death six years before she passed away.

"Sister Thomas was also a Christian minister." She became a member of the North Carolina Conference in 1948.

"Sister Thomas was a Christian mother." In spite of her busy life as a minister and a minister's wife, she still had time to show love and affection to her children.

Her labors may not have been fully compensated in this life, but she has gone to be with the Lord to await the rewards reserved for those who have served the Lord in full commitment.

Her death came as a result of injuries received in an automobile accident. She died on April 10, 1991. The funeral was held at the Kenly North Carolina Church on April 13. Interment in the Moore's Chapel

Pentecostal Holiness Cemetery followed as her body was laid to rest next to her beloved husband.[37]

"MEMOIRS AND MEMORIALS COMMITTEE REPORT"

"One of the most beautiful things that I have ever seen is the final phase of a setting sun as it casts its brilliant colors of gold and amber against the western sky, creating a breathtaking afterglow. Ten of our finest soldiers are absent from our midst today, yet we bask in the afterglow of their beautiful lives," writes Rev. Hazleen Graham about the ministers and/or their wives who had died during the previous year in that conference. Rev. Lila McCutcheon, who was ordained, is listed among them.[38]

Rev. Lessie Driggers Polston

Warren and Hattie Driggers of Clio, South Carolina became the parents of Lessie on April 30, 1906. She was saved early in life and received the call to preach in 1927. She was an ordained minister in the North Carolina Conference. She pastored two churches in South Carolina before moving to North Carolina, and in her twenty-nine years of pastoring, sixteen of those were at the Gum Chapel Church.

"After several years of failing health, she was called to receive the 'crown of life' on July 22, 1992." [39]

Rev. Mrs. Lacie Vick

Lacie was born on September 6, 1929, to W. E. and Polly Bass of Johnson County, North Carolina. She became a Christian at the age of eighteen and responded positively to the call to Christian ministry by entering Holmes Bible College in Greenville, South Carolina, where she earned a bachelor of sacred literature degree. She was also a licensed practical nurse and worked at the Johnston Memorial Hospital in Smithfield, North Carolina.

As a licensed minister of the North Carolina Conference, she pastored three churches: Micro, Taylor's Chapel, and Antioch Mission.

Services in her honor were conducted at the Parrish Funeral Home in Selma, North Carolina on October 14, 1992. Interment was in the Jones' Family Cemetery near Kenly.[40]

Rev. Margaret H. Russell

A private graveside service was conducted by Rev. T. Elwood Long, Superintendent of the North Carolina Conference on November 5, 1993, for Rev. Margaret Russell. The funeral service was held earlier in the day at the First Pentecostal Holiness Church in Goldsboro, North Carolina.

Margaret was born and reared in Raleigh, North Carolina. It was there that she met and married Joe L. Russell, Sr. The couple attended a city-wide evangelistic campaign in Fayetteville where they both were converted and joined the First Baptist Church. While in the city, they met Carl and Lila Isaac, who had received the Pentecostal experience, and through the Isaacs' prayers and guidance, they believed and accepted this wonderful baptism.

Feeling the call of God into ministry, Mr. Russell enrolled in Moody Bible Institute in Chicago. Margaret later felt her call as definitely as her husband had. After they completed their studies at Moody, they returned to Fayetteville and joined the Person Street Pentecostal Holiness Church, where Rev. Eddie Morris was pastor.

They purchased a large tent and evangelized for seven years. After joining the North Carolina Conference, they were assigned the Elizabethtown and Boardman churches, but they continued their evangelist work where possible. In 1941, they founded the Peniel Church and served as its pastors.

Mrs. Russell joined the conference in 1950 and assisted her husband in pastoring six additional churches. While they were at the Tabernacle Church in Goldsboro in 1969, Margaret's husband passed away; she assumed full responsibility as pastor for more than a year to complete the assignment.

In 1970, she was assigned to pastor the Pikes Cross Roads Church and was there for eight years. Her efforts were blessed of God in that the membership grew and a beautiful sanctuary and educational building were completed and paid for in full when construction was finished. Also, a parsonage was begun and almost completed before she left the church.

In addition to her pastor duties, Mrs. Russell was always very active at every level in the Woman's Auxiliary of her denominational fellowship. Besides leading her ladies at the local church, she served in many official capacities in the North Carolina Conference Woman's Auxiliary including serving as its Secretary-Treasurer for several years. She was affiliated with the women's work on the general level in some capacity from 1957-1977.

Her other duties have included serving as Director of the Eastern Educational Zone from 1957-1969; she promoted the Ministers' Wives Fellowship, the Sharing Sister Program, and the Feast of Ingathering, introducing bus trips to church schools to promote the work. She wrote Woman's Auxiliary (WA) programs for eight years, and the first study courses on "Church Discipline" and "Stewardship" which were published in *The Helping Hand*, the official publication of the Woman's Ministries Department of the Pentecostal Holiness Church. She introduced the idea of appointing directors at the general, conference, and local levels for Missions, Education, and Woman's Auxiliary Day. She designed the emblem and suggested the words in the motto of the women's group. Through her efforts in initiating the Gold Bond Stamp Drive, Falcon Children's Home was able to get a 38-passenger bus and a walk-in freezer.

When Margaret Russell decided to retire from active ministry, she was graciously honored by the women she had served so well through the years and "received accolades from every level of the church for her labor of dignity, grace, and charm. She was indeed a marvelous, gracious, multi-talented servant of God and shall long be remembered as one who gave her all to the Lord Jesus Christ, whom she loved and served well."[41]

Rev. Lucille Rogers

The memorial service for Rev. Lucille Rogers was held November 17, 1993, at the Northwood Pentecostal Holiness Church in Fayetteville, North Carolina. Rev. Mark Potter officiated, highlighting her ministry and service years in the conference and presented her family with a bronze medallion to be place on her headstone. Rev. Wayne Windham delivered the eulogy. Interment was in Mt. Hope Cemetery. She was a licensed minister in the South Carolina Conference.[42]

Rev. Ruth Williamson Kirby Goude

Rev. Ruth Goude's funeral service was held at the Ebenezer Pentecostal Holiness Church, July 18, 1994. Conference Superintendent Mark Potter, Jr., and Pastor Chesley Floyd officiated. She was a licensed minister in the South Carolina Conference.[43]

Rev. Shirley Persinger

Rev. Persinger, 75, of Hot Springs, Virginia, died January 24, 1995, at Bath County Community Hospital. She transferred from the Freewill Baptist Church to the Appalachian Conference of the IPHC in December 1976.

The funeral was January 28 at Life Line Ministries in Mitchelltown, and burial was in Union Chapel Cemetery.[44]

Rev. Mary Frances Akers

A funeral service was held on January 25, 1995, at the Dudley Memorial Church in Bluefield, Virginia for Rev. Mary Frances Akers who died January 22 at her home at the age of fifty-two. She was an ordained minister in the Appalachian Conference, where she pastored the Faith Assembly Pentecostal Holiness Church in Bluefield for seventeen years. Interment was in Grandview Memorial Gardens.[45]

Rev. Donna M. Allen

After a long illness, Rev. Allen, age seventy-nine, was called to her heavenly reward March 22, 1995. She was an ordained minister in the conference, and pastor/co-founder of Community Pentecostal Holiness Church, Vago, West Virginia. Services were Saturday, March 25 at the Community Church, and burial was in the church cemetery.[46]

Rev. Mrs. Carrie Bullard

Rev. Bullard was born in Columbus County, North Carolina on April 16, 1932, and became a born again Christian in 1949. She was an ordained minister in the North Carolina Conference until the time of her death, having served in a pastoral ministry for twenty-one years. "Sister Bullard was an inspiration and encouragement to everyone who knew her. Her sterling example and radiant smile always served as a reminder of God's love and presence in the lives of His people." She went home to be with the Lord on June 12, 1995.[47]

"SONG OF THE SOUL"

"Rev. Carrie Bullard is no stranger to suffering and pain. Several months ago she learned that she had cancer, and since that time she has had surgery and treatments for the disease. Her family, her church, and her friends have surrounded her with their love, prayers, and devotion . . .

"During the last several months there is one thing that has been revealed to all of us who know and love Carrie Bullard. Her faith in the Lord has come shining through the darkness of the struggle. Never once have I heard her complain. Never once have I heard her question the Lord. Never once have I heard her ask, 'Why me, Lord?' even though it would have been perfectly normal to ask such a question. She has prayed for healing but has accepted whatever lot God has for her.

"I have known many ministers in my life, many men and a few women. However, I have never known one as dedicated to the Lord, the Church, and His kingdom as Carrie Bullard. She has been an excellent pastor, preacher, and minister. She really deserves the title bestowed upon her by the Church and the title which signifies her high calling. Carrie Bullard truly deserves to be called Reverend, because she has exemplified the character of her Master.

"With my own eyes I have beheld one of the greatest sermons which has been heard or seen. That sermon has come not from the pulpit but from the heart.

"In England there is a little bird, the sedge warbler, who hides in the hedges at night. It sings a singular medley of notes, chirps, and thrills called warbles. However, in the blackness of night when the little bird is disturbed and frightened, it sings its most beautiful song.

"Rev. Carrie Bullard has sung many songs in her churches through the years, but her most beautiful song has come through the dark night of pain, fear and suffering. Her music is the divine music which comes from within. Her music is the song of the soul. God has taught her to sing in the darkness, because 'He gives songs in the night.'"[48]

Rev. Callie Johnson
July 13, 1904 – July 19, 1996

Mrs. Johnson was saved, sanctified, and filled with the Holy Spirit in her teenage years. She graduated in 1925 from Franklin Springs Institute (now Emmanuel College), in Georgia. After she married Rev. Harold Johnson, she served with him in the pastorate in South Norfolk and Lincolnia, Virginia until they went to South Africa as missionaries in 1936.

Upon returning to the Eastern Virginia Conference in 1948, she was assistant pastor with her husband in Newport News, Norview, and Lincolnia in Virginia and in Elizabeth City, North Carolina until she retired.

She was active in the Woman's Auxiliary, serving as conference president and as secretary-treasurer where her leadership skills were evident. She will be remembered "as an elegant lady, a gracious hostess, and an excellent role model for all who knew her."

Callie was called home by her Heavenly Father on July 19, 1996. Her funeral service was held on July 22 at the Wood Mortuary in Greer, South Carolina, with burial at the Gum Springs Pentecostal Holiness Church. Dr. Kenneth Benson, President of Holmes Bible College; and the Rev. Larry Jones, Assistant Superintendent of the Eastern Virginia Conference, officiated.[49]

Rev. Irene Gaskins Ellenburg
August 9, 1917 – October 15, 1996

Irene Ellenburg was a native of Pitt County, North Carolina. She was converted in 1931, graduated from Holmes Bible College in South Carolina, and attended Emmanuel College, in Franklin Spring, Georgia and Erskine College in Due West, South Carolina. She was licensed to preach in the Eastern Virginia Conference in 1958, after which she conducted revival meetings along the East Coast as a part of the Gaskins-Faircloth Evangelistic Party. Irene was pastor in Arlington, Virginia for five years.

After marrying Rev. James Ellenburg in 1961, she assisted him in pastorates in Irmo and Langley, South Carolina and in Sharon, Pennsylvania. Her ministry in the Pentecostal Holiness Church exceeded half a century.

When her husband died, she moved to Kinston, North Carolina and transferred her conference membership from Pennsylvania to the North Carolina Conference. She continued to preach until her health declined.[50]

Rev. Fannie Mae Morris Jones

Fannie Mae Morris was born December 9, 1915, to Rev. Edward David and Nora Meeks Morris of Pit County, North Carolina. Her conversion to the Lord Jesus Christ occurred in the early 1930s at Rocky Mount, North Carolina. She attended Holmes Bible College in South Carolina in preparation for Christian service as an evangelist and later as co-pastor with her husband, Rev. John Paul Jones.

Prior to her being licensed by the North Carolina Conference in 1940, she served as an evangelist. Her preaching appointments carried her into six conferences of the Pentecostal Holiness Church. Her revival work spanned about fifteen years, but her total years of active service in the ministry were nearly fifty-three. Even though her assignments from the conference where officially over when she retired, she continued her active service for the Lord.

"Mrs. Fannie Mae Morris Jones was known for her courageous spirit, contagious enthusiasm, and tenacious work ethic. She won more souls to Christ than most."

Her funeral was held on August 19, 1997, at the South Henderson Pentecostal Holiness Church; interment was at Thomas Chapel Pentecostal Holiness Church Cemetery.

(**Author's note:** The following comments were gleaned from the remarks Pastor Frank Sossamon made at the funeral of Rev. Jones.)

"Independent, Energetic, Determined, Committed, Protective, and Caring are but a few words that can be used to open up some windows into the life of Rev. Fannie Mae Morris Jones."

Sister Fannie Mae was known to be her own woman. She was not owned by anyone; she was not for sale. As Sister Jones got older, she would go to sleep during the worship service at times. After the service concluded, she would say to Brother Sossamon, "Well, I know you noticed that I went to sleep this morning in the service. I only did that because I trust you. I know you'll preach the truth so I went to sleep."

She was described as a determined and energetic woman who went non-stop for the Lord and ministry. In her prime year, she experienced revivals that went on for weeks and weeks. Large numbers of spiritual experiences occurred, and the church would be packed with hungry worshipers. She would lock herself up in her room and pray and study until church time.

Time took its toll on her as her voice got weaker, as her body began to break down. All this was due to her going around the clock non-stop to do ministry. Yes, Rev. Fannie Mae Morris Jones gave relentlessly all she had.[51]

Rev. Grace Robinson

Grace Marie Robinson, 41, of Dublin, Virginia, an ordained minister in the Appalachian Conference since 1993, was called to her heavenly home on July 18, 1998, at Carilion Radford Community Hospital in Virginia.

A graveside service was held on July 21 at Highland Memory Gardens, Dublin, Virginia with Rev. Russell Payne and the Rev. Tony Brescia officiating.[52]

Rev. Mozelle Huggins Dowd
1916 – 1999

Mozzell was born Daisy Mozelle Jones to W. T. and Clara Mellette Jones on July 4, 1916, in Fayetteville, North Carolina. She was educated in the Fayetteville City schools and took her bachelor's degree from Southwestern College of Christian Ministries.

In the mid-1920s, Rev. John and Mrs. Lila Berry came to pastor the Person Street Pentecostal Holiness Church, and, under their guidance, Mozelle came to know the Lord as a young girl of about eight or ten years old. At the age of thirteen, the tragic death of a young girl she knew caused her to plead with God for someone to tell all young people everywhere that happiness is in the Lord. God chose her to take this message.

She was licensed to preach by the Pentecostal Free Will Baptist Church in December 1929, but she transferred her membership to the North Carolina Conference in 1950. She preached her first revival in Bennettsville, South Carolina at the age of sixteen and became known as the "Wonder Girl Preacher." So many people were saved that the small church could not accommodate the people, so the revival continued at the local courthouse auditorium. She was a holiness preacher most of her life. Mozelle holds the distinction of being the first lady minister to be ordained in the North Carolina Conference.

Through the influence of Rev. Eddie Morris, she joined the Pentecostal Holiness Church and served the Person Street Church as secretary for many years. She married Isaac Huggins, and together they reared six children, who are active in their respective churches.

In 1950, she organized the Stedman Church and brought it into the North Carolina Conference. Five years later, she was assigned to the West Area Church, with only eight members. There she began what would be a twenty-four year tenure encompassing a major renovation of the church, as well as the building of a parsonage and a free-standing fellowship building. In 1977, the congregation relocated to some property that had belonged to a United Methodist church.

While pastoring in Fayetteville, she was active in civic affairs and, in 1970, was presented the "State Leadership Award" from the Extension Homemakers of North Carolina. Pastor Dowd served the Conference Woman's Auxiliary as District Director and member of the board.

After retiring from the pastorate, she entered a new field of service, joining the staff of Southwestern College of Christian Ministries as a Student Counselor, a position she held for three years.

In an interview with Rev. Eddie Morris, she left these memorable words of support to young ministers: "Be sure you preach the Word. The Word needs no defense."

Her memorial service was held at the Baywood Pentecostal Holiness Church on October 4, 1999.[53]

Rev. Jacqueline Strickland
1934 – 2000

A memorial service for Mrs. Strickland was held Sunday, March 5, 2000, at Herndon and Sons Funeral Chapel in Walterboro, South Carolina. Interment was in Doctor's Creek Baptist Church Cemetery in Walterboro.[54]

Rev. Mary Thelma Green

Thelma was a licensed minister in the South Carolina Conference since 1935. She attended Holmes Bible College in Greenville, then she ministered with her husband in Virginia, West Virginia, and North Carolina, beginning even before she was received into the conference.

A funeral service for the ninety-three year old preacher was held October 22, 2001, at New Life Temple Pentecostal Holiness Church in Roanoke with the Rev. Walter Wood officiating. Interment followed in the Appalachian Conference Cemetery in Dublin.[55]

Rev. Virginia Waters Bridgman
January 5, 1931 – December 23, 2001

Sister Bridgman was a special Christian lady and minister in the North Carolina Conference. She was licensed in June 1981. "Her ministries as a Christian worker include a broad range of activities."

> **She was a Sunday school teacher for more than twenty-five years.**
> **She was a deaconess for two years.**
> **She served as secretary-treasurer of the Swanquarter Church for more than thirteen years.**
> **She was Lifeliners Director [Youth] for four years.**
> **She pastored the Swanquarter Church twice for a total of ten years.**
> **She pastored the Pinetown Church for a total of four years.**

Virginia "served God and her church well. She ministered faithfully in a time when some did not accept lady preachers," but she preached from Africa to North Carolina and was a warrior of the faith. She won a soul to Christ the day before she died on December 23, 2001.[56]

Rev. Sylvia Hill

The Rev. Hill went to be with the Lord August 12, 2002, at Princeton Community Hospital in West Virginia. She was born March 3, 1921, in Beckley and was the daughter of Quincey and Zella Fox Cochran. She was an ordained minister in the Appalachian Conference who pioneered and pastored the Wolf Creek Pentecostal Holiness Church in Narrows for eighteen years. Other churches Sylvia pastored were Crandon in Bland; one in Bluefield, Virginia; and the Christian Ridge Tabernacle in Elgood.

In addition to her pastorates, she was a volunteer musician at a Princeton retirement facility and was a member of the Mercer County Historical Society.

The funeral service was held at the Rowland H. Bailey Funeral Chapel of the Bailey-Kirk Funeral Home in Princeton with the Rev. Otuce Huffman, Sr. officiating. Burial followed at Roselawn Memorial Garden Mausoleum.[57]

Rev. Betty Ethel Glover Bailey
1920 - 2002

Sister Bailey was born in Johnston County, North Carolina on October 19, 1920, to Wilson and Lillie Glover. She was one of ten children. Ethel came to know the Lord in a cottage prayer meeting in 1929 and was licensed to preach in the Western North Carolina Conference (Cornerstone) on June 6, 1958. She later transferred to the North Carolina Conference. While a member of the latter conference, she pastored four churches: Deaver's Chapel, 1959-1961, Black Creek – 1961-1962, Middlesex – 1962-1976, and 1980-1990, and Airboro – 1976-1979 for a total of thirty-one years. In her later years, she founded Pine Valley Holiness Church.

Rev. Chris Thompson, Conference Superintendent writes, "Sister Bailey loved people and spent many joyous hours in gardening or going fishing. Her life was devoted to her family and the Lord, especially in the ministry to which she felt so dedicated. She was a special lady, loved by all who knew her. In a time when women preachers were not readily accepted, she not only preached but pastored. She made a difference!"

Her funeral was held October 12, 2002, at the Shumate Faulk Funeral Home near Goldsboro, and her body was laid to rest in Wayne Memorial Park.[58]

Rev. Theola Ammons
1919 - 2003

A memorial service for Mrs. Theola Ammons was held March 23, 2003, at the Johnsonville, South Carolina Pentecostal Holiness Church. Rev. Terry Fowler and Rev. Billy Miles officiated. Interment was at the Garden of Devotion Cemetery.

Sister Ammons was a precious handmaiden of God, who had a meek yet strong spirit. She lived a life of Christian character and integrity.

Her loving ways endeared her not only to her family but to all who were privileged to know her.[59]

Rev. Shelley Katri McDonald
July 6, 1980 – May 15, 2003

In August 2002, Shelley, a rising senior at Emmanuel College, met with the North Carolina Conference Board for an interview and was approved for license in the conference. She became the youngest member of that body. On May 15, 2003, she was killed in a tragic car accident.

While at Emmanuel College, she won the Distinguished Preacher Award for 2002. She also was active in the S.O.S. Soul-Winning Society. "Those who knew her speak of her creative ways to serve the Lord and her ever-increasing zeal for Him!"

The celebration service for Miss McDonald's promotion was held at the Whiteville Church on May 19. The church was filled to capacity. Her pastor, Dr. Lyndon Purifoy, led the service. Representatives from Emmanuel College and the North Carolina Conference were present.

"Shelley will be missed, but she is not lost. We know where she is – wherever He is. May the Lord bless her memory to our lives. May the model of her life be to all an example of His goodness and blessings."[60]

Rev. Wilma Carnell

The Rev. Wilma Stoneman Carnell, 87, of Pulaski, Virginia died June 29, 2003, in Pulaski Community Hospital. Born in Carroll County, Virginia on December 28, 1915, she was the daughter of Sidney and Mary Stoneman. Wilma had been a member of the Appalachian (Virginia) Conference since 1972.

The funeral service was held July 3, 2003, at Stevens Funeral Chapel with burial in the Shiloh cemetery in Pulaski County.[61]

Rev. Laura Lynette Windborne Mosley
August 23, 1928 – September 12, 2003

Sister Mosley heard the call early on Friday morning, September 12, to go to be with her Master. She had received earlier calls in her life, beginning with the one to be saved in 1947 at the Vaughan's Chapel Church. Thus began her walk with the Lord.

She heard another call and joined the North Carolina conference as a minister ten years later. Her ministry covered a span of seven years as an evangelist and twenty-two years in which she pastored eight churches.

Lynette's celebration service was conducted September 14, 2003, at Joyner's Funeral Home. Burial followed at Evergreen Memorial Gardens. She is described in the obituary as "a lady who was a faithful wife, mother, and preacher." Further, she "was a delightful person and energetic minister of the gospel."[62]

Rev. Brenda Gail Green

Rev. Brenda Green, 50, of Kimball, West Virginia, went to her heavenly home on November 20, 2004, at Welch Community Hospital following a sudden illness. She was born October 3, 1954 to Isaac and Dorothy Lambert. At the time of her death, she was pastor of the Mohegan Pentecostal Holiness Church, a homemaker, and a resident of the Vivan/Kimball area most of her life. Her ministerial membership was in the Appalachian Conference since 1988.

The funeral service was held November 15 at the Widener Funeral Home Chapel, Kimball, with the Rev. Rebecca Cardwell and Rev. Martha Boyd officiating.[63]

Rev. Lois (Jay) Linton
August 2, 1942 – January 5, 2005

Jay considered her primary ministry as one of song, because she enjoyed singing the gospel. She served as music director for a while at her home church and often sang at the Piney Grove Camp Meeting.

Rev. Linton joined the North Carolina Conference in 2000 when she was given the minister of music license. She was always faithful and diligent in her conference responsibilities.

Her funeral was held at the Chapel of Paul Funeral Home on January 8, 2005. The body was laid to rest at the Linton-Clark family cemetery.[64]

Rev. Vela Sizemore

Vela R. Sizemore, 83, of Austinville, Virginia, passed from this life to her heavenly home on April 1, 2005, at Waddell Nursing Home in Galax, Virginia. She was born January 27, 1922, in Carroll County to Jackson and Mary Etta Jennings.

Her ministry work began in the Western North Carolina Conference (Cornerstone), but she was later licensed and ordained in the Virginia (Appalachian) Conference. She retired in 1987, having pastored Gravley Memorial and Pine Mountain churches and having served as an evangelist for several years.

The funeral service was held April 3, 2005, at Woodlawn Pentecostal Holiness Church with interment in the Coulson Church cemetery.[65]

Rev. Mary Ruth Heath

Sister Ruth Heath was born on January 5, 1920, in Pender County, North Carolina to William and Lessie Heath. She was converted at the age of fourteen and began her ministry at the age of twenty when she entered Holmes Bible College, Greenville, South Carolina. She remained at Holmes for twelve years. She graduated during that time and taught at the school and also served as Dean of Girls. While working at the school, she attended Furman University.

Ruth joined the North Carolina Conference in 1948 and assisted in pastoring five churches. She worked at Falcon Children's Home for three years and worked faithfully in Vacation Bible School for twenty years.

She died on April 15, 2005 at the age of eighty-five.[66]

Rev. Lida Mae Hales Rogers

Lida Mae Hales was born on December 1, 1925, in Johnston County, North Carolina, the daughter of William and Nempie Hales. She graduated from Glendale High School in 1944.

She was a member of the North Carolina Conference involved in multiple ministries throughout her career. She served as a Sunday school teacher, Women's Ministries president and vice-president, full time pastor, and fill-in pastor for various churches over the years. She held home prayer meetings and revivals in many areas of the denomination and was a speaker at Women's Ministries meetings and numerous outreaches.

Rev. Rogers and her husband started the Sunday School Extension Outreach at Smithfield Manor in 1976, and it is still an ongoing mission work through the Bizzell Grove Church. She "was a living example of God's glory with a pure heart filled with His grace; she was the light in the darkness of those who knew her, forever leaving a piece of her heart in their memories."

Lida Mae passed away on April 19, 2005, at Good Hope Hospital in Erwin, North Carolina. The celebration service was held at Parris Funeral Home in Princeton on April 22, 2005.[67]

Rev. Luetta Paschall Morris

"Many people live lives or exist in various states of desperation – not Luetta Paschall Morris. Most Christians live on the fringes of joy, contentment, and happiness – not Luetta Paschall Morris. Most Christians live under the quilting frame. They know there must be a pattern to it all but they can't seem to put it all together – not Luetta Paschall Morris," reads the obituary.

She was described as a lady that knew the pattern. She was able to find and discern the Master's purpose; she was able to see the quilt above the frame. She exemplified this spiritually, figuratively, and literally. Death was not an exit for her, but an entrance because of the way she lived.

Sister Morris was born on February 10, 1916, was saved at the age of eight, attended Holmes Bible College in Greenville, South Carolina after graduation from high school, and worked on the staff at the college after earning her degree there. She also received a B.S. degree in history with a minor in English from Furman University also in Greenville.

In 1943, she received her license to preach and often ministered in the Pentecostal Free Will Baptist Church and in the Upper South Carolina Conference of the Pentecostal Holiness Church. She transferred to the North Carolina Conference in 1952.

She organized the Garland (NC) Church in 1954 and remained there as pastor for nine years. Under her leadership, the congregation built its first church. Even later, she was a major factor in helping the church build a new sanctuary.

In 1963, "Miss Lu," as she was affectionately known, was assigned to pastor the Peniel Church in the North Carolina Conference. She led them in a large building project and relocation, during which they were able to construct a new church and parsonage. The membership tripled in size under her capable guidance, which lasted twelve years.

While pastoring, she taught public school for twenty-three years, conducted Vacation Bible Schools, and worked in the conference youth camps for years.

In 1975, she married Rev. Harvey Morris. On their retirement to Falcon, she served on the town council for four years and as mayor for twelve.

Sister Morris entered the presence of the Lord on April 27, 2005. Her celebration service was conducted in her beloved Peniel Church three days later.[68]

Rev. Georgia N. Osborne
April 28, 1925 – December 20, 2005

Rev. Mrs. Georgia was relieved of her suffering and promoted to heaven on December 20, 2005. She had battled with triumph through an extended illness and died as she lived, with grace and victory in the Lord.

She was born April 28, 1925, in Dillon County, South Carolina to William and Nealy Norman. Georgia was converted to the Lord in 1934 at the Lake View Pentecostal Holiness Church. In 1955, she was called to preach and was licensed by the South Carolina Conference two years later. In 1975, she was ordained by the North Carolina Conference at Falcon.

"Rev. Osborne served the kingdom well as an evangelist for over 30 years. She faithfully pastored for 10 years until her health prohibited her continuing." Her pastorates took her to the Hope Mills and the Abbottsburg Churches. During her tenure, both churches grew. While at Hope Mills, she led the church in a building project and in relocation.

A special service of thanksgiving and remembrance was held December, 23, 2005, at the Lumberton First Church. The service, like Sister Osborne, was warm, encouraging, and inspirational. Her body was laid to rest at the Lake View Pentecostal Holiness Church Cemetery, Lake View, South Carolina.[69]

Rev. Mary Thomas

Mrs. Mary Eloise Lucas Defibaugh Thomas was born September 15, 1920, in North Carolina, the daughter of Coleman and Lena Lucas. She attended Campbell College, Holmes Bible College, Radford College, Virginia Polytechnic Institute, Miami University, Longwood College, Lynchburg College, and the University of Virginia from which she received associate, bachelor's and master's degrees.

Her interests were playing the piano, teaching children, caring for animals, and being of service in her church. She was an ordained minister in the Appalachian Conference, pastoring alongside her husband when he was assigned to churches in Bluefield, Welch, Princeton, and War, West Virginia; Meadowview, Radford, and Lynchburg in Virginia. She also worked as an evangelist from 1937 to 1943 with the Freewill Baptist Church.

A celebration of life service was held February 19, 2006, at Tree of Life Ministries, Lynchburg. A private graveside service for the immediate family was held at the Appalachian Conference Cemetery, Dublin.[70]

Rev. Cora Hudnell

On November 25, 2006, Sister Cora Hudnell's funeral was conducted at the Paul Funeral Home in Washington, North Carolina. It was a service of celebration because Sister Hudnell was a very special lady, who left a legacy of honor and victorious life for her Master. She was a woman of prayer and one who valued all her commitments.

Cora was a preacher and a pastor's wife. The couple began pastoring the Kenly Church in 1942 and went on to pastor eleven other churches during their careers[71]

Rev. Sarah Thelma Player
1911 – 2007

Sarah Thelma Player of Rockingham, North Carolina, born July 28, 1911, daughter of Louis and Della Lisenby Jacobs went to be with her Lord October 12, 2007, at the age of ninety-six. At the time of her death, she was the oldest serving pastor in the entire denomination.

She was ordained in the South Carolina Conference in 1965 and enjoyed sixty plus years of ministry. She always was held in high esteem by her minister colleagues, not only in the Pentecost Holiness Church, but in many other religious denominations.

In the Rockingham area, where the majority of her ministry took place, she was recognized by the Richmond County Ministerial Association and the Richmond County Council as one of the most loyal and faithful ministers in the community.

She pastored four different churches during her ministry.

Ellerbe	1949-1958
By Way	1959-1986
Cordova	1990-1994
Living Waters (founded by her)	1980-1994
Living Waters	2006-2007[72]

Thelma still was actively involved in pastoral ministry when the Lord took her home.

In a report in *The Challenge*, October 7, 2001, she was mentioned as third runner-up of the Pastor of the Year Award for 2000.

(**Author's note:** Apparently, Thelma pastored two churches at the same time as the dates above overlap.)

"By faith [she] still speaks, even though [she] is dead" – Hebrews 11:4c-NIV. Death has silenced these voices, but the lives of these ladies continue to speak through the influence they made on countless individuals whose paths crossed with one of them. That contact was not incidental, by chance, or happenstance. God in His providence directed the meeting whether in a home, on the street, or in a church service. One of these women may have preached a sermon that moved the heart of someone who today is standing in the gap to spread the Word, the Gospel, the Good News of salvation through God's only begotten Son, the Savior of the world. Someone may be on the mission field now because they felt the call of God during a service conducted by one of these anointed preachers. Some child may have become an adult who is now teaching Sunday school because Sisters Robinson, Park, Burnette, Jones, Sullivan, Byrd, Carnes taught them well. Or what about Beadie, Marie, Eugenia, Doris, Henrietta, Lula Mae, or

Margaret? What a good reputation they left behind! Lips **are not** silent; they continue to voice the Truth through others.

Words that stand out in the obituaries written about these lady ministers are noteworthy: determined, inspiring, enthusiastic, committed, meek, sober, loyal, faithful, dedicated, consecrated, knowledgeable, honest, dependable, multi-talented, pure, courageous, gracious, effective, successful, capable, caring, energetic, loving, zealous, warm, living examples, prayer warriors, crusaders for the Truth, and servants who always were ready to minister.

Servant is used last, but certainly is not the least descriptive word for what occurred in the lives and ministries of these precious saints of God. *Servant* is a word literally translated from the Greek as a *bond-servant* or *slave*. Paul often applies the word to himself, as well as to believers in Christ. "The word involves the ideas of belonging to a master, and of service as a slave." The former is meant in Paul's use of the term, since Christian service, in his view, is the expression of love and of free choice. It relates to freedom and sonship. "On the other hand, believers belong to Christ by purchase and own Him as absolute master."[73]

Each one of the lady ministers named in this chapter were servants of the Lord Jesus Christ as much so as the Apostle Paul.

---

[1] Lois Tripp, "Winter . . .then Spring – Summer . . . Sunset," *The Helping Hand*, May-June 1986, p. 3.
[2] Doris Moore, "My Friend . . . My Spiritual Mother," *The Helping Hand*, May-June 1986, p. 3.
[3] Jewelle Stewart, *IPHC Experience*, September 2006, p. 9.
[4] A. E. Robinson, *The Advocate*, May 31, 1917, p. 7.
[5] "Our Sainted Dead," *Yearbook of the Pentecostal Holiness Church*, 1946, p. 7.
[6] Rev. W. Eddie Morris, *The Conference Evangel*, North Carolina Conference, 1949, p. 6.
[7] James R. Williams and Mrs. Vernon Clark, "Memoirs," North Carolina Conference Minutes, August 1950.
[8] *The Co-Worker*, August 1960, p. 3.
[9] Rev. Melvin Narron, *The Conference Evangel*, January 1964, p. 11.
[10] *The Conference Beacon*, September 1967.
[11] *The Conference Evangel*, April 1969, p. 3.
[12] *The Conference Evangel*, July 1969, p. 3.
[13] Memoirs Committee Report," North Carolina Conference Minutes, 1969, p. 23.
[14] *The Advocate*, October 24, *1970, p. 10.*
[15] "In Memory," *The Challenge*, Summer 1971.
[16] *The Challenge*, Spring 1972, p. 7.
[17] *The Advocate*, April 7, 1973, p. 5.

[18] *The Challenge*, Spring 1974, p. 5.
[19] *The Evangel*, August 1975, p. 4.
[20] *East Oklahoma Conference News*, October 1975, pp. 2, 4.
[21] A. M. Long, "Katie Campbell – Awake in Glory," *The Advocate*, September 1975, p. 10.
[22] *The Challenge*, Fall 1975.
[23] *The Challenge*, Fall 1975.
[24] "Committee Report on Memoirs," Eastern Virginia Conference Minutes, 1978, p. 29.
[25] "Memoirs Committee Report," North Carolina Conference Minutes, 1978, p. 57.
[26] Rev. Blonnie Johnson, *The Advocate*, July 23, 1978, p. 11.
[27] "Deceased Ministers," South Carolina Conference Minutes, 1981, pp. 28-29.
[28] Rev. Tim Henry, "In Memoriam," *The Evangel*, December 1983, p 3.
[29] Rev. James O. Evans and Rev. Thad White, *The Evangel*, February 1985, pp. 3, 5, 11.
[30] Rev. J. Doner Lee and Rev. W. Eddie Morris, *The Evangel*, October 1985, p. 3.
[31] Rev. Eddie Morris and Rev. W. M. Watkins, *The Evangel*, February 1986, p. 3.
[332] Rev. Horace Warwick and Rev. Tim B. Henry, *The Evangel*, July 1986, p. 3.
[33] The Challenge, Spring 1988.
[34] Rev. T. Elwood Long and Rev. Jimmy Whitfield, North Carolina Conference Minutes, September 1990, p. 3.
[35] Eastern Virginia Conference Minutes 1991-1992, p. 18.
[36] "Memoirs and Memorials Committee Report," South Carolina Conference Minutes, 1991, p. 15.
[37] *The Evangel*, July 1991, p. 3.
[38] "Memoirs and Memorials Committee Report," South Carolina Conference Minutes, 1992, p. 15.
[39] "Memoirs Committee Report," North Carolina Conference Minutes, 1993, p. 63.
[40] *The Evangel*, January 1993, p. 3.
[41] *The Evangel*, January/February 1994, p. 3.
[42] *The Challenge*, Fall 1994, p. 3.
[43] *The Challenge*, Fall 1994, p. 3.
[44] *Appalachian Conference Messenger*, March 1995, p. 2.
[45] *Appalachian Conference Messenger*, March 1995, p. 2.
[46] *Appalachian Conference Messenger*, April 1995, back page.
[47] North Carolina Conference Minutes, 1995, p. 72.
[48] Dr. Ray Lundy, "In Memory," *The Evangel*, July 1995, p. 3.
[49] Minutes of the Eastern Virginia Conference, 1997-1998.
[50] Minutes of the North Carolina Conference, 1997, p. 70.
[51] *The Evangel*, October 1977, pp. 3, 13.
[52] *Appalachian Conference Messenger*, September 1998, p. 2.
[53] North Carolina Conference Minutes, 2000, p. 77.
[54] *The Challenge*, Spring 2000.
[55] *Appalachian Conference Messenger*, December 2001.
[56] "Memoirs Committee Report," North Carolina Conference Minutes, 2002, p. 111.

[57] *Appalachian Conference Messenger*, October 2002, p. 3.
[58] *The Evangel*, December 2002, p. 3.
[59] *The Challenge*, Spring 2003, p. 3.
[60] *The Evangel*, July 2003, p. 4.
[61] *Appalachian Conference Messenger*, September 2003, p. 3.
[62] *The Evangel*, November 2003, p. 3.
[63] *Appalachian Conference Messenger*, February 2005, p. 3.
[64] Rev. Chris Thompson, *The Evangel*, March 2005, p. 3.
[65] *Appalachian Conference Messenger*, June 2005, p. 3.
[66] North Carolina Conference Minutes, 2005, p. 83.
[67] North Carolina Conference Minutes, 2005, p. 88.
[68] North Carolina Conference Minutes, 2005, p. 87.
[69] Bishop Chris Thompson, *The Evangel*, February 2006, p. 3.
[70] *Appalachian Conference Messenger*, April 2006, p. 3.
[71] North Carolina Conference Minutes, 2007, pp. 110-111.
[72] Archives of the South Carolina Conference.
[73] Dr. Marvin Vincent, "The Epistle to the Romans," *Word Studies in the New Testament*, p. 2.

CHAPTER 10

Write it Before Them

"Now go, write it before them in a table, and note it in a book, that it may be for the time to come for ever and ever" – Isaiah 30:8.

SERMONS

(**Author's note:** The sermons that follow were sent in by ladies who filled out the information forms I sent them and responded to my request to furnish this material for publication. They have been edited for spelling and punctuation, but not for format or content. The inclusion of these sermons does not necessarily reflect my views, beliefs, or interpretation of the Scriptures. They are reprinted here with permission.)

The sermons that follow reflect a variety of styles and forms. Some are masterful; some are simple. The important thing is that they represent the Truth. Each minister, in her own way, endeavored to be a good ambassador of Christ. She worked to lift Jesus up for the world to see. Through her preaching, she tried to reach the lost and encourage believers to press on. The topics and texts are profound, for they move one to become more like the Master. They reflect God's presence in the lives of those in Bible times; they demonstrate the danger of human weakness and temptations of the flesh. They demonstrate the power of the Almighty to transform individuals; they point one to the ultimate source of strength--spiritual strength--and suggest that we follow in the way they have walked because it is proven to be THE WAY.

God has used these frail temples as instruments of righteousness in His vineyard. Frailty, however, does not suggest weakness. They have been and are spiritual giants among us. Heed their words!

THE LIFE AND TIMES OF DAVID
The Background
1 Samuel 16:1-13
Rev. Kitty Mears

I. Samuel
   A. From birth he was dedicated to God's service.
   B. Lived in the tabernacle with Eli
      1. Eli was not a good role model of a father.
      2. Eli's sons openly sinned against God.
      3. Samuel was still a child when the Ark of the Covenant was taken into Philistine territory.
      4. The Philistines had authority over the Hebrews.
   C. Relationship with King Saul
      1. God withdrew His favor from Saul.
      2. Samuel mourned for the spiritual condition of Saul and Israel.
   D. Ramah became the abode of Samuel.
      1. Ramah – "height"
      2. It is there that Samuel tried unsuccessfully to train his sons for God's service.
      3. Samuel built a "School of the Prophets" to train young men for God's service.

II. Jesse
   A. Son of Obed – son of Boaz and Ruth
   B. Nothing has been written concerning "a great man of wealth" as his grandfather Boaz.
   C. Jesse's wealth consisted of
      1. Sheep
      2. Eight sons
      3. David's care for him during his last days in Moab while Saul was pursuing David

III. 1 Samuel 16:1-13
   A. The anointing
      1. A public show of God's endowment for a special service
      2. A symbol of filling of the Holy Spirit
   B. Samuel's fear of Saul
      1. An evil spirit had control over Saul's emotions

        2. Saul had become a man of violent anger – moody.
        3. God's response
            a. Go offer a sacrifice
            b. Go to Bethlehem
            c. Go sanctify the household of Jesse
    C. Samuel's response
        1. Looked at outward appearance
        2. Listened to reasoning of God
            a. "Look not on the outward – look on the heart."
            b. Virtues of the soul, not the flesh
                (1) Righteousness
                (2) Respect for God
                (3) Obedience
    B. The calling of David
        1. Ruddy complexion
        2. Possibly red hair
        3. "Red" complexion – maybe sunburned
        4. According to Josephus
            a. Samuel whispered privately into David's ear God's intent for the throne.
            b. God's promise to have David's descendants forever on the throne only through his obedience.
            c. David would overthrow the Philistines.
            d. His house would be of great splendor and celebration throughout the world.
            e. At that time, the divine power left Saul and abode upon David.
IV. The favor of God
    A. God looks on the heart, not the physical appearance.
        1. Attitude toward God and holy living
        2. Pride vs. humility
        3. Self preference vs. looking out for the welfare of others
    B. True worship
        1. David vs. Saul
            a. A heart of love vs. "my way"
            b. Same attitudes compared with Cain and Abel
        2. A love of God produces righteous duty vs. a duty that stemmed from a love of one's self. (What am I going to get from this service of worship?)

C. Our attitude concerning service
   1. Right motive vs. wrong motive
   2. Eternal vision or "near sighted" (thinking only of one's self)

WHERE HAS THE POWER GONE?
Acts 4:31-33
Rev. Debra Whitside

In Acts 4, it is apparent that Peter is addressing the rulers of the people and the elders of Israel. The disciples had been threatened not to speak or teach in the name of Jesus. That sounds much like today's headlines. It is all right to pray to any other god in public, except in the name of Jesus Christ, but it is only by that name that we have salvation, healing, deliverance, and wholeness.

We have become too tolerant in the body of Christ. We have become weary in the body of Christ. We have become complacent in the body of Christ. In the church world, we have our Sunday morning crowd, our Sunday night crowd, and the Wednesday night folk. Guess which one has the most in attendance? Why? Where has the power gone?

If faith produces faithfulness, what is wrong in the body of Christ that we are not faithful to God's house? It's called stewardship. That means our time – don't be late; that means money – pay your tithes and give your offerings. That means our bodies. The hand of stewardship shakes the hand of sanctification, which means set apart for the Master's use.

Sanctification means to clean up. It's time for the body of Christ to clean up its act, so it can be used of God. From drunkenness to gluttony, from habits of tobacco use to greed and lust, we need a cleaning. If we will not sanctify ourselves from the works of the flesh, we will not have the power of God.

You want to know why some people will not receive the baptism of the Holy Ghost? It's because some are not sanctified; they are not holy unto the Lord. This is not what we might call holy but what God calls holy.

Where has the power gone?

QUENCH NOT THE SPIRIT
1 Thessalonians 5:19
Rev. Pauline Knowles

The Bible tells us about two fires: Holy Ghost fire and hell fire. One cannot be quenched, and the other should not be. When John the Baptist preached repentance to the people at the Jordan River, he told them one would come after him who would baptize them with the Holy Ghost and fire. This is the Spirit Paul warns us not to quench.

Jesus tells us about a fire that never will be quenched. He says it is better to go through life maimed, halt, and blind than to have all the members of our body and be cast into hell, into the fire that never will be quenched (Mark 9:45).

I am sure the devil would like nothing better than to quench both fires. He has tried down through the years, through false doctrine, to get people to doubt hell fire. He also works in various ways to quench the Holy Ghost fire that burns in the hearts of God's people. Let us focus our attention on the Spirit that Paul said not to quench.

I am afraid many of us are not aware of the importance of this Holy Ghost power that Jesus sent to His followers on the day of Pentecost. They were commanded to return to Jerusalem and tarry until they were endued with power from on high. Joel had prophesied that in the last days, this would come to pass. Jesus had told His disciples not to be troubled at His going away for He would pray the Father to give them another Comforter who would abide with them forever.

How sad that many have believed the lie of the devil about the baptism of the Holy Ghost. He has told people this experience was only for the early church. Peter does away with that statement when he declared, "For the promise is unto you, and to your children, and to all that are afar off, even as many as the Lord our God shall call" (Acts 2:39).

If we hunger and thirst after righteousness, we shall be filled. Seek, and ye shall find. The devil has always had a counterfeit for God's blessings. When you desire spiritual gifts, be sure you come God's way, which is the way of holiness. Do not be side tracked by taking a shortcut. Old Satan has always tried to get people, even Jesus Himself, to bypass the cross. You will never experience this beautiful baptism of power until you have been to Calvary and your soul, mind, and body have been purified by the blood of Jesus.

<u>The Holy Ghost can be resisted</u>. Stephen accused those who were stoning him of being stiff-necked and uncircumcised in heart and always resisting the Holy Ghost as their fathers did. When you refuse to obey the convicting Spirit of God, you are resisting Him. When you feel convicted of sin, it is the Holy Ghost trying to lead you to Christ. Don't resist Him; obey Him.

<u>The Holy Ghost can be lied to</u>. If we could call Ananias and Sapphira back from the dead, I am sure they would warn everyone not to lie to the Holy Ghost. They thought they were lying to Peter, but he told them they were lying to the Holy Ghost. Some times we feel that the church just started having hypocrites, but not so. The early church had these too, and God used them for an example. Be sure your sin will find you out. It pays to play straight with God.

<u>The Holy Spirit can be grieved</u>. We are told in Ephesians 4:30, "And grieve not the Holy Spirit of God, whereby ye are sealed unto the day of redemption." When we do and say things contrary to the will of God, we grieve Him. I am sure with the lukewarmness among God's people today, the Spirit is grieved.

<u>The Holy Ghost can be blasphemed</u>. Jesus said in Matthew 12:31, "Wherefore I say unto you, All manner of sin and blasphemy shall be forgiven unto men, but the blasphemy against the Holy Ghost shall not be forgiven unto men. And whosoever speaketh a word against the Son of man, it shall be forgiven him, but whosoever speaketh against the Holy Ghost, it shall not be forgiven him, neither in this world, neither in the world to come."

<u>The Holy Ghost can be received</u>. Thank God for this! The Holy Ghost is given to those who obey Him. He is not given to the world; for Jesus said, "The world cannot receive Him because it seeth Him not, neither knoweth Him, but ye know Him, for He dwelleth with you and shall be in you." Since our bodies are the temple of the Holy Ghost, we must present it holy unto the Lord.

I am fully convinced that when the Holy Ghost comes in, there will be inner joy and the outward manifestation of speaking in other tongues. This will be a supernatural act apart from man's wisdom.

We do not seek for tongues when we seek the Holy Ghost. When Paul went to Ephesus, he did not ask those twelve disciples if they had received tongues. He asked them if they had received the Holy Ghost and spoke with tongues and prophesied. They had not even heard anything about the Holy Ghost, but Paul laid his hands upon them, and they received the gift and spoke with tongues and prophesied. The same thing happened when Peter was at the home of Cornelius. While he yet spoke, the Holy Ghost fell upon them, and they began to speak with tongues and magnify God. When the Holy Ghost comes in, He will speak for Himself. That is the evidence He is abiding within. We must yield ourselves to the manifestations of the Spirit. If we fail to do so, we become guilty of quenching the Spirit.

There are two ways to quench fire. You can smother it out, or you can refuse to put fuel on it, and it will go out. The same is true with this Holy Ghost fire. If we want this fire burning as it should be, we must keep it stirred by reading God's word and praying in the Spirit. Many are not free to praise God and glorify Him in the house of God. You don't feel the joy in your heart you once had. What a shame! Whom the Son has made free is free indeed.

Not only can we quench this holy fire by neglecting to feed it, but sin and worldliness will smother it out. My, how we need to lay aside every weight and sin that does so easily beset us.

SPIRITUAL HOLINESS
"The A List"
Jennifer Oliver

I. Introduction: To be on "The A List" used to mean you were the best athlete in school or the most popular girl in town. To make "The A List" academically meant you made all A's on your report card. To make "The A List" regarding music refers to those who sell the most CD's. "The A list" simply has a connotation of just being the best, but what does it mean to be on God's A List? How can we be our BEST for Jesus Christ?

II. Sermon Body

   A. <u>A new Aspiration</u>

      1. When we accept Jesus as our Savior, the next logical step should be a change in our desires and aspirations. Our highest aspiration should be to live a life of holiness. That holiness springs out of a personal relationship with Christ Himself.

      2. John 15:4, "Abide in me, and I in you. As the branch cannot bear fruit of itself, unless it abides in the vine, neither can you, unless you abide in Me."

B. <u>A new Association</u>
   1. Revelation 21:5, "Behold I make all things new."
   2. We have to remember who we belong to now. We belong to God when we are saved. Our association changes. Our lives should no longer be about selfish desires but should be about what He wants us to be. He has given us a clean slate to start new in Him. A life with Him will be far better than anything this world has to offer.

C. <u>A new Accountability</u>
   1. Why is it important to pray for sanctification as a separate work and declare oneself as saved, sanctified, and filled the Holy Spirit? There are several reasons, but one excellent one is that of accountability. If we have confessed our sins to the Lord and asked Him to begin a new work within us, then our life should reflect some changes. We should make ourselves accountable to a pastor, leader, friends, Sunday school classmates – someone who truly cares.
   2. James 5:16, "Confess your faults one to another, and pray one for another that ye may be healed."

D. <u>A new Attitude</u>
   1. The question for many of us is how do I go about this change? God can give us the desire, but isn't there something we need to do? Yes, and it begins deep within us. The search for holiness is within the Christian anyway. A new attitude about our life can make all the difference. We must become godly minded.
   2. 1 Peter 1:14-16, "As obedient children, not fashioning yourselves according to the former lusts in your ignorance; but as he which hath called you is holy, so be ye holy in all manner of conversation; because it is written, Be ye holy; for I am Holy."

E. <u>A new Action</u>
   1. Finally, the day-to-day fruit we bear will change. Yes, we will make mistakes and fail in our actions. Perhaps our actions will not always be holy, but if we are faithful to ask for the Lord's help, He will in turn be faithful to bring that perfect work of sanctification to pass in our lives.

2. Philippians 1:6, "Being confident of this very thing, that he which hath begun a good work in you will perform it unto the day of Jesus Christ."

3. We also must remember that our actions are important to our witness. We are to be the light of Christ in this sinful world. That means that we are to be set apart in certain ways that will bring glory to His name. It's not us that the world needs to see; it's Jesus Christ within us that the world is desperately searching for.

III. Conclusion: D. L. Moody said: "A holy life will make the deepest impression. Lighthouses blow no horns; they just shine." When we strive for holiness, everyone benefits. We will find more satisfaction, and God will be better able to use us. No doubt, our families will be happier with us, and we can be a light to people we know and even some we don't know. Holiness is a win-win situation.

LIVING WATER
John 4:1-29
Marie Haydock

I invite you to take a journey back in time with me to be eye witnesses to a conversation between two people: Jesus and the Samaritan woman. Let's listen closely to what is being said.

Jesus came down to earth and took upon Himself the form of a human. He felt all that we feel. He wept. He got angry. He got hungry. He needed sleep and rest. He got tired and weary. Jesus said He needed to go to Samaria, not because of geographical consideration, but because of Divine compulsion.

As Jesus sat by Jacob's well to rest from His journey, a Samaritan woman came to draw water. The Bible doesn't name this woman, but I've named her Miss Jane to make it more personal. (The gospel according to Marie.)

Alone and lonely, Miss Jane came to the well. She felt empty in body and soul as she walked to the well in the noonday heat. Miss Jane lived for carnal pleasures and had not given a thought to her soul. Her sandals pounded heavily on the cobblestone. Her feet burned from the heat through the worn and loosely fitting sandals.

She probably wore a faded cotton robe fitting loosely about her. Her head dress of another color flowed around a once pretty face that had now grown hard and was then sad. Her body showed age and weariness.

She, no doubt, lived a life filled with pain and heartache. She longed for a new way of life, but thought it was too late. However, that day she sensed a new weariness of spirit she never felt before.

As Miss Jane approached the well, she saw a gentle faced man sitting resting. Jesus' journey had been long over hot sands and rock. He had walked twenty miles in the heat. He asked the woman for a drink, which probably surprised her.

Jesus spoke to her about living water, but the woman was puzzled because the only water she knew about was in the well. He also told her to call her husband because a man couldn't hold conversation with a woman alone.

Miss Jane left her water pot at the well and ran into the town and told the men to come see a man who told her everything she had done. Could this be the Messiah?

THE RIGHT NAME AND THE RIGHT ACTION TO GO WITH IT
Acts 3:6-7
Becki Hudson

When Peter and John came to the temple at the hour of prayer, they fixed their eyes on the lame man by the Beautiful Gate and Peter said, "Look on us." He didn't want this man to be distracted. If a person gets distracted, he can miss what God has for him.

Peter wanted this man to pay close attention to what he was about to do. He wanted him to really hear him. I believe he got right down into the face of that man and locked his eyes on that man's eyes, so that everything else in that lame man's awareness was shut out.

That's the way we need to be. That's the way we need to look at Jesus. We need to get so close to Him, and look so directly into His eyes, that we don't see anybody else; we aren't aware of anybody else; we don't hear anybody else. We only hear and see Jesus.

Then Peter spoke to him with a name. Every one of us needs a name that is stronger than the devil's name, a name that is stronger than your problem, a name that is more potent than your pain. That name is Jesus.

Paul wrote, "That at the name of Jesus every knee should bow, of things in heaven, and things in earth, and things under the earth; And that every tongue should confess that Jesus Christ is Lord, to the glory of God the Father" – Philippians 2:10-11.

Also, in Hebrews 7:26 we read that the name of Jesus is higher than any other name. He is "holy, harmless, undefiled . . . and made higher than the heavens."

There is no other name that can make whole the part of you that is lame. Only power in the name of Jesus can do that. Then Peter went beyond words. He did what needed to be done. This lame man heard what Peter said, but the words themselves had no visible effect on his life.

You may hear a sermon and in your mind say "amen," and then find that nothing changes in your life. People in great need all around you may hear about the love and mercy of God, the blood of Jesus, and the power of the Holy Spirit and yet not experience any of it for themselves.

Peter put the name of Jesus into action. He reached down and took the lame man by the hand and lifted him up. It was as Peter pulled the man to his feet that the lame feet and ankle bones received strength.

This man who had never walked didn't need any help walking. He only needed help getting up on his feet. Instantly, he was standing, walking, and leaping about as he praised God. We need the name of Jesus, and we can use the name of Jesus to get on our feet spiritually and emotionally and, in some cases, physically and materially.

It is your hand reached out to Jesus in faith that will help you stand. You don't need a crutch. You don't need to spend the rest of your life thinking you are helpless, but you do need to pull yourselves to your feet so that God can heal and strengthen the lameness in your lives. Rise up in faith on the inside.

Don't place your confidence in something else. Put your trust in the name of Jesus. He is the one who will heal you of lameness, strengthen you in your weakness, and cause you to walk in boldness. He alone is the One who can make you whole.

Matthew tells us that He called His disciples to Him and gave them authority to drive out evil spirits and heal every disease and sickness. You have to understand that what Jesus gave these disciples, He expects us to walk in also. They were not the only ones who got something; He also gave us that power. "I can do all things through Christ who strengthens me" – Philippians 4:13.

God doesn't help us and bless us and do things for us because we deserve it, because we've earned it, or because we're good. He does it because we believe in Jesus and because He died for us.

One of the best examples in the Bible about someone who could have had everything and yet continued to do without and have nothing was Mephibosheth. It was all because of how he felt. He felt bad; he felt guilty; he felt worthless; he felt that he had no value; he felt that nobody wanted him, and so he hid in a poverty stricken place called Lodibar.

Some of us need to get out of Lodibar and start knocking on the king's door and asking for our rights in Jesus' name. I come in Jesus' name, and I ask you to help me, bless me, favor me, and take care of me. I don't go in my name. My name wouldn't get me anywhere in heaven. I go in Jesus' name.

The name of Jesus is available to us, but we need to get committed. We need to get serious about our walk with God. When we make a commitment and we're serious, God honors that. Thank God when we make mistakes, there is no condemnation to those who are in Christ Jesus.

We need to put on that armor of God, so that when the devil comes at us, we say, "No, devil, I have been made the righteousness of God in Christ." The devil works through anything he can work through, and we have to stand firm and take back what belongs to us.

Life is supposed to be difficult. It enables us to grow as Christians. If everything was handed down to us, we would never learn or grow in Christ. Yield every area of your life. Take your eyes, your ears, your hands, your feet, your thoughts, and your heart, and go completely into the face of Jesus.

To know Christ is to have riches and a place in the Kingdom of God. Don't give Him part of you; give Him all of you. Surrender all to God in the name of Jesus and know that all things are possible. We have to make that stand. It is our right before God that we can ask and receive in Jesus' name.

What is it that you need in your life tonight? Whatever it is, know that you can make that stand. You have the armor of God for whatever comes against you. You have the name of Jesus. Go boldly before God, believing in Jesus' name. Ask, believing, and it shall be given to you.

FIVE MEANINGS OF MERCY
Lamentations 3:19-33
Betty Walling

Evangelist Luis Palau tells how a mother once approached Napoleon seeking a pardon for her son. The emperor replied that the young man had committed a certain offense twice and justice demanded death. The mother answered with "But I don't ask for justice; I plead for mercy!" The emperor replied that her son didn't deserve mercy. Again, the mother pleaded for mercy with this statement: "It would not be mercy if he deserved it, and mercy is all I ask for." Then, the emperor granted her request.

God's mercy has a five-fold meaning.

I. The meaning in affliction – vv. 19-21
   Affliction teaches us lessons we never forget.

II. The endurance gives us hope to face tomorrow – vv. 22-23
    Endurance gives us hope to face tomorrow.
    A. God's compassion is one of His main attributes.
    B. His compassion remains ever new.

III. The resignation of anticipation – vv. 24-25
     A. Silence nourishes the soul that trusts in the Lord.
     B. Suffering disciplines the soul that trusts in the Lord.

IV. The courage to face persecution – vv. 26-30
    A. It takes courage to be silent.
    B. It takes courage to be non-violent.

V. The yearning of restoration – vv. 31-33
   A. God always tempers grief with mercy.
   B. God always avoids unnecessary pain.

"His compassions fail not" – v. 22. (cf. Psalm 78:38).

In Lamentations 3:1 we see the analogy of the rod (God's punishment). Jeremiah is depicted as sick, injured, dead, buried, slow-moving, a prisoner, tortured, attacked by animals, a target of arrows, an object of ridicule, and forced to eat bitter and contaminated food. He had almost given up hope, but then he recalled something that restores hope: the mercies of God. Mercies in some translations are covenant love, steadfast love, linked with truth, faithfulness, and goodness.

Psalm 103:4 links mercy with compassion; Exodus 34:6 links mercy with graciousness and longsuffering; Psalm 23:6 links mercy with goodness. The ability to offer sacrifices was gone. It seemed so hopeless, but God's mercy remained. Looking at v. 24, Jeremiah states, "The Lord is my portion."

The book of Lamentations calls attention to God's faithfulness and righteousness in judgment. God loves us and allows calamity as a last resort to restore us with mercy. Judgment is the fruit of sin and rebellion. Wait on the Lord expecting daily expressions of His mercy. Know God does not enjoy judgment and wants to give mercy at all times. Seek the Lord; expect Him to bring good things to pass for you. Wait for Him to show mercy in distress. It is never too early to begin spiritual development. So often in fact, too many times people wait too long. Do not complain about adversity in your life. Accept God's discipline as an expression of His love – love that will turn us from rebellion to obedience. If we do not deal with sin, God will hold us responsible for judgment that will follow.

AN ANOINTING FROM THE HOLY ONE
1 John 2:20-27
Karen Atkins

It's important to know what the Scripture was saying to them in the day and time in which it was written, so I spent some time studying about the subject of anointing. The Bible has two words translated "anointing."

1. The Hebrew word is "meshiach," which means to rub or smear with oil, to cover over, to consecrate. This is the root for "Messiah" – the Anointed One.
2. The Greek word is "chiro." It means to rub with oil or to cover over. It is always used for rubbing, pouring, or sprinkling with oil in a religious sense. "Chiro" is the word from which we get the word "Christos" or Christ – the Anointed One.

In the Old Testament, the coming of the Messiah, or the Anointed One, is foretold; in the New Testament, it was fulfilled in Jesus Christ, the Anointed One. They are one and the same.

In the Scriptures, anointing is either material or spiritual.
1. Material can be of three types.
   a. Ordinary – anointing the head or body with ointment was an ordinary custom for the Jews and other nationalities of that time – probably because of the dry climate. It also seemed to be a sign of respect sometimes paid by a host to his guests.
   b. Official – it was a rite of inauguration. Prophets, priest, and kings were anointed. Oil was poured on the head of the person being anointed.
* The Old Testament records two instances of the anointing of a prophet.
* When God instituted the priesthood with the tribe of Levi, beginning with Aaron and his sons, all were anointed. Later, it seemed to be especially reserved for the high priest only.
* Kings were set apart through the ritual of anointing, which was performed by a prophet who acted in God's power and authority (1 Samuel 15:1). The purpose of anointing is to authorize, or set apart, a person for a particular work or service (Isaiah 61:1). The anointed person belonged to God in a special sense. The phrases, "The Lord's anointed" and "God's anointed" are used of men such as Saul, David, and Solomon in the Old Testament. David, for instance, was anointed three times.
* Also, inanimate objects were sometimes anointed to signify that they had been set apart for a holy use – the serving utensils and furniture in the temple were anointed.
   c. Ecclesiastical – in the New Testament, anointing with oil was often used in healing the sick, as James instructed (James 5:14), and as demonstrated by the twelve in Mark 6:13.
2. Spiritual
   a. In the Old Testament, in Psalm 2:2 and Daniel 9:25, 26, a Deliverer is promised under the title of Messiah, or Anointed One. His anointing is described as spiritual, with the Holy Ghost, in Isaiah 61:1. **(Read)**

Jesus Himself found it necessary to be anointed by the Holy One if He was to carry out His assigned mission. He also quoted this Scripture from Isaiah when he began His ministry, and He told them it was in reference to Himself. He was the fulfillment of that prophecy.

In the New Testament, Jesus of Nazareth is shown to be the Christ, or Messiah, or the Anointed One foretold in the Old Testament, and His being anointed with the Holy Ghost is a documented historical fact. Jesus Christ was anointed as prophet, priest, and king.

    b. Spiritual anointing with the Holy Ghost is also conferred upon Christians today. – (2 Corinthians 1:21-22-NIV and 2 Corinthians 1:20-22-NLT). He has identified us as His own. How? By putting the Holy Spirit in our hearts as a guarantee, as the first installment of everything that is to come – everything that He will give us. This is what His anointing does for us. Anointing expresses the sanctifying influences of the Holy Spirit upon Christians, who are priests and kings unto God.

Read 1 Peter 2:9-10-NKJV. We are chosen and set apart that our very lives of obedience are a praise to Him.

Read Revelation 5:10- NKJV. This is God's plan for our lives. He will give us a kingdom, and we will serve Him as priests, and we shall reign as kings on the earth. Maybe you aren't feeling too kingly these days. Maybe you don't feel as though you've been reigning over anything lately. Maybe you would feel you have something in common with the man in this story.

Dr. Bill Bright of Campus Crusade for Christ tells this story of a famous oil field called Yates' Pool. During the Depression, this field was a sheep ranch owned by a man named Yates. He wasn't able to make enough on his ranching operation to pay the principal and interest on the mortgage, so he was in danger of losing his ranch. With little money for clothes or food, his family had to live on government subsidy. Day after day, as he grazed his sheep over those rolling west Texas hills, he was no doubt greatly troubled about how he would pay his bills. Then, a seismographic crew from an oil company came into the area and told him there might be oil on his land. They asked permission to drill a wildcat well, and he signed a lease.

At 1,115 feet, they struck a huge oil reserve. The first well came in at 80,000 barrels a day. Many subsequent wells were more than twice as large. In fact, 30 years after the discovery, a government test of one of the wells showed it still had the potential flow of 125,000 barrels a day. Mr. Yates owned it all. The day he purchased the land, he received the oil and mineral rights. Yet, he'd been living on relief. He was a multimillionaire who was living in poverty. What was the problem? He didn't know the oil was there, even though he owned it.

Many Christians live in spiritual poverty. They are entitled to the gifts of the Holy Spirit and His energizing power, but they are not aware of their birthright. You have an unction – an anointing from the Holy One. What we need today is to recognize our anointing. The anointing is being separated for service, set apart for a holy purpose.

* The anointing is the power to do what God has called you to do.
* The anointing is being in the same mind as the Spirit.
* The anointing is being in tune with the Spirit.
* The anointing is having the discernment of the Spirit.
* The anointing is being used by the Spirit.

The explorer, Richard Byrd, said, "Few men during their lifetime come anywhere near exhausting the resources dwelling within them. There are deep wells of strength that are never used." I am convinced that each of us has deep wells of strength within us, but not our own strength. We have an anointing from the Holy One, and we can operate in His strength.

Read Colossians 1:11-TLB; Colossians 1:11-12-The Message; Colossians 1:28-29-NIV.

This makes all the difference not to try to struggle along in our own puny strength but to be able to operate in His mighty power – His awesome strength. How do we tap into that strength?

Mother Teresa said, "To keep a lamp burning, we have to keep putting oil in it." Seems really rudimentary, but it's amazing how many people gave up on their Christianity or how many Christians are living a defeated life because they neglected to tend their lamp. How? It's the same list you've heard time and time again, but it bears repeating because it's so essential to our spiritual health.

1. READ THE WORD – "Get into the Word, and let the Word get into you." The Word will build you up. The Word will light your path. The Word will keep you from sinning. The Word will convict and encourage and strengthen. It is our bread and our water. Spiritually, we cannot live without it. Your spiritual life will only be as strong in proportion to how much time you give to the Word. No more, no less. Remember, the Word is living. When you get into the Word, and the living Word gets into you, it grows and develops and takes the place of useless clutter and debris and trash and junk and everything you don't want or need. It will fill you up and satisfy you.

2. PRAY – It is still amazing to me that the God of the universe will take time for me, wants to have a relationship with me. My relationship

with God is like any other: invest in it, and it will grow and flourish. Neglect it, and it will wilt and die. Set aside some time to come apart to pray, but use the other opportunities that He gives you throughout the day to call on Him and discuss whatever is on your mind or on His. Do you have trouble thinking what to pray about? Whatever is important to you is important to Him. You start praying, and He'll bring to mind whatever you need to pray about. Do you feel guilty because your mind wanders when you are praying? John White, in his book The Fight says that we should use that as an opportunity to thank God. When we realize our mind has been wandering, we should say, "Thanks, God, for calling me back to you," then go on with your prayer. Just make it work!

3. PRAISE AND WORSHIP – This should be done in the service and on your own. God inhabits the praises of His people. Praise is comely for the upright. In other words, to God, praise looks good on you. He likes it; He commands it; He rewards it. Those are good enough reasons. Praise and worship is also how God gives us victory in a spiritual battle. It is a mighty effective weapon against the devil. Praise and worship isn't about what or how you feel; it's all about what you will. We must will to do it, regardless of how we feel. That's why in Hebrews the writer refers to it as a sacrifice of praise.

4. FORGIVE – Don't allow anything to stay in you life that will steal your anointing. An unforgiving spirit is a robber and a thief. Jesus Himself said we can't get an answer from God to our petitions until we've first reconciled with our brother. Not forgiving will cause bitterness if we believe we have a right to it or guilt if we don't. It will give birth to jealousy or envy or wrath or hated or spite or other debilitating sins. Whatever it is, let it go. It costs too much to keep it.

5. RELEASE YOUR PAST – When I speak of letting it go, that includes not only what we hold against another, but what we hold against ourselves. Sometimes we just mess up badly; there is no need of covering it up or pretending it didn't happen. We're just wrong, and we know it, and we know everyone else knows it too. It's hard to get over. Romans 8:1 tells us there is no condemnation in Christ Jesus, so if He, the only one who is worthy, doesn't condemn us, who is making us feel so guilty? Satan and ourselves. We need to give it to Him. Someone once said, "I decided to give up my past in order to live my future." This quote is attributed to Johnny Cash: "Close the door on the past. You don't try to forget the mistakes, but you don't dwell on it." After we ask God's forgiveness, we need to forgive ourselves and go on, not give up.

6. GIVE BACK TO GOD – This can be done with tithes and offerings. Read Malachi 3:8-11-KJV. If we want the anointing of God in our lives, we must not shut up the windows of blessing that He longs to pour out on us, nor do we want to tie His hands for rebuking the devourer. We don't want a curse; we want blessings!

7. SHARE – We are anointed for a purpose: to do His kingdom work. God designed us to be rivers, not cisterns. The trouble with a cistern is that the water can get old, and it can become stagnant and stale. A river, however, has a constant flow – old water out, new water in. That's how we should be. Whatever the Holy Spirit has give us, we need to give it out, and that will empty us so He can fill us again. Ephesians 5:18 tells us to be filled with the Spirit, but in the original language, the grammatical structure actually says "keep on being filled with the Spirit" – over and over – a fresh flow. There're a whole lot of lost people out there who would love to have some answers, would love to have some place to turn with their problems. They are just aching for someone to give them hope. We have to be about our Father's business.

8. SERVE – Everyone has his own anointing; everyone has his own giftedness; everyone has something to do, something that is uniquely suited to them, something nobody else can do quite the same. Everyone has a job to do in the body, so why aren't we doing it?

* We are too ready to let someone else do it.
* We are too ready to see our own limitations.
* We are too ready to put it off until we have more time.
* We are too ready to think we need to be more qualified.

How much more qualified do we need to be? After all, we have an anointing from the Holy One. We can operate in His mighty power and strength.

Some years ago, I came to the conclusion that there are two very effective little demons at work in the spirit world. (There are others, of course, but I want to look at these two, because they are so effective in hindering our spiritual lives.) These little demons are tireless and relentless. I wish we had their energy and sense of purpose.

1. **Harassment** – This little demon just makes it tough on us. He whittles away at our self-esteem, telling us that we aren't talented enough for anything, or that everyone else thinks someone else could do it better, or causes someone to criticize us, or uses any number of other ploys. The reason he is so effective is that it all seems like small decisions, small choices, small rationale, but combined they have disastrous effects on us. We need to quit listening to him and start listening to what God says

about us. God tells me in Philippians 4:13 that I can do all things through Christ who strengthens me. God tells me in Philippians 1:6 that we can be confident of this very thing, that He who has begun a good work in you will complete it until the day of Jesus Christ. And God says in Philippians 2:13, "For God is working in you, giving you the desire to obey him and the power to do what pleases him"-NLT. God has given us many more encouraging words in the Bible. We need to listen to them rather than this little demon.

2. **Distraction** – This little demon, I believe, has the job of putting stuff in our life that gets in our way. He keeps us so busy thinking about and dealing with stuff that we lose sight of what is important. This reminds me of a management class I took once. The instructor explained that there is stuff that is important to do, and there is also stuff that is urgent. The urgent is the stuff that clamors for time and attention. It makes such a racket that we take care of it first, even though, if we stopped to ask ourselves, it may not be that good or helpful; it's just loud. Meanwhile the important stuff gets left in the dust. We need to operate as the apostle Paul said in Philippians 3:13-14, "But this one thing I do, forgetting those things which are behind, and reaching forth unto those things which are before, I press toward the mark of the prize of the high calling of God in Christ Jesus"-KJV. This one thing – the important thing – not these 50 things I dabble in. We need to get our priorities in order and give the demons Distraction and Harassment the boot!

Before I went off on the tangent about the demons, I was talking about ways to fill up our spiritual lamps, to tap into His might power, to be filled and keep on being filled with the Spirit, to be anointed by the Holy One. I want to encourage you to plunge in to these areas in your spiritual life:

* READ THE WORD
* PRAY
* PRAISE AND WORSHIP HIM
* FORGIVE
* RELEASE YOUR PAST
* GIVE BACK TO GOD
* SHARE WITH OTHERS
* SERVE HIM IN YOUR AREA OF GIFTEDNESS

This isn't an all-inclusive list by any means. I could name other things that would help us fill our lamp, but you get the idea. We need the anointing of the Holy One, and we know that we have it. Let's look at a couple of verses from our text again.

1 John 2:20 - "But you have an anointing from the Holy One, and you know all things."-[NIV]. John wrote this to counteract a philosophy called Gnosticism prevalent at the time. The word Gnosticism means "in the know." Proponents of Gnosticism said they had a new revelation, a new illumination. If you weren't a Gnostic, you weren't "in the know." They were challenging the teachings of the early Christian church and confusing many members. John was saying here that the Holy Spirit had anointed them for life and for service, and that the Holy Spirit would confirm in their hearts that what they had been taught from the beginning was the truth. This is true for us today as well. We are anointed with the oil of grace, with gifts and spiritual endowments, by that Spirit of grace. We are anointed as subordinate prophets, priests, and kings unto God. He anoints us to make us like Him. Verses 21 through 26 are speaking about the liars and deceivers who would try to lead us astray. So the anointing is also like a spiritual eye salve; it strengthens the eyes of the understanding. It is durable and lasting, for oil is not soon dried up.

Verse 27 tells us that the anointing abides in us; it dwells within us; it tabernacles with us; it is constant.

* Temptations arise
* Trials arise
* Snares arise
* Seductions arise
* Problems arise
* Disappointments arise
* **BUT THE ANOINTING ABIDES**

The Holy Spirit and His anointing is our constant companion. "Lo, I am with you always."

What else does this anointing do in our lives?

* Makes holy – Exodus 30:32 (used to consecrate priests only; not ordinary use)
* Makes a covenant between us and God – Exodus 40:15 (perpetual priesthood)
* Releases us to minister – Leviticus 7:35-36 (makes provision for material needs to free for ministry)
* Sanctifies – Leviticus 8:10 (sets us apart for holy use as the temple implements and the priests)
* Breaks bondages and frees the sinner – Isaiah 61:1
* Heals the sick – James 5:14 (call the elders)
* Abides and teaches the truth – 1 John 2:27

When we form a visual image of a priestly anointing as David gave us in Psalm 133:2, we see that "It is like the precious ointment upon the head, that ran down upon the beard, even Aaron's beard: that went down to the skirts of his garments"-KJV. It covered him from head to foot. As I said before, Jesus Himself was anointed by the Holy One. Jesus is the head of the church, and as He was anointed, it flowed down from the head, and covered the entire body. No part is left out! His anointing is our anointing. What He accomplished under the anointing, we can too.

We must have the anointing before we can start our service to God. We have to be set apart and consecrated for His service. If we try to minister on our own without anointing, we are saying,

- * We don't need God and that we can do it in our own strength. This is **humanism**.
- * Our ideas are good enough and worthy in themselves. This is **idolatry**.
- * We will go our own way instead of God's way. This is **rebellion**.

We need the anointing of the Holy One if we expect to be fruitful. We need to serve the Lord with excellence.

Educator Marva Collins said, "Excellence is not an act but a habit – the things you do the most are the things you will do the best." We have to keep on doing the right things, day after day, when someone is watching and when they are not, when we feel like it and when we don't. It has to be a habit so ingrained that we can't separate our habit from who we are. Only when we do the right things the most will we do them the best.

Sometimes we just need to change our focus. I recently read a story that illustrates this. Teresa Barbella, an art teacher, tells this story: "It had been a week – one of those weeks where around every corner is a new problem, a new worry, I was in the art studio, 30 minutes into my after-school class, when a new student came in – 6 year old Travis. I gave him a set of watercolors and said, 'We're painting today – whatever you like.' He smiled and began painting. My mind drifted back to the week's problems.

Suddenly, Travis stopped and a look of pure wonder came on his face. 'I made purple!' he exclaimed. 'It's my favorite color, and I made it!' He was enchanted as only a 6-year old could be. His delight was contagious and soon the other children began mixing paint to see what new colors they could create.

'Can you make purple?' he asked me.

'Yes, I can,' I replied, 'but not nearly as magnificent as your purple.'

'I like my purple.' He smiled, satisfied.

It was at that moment that I realized that age or occupation or level of accomplishment has little to do with what really matters. Maybe I can't make ends meet, or make people like what I do, and maybe I can't paint a famous portrait, but I Can Make Purple!"

We must change our focus. Instead of naming off our inadequacies, look at what we can do. We need to remember, "Whom God calls, He equips." It isn't our job to find our own resources or to figure out how to do a task; that's God's problem. Our job is to obey.

In closing, let's look at our text once more, this time from the MESSAGE. (Read 1 John 2:20-27.) Life isn't measured by the number of breaths we take, but by the moments that take our breath away.

Ask this question daily: Which is stronger: my urge to grow or my resistance to change?

- * Can we find the courage within us to believe what God says?
- * Can we find a place within the body where we can minister?
- * Can we examine our life and see where our priorities ought to lie?
- * Can we see our place in the kingdom of God for the glorious adventure He intends it to be?
- * Can we smell the sweet aroma of the Holy One covering our lives?
- * Can we feel the power of the Holy One energizing us to do His will?

I believe we can, for we have an anointing from the Holy One – and we know all things!

WATCH THE CLOUDS!
Numbers 9:15-23
Jewelle Stewart

Part of the daily routine of millions is to turn the television on to the weather channel. We are weather-watching people. This source helps some know whether sunny or overcast skies are expected or if a storm is on the way. In my brief sojourn in the heartland, I've learned that quite a variance of weather patterns can occur in a short period of time. Strong winds abound. Clouds form quickly, and rain pelts down at a fast and furious pace. I watch and prepare accordingly.

Numbers 9 records how the children of Israel had to become "cloud watchers." This supernatural atmospheric phenomenon of the cloud by day and fire by night covered the tabernacle and lasted for the duration of their desert wanderings – an amazing feat that no modern-day weather pattern can rival.

In the natural, we know clouds bring refreshing showers, as well as storms. They give cover and can shield the earth from the harsh rays of the summer sun. Low-lying clouds or fog can cause such a thick covering that vision is obscured. We understand also the nature of fire. A warm fire on a cold wintry day invites one to draw closer and partake of its comfort. Both clouds and fire contain elements necessary for life: oxygen, water, light, and energy/heat. Both have life-enriching capabilities; both, too, have the capability to destroy.

The account of the cloud in Numbers is unlike anything today's weather-watchers have seen. This cloud, called a "theophany," was a manifestation of the presence of God and first occurred on the day the tabernacle was set up (Numbers 9:15). It appeared on the sixth day following the second Passover (the date allowed only for those who had not been able to partake of the Passover of the previous month). I believe there is a direct correlation between man's creation on the sixth day and the fact that is was six days after Passover when the tabernacle was readied and the cloud of God's presence came down. It hovered over the tabernacle.

In the Garden, God came daily to fellowship with Adam and Eve, but their sin separated them from God's presence. Here, at the erection of the desert tabernacle, God again comes to provide for and lead His people. On this occasion they were charged "Watch the Cloud! When it moves, you move. When it rests, you rest. One day or year, watch the cloud and move when and only when it moves."

Watching the cloud was vital to their existence. I believe it was of such importance that some became "cloud watchers"; or "discerner of times," responsible for alerting the priests and the camp at the slightest movement of the cloud or pillar of fire. Scripture does not record it, but I believe it possible that some of Issachar's tribe developed a keen sensitivity to the activity of the cloud. Parents were told to teach their children, and their children were to teach the next generation and so on. It is recorded in 1 Chronicles 12:32 about the sons of Isaachar that they were men that "had understanding of the times, to know what Israel ought to do." The charge to Israel in Numbers 9 was "Understand when the cloud begins to move and move with it.

When the cloud began to lift, the cry went out, "Let God arise, let his enemies be scattered" (Psalm 68:1), and the entire camp went into action. No one stood still. No one decided, "I want to stay here a little longer." Together they went following the cloud of God's presence.

Many years ago, I heard Judson Cornwall say, "The cloud went fast enough for the ones who desired to move fast but slow enough to cover the weak and infirm." All were included. As they moved out, Judah (praise) led with Issachar (reward) following close behind (Numbers 10:14).

There were many rewards of watching and moving with the cloud:
1. Israel was kept under the divine covering and provisions.
2. They had direction (v. 17).
3. They had unity of purpose and order in the camp (9:13; 10:14).
4. It was shelter and comfort (9:15-16).
5. It afforded protection from their enemies (10:35).
6. There was release and increase of the prophetic voice (11:25).
7. Leadership was confirmed (12:5-10).
8. The congregation came to places of rest (9:23).

Another theophany involving the cloud occurred at the dedication of Solomon's Temple (1 Kings 8:10; 2 Chronicles 5:13-14). When it was completed and the priests had everything in place, the cloud of God's presence so filled the temple the priests could not even stand to perform their duties. After the dedication prayer, fire came down and consumed the offerings. All the people saw the fire and the glory cloud above the temple. Everyone fell to his knees and worshiped together. Music and singing filled the temple and surrounding areas. There was much rejoicing.

Acts 2 records another theophany. This one involved wind (associated with cloud movement) and fire (tongues of fire). Christ's core group had obediently gathered as He instructed and were awaiting the promise of power from on high. One hundred and twenty were unified in their mission, obedient to their purpose, and they recognized their existence and progress would depend on God moving in their midst with power. When the Holy Ghost came, they were filled with power and might and became living temples. Instead of a tent where a select few could enter, or the temple that accommodated larger crowds, these became individual temples, thrust from the small gathering place (the upper room) and out into the nations.

Just suppose that one day when the cry was sounded, "God is arising, let his enemies scatter," Sister Aaron said, "I'm tired of moving. This is where I'm comfortable now. My flowers look good and the vegetables will be coming in before long. I'm just not moving this time." Nothing Aaron said budged her, so they stayed. At night they experienced cold like they'd never known. As the day passed, the heat was so intense they could hardly breathe. Flowers and fruit burned up, and wild beast came to their tent at night. Emotions ran high, and disaster struck at every turn. No, it did not happen to them.

What about when the temple was finished, Solomon just sprinkled a little water around, smeared a little oil on the altar and said a simple prayer, and everyone went home. What if, on the ninth day, someone in the upper room said, "Nothing is happening around here. Let's go to another place and see what we can do to get this group going?"

Even in our day, there may be those who would say, "I don't agree with that. I'm not doing it just because that leader says to," or perhaps some who would show another form of resistance to the moving of God. Could that explain why some experience lack of divine covering or direction? Could this be why homes are breaking apart? Could this be why ministries seem to lack unity of purpose and order, why peace is absent from church meetings, and why rebelliousness to leadership is still present among the people of God? Perhaps this explains why the prophetic voice is weakened and sometimes silenced.

The charge still is "watch the cloud!" Yesterday's move is not where we are going today. God is calling us to turn our eyes again and again to the cloud of His presence. The church at Laodicea (Revelation 3:18) was admonished to anoint their eyes with salve so their sight could be restored. Our responsibility is to keep our spiritual eyesight clear so we can see and understand God's directions daily. Watch the cloud! His presence and power and work in our temples require diligence. Like the sons of Issachar, our responsibility is to be sensitive to the moving of God's presence and to understand the times. That is the place of overcoming victory, but it will not happen until we develop cloud-watching mentality.

May our prayer be, "Return, O Lord, in power among your people. Rise up and let your enemies be scattered and let them that hate thee flee before thee. Make known to us the path of life; fill us with joy in your presence."

PERSUADED: ONE WHO BELIEVES AND SPEAKS
Roberta Trujillo

(Hosea: Minor Prophet)
1. The mind of God is revealed to this prophet
2. He prophesies in Israel during a time of prosperity
3. During his reign (began when he was very young until he was very old) he was constant in the call of God as prophet.

4. Some kings like him and some kings did not.
5. Hosea speaks to Israel of their sin and of their destruction.
6. The word of the Lord came to him, and he was to tell the children of Israel that they were an evil and adulterous generation.
7. Hosea's life was used as a mirror to show them their sins.
8. Hosea is ordered to take unto him a wife of whoredoms and children of whoredoms.

Hosea 4:1
"Hear the word of the LORD, <u>ye children of Israel</u>: for the LORD hath a controversy with the inhabitants of the land, because there is <u>no truth, nor mercy, nor knowledge of God in the land.</u>"

Controversy
Nutshell: You're saying one thing and doing another thing, and I've got a BIG problem with this.

* **Because the people "strove" with the priests, they were destroyed for lack of knowledge.** (Hosea 4:6 says, "My people are destroyed for lack of knowledge; because thou hast rejected knowledge, I will also reject thee, that thou shalt be no priest to me: seeing thou hast forgotten the law of thy God, I will also forget they children.")

<u>Those who rebel against the light can expect to perish in the dark. The children of Israel had yet to be persuaded.</u>

Persuaded
1. to successfully urge somebody to perform a particular action, especially by reasoning, pleading, or coaxing
2. to make somebody believe something, especially by giving good reasons for doing so

READ Psalm 116:1-8
* Verse 10 – "I believed, therefore have I spoken...."

Paul references David's word. He knew what David was talking about.
* 2 Corinthians 4:13 – "Yet we have the same spirit of faith as he had who wrote, I have believed, and therefore have I spoken. We too believe, and therefore we speak."

Your life must reflect your "persuasion" of the Gospel of Jesus Christ. Hebrews 11:13-14 says, "These all died in faith, not having received the promises, but having seen them afar off, and were persuaded of them, and embraced them, and confessed that they were strangers and pilgrims on the earth. For they that say such things declare plainly that they seek a country."

SPIRITUAL EMPOWERMENT
Christ the Liberator
Philippians 4:13
Geraleen Talmadge

EMPOWER: TO GIVE STRENGTH

GIVE THE RIGHT OF AUTHORITY

Philippians 4:13 – **"I can do every thing through Him who gives me strength."**-NIV

(**READ**: Joel 2:28-29)

We are not concerned in this meeting with secular empowerment. We are speaking of spiritual empowerment for all mankind, but especially we speak of spiritual empowerment for women.

We can trace the history of women back through the years of paganism and the time of the Greeks, Romans, and even into Judaism and we find that their plight during those years was very different from conditions or circumstances that we are under today.

In the early history women were considered very little above the status of a slave in the household, under the complete authority and control of the husband. In Greek society, the woman's main task was to produce sons for her husband, so they could be superior warriors. When her child-bearing years ended, the husband could easily get a divorce with no legal process needed.

It is interesting to note that during this time, the government passed a law making it illegal for women to have more than a half ounce of gold or certain rich clothing items they weren't supposed to wear.

History tells us that the women really objected to these measures. I don't know if they toyi-toyied (a special march that was used in South Africa during the days of apartheid) or what they did, but their power was sufficient to have the laws repealed. During that era, laws became lax and morals dropped. Divorce became a common occurrence. It was said that the noble ladies counted their age not by the passing of years but by the number of divorces they had.

In Old Testament times, the position of women in Israel was very different from those of women in the heathen nations. Israelite law sought to protect women, to safeguard her rights and guarantee her freedom. In Proverbs 31, we read high and lofty and beautiful words describing woman at the height of her excellence. It is declared that her price is above rubies.

Under strict Judaism, women had a place of dignity in the home. She was the husband's conscience, encouraging him to a life of holiness. Although children were the special charge of the mother, the father also had responsibility in their training.

THE COMING OF CHRIST

The life and ministry of Jesus was the turning point in the history of women. He insisted on protecting the sanctity of their personal lives and promoting the activity of their religious lives.

The Jewish rabbis didn't teach women publicly, as education was for men. The only education the women were allowed was that which had to do with the home. During the ministry of Jesus, however, it is evident that He taught women privately and in His public ministry. Women, as part of the multitudes, received His teachings.

He visited the home of Mary, Martha, and Lazarus many times, but on the first occasion, we see Mary sitting at His feet listening to His teachings. He even stated to Martha that Mary had chosen the better part.

Jesus spent time with the Samaritan woman at the well having a long theological discussion with her (a harlot at that). In the parables that He taught, He often alternated using women and men in His illustration. (Refer to Luke 15: the man and his sheep; the woman and the lost coin.) He spoke of the lilies of the field that do not toil (men's work) and spin (woman's work).

When Lazarus died, Jesus went to the home again, and it was to Mary and Martha that He revealed the truth of the resurrection as it related to Him, not just an event of the end time.

He used women in His teaching also. The sacrificial giving of a widow was used to teach the disciples that true value is based not on quantity but on quality. Therefore, we see that the Lord held up to men the lives and examples of women. The fact that Jesus would do this indicated not only His interest in women but showed His appreciation for their intellectual capacity, but also of their spiritual capabilities.

On two occasions, Jesus allowed women to anoint Him. These are just a few instances, but they should serve to show us that Jesus raised the level of womanhood considerably by His mentioning of them in His messages and also by association.

WOMEN AS MINISTERS TO JESUS:

In Luke 8:2 we learn of certain women who ministered to Jesus of their substance. These were women from Galilee who seemingly followed Him and assisted Him in a financial way.

Today what is expected? Women are to follow the example that they see in the Word of God.

A. Homemaker or homemaker/business woman

Throughout the Bible we have examples of God-fearing mothers. Someone has said "The hand that rocks the cradle rules the world." Proverbs 31 gives a good picture of a homemaker. She cares for all the needs of her family. At a time when clothing couldn't be purchased at Woolworth's or Ackerman's, she had to weave the materials and then make the garments. This woman has been held up through the centuries as an ideal mother. Remembering that it isn't enough to feed the children physical food, but like Lois, Timothy's grandmother and Eunice, his mother, we must pass on to our children the faith that has been received by us.

Through family devotions, through taking the children regularly to church, Sunday school, and youth services; by living exemplary lives before them also, we help them see and learn the gospel more readily. We can't teach them one thing and then live another in front of them. "Actions speak louder than words."

Is this the way it is in your home? Mother is the keeper of all things. When anything is lost, who is approached to ask where it is? She is the knower of all things. It is the mother who must decide if the child is ill enough to take him to the doctor. She is the one who knows when to be quiet rather than speak. She is also the maker of all things. She prepares the food that the family enjoys. She is the peace keeper in the family. She makes the children smile, etc. She has no sick leave, no days off, works lots of overtime, and gets no pay.

B. The church

As a member of the body of Christ, we have a part to play in the workings of the body. (**READ**: 1 Corinthians 12:12-27.) Each part of the body has its own function. If one part doesn't render its service, it puts pressure on the rest of the members. As a Christian, you have a responsibility to use your gifts and talents in every way you can in your local church.

So often, women think that only men can be used of the Lord. When the devil tells you that, take the Word, and show him differently.

- * The Shunamite woman showed hospitality to Elisha. She housed and fed a man of God, and God rewarded her with the promise of a son (2 Kings 4:8).
- * A young captive maid brought a message to Naaman of the possibility of healing for his leprosy (2 Kings 5:2).
- * Deborah was a homemaker, a judge, and led the army into battle (Judges 4:4).
- * Esther, a young Jewish orphan, at the risk of her own life, fulfilled God's purpose in her life and saved her nation from being destroyed (Esther 1-10).
- * Mary, a young sixteen year old girl, submitted to the will of God. "Behold the handmaid of the Lord, but it done unto me according to they word (Luke 1:30). God used her to give birth to the Savior of the World.
- * Women in Luke 8; Mark 15:40.
- * Anna – Luke 2:36-38 – Prophesied at the age of 84; God used her to confess Jesus Christ as the Redeemer of the world.
- * Priscilla – Acts 18:24-28 – teacher.

There are classes to be taught; there is music to be made; there is the church to be cleaned, visitors to greet, flowers to bring, prayer to be offered, and Women's Ministry to be promoted and enjoyed.

There are husbands who are ministers or whatever work they are in that need your support, your prayers, and your love, devotion and faithfulness.

C. Your community

There is a world out there that also needs you ladies. They will die without Christ and their blood will be on your hands if you don't do your part to win them to Christ. Pray for their souls.

Pray to the Lord of the harvest for workmen in the fields. Raise monies for the Feast of Ingathering so men and women can be trained to go as ministers and missionaries. Be willing for your sons and daughters to be used of the Lord. This is the challenge that I leave with you today. You are first class citizens; you are loved by God. He needs you to do the very best that you can for the world's dying millions in your home, in your church, in your community.

(**Author's note:** The sermon above was used in WM seminars across Africa.)

YOU MIGHT BE IN THE MIDDLE OF A MIRACLE
Hebrews 2:4
Sharon Hartman

We read in the Bible about all the miracles that were performed. Some were accomplished by people in the Old Testament through God, and some by people in the New Testament. Christ performed many. Why is it that it seems not as many are taking place today?

Let's look at some miracles and see.

I. When did miracles occur?
   1. When there were concerns over needs.
      a. Jesus fed the 5,000 with 5 loaves and 3 fish; <u>they were hungry</u>.
      b. He turned the water into wine; <u>He supplied a need</u>.
      c. Moses struck a rock to get water and prayed for manna and quail. <u>The people were hungry and thirsty</u>.
      d. Elijah prayed for rain when there was a drought. <u>The people needed rain for survival</u>.

Why do we need a miracle today? Are we hungry? Do you have a need for God to supply? Are you thirsty? Do you need something for survival? These are basic needs. Jesus said in Matthew 5:6, "Blessed are those who hunger and thirst after righteousness, For they will be filled." In Matthew 6:33, He said: "But seek ye first the kingdom of God and His righteousness, and all these things shall be added unto you." These are needs that we have for survival. If today you are sitting here with a need – you are hungry, thirsty, or you need a financial miracle, you may be sitting in the middle of a miracle. Jesus said ask and ye shall receive. As we have seen in these verses, we need to seek something else first: His righteousness and the kingdom of God. When we come to Him genuinely seeking Him, then He will provide the miracle, both spiritually and physically.

2. Healing miracles occurred.
   a. Blind man
   b. Peter's mother-in-law
   c. Man with withered hand
   d. Woman with the issue of blood

Many healings occurred that were miracles. People looked in awe upon those miracles that were performed. Why did Jesus heal? He was <u>compassionate</u>; people had <u>faith</u>. What do we see in people these days? Let's step on him so we can go up the ladder. Oh, he's sick – too bad. Sometime I'll pray for you. We say it, but no prayer comes forth.

We've seen miracles here at Faith Central Fellowship. Ray Scruggs had his back healed. Mr. Reich was healed. I could ask right now how many of you have had a healing touch in a service here, and I'm sure we would have many hands go up. What is your thinking? They probably weren't that bad to start with, or it probably hurt again when they got home. Look deep within. Why do we not have miracles? Are we compassionate as Jesus was? When you see someone sick or maimed or whatever, do you turn away and not want to deal with it or do you have compassion?

Do you want to see them healed? Do you go on your knees and intercede for that person? Or better yet, do you lay hands on them and pray that they will be healed? You might say, "I don't have the gift of healing. I can't lay hands on one and they be healed." How do you know? Have you tried it? Compassion and faith are the two things that help it work. The hardest one is faith. Do we really believe Jesus can heal? Do we expect Him to do it? We're afraid that He won't. Even if it doesn't come immediately, the healing may be in progress. We have to step out, have compassion and faith, and we may see miracles begin to happen in this place.

God honors us when we are sincere and trust in Him. Another thing is motive. Do we want them to be healed so that everyone can see you have some special spiritual power, or do you want them to be healed so that all can see the glory of God and fall down on their knees before Him and accept Him as Savior and Lord?

3. Jesus heals our hurts.

      a. Barren women
      b. Woman of Samaria
      c. Mary Magdalene
      d. The storm

Many women prayed to God in the Bible because they were barren. A few examples are Sarah, Hannah, and Elizabeth. These women went through shame in those days. They longed for a baby for years and never had one. They were ridiculed, but God saw their hurt and reached down to touch the womb, and they gave birth. God sees what our concerns are. He perfects that which concerns us.

The woman of Samaria didn't even know who Jesus was; He sought her out. She had had five husbands and was living with someone else at the time. Jesus revealed to her what was going on and told her to drink of the "living water." Jesus is concerned about us no matter where we are. If you have sinned greatly, He says, "Come. I have a miracle for you. I'm concerned about your hurts and only through me can you receive the healing you need."

We see Mary Magdalene, a prostitute who Jesus reached down and touched. Her life was full of sin, shame, and hurt. She was the first woman to share the good news of Jesus. God sees your hurts today. He wants to give you a miracle.

Jesus calmed the storm. Maybe today there is a storm raging in the midst of your soul. It could be sin; it could be circumstances. Whatever that storm is, Jesus wants to say, "Peace be still." When He commands, even the wind and waves obey. What are the hurts in your life today? Jesus can take care of them. Right now you are in the middle of a miracle; let Jesus perform it in your life.

   4. Gifts of the Spirit
      a. Peter walking on the water
      b. Holy Spirit being outpoured

The Lord gives us miracles sometime that are not concerns, healings, or hurts. When the storm was raging, Jesus was walking on the water to His disciples. He came to take care of the storm, but Peter wanted to come to Him. Jesus said, "Come." The Holy Spirit took charge as Peter stepped out of the boat. This morning, you may be at a point in your life where you might just need to step out of the boat. God may be calling you to new dimensions in your life. As long as you hold on to the old, nothing can be manifested through the Spirit.

Jesus is calling you this morning, "Come, step out of the boat." You may be afraid; your faith may waver. There may be times when He has to reach down and pick you up as you are sinking, and He will. Step out of your comfort zone and come to Him. He will come through for you.

One of the greatest gifts and miracles that we have is the outpouring of the Holy Spirit. In John 14 and 15, Jesus told His disciples that He was going away and He would send a comforter to be with them. He didn't leave them by themselves. He told them that they would do greater things than He had done because they would have the Spirit of Truth.

In the book of Acts, we have the story of the outpouring of the Holy Spirit. The saints of God were gathered in a room, and they were praying. (**Read** Acts 2:1-4.) The Holy Spirit came for several reasons. First, Jesus had promised them; second, because they were prayed up; third, because they were in one accord. This was a great miracle. People spoke in other tongues, and people from other places could understand. Now, let me say the tongues were just the evidence that the Spirit was there.

The Holy Spirit came to give power. After the Holy Spirit was manifested, they were changed. No more did they have to hide in a room and pray. They boldly stood in the street and preached the gospel of Jesus. Thousands were saved.

Peter stood before the multitudes and proclaimed the gospel of Jesus. We see him in prison and ultimately giving his life. Before he was afraid to say he knew Jesus. Why the change? Because the power of the Holy Spirit was flowing through him.

If you have accepted Christ as your Savior but you are still sitting back and are afraid to do anything for the Lord, then accept this gift. He wants to give you power and boldness. The Holy Spirit was not just for those people a long time ago. He is for us today. There is no way I could stand up here before you and proclaim the power of the Holy Spirit in my life without that gift. That power gave a shy girl like me boldness to stand up here and proclaim the gospel to you. Still, sometimes when I think about it, it scares me, but when His anointing is flowing through me, there is nothing like it.

If you are afraid of the Holy Spirit, let me tell you, it's like no high that you could ever have in the world. It's a great miracle, and you only have to ask to receive for Him to come into your life.

5. Salvation

(**Read** John 3:1, 2.) Here is a sinner who was a great ruler of the Jews. He was afraid to come to Jesus by day, so he came by night. He knew

Jesus had to be from God because he recognized the miracles. However, Jesus told him that the greatest miracle of all was being born again. He explained that when a person comes to Christ, it is like having a brand new life. It is like being born again. Sometimes we wish we could go back and change things in our life. We can only change them by accepting Christ. Others may still remember what we've done, but Jesus wipes the slate clean. God puts those sins into the sea of forgetfulness to remember them no more. This is the greatest miracle of all: that Jesus could take a sinner like me and give me a brand new life with Him. The best part of it is that one day we will be in heaven living forever with the King of kings and the Lord of lords.

II. Why did these miracles occur?
   1. To manifest the glory of God – In John 11:4 Jesus said, "This sickness is not unto death, but for the glory of God, that the Son of God may be glorified through it."
   2. To show the works of God – In John 9:3 Jesus said, "Neither this man nor his parents sinned, but that the works of God should be revealed in him."
   3. To fulfill the divine commission – Mark 16:15 states "Go ye into all the world, and preach the gospel to every creature."
   4. To fulfill prophecy – (**Read** Joel 2:27-29.) It was foretold. He will never put us to shame. He is pouring out His Spirit on us, both menservants and maidservants – men and women. He is working through His Holy spirit. These are the last days, and signs are pointing to them today. We don't know when He will come, but we know many signs have been fulfilled. We hear about earthquakes, hurricanes, Tsunamis, seasons mixed up, and so many things. Miracles are all around us.

How can we see miracles happen today?
1. Be hungry and thirsty
2. Be sensitive to needs
3. Have compassion
4. Have faith
5. Give your desires over to Him
6. Yield disappointments and hurts to Him
7. Pray
8. Turn from sin

Jesus is here this morning. You might be in the middle of a miracle. What miracle do you want God to perform for you? Do you need the miracle of salvation? Do you have a need that He can supply? Do you need healing? Is there a hurt or a storm that is raging inside of you and you need Jesus to calm that storm and say, "Peace be still." It doesn't matter how big the hurt or sin; He can take care of it. Do you need the baptism of the Holy Spirit to provide boldness and power in your life? Do you need to step out of your comfort zone and do what God is calling you to do? Step out of the boat. You are in the middle of a miracle; let God perform it for you.

WHAT KIND OF PATTERN ARE YOU?
Acts 2:32
Jane Blass

Patterns:
- * What do these all have in common? Show three packages of patterns.
- * Any of you ever sew or make a craft? You need a pattern.
- * Learn quickly in life: each gets bigger if original is not used.

Original pattern is Jesus:
- * He knows we are human and need flesh and blood to see to follow.
- * We have apostles, prophets, evangelists, pastors, teachers.
- * The Bible is careful to tell us what a good pattern is.

Titus 2:1-5	Show yourself a good pattern.
1 Corinthians 4:15-17	Imitate me.
1 Corinthians 11:1	Imitate me as I imitate Christ.
Philippians 3:17-19	Follow my example – you have us for a pattern.

- • According to Titus, you and I are one of those patterns.
- • It is an awesome responsibility to be a good pattern.
- • Almost all come to Christ under the influence of another human being.

Story:

The story is told of Gordon Maxwell, missionary to India, that when he asked a Hindu scholar to teach him the language, the Hindu replied, "No, Sahib, I will not teach you my language. You would make me a

Christian." Gordon Maxwell replied, "You misunderstand me. I am simply asking you to teach me your language." Again the Hindu responded, "No, Sahib, I will not teach you. No man can live with you and not become a Christian."

* We can only be good if we model exactly after the original.

God gives us patterns as we read the Scriptures.
* We must be certain they are following Christ according to the Word. They are no substitute for us personally seeking the face of God and learning from the original ourselves.
* <u>Final Quest</u> by Rick Joyner – White Throne
* God has given you pastors and teachers in your own church. You can know them and their lifestyle, and how they live the Word before you.
 < TV personality would be shocked!
 < Preachers divorcing and congregations applauding

What makes us a good pattern after Jesus?

Let me help you in this self examination and help myself as well by putting a few personal questions to you which we could all consider as we walk with Christ.
* Am I Spirit filled and lead; are the gifts of the Spirit in my life?
* Do I cherish the face of God more than His hands?
* Am I clean in thought, word, and deed?
* Is Christ (so far as I can make Him) the head of my home?
* As a husband, do I love my wife as Christ loved the church?
* As a woman, am I showing respect to my husband?
* Am I walking humbly before God and men?
* Do co-workers know I'm a Christian?
* Would my neighbors and family be drawn to Christ by knowing me?
* Do I make time each day for prayer and study of my Bible?
* Do I go to church regularly and take communion?
* Do other Christians find it easy to work with me?
* Do I tithe and give freely and cheerfully to the kingdom of God?
* Can other see I'm growing in Christ?

Story:

Around the turn of the century in rural Tennessee an old man crippled with arthritis was very faithful in his assembling with the saints. Twice on Sunday and on Wednesday nights a little girl watched from her window as the old man with his cane painful made his way down to the little church on the corner. The old man went to his reward never realizing just what an impact he had made for the cause of Christ. Because of his godly influence, many will go into heaven with him. There can be no greater joy than to reach heaven and to hear someone say, "I am here because you have shown me the way."

The Christian sees through kinder eyes – like Jesus.
He gives from a bigger heart – like God.
He speaks with a purer tongue – like Christ.
He serves with more willing hands – like Jesus.
He walks with a greater faith – like his Lord.
He loves with agape love – like the Father in heaven.
He thinks with a spiritual mind – like Christ.
He sees the needs of others with a compassionate view – like Jesus.
He heals the wounds of other with love – like the Master.
The Christian is different only when Jesus rules his life.

MARY IN A MARTHA WORLD
Luke 10:38-42
Nelle Goodman

1. What did it mean to be like Martha?
2. What did it mean to be like Mary?
3. Notice that Jesus was visiting both.
4. Martha received (invited) Jesus into her house.
   a. She invited Jesus and the twelve disciples.
   b. She was very industrious like the woman in Proverbs 31.
      1. She was virtuous.
      2. She cared for her home well.
      3. She was a good cook.
      4. She was wise about business affairs.
      5. She was very smart – a worker.
      6. She cared for others.
      7. She was very brave.

        8. She was trustworthy.
        9. People came to her for advice.
        10. She had a great influence on others.
    c. With all these good traits she was still human.
        1. Fidgety (nervous)
        2. Busy
        3. Bossy
        4. Orderly
        5. Perfectionist
        6. Complainer
        7. Need an attitude adjustment
        8. Thought no one cared how hard she worked
        9. Time was of great importance
        10. Wanted everything to be just right
5. Mary
    a. She loved Jesus – Matthew 6:33.
    b. She was meek and humble.
    c. She had a submissive spirit.
    d. She was a peacemaker.
    e. She was pleasant to be around.
    f. She was compassionate.
    g. She hungered after righteousness.
    h. She was willing to endure criticism.
    i. She was committed to Jesus.
    j. She was pure in her heart.
    k. She was salt in attitude and actions.
    l. She was light. People saw her as a caring person.
    m. She knew that life was more than raiment.
6. Mary and Martha made deliberate choices.

Martha	Mary
Loved Jesus	Loved Jesus
A talker	A listener
Fretful	Calm
Discontented	Contented
Complainer	Held her peace
Worrier	Concerned

Worked for people (cooked, etc.)	Interested in people
Chose to feed the body	Chose to feed the soul
Chose to run around	Sat at Jesus' feet
Chose to be a worker	Chose to be a worshiper

7. Both made good quality choices.

They both loved Jesus, had compassion, loved people, were considerate of Jesus and the disciples, and were willing to go the extra mile for others.

MISSION IMPOSSIBLE
[Scriptures cited in the body of the sermon.]
Carolyn Wade

<u>Mathew. 19:26 (NKJV)</u>
After being questioned by His disciples on many issues, Jesus made this statement, "With men (humanly speaking) this is impossible, but with God all things are possible."

<u>Luke 18:27 (NKJV)</u>
"The things which are impossible with men are possible with God."

<u>Genesis 18:14 (NKJV)</u>
Abraham and Sarah when faced with having a child past child bearing age asked this question: "How can a worn-out woman like me have a child when my husband is also old?" Her question was answered with a question: "Is anything too hard for the Lord."

<u>Jeremiah 32:17 (NKJV)</u>
"Ah, Lord God! Behold, You have made the heavens and earth by Your power and outstretched arm. There is nothing too hard for You." NOTHING IS TOO DIFFICULT FOR YOU.
> When we truly make Him Lord over every area of our lives He becomes to us the Lord of the impossible.
> Think of a specific area of your life right now where you are overwhelmed and ask yourself if anything is too hard for God.
> Is this habit I'm trying to overcome too hard for Him?
> Is this illness in my body too hard for Him?

> Is this problem I'm struggling with too hard for Him?
> When the enemy attacks you with a variety of things, remember to make it a habit to ask yourself this question: Is this too hard for God to handle? No, of course not, so let Him.

Isaiah 59:1, 2 (NKJV)
"Behold, the Lord's hand is not shortened, That it cannot save; Nor His ear heavy, That it cannot hear. But your iniquities have separated you from your God."

The people in Isaiah's day were saying that God no longer answered prayer. "No, Isaiah declared;" the trouble isn't with God; the trouble is with you. The hindrance isn't on God's part; it's on yours." If you are facing an impossible situation, let me tell you on the highest authority that with God all things are possible; the impossible is on your end.

Moses: From the time he entered Pharaoh's court, threw his rod to the floor and it became a serpent which swallowed up the serpents of Pharaoh's men, that rod became known as the Rod of God in the hand of Moses. Miracle after miracle occurred. When they were at the Red Sea, the army of Pharaoh was coming fast behind them. Was the mission impossible? I don't think so. Moses lifted up his rod over the sea at God's command and declared, "Fear not, stand still and see the salvation of the Lord. The Egyptians whom you have seen today you will see them no more forever." – [Exodus 14:13-NKJV]

The pillar of fire moved between Israel and Egypt; God caused a wind to divide the sea, and Israel went over on dry ground. When the Egyptians followed, the sea returned to normal and swallowed up the entire army of Pharaoh.

> Are you between a rock and a hard place?
> Are you facing impossible situations?
> Is there trouble on every hand?

The Word of the Lord for you is this:
* Fear not…stand still.
* Quit trying to work things out.
* Still your efforts.
* Still your emotions.
* Still your flesh.
* Be still and know that He is God, and let him work for you.
* As long as you're trying to work things out, God won't.

- He will bring about a separation between you and your enemy.
- He will cause the winds of the Spirit to blow upon that situation until it is dried up and you can walk right out of it.

Exodus 15:23

Traveling in the wilderness, the children of Israel became thirsty; there was not water for three days. They came to Marah and finally found water, but it was too bitter to drink. The people murmured to Moses; Moses cried out to God which became a pattern. Was the mission impossible? I don't think so. God showed Moses a tree, which he was to cast into the bitter waters, and they became sweet.

I'm here to tell someone that when you are thirsty, dry, and bitter, let me show you a tree. "Mercy there was great and grace was free. Pardon there was multiplied to me. There my burdened soul found liberty." Where? At Calvary. It is the cure for all that ails you.

2 Kings 6:5

The sons of the prophets were cutting down beams to build a new meeting palace when an axe head fell in the water. The young man was distressed for the axe was borrowed. They called Elisha and showed him where it had fallen in. Was this a mission impossible? I don't think so. Elisha cut down a stick and cast it in the water where the axe head fell, and behold, the iron swam.

Are you heavy burdened? Are you sinking to the bottom? Are you distressed over many things? What God wants us to see in this story is that He cares about the little things as well as the big thing, everyday stresses that come our way. Casting a stick in the water is casting our care on the Lord for He cares for you. He will cause that heavy burden you're carrying to become light. "Take my yoke upon you," Jesus said, "and learn of me for my yoke is easy and my burden light." – [Matthew 11:29, 30-NIV].

The virgin birth of Jesus as recorded in the gospels is still debated today. Was that mission impossible? I don't think so. Some would say so, but by faith we believe Luke 1:37, "For with God nothing shall be impossible." In the natural this would be impossible.

Are you trying to birth something in the natural which is an impossible situation? Move it from the natural to the supernatural, and watch God perform the impossible. Cease from your labor and rest, and let God be God. Hey, there are some things that God doesn't need your help with – only your trust.

Acts 16:16-34

Paul and Silas were thrown in jail for casting out the demon of divination from a slave girl who was making her masters much money through fortune telling. Her masters had Paul and Silas thrown in jail, stating that these Jews were causing exceeding trouble in the city. They were fastened to the wall with their feet in stocks in a dirty smelling dungeon, and what do we find them doing? They were praying and singing praises to God. Amazing! Was this mission impossible? I don't think so.

When life has your back against the wall, you have no way out. Take a clue from Paul and Silas, who at midnight prayed and sang praise to God. Then watch the impossible situation become possible.

I could go on with impossible situations recorded in the Bible that God through faith, trust and patience made possible, but I leave you with this story.

Luke 11:2

Mary and Martha's brother, Lazarus, died. They sent for Jesus, but He delayed his coming. Was this mission impossible? I don't think so. Jesus called Lazarus out of the grave after he had been dead for four days and released him from his grave clothes. His sisters received him alive and well. Perhaps you have some dead issues. Things are lifeless; you have no joy; you are just going through the motions. Let me tell you Jesus is here now, and He is calling to you as He did to Lazarus: COME FORTH.

Come forth if you believe you will experience the glory of God. (Everything you need flows in His glory.) Come forth and rise above all that the enemy has put in your way to stop you. Come forth and rise to the challenge to fulfill God's purpose in your life and watch the glory of the Lord invade your space. Come forth and cast all your burdens and cares upon Him. Come forth for He is calling you right now.

WHAT SHALL THE END BE?
1 Peter 4:17
Ruth Powell

Several years ago, I heard Terry Trammel preach on heaven and hell and began studying about both places. (Reference Isaiah 66 and Ezekiel 48.) Isaiah wrote many things in his sixty-six chapters, but notice the last thing he writes about in the last verse of his prophecy: a place where the "worm shall not die" – Isaiah 66:24. Ezekiel also wrote many things, but we want to look at the last verse of his book where he saw a place where "the name of the city from that day shall be, The Lord is there" – Ezekiel 48:35. They were talking about two very different places. Each of us will end up in one of these places. What shall the end be?

As far as we know, there are only three places where men have lived, now live, or will live: heaven, hell, and earth. A lot of people seem to think they are not good enough for heaven and not bad enough for hell. They hope for an alternative, which isn't so, except for this earth. What we do here will determine our destiny, our end.

There was a time when we didn't exist, but that will never be true again. We are eternal beings, so we will live forever somewhere. The history of man is that he was born, lived and died. As we near the end, there should be much preaching and interest in our future because time is uncertain. We hear no preaching on hell in these days.

Many people don't really believe in hell and often use the word in a joking way, but it is no laughing matter. It seems the majority of mankind is on the broad way that leads to hell – Matthew 7:13.

The Bible has one thousand passages that call out with warnings and invitations. There are two hundred thirty-four warnings in twenty-seven books. That's like driving twenty-seven miles and seeing two hundred thirty-four signs warning against hell. Signs that point out you are going the wrong way. You have to love a God who puts roadblocks, people, and pastors to warn the unsaved. We may be a nuisance as we keep calling and praying.

The Holy Spirit is One who deals with you, wooing you. Also the cross is the greatest roadblock. Gehenna, the place for burning garbage, was half way between Jerusalem and Mount Calvary. The cross stands between heaven and hell as a warning. If you choose to go to hell, you will go in spite of the cross. You will walk past it.

What a contrast between heaven and hell, but there are several similarities. Both will be inhabited by conscious people who will hear, see, feel, and remember. Both are eternal. Both are prepared places. Hell was prepared for the devil and his angels. God never prepared hell for man or man for hell.

They are also different. Heaven is glorious for what's there and for what isn't there. We read in Revelation of a lot of "no mores." No more night, death, tears, sorrow, separation, or sickness. Everything heaven doesn't have, hell does. Hell has no exits and is a bottomless pit. Heaven has gates of pearl, streets of gold. What men worship here, we will walk on there. Heaven has light; hell is a place of outer darkness. Heaven has health, music, worship, and rejoicing. Hell is a place of weeping and wailing. Heaven is a place of eternal rest; hell is torment forever.

Four reasons why I want the last chapter of my life to be like the last verse of Ezekiel's prophecy, rather than Isaiah's.
1. Because of the welcome
2. Children
3. Family
4. Name of the city

Notice a difference in the welcome. Think what your end will be if you die and don't know the Lord. You will be in hell at once at death, at your funeral. The moment you die you go to your eternal home. How awful is hell! Isaiah wrote in 14:9, "Hell from beneath is moved for thee to meet thee at thy coming: it stirreth up the dead for thee...." The inhabitant may get excited for a moment thinking you can help, but there is no help, no hope. What an awful feeling to realize that is forever and ever!

When the child of God leaves this world, the welcome is a wonderful thing. The Bible says, "Precious in the sight of the Lord is the death of his saints" – Psalm 116:15. Jesus will welcome us and say "well done." Paul wasn't fearful when he wrote, "For I am now ready to be offered, and the time of my departure is at hand" – 2 Timothy 4:6. Stephen saw heaven open and knew he had fought the last battle, had gone the last mile, and knew there were joys that awaited him.

Thirty-three million babies have been aborted. Every infant will be in heaven, for of such is the kingdom of heaven. How horrible to spend eternity with the ungodly like Pharaoh, Herod, and Hitler, but no children. Don't you love little children? Can you imagine eternity without them?

I love my family, and I want to be with them. Can you imagine being separated forever from your family? Hell won't just separate saint and sinners, but husbands and wives, moms and dads and children. Choose heaven because of family.

Then the name given to heaven is significant: "The Lord is there." The best thing about heaven isn't the mansions or the gold, but Jesus. Even if there are no gold streets or gates of pearl, even greater than children or family is that Jesus is there. If He is there, that will be heaven. "Behold, the tabernacle of God is with men, and he shall dwell with them, and they shall be his people, and God himself shall be with them, and be their God" – Revelation 21:3. The choice is yours.

(**Author's note:** The statistics about the number of aborted babies used above are out-dated, as the sermon was preached in 1997.)

A PROMISE GIVEN
Genesis 3:15
(Mother's Day 2007)
Marie Cardenas

God gave mothers a promise that began with Eve in Genesis 3:15. There God is speaking to the serpent (and Eve surely hears) when He says: "And I will put enmity between you and the woman, and between your offspring and hers; he will crush (or bruise, disable) your head and you will strike his heel."-[NIV]. In looking at this verse, we quickly think of Jesus who bruised the head of Satan when He willingly went to the cross to die for us. When Jesus rose from the tomb, Satan was defeated, and he no longer had authority over us. Our part is to continue to walk by faith and by the Spirit to keep from falling under the influence of our enemy. In other words, we have to continually keep Satan under our feet, bruised and without power until Jesus returns.

We need to look more closely at the words that God spoke to the serpent: "And I will put enmity between you and the woman and between your offspring and hers." The word "offspring" (NIV), or "seed" (KJV) means posterity, which means "all future descendants or generations." God was speaking here of every believer who would come from Eve. There are two kinds of offspring in this verse: one is Satan's; the other is Eve's.

Jesus spoke of the offspring of Satan when He said to the Pharisees in John 8:44, "You belong to your father, the devil, and you want to carry out your father's desires. He was a murderer from the beginning, not holding to the truth, for there is no truth in him. When he lies, he speaks his native language, for he is a liar and the father of lies."-[NIV]. The offspring of Satan would be those who would not hear the truth spoken by God through Jesus. The offspring of Eve would be those who followed the truth: Jesus.

God has blessed motherhood with a promise through this passage relating to Eve. Though Eve was deceived by Satan and sinned, God already had a plan of forgiveness and redemption that would include her offspring. That plan was through the motherhood of Eve. Her true descendants would be the believers, those who would follow God with all their hearts.

There is a natural enmity between Satan's children who turn away from God and Eve's children who carry and give birth to the next generation that will live for God. Why do you think that there is such a huge fight over our unborn children? Why are they being aborted? One answer is that Satan would like nothing better than to see the next generation of believers destroyed and unable to live for God. Satan would like to make God's promises null and void. This is the promise that God gave Eve and all women who serve God: the serpent's head would be crushed. This cannot take place if her children are destroyed. Though Jesus has already won the battle and bruised the enemy, Satan would like nothing better than to disable the kingdom of heaven on this earth by destroying our children. However, God's plan is for motherhood to be a blessing and a glorious honor to Him.

In Genesis 3:20, Adam called Eve "the mother of all living." The word translated "living" comes from a Hebrew word that means "to revive." Eve can be considered the mother of all people, but we are all dead spiritually until we come to believe and accept the one true God. When we accept what Jesus did for us, we are dead no longer but revived and alive in Him. Adam makes a distinction between the physical and spiritual children. Eve is the mother of all who would be revived – those who were dead and now are alive to God. These revived man and women would be the offspring of Eve. Those would be the ones who would be Satan's enemies. Adam understood, Satan understood, and Eve understood that God had given Eve a promise for descendants who would be reconciled to God and walk with Him again, as Adam and Eve had done in the garden before the fall.

God made Eve a promise that was fulfilled through her offspring. Let's look at how the Bible demonstrates this promise in some of the mothers we find in the Bible. Sarah became the mother of nations because the promise made to Abraham could only take place through her. In Hebrews 11:11 we read, "Through faith also Sara [Sarah] herself received strength to conceive seed, and was delivered of a child when she was past age, because she judged him faithful who had promised." The promise made to Abraham and Sarah was none other than the promise made to Eve. God chose them because they had faith in Him and followed Him wherever He sent them. They had faith, and they were obedient. Their posterity would be taught to follow God in faith, and they would disable Satan's plans to destroy Israel. The child that Sarah bore would be a part of the genealogy of Jesus and a partial fulfillment of the promise made to Eve that her offspring would be enemies of Satan. Their very faith made them the offspring of Eve and the enemies of Satan.

In Genesis 21:8-12, we find Sarah protecting the promise that was made to her and her child. God had promised that through Isaac He would make a great nation, a nation that would follow God. That promise could not come through a slave from Egypt who worshipped other gods. The promise had to be fulfilled through the free woman who worshipped the one true God. As she protected her son from the mocking of Ishmael, who thought he was be heir to Abraham's fortune, she also protected the promise God had given her and Abraham – (and Eve hundreds of years before); the promise that through Isaac, there would be many who would be enemies of Satan. That is why Abraham is told by God to listen to his wife and send Ishmael away.

In 1 Samuel, we find the story of another woman, Hannah, who prayed that she would cease to be barren and have a child. I am sure she had prayed many times to get pregnant, but it didn't happen until she promised to give that child back to God. He gave her the joy of having a child and then blessed her gift to Him by making Samuel a great prophet among God's people. Hannah was a woman of prayer, and I believe she never stopped praying for Samuel. The promise given to Eve was fulfilled again in a descendant, Hannah, as Samuel helped to disable Satan's plans against God's people.

In Luke, we find Elizabeth, the mother of John the Baptist. When the angel announced his birth, he said that John would be a joy and delight to Elizabeth and Zechariah. Isn't that the way it is? Our children are a joy and a delight to us, and isn't it a greater delight to know that they are following the plan that God has set before them? I believe that every child has a future planned for them from their mother's womb just as Isaac did, and Samuel did, and John did. There were bumps in the road for each of these mothers and their children, but they managed to get through them, and the only things we remember are the great things that were done by them.

The promise made to Eve was fulfilled in Elizabeth when the angel said, "Many of the people of Israel will he [John the Baptist] bring back to the Lord their God." – [Luke 1:16-NIV]. (These are the revived ones!) John the Baptist disabled Satan's plans when the people listened to his preaching and turned their lives around to follow God.

Mary was given the greatest honor of all in fulfilling the promise made to Eve. She became the mother of Jesus, who would ultimately destroy Satan's power over humankind. Because of Jesus, we have power through faith in Him to destroy, not just disable, the plans of Satan in our lives. The promise given to Eve is not completely fulfilled yet. That will not be until all the offspring of Eve are in the kingdom or all are revived that will be revived.

Godly mothers are Satan's enemies because they bear children who will follow after God. These mothers believe the promise of God made to Eve saying that her descendants, her righteous descendants, would bruise the head of Satan. Though Christ did His work on the cross, He has told us to continue to make disciples and obey His commands. We are to continue the work He entrusted to us, and as we do, we keep the enemy under our feet.

Mothers, both future and present, God have us a wonderful promise through Eve that our descendants would be Satan's enemy. Satan may have caused the fall in the Garden of Eden, but God promised a godly posterity that would eventually be reconciled to their God and live again in intimacy with Him. Mothers, you are Satan's enemy. Enmity means hatred. Satan hates you and your children. In Genesis, God said there would be enmity between Satan and the woman. That means that you should hate him as much as he hates you. That means that you can stand between Satan and your children as his enemy, warring against him for your children.

There are three ways that we as mothers can disable the enemy in the lives our children. One, we must believe our children are the children of that promise that was given to Eve and to us and that our children will rise up in faith and obedience to God.

Second, the guidance, the teaching, and training that godly mothers give their children will be a blessing to God and a bane to Satan. In 2 Timothy 1:5, Paul commended two women: a mother and a grandmother. He is talking to Timothy when he says, "I [have been] reminded of your sincere faith, which first lived in your grandmother Lois and in your mother Eunice and, I am persuaded, now lives in you also."-[NIV]. These women believed that Timothy would be a man of faith. They modeled their own faith before him. They taught him about their God.

Finally, the third thing is that they prayed for him. Prayer that goes into raising each child will not only protect him or her from the enemy, but will keep them on that narrow path. Timothy is an example of the descendants of that promise to Eve; he was one who was revived because of the influence of a godly mother and grandmother.

Eve, Sarah, Hannah, Elizabeth, Mary, Lois, and Eunice all believed the promise of God. They believed that God would keep His promise.

They believed that their child would be a child of that promise, a child that would further the kingdom of God and disable the enemy in ways they may never have understood completely. These mothers looked toward their God and believed Him. There was joy in their hearts over their children. They protected their children through prayer and taught them the ways of God. God moves when we pray, and I believe that He, understanding the way of love, moves even more quickly to a heart crying out in love for their child – father or mother.

There are many mothers here today who are beautiful in the sight of their children, who have believed the promise of God for them and continue to guide and pray for them. I honor you today just as God honors you for your hard, wonderfully rewarding work as mothers as you fulfill the wonderful promise made to Eve thousands of years ago. By some chance, if you haven't believed the promise of God for your children, there is no time like the present. Believe and pray. God will do a great work in your children as He fulfills His promise. God bless you.

SOAR LIKE AN EAGLE
Isaiah 40:31
Eilish Ayento

Life can be tough with troubles, problems, and hardships that enter into our comfort zones at any time. When faced with an adversary, and it doesn't matter what form it takes, the way that we handle it depends upon our relationship with Jesus Christ and our grounding in His Word. The passage that I read uses the metaphor of an eagle. Let us examine God's Word today.

1. Why an eagle?
* When we are going through a hard time we need strength.
* The eagle, especially in America, is a symbol of strength.
* With the truth, the right thoughts, the right attitude and altitude in the Lord Jesus Christ, you can soar above your troubles.
* To be able to do this we must wait upon the Lord.
* It is important that you develop a quiet time with God so that He can give you the spiritual strength that you need.
* Exodus 19:4-6 (**read**)
* Common sense and a moral life in following God's holy Word.

2. Attributes of an eagle:
- They fly alone and make a nest high in the treetops. They have one mate and make strong nests lining the inside with soft feathers from their body.
- Deuteronomy 32:11-13 (**read**)
- When young eagles grow, the mother shakes the nest and puts the babies on the edge of the nest, then drops them. She then flies around them and scoops them up to safety on her back. They soon learn to fly. They discover their wings and are no longer earthbound.
- We can learn to fly by becoming over comers and living a victorious life.
- When an eagle is wounded in the wing, he flies high to a rock in the mountains. There he spreads his wing and stays there for the sunshine and healing.
- We need to be on the rock Christ Jesus, the son shine from God.
- Romans 13:11-14 (**read**)
- Put on Christ.
- Eagles have keen eyesight. We need the Holy Spirit giving us discernment to know our enemy.

3. The eagle has landed.
- This is a great quote from the men that landed on the moon nearly thirty years ago in an area known as the Sea of Tranquility.
- After an eagle has flown through many storms, the feathers of his wings become ragged. The noise in flight can cause animals to hear it coming.
- His beak and claws have grown too long, and he can't perch on limbs to rest.
- The eagle doesn't consult with the sparrows. He flies high to the mountain rock. There he beats off the claws and his beak and pulls out all his feathers.
- There he sits naked and in a fasting condition until his beak grows, the claws return, and his feathers come in.
- With new strength and renewed, he is ready to meet any type of weather.
- We can learn from the eagle.
- 1 Thessalonians 4:11-12 (**read**)
- Patience and waiting in quiet on the Lord
- 1 Timothy 2:2-3 (**read**)

In closing, we can learn from the common sense in God's creation and the spending of precious time waiting on the Lord in patience and quietness.

(No title)
2 Chronicles 20
Dr. Marysue Huffman Freeman

In chapter 20, we find King Jehoshaphat confronted with three armies. He was told a great multitude was coming against him to battle. These armies were not only threatening him, they were already in progress. His strategists informed him that these kings with their armies had already marched past Syria and beyond the Sea of Galilee to Hazazontamar, which is En Gedi, which was west of the Dead Sea. The Dead Sea is less than 15 miles away from Jerusalem. In other words, the enemy was already almost right at their door.

En Gedi is the area where David effectively hid from Saul and more than 3,000 of his troops. No one could overrate this location as a place of refuge. Therefore, allowing the enemy a supposed secure, safe place to retreat in case their surprise attack was not as effective as they supposed. However, these enemies did not know the God of Abraham, Isaac, Jacob, and David. This was the God who showed David even the specific cave in which Saul was sleeping while his soldiers stood guard. He was the same God who protected David while he maneuvered through those troops to the cave where his enemy was and back out with the piece of his garment.

When Jehoshaphat heard of their impending attack, he realized that he was surrounded by the armies from Syria on the north, Ammon on the west, and Moab on the south. He was at a similar point as Moses at the Red Sea. Mountains were on one side of the sea, and Pharaoh's army coming up behind. Verse 3 tells us that Jehoshaphat feared.

He did not fear, as many of us do today when we hear the news that our enemies are at the door. It could be the enemy of broken health, lost finances, relationships, or many other enemies we encounter during our lives. However, Jehoshaphat did not only fear, he <u>set</u> himself to <u>seek</u> the LORD, and proclaimed a <u>fast</u> throughout <u>all</u> Judah.

There are times our enemies appear to be too strong for us. They seem to have out maneuvered us by keeping us from attaining our highest goals. Many times, the demonic forces that are strongholds in our lives can only be broken by seeking God and fasting. On one occasion, the disciples could not cast a devil out of an individual. They were surprised because, prior to that occasion, they thought all demonic forces were subject to them. When the disciples asked Jesus why they could not cast that spirit out, Jesus told them in Matthew 17:21, "Howbeit this kind goeth not out but by prayer and fasting." In Mark 9:29 He said, "This kind can come forth by nothing, but by prayer and fasting." Jesus frequently went apart to pray and fasted prior to His encounter with these forces of darkness.

In Isaiah 58:6, God asked Israel, "Is not this the fast that I have chosen?" In response we find the answer stated in the form of a question. "Is not this the fast that I have chosen? To loose the bands of wickedness, to undo the heavy burdens, and to let the oppressed go free, and that ye break every yoke?" In verse 7 we find the explanation as to why we need/must fast. Jehoshaphat knew that God would hear from heaven if he set himself to seek Him.

We see here that the king "set himself." To set requires one to arbitrarily do a thing; to place or put in the right place, position, or condition for us; put in proper order, or arrange. Even though Jehoshaphat was the king, the highest authority, he immediately placed himself under the authority of God. None of Judah rebelled at the king's decision. They gathered themselves together to ask <u>help</u> of the LORD. <u>All</u> the people in every city came to seek the Lord.

Why is it that everyone wants to go to church when trouble comes? Most of us are just like Jehoshaphat and these children of Israel. When trouble came, they all went to seek God. Thank God we know to seek Him. Thank God we have enough knowledge of Him to know He will hear us and answer if we will humble ourselves and seek Him.

The Holy Spirit is revealing to each of us here that the head of the household must take authority in time of crisis. Whether it is a rebellious teenager, a defiant spouse, a wicked employer or co-workers, creditors, tragic news from our physician, whatever the enemy brings, we are to turn to God, acknowledge His power and authority. In Nehemiah 5, he prayed, "so that none is able to withstand thee...." Nehemiah was asking God to spare the nation. Before asking, he reminded God of His standing.

In verse 7, King Jehoshaphat reminded God, "Art not thou our God, who didst drive out the inhabitants of this land before thy people Israel, and gavest it to the seed of Abraham thy friend forever." We are to remind God of His covenant that He has with us and acknowledge that we know

He is the one who has given us whatever the enemy is trying to take or has stolen from us.

Verse 9 does not question whether trouble will come in our lives. He prayed, "<u>when</u> evil cometh upon us as the sword of judgment...." The king knew that we as human beings sin and go astray from what God has commanded us to do. He also knew that, even when we have sinned to the degree that God finally brings judgment, we can fall on His mercy and cry out for His <u>help</u>, and He will hear and answer our cry.

IF GOD BE FOR US, WHO CAN BE AGAINST US?
Romans 8:31
Patsy Jones

Let's take this verse apart this morning.

IF – This word isn't a question, but a statement. It isn't a condition, but a certainty. Not if God is for us (like is He really for us?), but literally "Since God is for us."

IF GOD – Who is for us? God. Who are we talking about?

1. **THE ONE WHO CREATED US.** Isaiah 45:18 (**read**)

    * Lord – Jehovah – "the existing One." This is the proper name of the one true God.
    * heavens – sky, abode of the stars, as the visible universe, atmosphere, etc.
    * God – the true God.
    * formed – to form, fashion, frame
    * made – to attend to, put in order
    * established – to be set up, be stable, be secure
    * vain – that which is empty, nothingness, empty space
    * inhabited – to dwell, have one's abode

Jehovah created the universe, sky, the atmosphere, and the true God fashioned the earth, framed it not in vain – not empty, or in a state of chaos; He made it for people to dwell in. He took nothing and made the universe out of it. Then He hung His creation on nothing – Job 26:7b, "and hangeth the earth upon nothing." That is where it hangs today. The earth is hanging somewhere in a vast universe poised on its own weight. He fitted it and designed it to give to us – mankind."

Isaiah 40:26; 40:12 (**read**)

2. Isaiah 40:26 – "Lift up your eyes on high, and behold [look at, consider] who hath created these things…."

3. Isaiah 40:12 – He measured the waters in the hollow of his hand.

4. "And meted out heaven with the span [the distance from His thumb to the little finger on an outstretched hand] of his hand."

5. "Comprehended the dust of the earth in a measure." – comprehended means to hold. He holds the dry earth in his three fingers (thumb and two fingers – a pinch in cooking terms.

6. "Weighed the mountains in scales, and the hills in a balance." – It is like He holds scales in His hands and weighs the mountains and the hills. His power is unlimited and, no creature can compare with Him.

Matthew Henry

1. "He has a vast reach. View the celestial globe, and you are astonished at the extent of it; to him they are but a hand-breadth, so large-handed is he. View the terraqueous globe [consisting of land and water], and he has the command of that too. All the waters in the world he can measure in the hollow of his hand, where we can hold but a little water; and the dry land he easily manages. It is no more to him than a pinch, or that which we take up between our thumb and two fingers."

2. His strength is so vast that He holds the mountains and hills as if He weighed them in a pair of balances and put them into place as a ballast to the globe or a stabilizer to the earth. He put everything in just the right place to keep the earth hanging out there on its nothingness.

7. **BRINGETH OUT THEIR HOST BY NUMBER** – host – whole creation by count. **AND CALLETH THEM ALL BY NAMES BY THE GREATNESS OF HIS MIGHT** (abundance, greatness of his power, wealth, physical strength) **FOR THAT HE IS STRONG IN POWER; NOT ONE FAILETH** – is lacking.

He hung out all the stars in the universe and called them all by name – Isaiah 40:26.

PSALM 147:4 – HE TELLETH THE NUMBER OF THE STARS; HE CALLETH THEM ALL BY THEIR NAMES.

* This picture is like a general who draws out the squadrons and battalions of his army, of the knowledge he has of them; the stars come out each night just like God set them in order at the beginning. From day-to-day He brings them forth, making them to rise and set in their appointed times.
* He calls them all by names, proper names, and not one of them fails either to appear when He calls them or to do the work to which He sends them.

Does this give you a picture of how big God really is? Who is for us? Just God, the One Who was and is and always will be. He is the One we call by these names:

* **EL ELYON – GOD MOST HIGH, CREATOR, AND POSSESSOR OF HEAVEN AND EARTH; HE IS THE MOST HIGH GOD.**
* **EL SHADDAI – GOD IS ALL POWERFUL AND ALL SUFFICIENT.**
* **JEHOVAH-JIREH – THE LORD WHO SEES AND WHO PROVIDES** – He is the God who wants to supply my needs.
* **JEHOVAH-NISSI – THE LORD OUR BANNER (OUR BATTLE FLAG).** He is the God who will fight my battles.
* **JEHOVAH-TSIDKENU – THE LORD IS MY RIGHTEOUSNESS** – He is the Lord who wants to forgive my faults.
* **JEHOVAH-ROHI – THE LORD IS MY SHEPHERD** – He is the God who wants to lead, guide, and protect me.
* **JEHOVAH-ROPHI – THE LORD WHO HEALS** – He is the God who wants to heal my body and my hurts.
* **JEHOVAH-SHALOM – THE LORD OUR PEACE** – He is the God who wants to relieve my stress and give me peace.
* **JEHOVAH-SHAMMAH – THE LORD IS THERE** – He is the God who will never leave me nor forsake me.

Who is for us? What does it mean for God to be for us? Since God is for us that means He is on our side. God is on my side. God is for me.

Today God is for me. Tomorrow God is for me. Everyday from now to eternity, God is for me. Tell your neighbor that God is on your side.

GOD IS ON MY SIDE. God is interested in what is going on in my life. God is interested in everything that concerns me whether little or big. He is interested in the outcome of my struggles. Why He is not just interested; He is right in the middle of them with me.

Deuteronomy 20:1-4 (read)

God gave Moses some directions for the children of Israel, and these directions were how they were to conduct themselves in battles. This is how the army of the Lord was to behave.

1. When you go out to battle against your enemies and you see horses and chariots, and an army greater than your own, "**BE NOT AFRAID OF THEM: FOR THE LORD THY GOD IS WITH THEE.**"

2. Do not let your hearts faint. **DO NOT LOSE YOUR COURAGE.**

3. Do not fear. **DO NOT LOSE YOUR FAITH**.

4. Do not tremble or be terrified. **DO NOT WRING YOUR HANDS AND ASK "WHAT ARE WE GOING TO DO?"**

WHY? Because you are in the army of the Lord, and the Lord your God is He who goes with you to fight for you against your enemies to save you. God is for us; He is on our side. He's saying, "Do not be afraid, do not lose your courage, do not lose your faith, do not tremble or be terrified, because I am on your side, and I am going to fight for you, and I am going to deliver you."

It does not matter what the odds are; God is on my side. It does not matter if it looks hopeless; God is on my side. It does not matter if the situation looks bigger than you or me; God is on my side. **GOD IS ON MY SIDE.**

Psalm 118:6; Hebrews 13:6 (read) – Helper in Greek is a compound word which comes from **(boe)** which means a cry to help and **(theo)** which means to run. Put them together, and it means one who comes running when we cry for help. This Greek compound word paints a picture of the Lord as one who is poised and ready to rush to the relief of His oppressed children when they shout for His assistance.

Psalm 91:15 (read)

GOD IS ON MY SIDE.

Since God is on my side, who can be against me? Who? What? Which of my enemies and what weapon can be against me to prevail against me? Since God is on my side, that means He is between me and every foe or enemy. They have to touch Him before they can touch me. When the children of Israel stood before the Red Sea, the angel of God and the cloud moved their position from before them to stand behind them, and they separated Israel from Pharaoh's army. **Exodus 14:19-20 (read)**

Hey church, we have a champion on our side. He has never lost a battle; He has never been defeated.
* He has never seen a sinner He cannot save.
* He has never seen a disease He could not heal.
* He has never seen a problem He could not solve.

He has always been a winner, and He always will be because He is **GOD**.

Since God is on our side, who can be against us? No one, nothing that Satan throws at us, none of our enemies can defeat us because God is on our side. He fights for me, and He is between me and my enemies. He is my victory. You are not alone; God is on your side. Remember how the army of the Lord goes into battle the next time your enemy attacks you.

CONCLUSION

Matthew Henry – "God is for us – he is in covenant with us (has made promises to us, and does not break his promises) and he has engaged for all his attributes (what makes him God) and his promises for us. All that he is, and has and does is for us, his people. He performs all things for them; he is for them, even when it seems that he is against them. And if so, who can be against us so as to prevail against us or hinder our happiness? Be they ever so great and strong, ever so many, ever so mighty, ever so malicious, what can they do?"

WHILE GOD IS FOR US, WE MAY HAVE A HOLY BOLDNESS AND SAY TO ALL THE POWERS OF DARKNESS
* **Let Satan do his worse; he is chained. – 1 John 3:8 (read)**
* **Let the world do its worst; it is conquered. – 1 John 5:4 (read)**
* **Principalities and powers are spoiled and disarmed, and triumphed over in the cross of Christ. – Colossians 2:14-15 (read)**

Who then dares fight against us while God Himself is fighting for us?

GOD IS ON MY SIDE.

BLOW THE TRUMPET IN ZION
Joel 2:1
Charlene West

If I were Jewish, last Friday I would have made a special bread, and our family would have gathered around the table to celebrate the beginning of the Sabbath at 6:00 in the evening. Our table would have been prepared especially for this occasion, because besides announcing the Sabbath, we would be celebrating one of our national holidays – Rosh Hashanah – the day of the Feast of Trumpets or the blowing of the shofar (ram's horn). We would greet one another with L'Shanah Tovah (Happy New Year!). It would be celebrated with happiness and joy.

Psalm 47 would be read as it is still read in synagogues during this celebration. "Oh, clap your hands, all ye people; shout unto God with the voice of triumph. God is gone up with a shout, the Lord with the sound of the trumpet. Sing praises to God, sing praises; sing praises unto our King, sing praises. For God is the King of all the earth: sing ye praises with understanding" (47:1, 5-7). They had a place on their calendars for this celebration, because it is one of the seven major feasts of the people of Israel. We should not be surprised that the Israelites had a special feast for the sounding of the trumpets, but what did all this trumpet blowing mean?

I. FIRST, IT MEANT THAT A MESSAGE WAS BEING ANNOUNCED.
   A. The shofar was the most common trumpet for ancient Israel although they later made trumpets with silver.
   B. In the desert, they could only communicate with the people by the sounding of trumpets.
   C. The trumpet, nevertheless, had to be blown so that the people understood the message. Its sound could not be uncertain.
   D. Trumpets were blown to announce the <u>feasts</u>, the <u>new moon</u>, the beginning of <u>months</u>, over <u>sacrifices</u>, to <u>gather</u> the people, to call them to <u>war</u>, to <u>move</u> the camp, to <u>anoint kings</u>, to <u>destroy the wicked</u>, and to <u>sound an alarm</u> when an enemy was coming (Numbers 10:5-6).
      1. Every event had its own sound, and when the trumpet sounded, each group knew their sound and what the sound meant.

2. If it sounded an alarm to go to war, each tribe knew when to move. Each group moved according to its order.
 E. What is the message we, as a church, are announcing? It is a message given to us by the Lord: "Go ye into all the world and preach the Gospel to every creature." Our message must be clear an easily understood, and it is a message for every person.
  1. There is only one way to be saved.
  2. Without holiness no one shall see the Lord.
  3. By the stripes of Jesus we are healed.
  4. The baptism of the Holy Spirit is for all believers.
  5. Jesus is coming again.

II. **THE SOUNDING OF THE TRUMPET IS CONNECTED TO A "CALLING AWAY"** – a day of joy for the Christian.
 A. Isaiah speaks of this event; Paul and John connect it with the sounding of a trumpet.
  1. "Come my people, enter into thy chambers, and shut the doors about thee for a little moment, until the time of indignation be past . . ." – (Isaiah 26:20).
  2. "And after this I looked, and behold a door was opened in heaven, and the first voice that I heard, as of a trumpet, speaking with me, said: Come up hither, and I will show thee the things that will take place hereafter. And immediately I was in the Spirit . . ." – (Revelation 4:1-2).
   a. These verses speak of a people God is going to take from the world *before* the time when His wrath will be poured out upon the earth.
   b. The day of calling away follows an old Jewish wedding custom. After the engagement ceremony, the bridegroom left promising to return later.
   c. He would carry his bride to the home he had prepared for her. He did not tell when, but he would come secretly and take here away to be with him for seven days.
   d. Jesus said, "I go to prepare a place for you, and if I go . . . I will come again." – [John 14:1, 2]. He did not say when, just to be ready and watching for His coming. We do not know the day nor the hour when He will catch us away.
  3. Paul tells us of this event, "For the Lord himself shall descend from heaven with a shout with the voice of the archangel with

the trump of God, and the dead in Christ shall rise first, then we which are alive and remain shall be caught up together with them to meet the Lord in the air, and so shall we ever be with the Lord." – [1 Thessalonians 4:16, 17]. It will be sudden, without warning or announcement.

III. **THE TRUMPET ANNOUNCED THE BEGINNING OF THE 10 DAYS OF REPENTANCE BETWEEN ROSH HASHANAH AND THE GREAT DAY OF ATONEMENT.**
   A. For many long years prophets and preachers have announced the message of salvation.
      1. The message has been clear. Today is the day of salvation.
      2. Christ is coming to take us to the place He has prepared for us. "In my Fathers' house. . . .
   B. As I preach this message, the Lord still has not come, but He may come before I finish.
      1. We live in the time of His mercy when we can prepare ourselves.
      2. Are you ready for the coming of the Lord? Is everything up-to-date? Is there something of which you need to repent?
      3. This is the moment to do it!

IV. **THE TRUMPET SOUND ALSO ANNOUNCED THE DAY OF THE LORD – THE BEGINNING OF TRIBULATIONS (Joel 2:1, 10-11).**
   A. Ten days after the sounding of the trumpets, the Israelites celebrated the Day of Atonement – a day of fasting, repenting, and confessing.
      1. It was the only day the great high priest went into the Holy of Holies of the temple.
      2. The people could fast at any time of need (Nineveh, Esther, etc.), but there was an annual fast when everyone participated.
   B. It was a day when God forgave the sins of the people of Israel for another year – national repentance and national forgiveness.
   C. If we ever needed a time of national repentance in the USA, it is today.
      1. Because a world government is already being formed. We live in a global world.

2. The computer system with which the Antichrist will control the population of this planet is already set up. Are you planning to be here when he governs?

CONCLUSION: God is speaking to us. You do not have to be afraid if you have Christ. "God is our refuge and strength, a very present help in trouble. Therefore will not we fear, though the earth be removed . . ." – (Psalm 46:1-2a). Even now the Lord is walking among us to meet our needs. If you have not made a decision to accept Christ as your Savior, do it now!

THE ARMS OF JESUS
Isaiah 40:10-11
Janice Marshburn

My prayer is that, before the conclusion of this service, someone who Jesus hasn't had the privilege of holding for a long time will be resting in His arms. That as He holds you, He'll silence the cry within you, ignite a new hope within you, and reignite the fire of the Holy Ghost.

I believe someone is screaming from within, *I'm worn, weary, wounded, sick, and hurting. My strength to fight, my strength to press on is gone. I can't face another day, another demand or disappointment. I can't teach another class. I can't preach another sermon. I can't walk in my destiny or fulfill my calling.* There's a scream inside of me that no one understands, and no one can satisfy or silence except Jesus. Therefore, in my state of weakness, what I really need is for someone to help me get to the arms of the one Isaiah wrote about where he said, 'Behold the Lord God will come with strong hand, and His arm shall rule for Him: behold, His reward is with Him, and His work before Him."

This scripture tells us that God's arm (Christ) is a mighty arm for winning the battle. He encourages us that the battle isn't ours, for the Lord will fight for us, and we will hold our peace. All we need to do is stand still and see the salvation of the Lord. The passage goes on to tell us that His arm isn't only mighty but loving for carrying His wounded, weary lambs. Verse 11 tells us, "He shall feed His flock like a shepherd; He shall gather the lambs with His arm, and carry them in His bosom, and shall gently lead those that are with young." Not maybe, but He shall.

As we read these scriptures and the world spins around us to the point that it seems out of control, our heart begins to cry within us, *I want to get to the arms of this Great Shepherd who loves His flock with a tender, deep, true, patient, abounding love. I want to get to the One who loves in this manner because His flock is His own creation, a reflection of His image, who was purchased with the precious blood of the only begotten Son of God. I want to get to the arms of the One who cares enough for me to hold me close to His heart as He carries me to green pastures in high places away from the reach of the enemy, and to springs of water where there is life and refreshment. I want to be in the arms of the One who cares enough that even though He has a hundred sheep, if one goes astray, He would leave the ninety-nine and seek for the one lost until He finds him and then lays him on His shoulders rejoicing as He brings him back home again.*

Church, the Holy Spirit said in Isaiah 53:6, "All we like sheep have gone astray; we have turned everyone to his own way." We as sheep are continuously wandering into strange paths, or pastures that aren't good for us while the Great Shepherd, out of great compassion, constantly seeks us out and brings us back to the safety of His fold.

There's a scream inside of me that says *I want to get to the arms of the One who **guides** His flock as He gently leads us in paths of righteousness by going before us and pointing us in the way we should walk.* By our conscience or the influence of His Spirit, He keeps us in the right path and suffers us not to depart from it. Church, there's a scream inside me that says *I want to get to the arms of the One who sets His pace so those following Him will not fall behind. I want to get to the arms of the One who when He sees us struggling to get over the mountain that stands before us, when He sees the ascent is too much for our feeble limbs, He is immediately there taking us up in His arms holding us close enough to feel the beat of His heart and hear His whisper of love as He gently carries us the rest of the way.*

I want to get to the arms of the One who **guards** His flock, the One who never slumbers or sleeps but constantly defends us from spiritual threats. I want to get to the One who protects us from the wolf in sheep's clothing or from the roaring lion who walks around seeking whom he may devour. I want to get to the arms of the One who feeds His flock, the One who declares Himself to be the Bread of Life and promises that if any man should eat, he shall live forever.

This message was inspired by the Holy Spirit as I was reading a devotion by Smith Wigglesworth in which he talked about a screaming child who was separated from his mother. In an effort to get him back to his mother, he was passed from one person to another. The child was never satisfied until he reached his mother's arms. The distance between that child and his mother was frightening. The unfamiliar arms that were embracing that child as he was being passed from person-to-person was terrifying, but when he reached Mama, he recognized the voice that he had become familiar with even while in the womb. He recognized the warmth of the hands that held him close since the day he was born into this world. Suddenly the cry was silenced.

I believe someone hearing this message is that child. There's a distance between you and God. You're screaming from the inside *would someone through love and intercession pick me up and pass me over the things that have crowded my world and lay me in the arms of God? Pass me to the arms of the I AM, the eternal, all-powerful Lord. Pass me to the arms of Jehovah Jireh, my Provider, Jehovah Shalom, my Peace; and Jehovah Rapha, my Healer.*

In Mark 10, we read of the little children who were brought to Jesus. Verse 13 says that "they" (probably referring to their parents or grandparents) brought them to Jesus so that He would touch them. His disciples rebuked them for doing so maybe thinking that Jesus' time was much too valuable to be bothered with children. Verse 14 tells us that when Jesus saw what the disciples were doing, He was displeased.

Church, He is displeased with anyone who tries to hold someone back because he feels that person is unworthy or unfit. The command is to go out in the highways and hedges and compel them to come in. We need to seek out the drunkard, the thief, and the harlot of every race, color, and age and bring them to the arms of Jesus. Our job is to invite all wanderers to come to His cross. Let us not displease our Lord.

Some writers feel Jesus actually became indignant as He said to them "suffer the little children to come unto Me, and forbid them not: for of such is the kingdom of God. Verily I say unto you, Whosoever shall not receive the kingdom of God as a little child, he shall not enter therein." We could preach all day about our responsibility of bringing people to the Lord – of our responsibility as parents, Sunday school teachers, and children's ministry workers bringing them to the knowledge of the Lord through prayer, through teaching them the truth, and by setting before them life and death, heaven and hell, mercy and judgment. We could preach on and on about how we must become humble, dependent, receptive, teachable, and as simple as a child to get to heaven. We can talk about how we must come to Jesus with a faith that trust Him just like a little child who trusts his father and just leaves all the problems up to daddy to solve. However, the point that I want us to focus on is in verse 16 where Jesus does more than the guardians had asked. They asked that He touch them. He did put His hands upon them bestowing His Spirit upon them; He did bless them with the spiritual blessings He came to give, but He also took them up into His arms. Underneath them were the everlasting arms of power and providence, pity and grace, strength and security. I believe some were infants, while others were young children, but regardless of their age, all were welcome.

I have envisioned again and again what happened there that day. In my spiritual mind, I could see a multitude of people all around Jesus. Maybe a few mothers had gotten through the crowd pushing their children closer and closer to Jesus and finally reaching Him, crying out for Him to touch them and bless them, desiring Him to convey His blessings on their **future** lives. I believe some had heard of Jesus' miraculous life-changing touch that could affect them **immediately**. I believe some brought their child hoping He would touch them and the generational curse of alcohol, drug abuse, or suicide would be broken.

I believe some had heard of Jesus' miraculous healing touch and brought the weak, sick ones who could not push their way through the crowd. As I studied the text, I could hear a mother saying *"I can't get through the crowd to hand Him my baby girl. Would someone carefully pass her over everyone else and into the arms of Jesus? Tell Him she has seizures and heart disease. Ask Him to touch her that she will be healed."* When that baby left the arms of his mother, he started screaming in fear of the unknown, but that cry was silenced when he reached the arms of Jesus.

Another one is yelling, *"If you won't let me get through, please make a way for my child to get through. She was shaken by an angry father and now has brain damage. Please get her to the arms of Jesus, and ask Him to touch her that she will be made whole, and bless her that she'll have a prosperous future and wisdom to make right decisions.*" When that child left her mother's side, she started screaming as she saw unfamiliar faces and felt an unfamiliar touch, but that cry was silenced when she reached the arms of Jesus, for in His arms is a peace and satisfaction that only God can give.

Church, I'm seeing some frightening sights, hearing some unfamiliar sounds, feeling some unfamiliar feelings, and fearing the unknown. Some days, I'm even crying from within, *"I'm too weak to fight, to persevere, to press, and there's a mass of demons all around trying to hold me back. Would someone through prayer pick me up and pass me through the crowd to the arms of Jesus?"*

When the doctor says, "I've done all I can do" your soul screams out, "My *strength to press on is gone, someone please help get me to the arms of the One who said before they call, I will answer, and while they are yet speaking I will hear.* When the doctor says "There's no hope other than a miracle, you'll never conceive that child you have long for." Your soul begins to cry out, *"Somebody please help me get through this crowd to the arms of the One who can make the impossible possible. I'll never be satisfied until I feel the warmth of His embrace, for there's no one who can comfort like Him."*

When the layoff comes and you are just a few months from retirement, or you've just bought a new house and now you're in danger of losing it, or you've been diagnosed with a serious illness, and you desperately need the health insurance that you're going to lose, your soul begins to scream out *"I've got to get to the arms of Jesus, the One who can supply all my needs according to His riches in glory, the One who can make a way where there seems to be no way."*

The woman in Mark 5, who had been hemorrhaging for twelve years and had spent all her money on doctor bills but was worse, was screaming on the inside, *"I've got to get to Jesus even if it's just to touch His cloths. I want to be released from these arms of affliction, embarrassment, isolation, and loneliness and rest in His healing arms."*

At the empty tomb of Jesus, Mary's heart was screaming as she spoke to one who she thought was the gardener, *"Sir, if you're the one who took Him, please tell me where you put Him, and I will take Him and care for Him. I've just got to see Him again. I've just got to experience His touch one more time."*

In Mark 10[:47], we find a blind man crying out, "Jesus thou Son of David, have mercy on me." In other words, *I've got to get to the arms of the only One who can release me from these arms of blindness.*

In Psalm 18, David wrote, "The sorrows of death compassed me [or death bound me with chains]; the floods of ungodly men made me afraid. The sorrows of hell compassed me about; the snares of death prevented me. In my distress, I called upon the Lord [or I screamed out to the Lord], and cried unto My God: he heard my voice out of his temple, and my cry came before him, even into his ears. He sent from above, he took me; he drew me out of many waters. He delivered me from my strong enemy, and from them which hated me for they were too strong for me. They prevented me in the day of my calamity; but the Lord was my stay. He brought me forth also in a large place; He delivered me, because he delighted in me." – [vv. 4-6, 16-19]. The cries of David's heart reach the heart of His God, and today yours will too. He delights in you, and He will take you and draw you out of the MANY troubled waters of this life. He will prevent you from being destroyed. He will be your stay. He will deliver you.

Today, someone is crying, *"I want to be released from the arms of this world that feel so cold and foreign, from the arms that have been holding me down or back, from the arms that are squeezing the very life out of me. I want to get to the arms of Jesus. I want to be released from the arms of fear and rest in the arms of Jesus where there is peace. I want to be released from the arms of doubt and rest in the arms of Jesus where there is assurance. I want to be released from the arms of affliction and rest in the arms of Jesus where there is healing. Today my soul is crying to be released from the arms of addiction and rest in the arms of Jesus where there is deliverance, to be released from the arms of death and rest in the arms of Jesus where there is life. I'm so worn and weary because I have tried in my own strength; now I know that nothing else can satisfy me, that no one can silence this cry within me except Jesus. Will someone through compassion and prayer please help lift me over that which has crowded me out or held me back and help me get to the arms of the Sustainer."* All it takes is child-like faith. Just believing that He will and not just that He can.

Before closing, let me remind you that God said in Revelation 20:12 that He is coming and His reward shall be with Him. Also, in Mark 10:15, Jesus said, "Whosoever shall not receive the kingdom of God as a little child, he shall not enter therein." This means that those who aren't willing to accept His embrace, rest in His arms, look into His eyes, seek His forgiveness, obey His commands, or allow Him to be Lord and Master of their lives, cannot enter heaven. Heaven will never be their home, and they will never experience everlasting peace and rest, but shall forever experience the weeping, wailing, and grinding of teeth in the flames and torments of hell.

The challenge is to come to the arms of Jesus. He is willing to receive you for He said, "He that comes to the Father He will in no wise cast out." Come to Him, and He will silence that cry of guilt and shame. He will silence the voice of that demon who says your life isn't worth living. Let Him take you up into His arms, put His hands upon you, impart His Spirit within you, and bless you with the spiritual blessing He came to give. Let Him silence the cry that is within you.

RESOURCES: THE BIBLE EXPOSITION COMMENTARY, SMITH WIGGLESWORTH DEVOTIONAL, PULPIT COMMENTARY, BIBLICAL ILLUSTRATOR

BLAMELESS AND HOLY WHEN HE COMES
1 Thessalonians 3:13; 5:23, 24-NIV
Jeraldine Posey, D. Min.

Both of these passages of Scripture speak of being blameless and holy at the second coming of Jesus. To better understand the subject, we need to know what a life of holiness or heart purity or sanctification really is. Two thoughts are prominent in the definition: separation from evil and dedication unto God and His service. Sanctification as separation from the world and setting apart for God's service is a concept found throughout the Bible. Spoken of as *"holy"* or *"set apart"* in the Old Testament were the land of Canaan, the city of Jerusalem, the tabernacle, the Temple, the Sabbath, the feasts, the prophets, the priests, and the garments of the priests.

As Christians, we are commanded to *"be holy"* (Leviticus 11:44; 1 Peter 1:15, 16); to *"be perfect"* (Matthew 5:48); and to *"offer (our) bodies as living sacrifices, holy* and pleasing to God" (Romans 12:1). The terminology used in these verses indicates that we have a responsibility in the matter, but we also know the means is divine. Paul expressed a prayer for the Thessalonians in one of the passages I read: "May God himself, the God of peace, sanctify you through and through" (5:23). The text concludes with this assurance: "The one who calls you is faithful and he will do it" (5:24).

Someone has said "Christianity is supremely the champion of purity." The reason is because its God is holy and pure, and He wants us to be like Him. One of the Beatitudes that Jesus used in the Sermon on the Mount recorded by Matthew and Luke states, "Blessed are the pure in heart, for they will see God." In this sermon, Jesus laid down the foundational principles of life and conduct for citizens of the kingdom of God. The traits which the Lord emphasized to His disciples were that they should be poor in spirit, should mourn and be meek, they should hunger and thirst after righteousness, be merciful, peace-makers, and be pure in heart. Jesus said people who do these things are "blessed" (happy).

The statement about purity is the most comprehensive of all the beatitudes. God means He is not satisfied with mere external show of religion, but we must strive to keep the heart and conscience void of offense. We must not only lift up to the Lord clean hands, but a pure heart. How can we do that? How can we be holy? Paul gave the answer in Galatians 2:20 when he wrote, "I have been crucified with Christ and I no longer live, but Christ lives in me." So, to be holy and blameless before God involves dying to self, turning over our self-centered lives to Him to become a Christ-centered individual. The self seeking "I" has surrendered and given place to the life and rule of Christ. It used to be "I, not Christ," but when we die to self, it is, "Not I, but Christ." It is Christ living in and out of me.

John Wesley put it this way: "In one view, it is purity of intention, dedicating all the life to God. It is the giving to God all our hearts. It is one desire and design ruling all our tempers. It is the devoting, not a part, but all of our soul, body, and substance to God. In another, it is having the mind of Christ, which enables us to walk as Christ walked. It is the removal from the heart of all filthiness, all inward as well as outward pollution."

So many scripture verses speak out on this doctrine of heart purity or sanctification with unequivocal clearness. They leave no room for speculation and doubt. The Bible supports this idea from Genesis to Revelation and in short shows us

* There is One who sanctifies.
* There are those who need to be sanctified.
* This experience forms a union with Jesus Christ.
* This union constitutes a society of holy people of whom Christ is not ashamed.

The teaching of being holy and set apart is no mere theory. The idea of a separated people has been in the plan of God from the beginning.

* It was seen in the case of the sons of God and the daughters of men. (Genesis 6)
* It was seen in God's desire for a people who would be called by His name.
* It was seen in God's instructions to Abraham not to take a bride for Isaac from among the heathen.
* It was seen in God's concern for Israel in Egypt, and in its relationship to other nations.

God always has insisted upon His people being a separate people – distinct from the world, a people marked by a certain way of life and attitude of heart.

Jesus prayed for His disciples to be sanctified through truth: "Sanctify them by the truth; your word is truth" (John 17:17). We are to be made pure and kept pure by the Word of God. Jude addresses his epistle to "those who are sanctified by God the Father" (vs. 1).

God cannot tolerate sin; it cannot enter heaven, and He wants all men to come to the knowledge of His will; therefore, He commands them to be holy. "Make every effort to live in peace with all men and to be holy; without holiness no one will see the Lord" is a command (Heb. 12:14).

We know God is holy; heaven is a holy place; we call this the Holy Bible, and believe it was written by holy men, as they were moved upon by the Holy Spirit. If we walk in this way called the highway of holiness, we must be pure in heart for no unclean things shall pass over it (Isaiah 35:8). Jesus is coming again and He will be looking for those who are pure and blameless.

(**Author's note:** The following sermons have previously appeared in various publications that will be cited in the endnotes. They are published here as they appeared in the referenced periodicals, except where noted, so the reader can better see into the nature of the writer and get a feel for what these women had to say. These are their words from the Heavenly Spokesman.)

GOD'S CALLING – HIS ENABLING
John 6:9b
Blanche L. King

In the story of the miraculous feed of the five thousand, the story from which the text is taken, there have been various interpretations of the statement Andrew made when he called the Lord's attention to the lad with the five loaves and two fishes. Judging his character from other incidents in his life, incidents which indicated that he had a more correct sense of values than we always find in those who occupy places of prominence, I believe that Andrew noticed a bright-faced little lad, and with a sense of discernment that revealed to him a wealth of possibilities in this youngster, his generous heart immediately yearned to bring another bright prospect into the service of his Master. Perhaps objections from other disciples to the seemingly ridiculous suggestion caused Andrew to reconsider and add, "But what are they among so many?"

Or it might have been like this: From the day that Andrew heard John the Baptist say, "Behold the Lamb of God," he had followed the Lord with implicit confidence. He had never known a need to arise that was too great for the Master to supply, sometimes by a miracle, but more often by the use of something at hand. Here was a need – the multitude was hungry – and here was a lad with his lunch, anxious to be of use to the Master, who had become his hero. Could the Lord bridge the gap between the great need and the scanty provision? Perhaps even Andrew's faith began to waver a bit, and he thought aloud, "But what are they among so many?"

Whatever the thought that inspired Andrew's suggestion, the Lord accepted the challenge to use the weak and seemingly foolish to accomplish His purpose. And from this incident we have the beautiful lesson that there is nothing small, or weak, or insignificant when dedicated to the Master's service and touched by His divine hand.

That we still have those who think of doing something for God in terms of natural ability we know by trying to enlist helpers in carrying on Christian work. The Sunday [s]chool superintendent, the Young People's leader, the Auxiliary president, the pastor, the conference superintendent, all have experienced difficulty in securing the assistance of their membership in the expansion of God's kingdom. In all groups the reply to a call for service is too often that the attempt would be foolish. What could they do with a task so great? "What are they among so many?"

There are a number of reasons for such a feeling of incompetence. We might consider first the attitude of indifference. There are among the Lord's professed followers those who fail to enter His service because their love for Him is so lukewarm they feel no response in their hearts to the need for laborers in His great harvest field. The cry of the lost, "Carest thou not that we perish?" or the question asked of Cain, "Where is thy brother?" or ever the Great Commission of the Lord to His followers – none of these reach their hearts, hearts into which the care of the world and the deceitfulness of riches have entered to choke the Word, rendering their lives unfruitful. Though such may have once known the Lord, they are dangerously near, if not already in, the condition of the savorless salt – fit to be cast out and trodden under foot of men.

There are also those who hesitate to enter the service of the Lord because of a fear of failure. There is a lack of confidence in their hearts, confidence in themselves; and, although they do not realize it, there is also a lack of confidence in the Lord who calls them into His service. They fear that reproach may be brought upon His cause by the poor service which they might render. The only remedy for such a condition of heart is perfect love, for "Perfect love casteth out fear." Someone has well said, "Perfect obedience would bring perfect peace, if only we had perfect confidence in the power we are obeying." "Without faith it is impossible to please, him" and without confidence in His wisdom in calling us into His service, be that service small or great, our response is only half-hearted, or less, and will be as ineffectual as the effort which we put into it is lifeless. The

Scripture speaks of the fearful and unbelieving, and though we may, in our imperfect human judgment, look upon these as among the lesser sins, we are told definitely that those in such a condition of heart have their part in the lake which burneth with fire and brimstone.

We also have those with a sense of false humility, those who rather pridefully declare, "I don't believe in putting myself forward." With this smug excuse they cover up their pride, while the work of God is neglected. They are more concerned about their reputation than about the souls of lost men and women. They will find themselves in the class of the unprofitable servant who hid his lord's talent under an excuse that had no foundation in truth.

Perhaps the class of excuse-makers who are easiest to "activate" in the work of the Lord is made up of those who possess a sense of sincere humility carried to the extreme. The Lord seems to be more patient with this class. Such an attitude was manifested by Moses when God called him to lead the children of Israel out of Egyptian bondage. What was Moses' answer? "Who am I, that I should go unto Pharaoh, and that I should bring forth the children of Israel out of Egypt?"

Moses had not always felt so helpless. Forty years before this time he had decided that his natural ability, which included his striking appearance, no doubt, as well as his superior learning, and his position as a prince in the royal household of Pharaoh, made, him, as he thought, the ideal one to deliver his brethren from slavery. In fact, his natural advantages at that time would have aided him immeasurably in the task for which God had saved him in infancy (and which calling Moses, doubtless, had felt since childhood) had he trusted in God rather than in these natural advantages. Physical beauty is a gift of God, but He rarely gets the benefit of such an endowment. Yes, beauty of countenance, combined with loveliness of Character, is one of the Creator's greatest gifts to humanity, but such a combination is also one of the prized targets of Satan. (And Satan has his allies in accomplishing the ruin of such lovely characters – flattering, fawning, carnal professors who are attracted by the physical more than by the spiritual.) Education supplemented with divine wisdom makes one learned indeed. And prestige attained by adherence to righteous principles, rather than by compromise with popular standards, is a mark of the truly great. But Moses thought too highly of his natural advantages, and because he did, God's people had to suffer forty years longer in rigorous slavery, waiting for Moses to arrive at a proper sense of values – to realize his nothingness and God's almightiness.

But Moses did learn, which is more than can be said of some who claim to serve the God of Moses today. And although God had some difficulty in persuading him that he could lead the Israelites out of Egypt, Moses finally went forth to perform this mighty task in the power of Jehovah with nothing visibly greater than a rod, a common shepherd's tool. In all the lonely years of his shepherd life Moses never realized that his insignificant rod, like unto which all the shepherds used, when energized by the power of God could strike terror to the hard-hearted monarch of Egypt. In his hand was the potential power to destroy the idolatrous hordes of Egypt and bring freedom to the people of God, but that power lay unused while Moses mourned over his failures and weaknesses, and the kingdom of God suffered violence. There in the desert Moses lived in solitude and his education enriched only his own life, and his handsome appearance made no impression upon the unimaginative Midianite shepherds, who grudgingly made small talk with the snobbish "Egyptian" in their midst. His former position in the royal household became a mocking memory as he labored with his sheep on the backside of the desert. The things that "might have been" were his constant mental companions, and it became clear to him why those possibilities had never materialized. Finally, he was convinced that he was nothing, and then he was in a position for God to use him.

We wonder if Moses could have arrived at his feeling of incompetence sooner. Was it necessary for him to brood over his failure forty years? What if he had repented at once, had acknowledged his need of God's help and power to accomplish his task, instead of going down to Midian and "sitting down by a well"? He might have avoided entanglements that caused him personal distress later, and God might have used him for a speedy deliverance of Israel, even though Pharaoh's secret police were after him. Whatever might have been, we can rejoice that Moses finally yielded to the call of God, and although Israel had only forty years of his leadership when they might have had eighty, those forty years were filled with demonstrations of God's power through His yielded servant, years of service in which Moses himself must have been amazed at what God could do with one so incompetent as he. Have you ever wondered as to when Moses discovered his voice? And if he ever decided that he might have gotten along better without Aaron's help? His farewell speech and his song which he "spake in the ears of all Israel," with the response on the part of those who heard him, bespeak an eloquence which belies his excuse in Midian that he was slow of speech. Tongues inspired by God become as the pen of a ready writer. Thoughts of sluggish minds become clear and established when committed unto the Lord. Yes, Moses was extremely humble. Yielded to God, he became "very meek above all the men who were upon the face of the earth," and the more forceful leader of ancient Israel.

Moses in his shepherd experience has many followers in at least one respect – those who doubt their ability to do great things for God. We find only a few, comparatively speaking, who in the beginning of their Christian lives overestimate their God-given ability. The greater number of us is without Moses' natural abilities, and, from the first, realizes our limitations – a realization that came to Moses after forty years. Our failure often comes after we have run well for a while. After God has accomplished something through us, too often we forget how helpless we were before He took notice of us and we yielded ourselves as instruments in His hands. We cease to be little in our own eyes, and as did King Saul, we become puffed up over our accomplishments, cease to depend upon God, and then become miserable failures. But in spite of the fact that there are still some Sauls in the land, we may thank God that there have been and still are those whose eyes have never turned into magnifying glasses when they behold themselves; those who like the great Apostle Paul consider themselves the least of all saints, and are determined to know, not their abilities and accomplishments, but counting these as refuse, they know only Jesus Christ, and Him crucified.

David was one of God's servants who demonstrated sincere humility. In considering David as a great king, we are apt to forget his humility as a lad. Those who dwell upon his military exploits forget the simplicity of his early life. Even in his day, there were more who sang about David's killing his ten thousands than those who remembered the gentle shepherd lad who wrote about the still waters, the green pastures, and the paths of righteousness. But it was in those years of quietness before God that David learned to depend upon the strength of Jehovah. He was unassuming, boasting only in God. He never mentioned the feats of strength he had performed with the lion and the bear, until the telling of it would open to him another opportunity to glorify the God of Israel. Though ridiculed by his brothers, belittled by King Saul, and disdained by Goliath, David with his shepherd's sling and five stones, under God's anointing, accomplished that which King Saul and his army could not do with their tested armor and instruments of warfare.

David's anointing for kingship by Samuel caused no feeling of self-exaltation. He returned to his sheep and waited God's time for his ascendancy to the throne. And when he was brought before Saul, he served the backslidden king as if he were only an ordinary subject, instead of the God-appointed successor to the man he served. David was faithful as a lowly shepherd and became the inspired poet and musician; he used his musical talent in soothing the tormenting fears of a demon-possessed king and won a friend in the king's son, a friend who saved his life and compensated fully for the fiendish jealousy of the king. David valued the love of a faithful friend more than the glory of a victorious battle or the throne of Israel. He refused to avenge himself of Saul's hatred, thereby to take a short cut to the throne. He waited for God to promote him and, in God's time, became the most beloved king of ancient Israel. There must have been times when David felt that he had cleansed his heart in vain, when he must have asked himself the question, "What are these (my ideals) among so many (corrupting influences)?" But he continued to serve God as he had opportunity, and his usefulness increased until he established a kingdom and became a man after God's own heart. "Little is much if God is in it."

In modern times, the outstanding success of Dwight L. Moody can be attributed to the fact that he determined to prove what God could do through one thoroughly consecrated to Him. What if Moody had said, "Who am I among so many learned and trained minister of the Gospel?" What if he had chosen to continue working as a shoe salesman, instead of making sure that he was shod with the preparation of the Gospel of peace? Had he been indifferent to the call of God, then multitudes that are either in heaven or living in the joy of sins forgiven, would be suffering the torments of hell or living in sin's dreaded bondage.

Many Christians are spending their lives hiding their talents or failing to take advantage of their opportunities for service, saying, "What are these among so many? What would my feeble efforts accomplish when sin is so rampant and the forces of evil hold such mighty sway?" If you cannot do great things, do little things and make them great. Someone has said that it is better to do small things in a great way than to attempt great things in a small way[.] So, if you cannot turn the world upside down, move the pebbles that obstruct your pathway to greater service. Remember Moses' rod and David's sling, and throw into the service of the Lord everything belonging to you, even the common tools that you use every day of your lives – your ability to testify, to sing, to pray, to speak, to make money, to make friends, your time to visit the sick and downcast, your opportunities to show hospitality, to perform kind deeds for those who need such. Do these things, not to gain to yourself friends and a reputation for goodness, but go under the anointing of God, seeking His glory, and see your life transformed into a powerhouse of spiritual blessing to humanity. The woman of Shunam consecrated her home and her bread tray to God's service, and a prophet was sheltered and fed. This kindness and consecration brought blessings to her household, and life to the son whom death had claimed. Dorcas consecrated her needle to God's service, and an appreciative community besought the Apostle Peter to pray for her, and she was brought back from the dead. An insignificant sewing needle, but consecrated to God, it meant blessing to her neighbors and life for herself. Andrew had an influence to bring this [his] brother Simon to Christ. Andrew is not credited with great accomplishments, but indirectly he brought great blessings to those in need. He brought the lad with his lunch to the Lord, and the multitude was fed. He brought his brother to the Lord, and the multitudes on the day of Pentecost, and through the centuries, have been fed on that Living Bread that came down from Heaven, through the powerful preaching and inspired writing of the great Apostle Peter.

You who are gifted and talented, keep humble and show to the world that God is still doing great things through those who are thoroughly consecrated to His cause and willing for Him to have the glory for what they accomplish. You who may be limited in your abilities, render what service you can give under the anointing and guidance of the Giver of all good things, and the world will marvel at what God hath wrought through so lowly a vessel.[1]

(**Author's note:** A poem was given at the end of this message which is not included here.)

OBEDIENCE
Hebrews 11:8-10
Miss Mary Ford

In the New Testament usage, to obey means to give earnest attention to the Word, to submit to its authority, and to carry out its instructions. The *promises* are given to *believe*, but the *commandments* are given to *obey*. In other word, we are to *believe* the *promises*, but we are required to *obey* the *commandments*. We hear so much in this day and age about *faith*, and that is well and good, but *obedience* and *faith* go hand in hand; they are Siamese twins, as it were; they are opposite sides of the same coin; it is impossible to separate them; split the coin and you have ruined it. The Bible knows nothing of salvation, nor any other blessing which we receive from God, apart from *obedience*. Study the lives and activities of the great characters of the Bible, who stand out as towering mountain peaks among the hills of time, and you will discover that they were men and women who strictly *obeyed*! Take the characters in our modern day who are accomplishing great things for God; you will hear, on every hand, of the great faith they have, but back of that faith is strict obedience to the slightest wish of the Master whom they serve, love, and worship. Study again the lives of such noble Christian characters as Savonarola, John Knox, John and Charles Wesley, George Whitefield, Charles G. Finney, and many others, and you will find back of their great faith and great accomplishments for the kingdom of God, wills completely submitted to the will of Him whom they loved better than life itself. Read again the life of the beloved Apostle Paul; enter with him into the 'place of hearing' before King Agrippa and Festus in Caesarea, and hear him declare, twenty-seven years after he had met the Master face to face on the Damascus highway, "I was not disobedient to the heavenly vision." I fear we usually become lost in all the maze of accomplishment of the mighty ones of God, both past and present, and lost sight of the fact of the most important part of all: that of strict *obedience* to our God and to His unchanging Word! And this strict obedience, which we are so prone to forget, if we ever even think of it, is that which brings about all the "faith" and the many wonderful accomplishments for the Kingdom of God.

The spiritual experience of Abraham was marked by four great crises, each of which involved surrender (obedience) of something naturally most dear:

First: The Lord commanded him to get out of his country, and from his kindred, and from his father's house. In the natural, his country, kindred, and loved ones were very near and dear unto him, as ours are to each of us. It meant something for him to obey this command of the Lord, and God alone knows the tears he shed, the heartaches he endured, the agony he suffered, and the praying he did to reach the place where he could make the full and complete surrender. I'm sure, could we have the privilege of conversing with our beloved pioneer ministers, who "blazed the trail" for this Pentecostal Holiness gospel which we so love and appreciate today, they would tell us, with tears coursing down their cheeks that they know how to feel with "faithful Abraham," and also know the fullest meaning of giving up home, loved ones, and friends for the 'Gospel's sake'!

Second: The parting with his nephew, Lot, especially dear to him by nature, and also as a possible heir, and as a fellow believer. When the land could no longer take care of their combined flocks and herds, and they had to separate, Abraham gave the choice to Lot, and no doubt with a sad and aching heart, watched him as he took his leave and "started toward Sodom."

Third: His own plan about Ishmael; when the Lord continued to promise to give him a son by Sarah, who now was ninety years of age, it apparently seemed incredible to him as it had to Sarah about twelve years previous to this time, so he desired the Lord to raise up the promised "seed" and the promised "nation" through Ishmael. Surely it was a heavy blow to his plans, and no doubt to his faith, when he finally realized the Lord would do no such thing.

Fourth: but by no means the least, was his test over his son Isaac. When Ishmael, his son by the Egyptian maiden, Hagar, was thirteen years of age, the Lord fulfilled His promise and gave Abraham a son by his wife Sarah, who was ninety-one years old at that time, and Abraham was one hundred! Utterly impossible from the natural standpoint, but always remember *there is nothing impossible with God.* When Isaac was nineteen or twenty years old the day came when the Lord spoke unto Abraham and asked him to take his son, his only son, Isaac, whom he loved, and get him to the land of Moriah, and offer him for a burnt offering! Can you imagine or realize what this great test meant to this dear old father, and this wonderful old Patriarch of God! Here he had waited (perhaps not too patiently nor believingly) for the birth of this lad, whom God has promised to send twenty-five years before he finally was born, and now, when he is the pride and rejoicing of their hearts and home, and apparently all the promises of the future, as far as Abraham and Sarah are concerned, are bound up in that young life, God demands his sacrifice! It seems we should lower the curtain here, and not gaze upon such a sad, sacred scene, but there is one mighty lesson in this for us, if we will dare to accept it. Well, as usual, Abraham OBEYED! We find him, with the servants and Isaac, arising early in the morning and taking the journey toward Mount Moriah. On the third day, when he gets a glimpse of the Mount, he leaves the servants there and he and Isaac proceed to the place of sacrifice! Oh, what a scene! After the beloved son of his heart is bound and placed on the wood on the altar, he draws the knife to take the life of that son of promise whom he loves dearer than life itself, but he loves God and His cause more, so he is still *obeying*! In the last minute of the "eleventh hour" GOD SPEAKS! Friends, listen to the words that came from Heaven: Genesis 22:13-18, but the last part of that 18th verse is where the emphasis is laid: "BECAUSE THOU HAST OBEYED MY VOICE!"

Is it by mere accident that he is called "Faithful Abraham," and the "Father of the Faithful"? Is it merely accidental that God selected him to be the head of a new nation whom God raised up through whom He planned to prove His holiness and power, and to bring forth the promised Messiah? Nay, but because he strictly OBEYED HIS GOD, who meant more to him that all his loved ones, family, friends, surroundings, personal plans, and EVERYTHING! He had completely said one eternal 'yes' to God, and he kept his promise and OBEYED regardless of the cost to him!

Would you like to have the "faith" that can move mountains? Do you have a yearning to really amount to something for God? Would you like to be able to successfully tell the story of a Savior's redeeming love so that thousands of men, women, boys, and girls, who are now traveling the broad road that leads down, *down*, DOWN to eternal despair and destruction, would be "changed from darkness to light, from death unto life, from the *power of Satan unto God*?" Have you tried to "have faith"? Have you tried to "believe?"[B]ut it seems the more you "try" the higher the doubts and difficulties mount? Listen, friends, try "Faithful Abraham's" way; start *obeying* in the little things; in *everything* that the Lord says do, regardless of how senseless it may seem to "people," or even to you; just begin to obey, and as your obedience mounts, so will your faith, and you will soon learn that the secret of great faith is *complete and perfect obedience*!

We are confident that our God, in this very day and age in which we live, is searching and seeking for that man, woman, boy or girl, who will lay all on the altar of complete and perfect obedience, in order that He may work through them, and once again prove to this poor, old sin-sick, sin-wrecked, sin-ruined world that He still "sits on the circle of the earth," taking note of the affairs of men and of nations, and through faith and obedience of His children, can even yet change the lives, manner and habits of individuals of all nations! Shall we, may we, DARE WE say as the poet did of old:

> Then in fellowship sweet, we will sit at His feet,
> Or we'll walk by His side in the way:
> What He says, WE WILL DO!
> Where He sends, WE WILL GO!

Never fear, only trust and OBEY!
Trust and OBEY, for there's no other way
To be happy in Jesus, but to trust and OBEY!

Abraham, when he was called to go out into a place which he should after receive for an inheritance, OBEYED, not knowing [where he was going.]²

THE WILL OF GOD YOUR SANCTIFICATION
Eulah Taylor
Colorado Conference

It is necessary in the study of Sanctification to know just what the term means. It is defined in the dictionary with several different shades of meaning: 1. To make holy; set apart for some sacred use; as God blessed the seventh day and sanctified it. 2. To purify (human beings) from sin.

The word "sanctify" has different shades of meaning, but in every phase of its meaning it carries the thought of purity, of holiness, of God-likeness. It certainly has no shade of meaning less than that. And in nearly all of its relationships it has a definite aspect, a definite act in its performance and accomplishment. It is God's will for His people from Genesis to Revelation; from beginning to end.

It was instituted by God, Himself, in the sanctification of the Sabbath. It was a day made holy, hallowed and set apart by God to be kept sacred, and for the purpose of rest and worship. It was to be a day of edification to both soul and body and was to be kept in commemoration of God's resting on the seventh day from all His labors. The Sabbath was made for man and not man for the Sabbath.

Sanctification was God's plan in eternity. He presented this plan to Moses, saying, "And look that thou make them after the pattern, which was shewed thee in the mount" (Ex. 25:40; Heb. 8:5)[.] This was imperative. Moses could not just slap the tabernacle together in any fashion, as some do the Gospel. It had a specific pattern to be followed and that was to be a type and shadow of heavenly things. It was significant in every detail. The instructions were specific. And though they might have been painful and tiring to carry out, it was to be done just that way. It is indicative of the process of working out our own salvation with fear and trembling. God has a plan and purpose for our lives. We must follow His plan, that is, that we should live soberly, righteously, and godly in this present world. How can one live godly unless he is first made godly by the power of God? Hence God's plan of sanctification not only embraced the Sabbath, but it included man in all his relationships to God. The tabernacle in its different departments signifies God's plan for His people – not only the Israelites but for all who through the centuries have embraced His covenants and promises, so that if we would please God we must do it according to His will and plan. And what was to one generation was to all. God's plan never changes. He fixed it so that it would fit all generations of every nation. All sacrifices used in connection with the tabernacle service were indicative and characteristic of His one supreme sacrifice in which He would give His Lamb, spotless and without blemish, - His Son – a ransom for many. God pitched this tabernacle and not man. And this tabernacle was Jesus Christ. It is written in John 10:36 (Jesus' own words), "Say ye of him, whom the Father hath sanctified, and sent into the world, Thou blasphemest; because I said, I am the Son of God?"

In relation to Jesus' sonship with the Father, He needed not to be made holy. He was infinitely and intrinsically holy as His Father, His progenitor. So sanctification must have another meaning in this respect. It seems to mean, having been set apart for a specific purpose, and that, primarily to please His Father. Thus it carries the thought of pleasing God. Anything or anybody that would please God must be holy, either intrinsically or as an experience passed upon one from an outside source (which source is God). Jesus is the only one intrinsically good.

Jesus was to please His Father in all things. This was understood before He came into the world. When God sanctified Him (set Him apart) He understood that He was to be the propitiation for our sins. Thus, was He to please His Father, and so He did. In Matt. 3:17, "And lo a voice from heaven, saying, This is my beloved Son, in whom I am well pleased." This was the first thing God had to say to the world about His Son. "He pleases me well." And unto whom would God say, This is my decree (I am fixed and determined) … "Thou art my Son; this day have I begotten thee," but unto Jesus? – Ps. 2:7. Thus He (the Father), set to His seal that He was His Son, begotten of Him, and beloved (dearly loved). Jesus pleased His Father well in all things (Matt. 3:17; 17:5; Mark 1:11; Luke 3:22, etc.)[.]

Paul tells us in 1 Thessalonians 4:1, how we ought to walk and to please God. From verses 1-9 he lines up the sanctified life:
1. It is the will of God for His people.
2. It will keep one from fornication.

3. Possession of one's vessel or body in sanctification and honor.
4. Does not permit concupiscence.[lust]
5. Does not permit defrauding, (cheating, deceiving, trickery).
6. Does not permit uncleanness.
7. It is holiness, purity of life and in heart.
8. Teaches us to love one another.

This is the life and it is required by God. It is the "living out" a sanctified life.

Paul speaks in verse 10 of this same chapter about increasing more and more. So it is a life that increases and does not diminish. It might be termed coming to the full stature of the fullness of Christ. Eph. 4:13, "Till we all come in the unity of faith, and of knowledge of the Son of God, unto a perfect man, unto the measure of the stature of the fullness of Christ . . ." Verse 15, "But speaking the truth in love, may grow up into him in all things, which is the head, even Christ." Verse 16, "From whom the whole body fitly joined together and compacted by that which every joint supplieth, according to the effectual working in the measure of every part, maketh increase of the body unto the edifying of itself in love." This is the development of the sanctified nature. It is entire sanctification. Another Scripture that points out the fact of entire sanctification is 1 Thessalonians 5:23, "And the very God of peace sanctify you wholly (completely; entirely; altogether); and I pray God your whole spirit and soul and body be preserved blameless unto the coming of our Lord Jesus Christ." Verse 24, "Faithful is He that calleth you, who also will do it." This is the blessed assurance of it. Also in 1 Thessalonians 3:13, we have another strong assurance, - "To the end he may stablish your hearts unblameable in holiness before God, even our Father, at the coming of our Lord Jesus Christ with all his saints."

Sanctification may be termed "the abundant life." Christ came that we might have life and have it more abundantly – John 10:10.

Paul tells us that the sanctified life is a life of increase. And if so, then this must have been what Jesus meant by the abundant life.

In John 17:17, 19, Jesus prayed that the Father would "sanctify them through thy truth, and for their sakes I sanctify myself, that they also might be sanctified through the truth," or as the note renders it "truly sanctified." Jesus is the truth, and He is made unto us wisdom, righteousness, and sanctification, and redemption – 1 Corinthians 1:30. Then if Jesus is made these things to us we must go to Him for them. These are all included in God's plan of salvation.

But how can one "live out" the sanctified life if he has never received the sanctified nature? And how do we receive it? Is it an experience definite and real? When do we obtain it? These are vital questions, and there is a Scriptural answer for all of them. Let us answer them in the order given.

Question 1. How do we receive the sanctified nature? In Romans 5:1, 2, we have a very definite answer: "Therefore being justified by faith, we have peace with God through our Lord Jesus Christ: by whom also we have access by faith into this grace wherein we stand, and rejoice in hope of the glory of God." The phrase "by whom" points to its antecedent, Jesus Christ. He is the one who makes it possible. Through Him we receive the experience. The word "also" is a conjunction connecting the two statements but differentiating between the two, meaning in addition to, or besides. If there were nothing further to be obtained then, what did Paul mean by this second verse? Why make such discrimination of it, if it means nothing? The word "access" means admittance, which pertains to the entrance or the act of entering: the obtaining of it, as passing from one state into another. The fact is that Paul means one is already in the state of justification by faith and is enjoying the peace of God in his heart. This is the natural result of being justified by faith. But he makes it clear that there is something to be obtained beyond this experience of grace. Another door of entrance is opened to us and that to something deeper, more glorious and grand. And it certainly is nothing less than the second work of grace wrought in the heart of the fully justified believer. Else, what do all these statements mean?

Paul also points out the fact that it is obtainable by faith: that we actually enter into this grace wherein we stand by a definite act of appropriating faith. So it must be obtained by faith. It must also be maintained by the same faith by which it is received.

John 10:9 – Jesus said, "I am the door: by me, if any man enter in, he shall be saved, and shall go in and out, and find pasture." John 14:6 – Jesus saith unto him, "I am the way, the truth, and the life: no man cometh unto the Father but by me."

In Acts 26:18, Jesus makes a definite statement: "To open their eyes, and to turn them from darkness to light, and from the power of Satan unto God, that they may receive forgiveness of sins, and inheritance among them which are **sanctified by faith that is in me** (Christ)." Here it is in concise form given by the Lord Jesus, Himself. Would anyone dare dispute His Word about it?

Eph. 2:18 – "For through him we both have access by one Spirit unto the Father." Eph. 3:12 – "In whom we have boldness and access with confidence by the faith of Him."

Heb. 10:19 – "Having therefore, brethren, boldness to enter into the holiest by the blood of Jesus." V. 20 – "By a new and living way, which he hath consecrated for us, through the veil, that is to say, his flesh." V. 22 – "Let us draw near with a true heart in full assurance of faith, having our hearts sprinkled from an evil conscience, and our bodies washed with pure water." V. 23 – "Let us hold fast the profession of our faith without wavering; (for he is faithful that promised)." It must be obtained when we draw near with a true heart in full assurance of faith. Else these Scriptures have no real meaning and the experience is unobtainable. It is an experience, definite, real and obtainable by faith through Jesus Christ our Lord.

[Question] 2. When do we receive it? It may safely be said that the moment we appropriate faith for it and come to Jesus for it, that instant we receive it. If it is obtainable by faith, as we have already pointed out – Rom. 5:2 – then it certainly is definite and instantaneous. There is a moment when one is not sanctified and there is a moment when he is definitely sanctified; faith has reached the point and made contact with the fountain head and has tapped the source that brought the blood of Jesus Christ trickling down into his soul, washing away, purging, cleansing his heart from all sin – 1 John 1:9. Hallelujah! The one sanctified knows when it takes place. Just as the peace of God came into his heart when he was justified by faith (Rom. 5:1), and he knew that, just that certain and sure is sanctification realized and acknowledged. Great joy comes into his heart and he feels that his heart is clean and pure. At no other previous time has he felt just like this. However it is his glorious privilege of walking with this consciousness ever present with him. Though tribulation and persecution arise, if he will let this grace in his heart "take over" and rule he will be still conscious that the blood of Jesus Christ cleanses him from all unrighteousness. Praise God. Isn't it grand to know this?

In Rom. 6:6, we read, "Knowing this, that our old man is crucified with him (that is, with Jesus), that the body of sin might be destroyed, that henceforth we should not serve sin." This is a climax. It is a crisis. Sin is dealt with here as a principle, a body as though it were alive and active and must be killed, slain, crucified. It must be eradicated, cast out. Ishmael was alive and active in the home with Isaac the heir, until he made so much trouble for Isaac that he had to be cast out of the home. Ishmael is the flesh life or the carnal nature, the old man, the Adamic nature typified. Isaac is the child of promise, the child of faith, the new man, the sanctified nature. As long as Ishmael, the old man, is in one's heart he will cause trouble for Isaac. He **must go out**! Isaac is the heir. He (Christ) must reign in this house. The two can't remain in the same house and at the same time. Christ may be in your heart at the same time the carnal nature is, but it can't remain so for long. One or the other must go out.

The word "henceforth" denotes that there is an instant when this is actually done and that from that very moment (henceforth) we should not serve sin. Let me repeat that it takes place at the very moment one appropriates faith for it.

Gal. 2:20 [reads] "I am crucified with Christ; nevertheless I live; yet not I, but Christ liveth in me: and the life which I now live in the flesh I live by the faith of the Son of God, who loved me, and gave himself for me." When He said, "I am crucified," he means my "nature," which is the nature of "Adam" who sinned in the beginning; the "body of sin"; and whatever name or term may apply in this respect is crucified or killed. It is actually put to death. Hence it is eradicated and I am made new after the image of Him who created me. Then it is no more I that live but Christ that liveth in me.

Gal. 5:24 – "And they that are Christ's have crucified the flesh with the affections and lusts." In other words they have experienced the death of the old man. Rom. 6:1-6 – The flesh here refers to the flesh life or the life that is lived after the flesh as described in Rom. 8:5-14, "For they that are after the flesh do mind the things of the flesh; but they that are after the Spirit the things of the Spirit. For to be carnally minded [or mind the things of the flesh] is death; but to be spiritually minded is life and peace. Because the carnal mind [minding things of the flesh] is enmity against God; for it is not subject to the law of God, neither indeed can be. So then they that are in the flesh cannot please God. But ye are not in the flesh, but in the Spirit, if so be that the Spirit of God dwell in you. Now if any man have not the Spirit of Christ he is none of his. And if Christ be in you, the body [flesh life or body of sin, the old man, the carnal nature] is dead because of sin; [It no longer has power in the life.] but the Spirit [nature of Christ] is life because of righteousness. [Righteousness now reigns in the life because of the Spirit that is alive.] But if the Spirit of him that raised up Jesus from the dead dwell in you, he that raised up Christ from the dead shall also quicken your mortal bodies, by his Spirit that dwelleth in you. Therefore, brethren, we are debtors, not to the flesh, to live after the flesh. For if ye live after the flesh, ye shall die; but if ye through the Spirit do mortify [kill, crucify, cause to decay] the deeds of the body, ye shall live."

In Romans we learn that sanctification is a crisis, bringing the "old man," "Adam's nature," to crucifixion. How can one serve God acceptably with Adam's fallen, depraved nature in him? It certainly cannot be done as seen in Rom. 8:7, 8. It must die. It must be eradicated. Sanctification is necessary. In Gal. 2:20 we learned that "I" or "Adam['s] nature" is crucified with Christ. Also Gal. 5:24. Paul recognized this nature in him which made him cry out in desperation. Rom. 7:24, 25 – "O wretched man that I am! Who shall deliver me from the body of this death?" (This body of death.) His answer is emphatic and convincing, "I thank God through Jesus Christ our Lord!" O glorious victory! What a wonderful sequence! This ends the argument.

Acts 15:8, 9 – "And God, which knoweth the hearts, bare them witness, giving them the Holy Ghost, even as He did unto us; and put no difference between us and them, purifying [or having purified] their hearts by faith." Paul says it was a fact in their lives, there was no doubt about it.

"1 Corinthians 1:2 – "Unto the church of God which is at Corinth, to them that are sanctified in Christ Jesus, called to be saints, with all that in every place call upon the name of Jesus Christ our Lord, both theirs and ours." He said they are sanctified. That is, they were in possession of that experience at that very moment.

In John 17:19, Jesus prayed, "And for their sakes I sanctify myself, that they also might be sanctified through the truth." Do you suppose that prayer was in vain? Not at all. Who was He praying for? In verse 9 He says, "I pray for them: I pray not for the world, but for them which thou hast given me; for they are thine." He was praying for those whom the Father had given Him. But He did not stop there. He makes it clear in verse 20, "Neither pray I for these alone, but for them also which shall believe on me through their word."

Acts 20:32 – "And now, brethren, I commend you to God, and to the word of his grace, which is able to build you up, and to give you an inheritance among all them which are sanctified." It must be a fact that some are sanctified. Acts 26:18, "To open their eyes, and to turn them from darkness to light, and from the power of Satan unto God, that they may receive forgiveness of sins, and inheritance among them which are sanctified by faith that is in me."

1 Corinthians 6:11 – "And such were some of you: but ye are washed, but ye are sanctified, but ye are justified in the name of the Lord Jesus, and by the Spirit of our God."

Eph. 5:25-27 – "Husbands, love your wives, even as Christ also loved the church, and gave himself for it; that he might sanctify and cleanse it with the washing of water by the word, that he might present it to himself a glorious church, not having spot, or wrinkle, or any such thing; but that it should be holy and without blemish."

To what extent does sanctification reach? It covers the whole being till he dies. 1 Thessalonians 5:23 – "And the very God of peace sanctify you wholly; and I pray God your whole spirit and soul and body be preserved blameless unto the coming of our Lord Jesus Christ."

How may we be assured of this? Verse 14 – "Faithful is he that calleth you who also will do it."

2 Tim 2:21 – "If a man therefore purge himself from these, he shall be a vessel unto honor, sanctified, and meet for the master's use, and prepared unto every good work."

Heb. 2:11 – "For both he that sanctifieth and they who are sanctified are all of one; for which cause he is not ashamed to call them brethren."

Heb. 10:9, 10 – "Then said he, Lo, I come to do thy will, O God. He taketh away the first [order of offering blood of bulls and goats] that he may establish the second. By the which will we are sanctified through the offering of the body of Jesus Christ once for all." V. 14 – "For by one offering he hath perfected forever them that are sanctified."

Heb. 13:11-13 – "For the bodies of these beasts, whose blood is brought into the sanctuary by the high priest for sin, are burned without the camp. Wherefore [for which reason] Jesus also, that he might sanctify the people with his own blood, suffered without the gate. Let us go forth therefore unto him without the camp, bearing his reproach." Verses 20-21 – "Now the God of peace, that brought again from the dead our Lord Jesus Christ, that great shepherd of the sheep, through the blood of the everlasting covenant, make you perfect in every good work to do his will, working in you that which is well pleasing in his sight, through Jesus Christ; to whom be glory for ever and ever. Amen."

All this is necessary because in Heb. 12:14 he [the writer] says, "Follow peace with all men, and holiness without which no man shall see the Lord."[3]

CHRISTIAN FREEDOM vs. PAGAN LICENSE
Beulah Taylor
Colorado Conference

Freedom as defined by Webster means personal and political liberty; independence – the quality of acting or thinking for oneself in regard to politics, art, literature, religion, etc. These four are the governing factors in one's life today.

A certain class of unregenerated think of freedom as unrestraint, license, immunity; unbridled; free to do as one pleases without check. The world clamors for license.

Christianity has given us the only true slant and meaning of freedom or license. For example, let us look at John 8:34-36. In this passage we are made to understand the true nature of sin. Sin makes one serve it instead of it serving the doer of it. On the other hand, he whom the Son makes free (from sin) shall be free indeed. The freedom spoken of here does not mean unrestraint or being unchecked; but one will be directed into the channel that leads to eternal freedom and liberty, but it is the worst form of bondage.

In 1 Thessalonians 4:1-12 we have a clear cut definition of freedom. Without exception it is the only definition of freedom. If it were not for this passage and others relating to and conforming to it, the world would have a right to drink deep and large the cup of sin and feel no compunction of conscience. Their philosophy, "Let me eat, drink and be merry; for tomorrow we die," would be without a flaw except that it would lead to the extinction of the human race. It would soon consume the pursuers thereof.

Mrs. V. A. Weaver, in a toast to the young people said:

> Now while life is raw and new,
> Let the moonlight's lunacy
> Tear away all cautions,
> Be proud and mad and young and free.

This certainly is a false concept of freedom. To it may be attributed the cause for youth delinquency and crime of all sorts. The right to live loosely leads to personal, social, moral, religious and political disintegration, resulting from undisciplined living.

Personally, I believe in the four freedoms: religion, government, speech and press. But I believe in them as they are defined in God's Holy Word. From the standpoint of religion, I believe we must worship God supremely and have no other gods. Politically speaking, I believe there is no better form of government existing than that which provides for "free enterprise" *of the people, by the people, and for the people*. I believe in free speech and free press, else I would not be able to express my feelings in regard to the subject I am engrossed in. Nevertheless, as much as I believe in Americanism as expressed in the four freedoms, I know there is a grave underlying danger that our conception of freedom along all lines will be directed in the channel that leads to eternal bondage unless governed by the true concept of the God who made freedom possible.

Jesus, in speaking on this subject, said "Thou shalt love the Lord thy God with all thy heart, and with all thy soul, and with all thy mind. This is the first and great commandment. And the second is like unto it, Thou shalt love thy neighbor as thyself. On these two commandments hang all the law and the prophets" – Matt. 22:37-40.

Those who heard Jesus on the occasion of the above declaration must have gone away feeling somewhat non-plussed by the astounding statements coming from one who did not profess to be a statesman, politician, diplomat, nor even a citizen of Rome. His was a new kind of philosophy, but it was *right then*! *It is right now*! It is the only enduring philosophy and policy. It will arise to supremacy when all other forms are crumbling to nothingness, and become extinct.

Young folk, what is your conception of freedom and liberty? Shall and will you be numbered with those who outride the chaos of licentiousness and debauchery? Or will you be in the throng who sink in despair beneath the waves of so-called freedom and license, after they have spent their force on your frail barque? Yes, this is also your "privilege," your "liberty," your "license." Which shall it be? The grace of God is the only solution in providing our freedom from the bondage of all sin.[4]

HIDDEN TREASURE
Ella Muncy

"God transferred his love to earth in human form . . . yet most of the world never found Him, for they sought for Him in elegant, but deceiving places."

All the world longed for His coming. The Jews awaited the birth of their promised Messiah. Even the Gentiles looked with longing for a deliverer.

Prophecies of This great One to come had been given many years earlier. From His virgin birth to His sacrificial death, His complete "prehistory" had been written.[1] But would they recognize Him? Would they find Him where they expected Him to be? Would they interpret the prophecies correctly and understand His redemptive purpose.

All heaven rejoiced.[2] A shining star proclaimed the birth of the long-awaited Saviour.[3] "Your King has arrived! Your Redeemer is born! The Messiah is come!"

As the darkened night was transformed by the glory of the Lord, a greater Light descended from the eternal heavens into a world filled with captivity and darkness. Now, the people who walked in darkness would see a great light, and upon those who dwell in the land of the shadow of death, this Light would shine forth.[4] Deliverance had come for the empty, darkened souls of mankind. But would man love darkness rather than light?[5] Time held the answer.

The world thought surely their King would be born in a palace to royalty where He would be pampered with earthly riches and schooled in worldly wisdom. But God's thoughts were not their thoughts.[6] His wisdom exceeded that of the carnally minded.

There, in a stable, the lowliest of places, the King of kings took His first breath as a human being. Before Him lay the road of humanity: the temptations, the trials, the rejections, and then His eternal gift to all mankind – His crucifixion. In humility, in a barn, the infant Lamb of God was welcomed by gentle animals into a world full of pride. Time would prove men, rather than animals, to be the true beasts as they would reject their King and subject Him to a brutal death.[8] Mary laid her Son to rest in a manger, a trough, the feeding place for animals. Later in His life, He would present Himself as the Heavenly bread[9] and the living water[10] for hungry lives and thirsty souls. He would fill them with joy and peace.[11]

"But God hath chosen the foolish things of the world to confound the wise; and God hath chosen the weak things of the world to confound the things which are mighty; And base things of the world, and things which are despised, hath God chosen . . . ."[12] The young mother wrapped her Baby in swaddling clothes.[13] Did she realize that her Son was the only person born specifically to die?[14] Would she understand that the cross was the reason for His being? Did Mary have the wisdom to know that this Child held the power to bring change to our hearts, our motives, our goals, our entire lives? All who would meet Him would be transformed. As the sun affects every object it touches, so would the Son of God.[15] Some would melt, others would harden, depending on the texture and quality of the object. Christ's presence would bring either subjection or rebellion. Though He remains unchanged, His objects respond differently.

The world had long awaited the arrival of a political king, one with worldly wisdom, fame and fortune. But God sent a spiritual King, despised and rejected.[16] He was clothed in royalty of His own righteousness. He was indeed a prince – the Prince of Peace.[17] God had transferred His love to earth in human form and gave us the greatest Treasure heaven ever contained.[18] Yet, most of the world never found that Treasure for they sought for Him in elegant, but deceiving places.

"For it is written, I will destroy the wisdom of the wise, and will bring to nothing the understanding of the prudent. Where is the wise? Where is the scribe? Where is the disputer of this world? Hath not God made foolish the wisdom of this world?"[19]

The world is still looking for Him. Day after day hopes are shattered, dreams fade, castles crumble. Lives are spent searching and waiting for that 'something' to fill the deep emptiness within. But the problem is that we still look for Him in the wrong places. The greatest Treasure is where we least expect to find Him.[20]

1. Isaiah 7:14; 9:2-7; 53
2. Luke 2:13, 14
3. Matthew 2:1, 2
4. Isaiah 9:2; Luke 1:79
5. John 3:19
6. Isaiah 55:8
7. Isaiah 53:3; Matt. 2:42
8. John 19:18
9. John 6:35, 41, 48, 51
10. John 4:14: Rev. 22:17
11. John 14:27
12. 1 Corinthians 1:27-28
13. Luke 2:7
14. Mark 10:45
15. Malachi 4:2; Rev. 1:16
16. Isaiah 61:1; Luke 4:18
17. Isaiah 7:16
18. John 3:16
19. 1 Corinthians 1:19, 20
20. 2 Corinthians 4:7 [5]

(**Author's note:** Ella Muncy is a licensed minister in the Virginia Conference. She attends the Pentecostal Holiness Church in Marion, Virginia. The footnotes are as they appear in the sermon. Footnote #7 is not in the text.)

"SONG OF THE SHEPHERD"
Psalm 23
Violet Curlee

(**Author's note:** Violet Curlee is a member of the Southern California Conference. She pastors Trinity Life Chapel, a Pentecostal Holiness church in Bakersfield.)

The power of the Twenty-third Psalm is not in memorizing the words, but rather in thinking the thoughts.

A shepherd lad watching his father's flocks bared his soul in a song of devotion to his sheep. That song surely was the Twenty-third Psalm.

The young shepherd's days, spent in solitude, reflecting upon God and man, helped shape him for his future role as king of Israel. His songs, or psalms, largely referenced the love and care of the Great Shepherd over the families of humanity.

The songs that flowed from David's heart expressed devotion and thankfulness for tender care, protection and guidance. He displayed blind, daring faith that would carry him from the sheepfold to the palace. David's care of his flock was motivated by God's wide shepherding of His sheep, mankind.

The King James translation is the best loved and most widely accepted version of the Twenty-third Psalm. Although it is not the language of the twentieth century, it is easily understood. Even people who do not accept the psalm's religious application appreciate its poetic beauty and structure.

In his book dealing with facets of this psalm, Charles L. Allen tells of a friend of his, a successful business man, who was nervous, worried, and sick. The distraught man's physician suggested that he talk with a minister and that he read Psalm 23 five times a day for seven days. The doctor went on to insist that the patient follow the prescription precisely: "Read the psalm the first thing every morning. Read it carefully, meditatively, and prayerfully. Reread the psalm after breakfast, lunch, and dinner, and finally, the last thing before going to bed."

It was not to be hurried healing. The patient was to contemplate each phrase, giving his mind time to absorb as much of the meaning as possible. "That prescription sounds simple, but it really isn't. The Twenty-third Psalm is one of the most powerful pieces of writing in existence, and it can do marvelous things for any person . . . It can change your life in seven days."[1]

Ralph Waldo Emerson said, "A man is what he thinks about all day long." Marcus Aurelius said, "A man's life is what his thoughts make it." The late Norman Vincent Peale said, "Change your thoughts and you can change the world." The Bible says, "As [a man] thinketh in his heart, so is he" (Proverbs 23:7).

Charles Allen goes on to substantiate his theory: "The Twenty-third Psalm is a pattern of thinking, and when a mind becomes saturated with it, a new way of thinking and new life results. It contains only 118 words. One could memorize it in a short time. In fact, most of us already know it. But its power is not in memorizing the words, but rather in thinking the thoughts."

The reflections of care in this psalm are many and varied:

The Lord is my shepherd; I shall not want. After World War II, hungry, homeless children were placed in camps where they were fed and cared for. Yet, they did not sleep well; they were afraid and restless.

A psychologist found a solution. After the children were put to bed, each was given a slice of bread. They could have more to eat if they wished, but this slice was theirs to hold. The result? The children would go to sleep, assured that they would have bread tomorrow.

He maketh me to lie down in green pastures. The shepherd starts the sheep grazing at about four o'clock in the morning. Then when the sun is beaming down, the hot, thirsty sheep are coaxed to lie down in green pastures. While they are still, they chew their cuds, which is nature's way of digestion. The psalmist said, "Be still and know that I am God" (Psalm. 46:10).

He leadeth me beside the still water. Sheep are timid creatures. Because they are poor swimmers, and because of the wool coat that could pull them under, sheep instinctively shun swiftly moving streams and will drink only from still waters.

The shepherd does not laugh at the sheep's fears. Instead, he watches for still waters where their thirst can be quenched. Likewise, God never demands of us anything beyond our strength and ability to perform.

He restoreth my soul. As sheep start to graze in the morning, each takes a place in line and holds that position all day. Sometimes during the day each sheep leaves that place in line and trots to the shepherd. He will then gently rub the sheep's nose and ears, perhaps whisper in its ear, reassuring and encouraging it so that it will return to its place in line.

Life has a way of squeezing the life out of a person like a housewife juices an orange. A person can become "only a shell." Dr. D. B. Robins said, "The psychiatrist's couch cannot take the place of the church in solving the problems of a frustrated society." "He restoreth my soul"; He revives life in me.

He leadeth me in the paths of righteousness for his name's sake. A sheep has no sense of direction. Dogs, cats, and other animals seem to have built-in compasses. This is not true of sheep. Since they can see only 10 to 15 yards ahead of themselves, they must be led, lest they fall over a precipice and die.

Some paths lead us, like sheep, up blind alleys, while other paths lead to green pastures. Notice that the psalm says, "He *leadeth* me." God does not drive us.

Yea, though I walk through the valley of the shadow of death, I will fear no evil: for thou art with me. Henry Ward Beecher called the Twenty-third Psalm the nightingale of the psalms. The nightingale sings its sweetest song when the night is darkest. And for most of us, death is the most terrifying fact of life.

My husband was a minister, a shepherd of men. The day he left us was a dark day for his family. He adored us, and loved his flock; but when I knew that he was leaving, I almost jealously watched as he said goodbye to an earthly flock to scamper into the fold of the Great Shepherd. "I will fear no evil: for thou art with me."

"*Thy rod and thy staff they comfort me.* Sheep are helpless, fearful animals with no weapons with which to ward off predators. But the shepherd of David's day carried a rod – a heavy, hard club two to three feet long – and a staff, which was about eight feet long with a crook on one end. If a lamb slipped and dangled helplessly on a ledge, the shepherd could retrieve it with the staff. It was a comfort to know he was equipped to meet the emergencies.

Thou preparest a table before me in the presence of mine enemies. The shepherd cleared the terrain of poisonous plants and thorn bushes each spring. The pasture became "a prepared table." Don't we try to take these kinds of precautionary measures for our children? God does the same for us.

Thou anointest my head with oil; my cup runneth over. As it grazes, a sheep is in constant danger of scraping its head on a stone, or of being injured by briars or thorns. At the close of each day, the shepherd examines the sheep and applies soothing, healing ointment to the wounded. Like a child that runs to his mother for comfort, we can run to God and the hurt will heal.

Surely goodness and mercy will follow me all the days of my life. Mary Martin sang, "I'm stuck like a dope, with a thing called hope, I can't get it out of my heart." Franklin D. Roosevelt said, "The only thing we have to fear is fear itself." Quit predicting disaster for yourself and the world. Say with the psalmist, 'This is the day that the Lord hath made; Let us rejoice and be glad in it' (Psalm 118:24).

And I will dwell in the house of the Lord forever. There is no place like home. People write and sing songs about home, sweet home. But home is not a house; it's family and love.

David closes Psalm 23 with a crescendo of faith: *I will dwell in the house of the Lord forever.* It is a great feeling to go home after shopping, work or even vacation, but what a thrill to know that one can go home at the close of life's day.

When a shepherd in Scotland was asked if his sheep would follow the voice of a stranger, he replied, "Yes, if they are sick; but never when they are well. A sick sheep will follow anybody."[2]

As long as a Christian keeps himself healthy by feeding on God's Word, there will be little danger of his following false teachers. It is when he has contracted itching ears that he becomes restless and dissatisfied with his master.

"And when he [Jesus] putteth forth his own sheep, he goeth before them, and the sheep will follow him: for they know his voice. And a stranger will they not follow, but will flee from him: for they know not the voice of strangers" (John 10:5, 6). No wonder the Twenty-third Psalm means so much to so many. What beautiful harmony we could make if we would but join together in the Song of the Shepherd, singing, "The Lord is my shepherd, I shall not want."

The Shepherd

The Lord is my shepherd	Guidance
I shall not want	Provision
He maketh me to lie down in green pastures	Peace
He leadeth me beside the still waters	Harmony
He restoreth my soul	Healing

He leadeth me in the paths of righteousness	Progress
For His name's sake	Purpose
Yea, though I walk through the valley of the shadow of death	Testing
I will fear no evil	Confidence
For thou art with me	Protection
Thy rod and thy staff they comfort me	Instruction
Thou preparest a table before me in the presence of mine enemies	Supply
Thou anointest my head with oil	Consecration
My cup runneth over	Abundance
Surely goodness and mercy shall follow me all the days of my life	Loving Care
And I shall dwell in the house of the Lord forever	Assurance

-Anonymous

[1] Charles L. Allen, *The Twenty-Third Psalm, A College Book of Verse*, C. F. Main, Wadsworth Publishing Company, Inc. Belmont, CA.

[2] "Dangerous Symptoms," *Herald of His Coming*, Box 3457, Terminal Annex, Los Angeles, California 90051."[6]

(**Author's note:** These end notes are as they appear in the original text of the sermon.)

INSPIRING THOUGHTS FROM THE PROPHETS
Mrs. Dessie McCurley
Georgia Conference

Isaiah was the gospel preacher of the old dispensation, and wrote the obituary of Jesus Christ seven hundred and twelve years before he [Jesus] was born. History says he [Isaiah] was a martyr for his faith in God, and was sawed asunder.

Jeremiah was the weeping prophet, and saw the church in a state of apostasy, and compared it to a piece of clay in the hand of the potter that was marred on the wheel.

Ezekiel was one of the greatest prophets of the old dispensation.

Most preachers tell us they get the inspiration they need from the faces of their congregations on Sunday morning, but suppose Ezekiel had depended upon the inspiration he got from his congregation, his sermons indeed would have been dry, for he had nothing to begin with but a valley of dry bones, and even the Lord Himself seemed to doubt that these could live, for He said unto him, 'Son of man, can these bones live?' and he [Ezekiel] said, "Lord God thou knowest." He was blessed with the great privilege of seeing the river of life flowing from beneath the altar, foretelling us that when Christ was slain and ascended to the Father, the river of the Holy Ghost would flow out to the world from the throne of God and the Lamb.

Daniel and the three Hebrew children have never been surpassed. Shadrach, Meshach and Abednego walked through the burning fiery furnace. Jesus (excarnate) come to their rescue, walked about in their midst, and they came out without the smell of fire.

Daniel read the hand writing on the wall, interpreted the wonderful vision of the king, purposed in his heart not to defile himself with the king's meat, was cast into the lion's den through one night. God locked the jaws of the lions and he came out without a scratch.

Hosea was one of the pre-exile prophets, [who wrote a] letter to a backslidden people, but they did not repent. He declared that piety and forbearance was soon to be followed by judgment, then follows the touching promise which assures the restoration of Israel and their re-establishment as the earthly representatives of Jehovah to glory and splendor in chapter 2. It is stated that she [Israel] shall call Christ (excarnate) "Ishi," – my husband.

Joel wrote only a short book of three chapters. The Spirit finds in an occurrence of the prophet's own time a suited time for the unveiling of far distant events, so he looked down through the stream of time eight hundred years and seeing the mighty Pentecost flooding the world with the Holy Ghost, sons and daughters prophesying and the great and final day of the Lord.

Amos writes [about] the necessity of God's judgments upon Israel, the certainty of Israel's desolation and pictures the famine that was to be in the land, not for bread and water, but for the hearing of the Words of the Lord.

Jonah was called of God to go to Nineveh; in disobedience he started for Tarshish. As disobedience always brings trouble, he found himself in one of God's submarines, as an administration of judgments. After traveling three days and nights in the mighty deep, he made the landing and started for Nineveh. Beware, dear Christians, lest we find ourselves in the submarine.

Obadiah, in his one chapter, preaches a wonderful sermon on pride and deceitfulness of the heart.

Micah looked through the telescope of time for more than seven hundred years and saw the glory of the church, the birth of Christ, His victory over the enemy and the final triumph of the church.

Nahum saw Christ in his first and second coming. In his first vision he says, "Behold upon the mountain the feet of Him that bringeth good tidings, that publisheth peace." In the second he saw the things that would take place in the preparation of the Lord.

Habbakuk was one of the greatest temperance lecturers of his day. He also believe in the Millennial reign of Christ, and rejoiced in the Lord. "Yet I will rejoice in the Lord. I will joy in the God of my salvation. The Lord is my strength and He will make me walk upon mine high places" – 3:17, 18, 19.

Zephaniah calls Jerusalem to repentance. He tells them to wail for the Salvation of Israel. In his last chapter he breaks forth in rejoicing and puts the daughters of Zion to singing and shouting, saying, "For the Lord thy God is in the midst of thee" – 3:17.

Haggai declares that because the people live in good houses and failed to respond to the building of the House of the Lord, that they should eat and not have enough, drink and not be filled, be clothed and not keep warm. They should earn wages and put them in bags with holes in them because of his house that was waste. He also would shut up the heaven from dew and the earth from bringing forth fruit, and would call for a drought upon the land. This should be a warning to God's children everywhere to look after the house of the Lord and His work first.

Zechariah was one of the post-exile prophets. Through his vision he saw the redemption of Zion and Christ as the "Branch." He gives us a beautiful picture of the Millennial reign. How holiness will be universal, even there shall be holiness upon the bells of the horses and the cook pots.

Malachi was the last prophet of the old Bible. He finished his prophecies three hundred and ninety seven years before Christ left us to grope our way in darkness for nearly four hundred years. He gives us a picture of backslidden people, and the nations robbing God in tithes and offerings, and promised if we would bring them in he would bless us. In the last chapter he describes the people of God as calves of the stall.[7]

Articles

(**Author's note:** This section contains articles that have appeared in various Pentecostal Holiness periodicals and were written by women ministers.)

"A Shelter in the Time of Storm" – Rita Wrenn

"Caring for a Flock of Suffering Sheep" – Ruth W. Johnson

". . . In Jerusalem . . . My Hometown" – Jeraldine Posey

"Let's Break Down Dividing Walls!" – Charlene West

"Holmes Bible College Report" – Ruth Heath

"Called to Abide" – Dr. Lydia Figueroa

"Rahab's Name was Listed with the Hero's of Faith" – Ruth Moore

"What A Great God We Serve" – Susan Wells

"Our Responsibility to the Great Commission" – Hazleen Graham

"Practical Ways to Support Our Military Heroes" – Chaplain Major Christy Sorrow

"A Hidden Threat" – Deborah Riley

"COMMERCIALISM: Digging out of the Tinsel" – Renee Ross

"Focus on Prayer" – Mrs. C. F. Isaac

A SHELTER IN THE TIME OF STORM
Nahum 1:3, 7
Rita Wrenn

Although it was late and I was tired, I couldn't sleep. Troublesome thoughts kept me awake.

"Lord," I prayed, "our son is fourteen today. He has been good thus far and there is no doubt he loves his family and wants to please us, but I'm afraid this is the lull before the storm. You know how all his life he has been headstrong, determined to do what he pleased no matter what anyone said.

"We must admit the experience he had with God at youth camp when he was twelve had a definite and lasting effect on his life. From that time until now he has shown a marked difference in his attitude. And all the changes have been good. He has shown maturity, submission, and respect that just weren't there before.

"But, Lord, You know that just any day now he will probably reach that stage of turbulence through which most teenagers go, when peer pressure might overrule what we've tried to teach him. I don't know if we're ready for that. It's hard for parents to know when to be loving and gentle, or firm and authoritative.

"The teenage years are so important! These next few years are formative, decisive years, years of choosing his life-style and of deciding what he will do with the life God has given him. As his mother, I'm scared. I'm sure his dad has some apprehensions, too. Will we give him the direction he needs?

"The impression that followed was too strong and too real not to have been the voice of the Lord."

"Do you remember the other day at the office when you and your friend were talking about storms? Both of you said you were not afraid of storms. Your friend said she enjoys standing by the window and watching the lightning play across the sky, seeing the wind gracefully arch and bend the trees back and forth, and hearing the rumble of the thunder. She said it testified to her of the great power of a great, big, wonderful Lord, and that it gives her an assurance there is nothing too great for Him!

"Then you said that you enjoy the storm because it gives you a feeling of security and of being isolated from the world, closed-in with God. You know He is in control, so you have a feeling of peace. You said that sleep was sweet and peaceful when the rain was pelting against the window panes.

"What you were trying to say is that you **trust Me**. You trust Me to take care of you even when there is potential danger all around you."

"That's right, Lord, that is what I was trying to say."

"Well, if you can trust Me in the weather storms, why can't you trust Me in the storms of life? Do you think the problems of guiding teenagers are too much for Me?' He asked."

"Lord, please don't be angry with me for making this observation. I know it sounds so doubtful, but isn't it true that **nature** obeys You perfectly? Humanity doesn't."

"Man is a part of **nature**. You can trust Me to give you the wisdom you need to guide your children. Do not be any more afraid of the turbulence of life than you are of the turbulence of the elements. I control it all."

Needless to say, I went to sleep that night. That was more than two years ago and I have lost no more sleep worrying over our children.

Sin may be raging, but "where sin abounds grace doth even more abound." We may be living in a changing society with many attitudes that threaten to undermine the moral foundations upon which we have built, but God's Word is still powerful, sharper than any two-edged sword. It will always be able to stand its ground against any theory, philosophy, or standard. The battle is still the Lord's! The government is still upon His shoulders.

We can trust Him. He will not fail.[8]

"CARING FOR A FLOCK OF SUFFERING SHEEP"
Ruth W. Johnson

"The herds mill about because they have no pasture; even the flocks of sheep are suffering." – Joel 1:18-NIV

As I passed the offering plate to Amy, my thirteen year old daughter, I smiled to see little Sylvia cuddled up next to her. Just the previous Sunday I had told Amy the background of Sylvia and her siblings. Five girls and a boy, ranging in age from four to ten [. . .] would be a handful even for Dr. James Dobson!

These kids were both willfully disobedient and childishly irresponsible. One teacher was at the point of quitting because of her inability to control the five-year-old girl. Seeking direction to reach these kids, I asked the neighbor who had invited them to church what she knew about their family life. The story she related was a heartbreaking one.

The children belong to a not-very-well "blended" family. Now living together, both father and mother were previously married and divorced. Four of the girls were from the mother's marriage. Sylvia and the boy were from the father's marriage. Because his wife was a crack addict, he got custody of the children.

The neighbor went on to tell me she hears crying, screams, and sound of beatings from the upstairs apartment where the family lives. Sylvia is often the target of the mother's rage. She is not allowed to play with the toys the other girls share, and when she tries, the mother makes sure they are taken away from her.

Knowing the situation the children face at home helped me understand their behavior and determine to show them the love of Jesus. When I explained to Amy the hurt Sylvia suffered at home, she felt compassion for her; and I felt blessed to see Amy reaching out to care for one of the suffering sheep in our little flock.

When God called our family to New York City seven years ago, He put a desire in our hearts to reach suffering people who were literally lost sheep without a shepherd. Our prayer was to find a neighborhood that really needed a church.

God certainly answered our prayers when He led us to this "square mile of urban blight in South Brooklyn," as Red Hook was described recently in the *New York Times*. Most of the traditional churches had given up on this area. We were able to lease an Episcopal Church building which was only being used one hour a week because the diocese could no longer find a priest to serve full-time in Red Hook. We hung a sign on the church and began to minister in the neighborhood.

Everywhere we looked – on the streets, in the schoolyards, in the towering government project buildings – we saw people suffering from the consequences of sin. Unfortunately, stories like Sylvia's are the norm rather than the exception in Red Hook. Almost 75 percent of the children in the elementary school a block from the church have at least one parent who is addicted to drugs. Well over half the children live in single-parent households. Lack of a decent education and unemployment are facts of life for many of the adults. Most of Red Hook's residents receive some kind of government assistance. For many, especially households headed by women, it is their only source of income.

Whereas every community has its share of drug addition, immorality, and poverty, these characterize the "normal" lifestyle in Red Hook. Many of the women in the area have listened to the life of government-sponsored family planners and have aborted their unborn children. Homosexuality is regarded as just an alternative way of life. Tuberculosis and AIDS are diseases common in the inner city and Red Hook is no exception.

In the beginning, few responded to the gospel message we shared so eagerly. Hardened hearts, hopelessness, and hate were frequent responses. We often wondered why we were here, but each time we asked that question, God sent an answer: a drug addict seeking help, a young mother shedding tears of repentance, a child's hungry hug.

God sent words of encouragement through a retired missionary: "If only one person is saved through your ministry in Red Hook, it will be worth it all." Sometimes we thought her words may have been prophetic – relating only to the future; but as we persevered, prayed, and were prayed for by saints who had made commitments to intercede for us, we saw hearts softened, hopes renewed, and hate give way to love. We have seen families restored, immorality renounced, and planned abortions canceled. The greatest joy comes when one of the lost, suffering sheep comes home to the Good Shepherd.

The almost 100-year-old church building is once again alive with children's voices, vibrant with praise and worship, and used steadily throughout the week for preaching, Bible studies, prayer, kid's clubs, and opportunities for fellowship. The church has become a pasture providing daily bread, living water, rest and comfort.

On May 15, [1994] Red Hook New Life Center was chartered as the first Pentecostal Holiness Church in New York City. Almost 100 people attend this service, and 32 members were received into the fellowship. Rev. James Leggett, executive director of Evangelism USA and vice chairman of the denomination, presided over the service and challenged the new congregation to be the church God was calling it to be.

Father Doug Norwood, the Spirit-filled Episcopal priest who had been instrumental in helping us acquire the use of the building, was present to express his thankfulness to Jesus for beginning a new work. When we contacted Father Norwood initially concerning leasing the building, he had told us he knew the Episcopal Church at the location was dying, but God had given him a vision of the church filled with children. Our first ministry endeavor was a successful children's church, out of which the other ministries developed.

As our family recalls the past six years, we realize how God has led us, provided for us, and protected us. We have renewed our commitment to reach out with Jesus' love to the lost and suffering people in Red Hook. The results are not always immediate (even after six years, we feel we have just begun to make a tiny difference), but for our family there is no greater satisfaction than ministering to and loving not only the bruised lambs like Sylvia, but a whole flock of suffering sheep."[9]

(**Author's note:** Ruth Johnson and her husband Randy pastor New Life Center in New York City. The church was organized on May 15, [1994].)

. . . In Jerusalem . . . My Hometown
Jeraldine T. Posey

Hopewell, Virginia, USA – my hometown! There is a wonderful blend of the old and the new here with historic roots which go back to 1607. Old City Point, now a part of the city, was founded by Sir Thomas Dale in 1613. It was incorporated as a town in 1824. General Grant had his headquarters at Appomattox Manor in City Point during the siege of Petersburg and the battle for Richmond. Abraham Lincoln spent two of the last three weeks of his life here. Today Hopewell is a modern, progressive city of approximately 25,000 people and is one of the great chemical centers of the nation.

More importantly – it is my Jerusalem! If I am to obey Jesus' command to be a witness for Him, I must begin right here. In the midst of all of this rich historical heritage, I must remember a greater spiritual heritage that is mine.

Jeremiah wrote: "Proclaim all these words . . . in the streets of Jerusalem . . ." (11:6). That means that I have a responsibility to evangelize my hometown by telling its citizens about Jesus.

What does the word *evangelize* mean? In too many instances it has come to suggest only the annual revival, and the word *evangelist* to mean only the preacher who conducts the services. With these views, however, the work of evangelism is limited to very few people and the result is that the greater majority of Christians conscientiously excuse themselves from the task which Jesus apparently meant should be shared by the entire body of believers.

Look at the first century Christians. Light is shed on the subject when we read Acts 2:46, 47: "And they, continuing daily with one accord in the temple, and breaking bread *from house to house*, did eat their meat with gladness and singleness of heart . . . And the Lord added to the church daily such as should be saved." (Emphasis mine).

In Acts 5:42, we see how far they pursued this concept: "And daily in the temple, and in every house they ceased not to teach and preach Jesus Christ." They evangelized all Jerusalem by going to the homes to proclaim the message of salvation.

Acts 20:20 indicates that the main thrust of New Testament evangelism continued. Paul's pattern was basically the same. "And how I kept back nothing that was profitable unto you, but have shewed you, and have taught you publicly and *from house to house.*" From Acts 2 until Acts 20 is a time span of about thirty years. Door-to-door evangelism was the continuous operation of the church of the first century.

In the second century, Christianity became entangled in theological controversy. A strong growth of apostasy characterized the third century. That apostasy became complete in the fourth century and Christianity was plunged into 1,000 years of darkness.

It was not until the time of Martin Luther that Christianity began to move out of that darkness through a theological reformation. Nothing was said about the evangelization of the world, however. In the 1790s William Carey brought this New Testament concept back to the forefront.

Mass evangelism reappeared about 200 years ago through the ministry of John Wesley. Unfortunately, the other form of New Testament evangelism (personal) has not yet made its re-entry into Christian history. It is talked about, people write books about it, and ministers preach fervent messages about the need for it. Yet, in the last 1800 years there has not been a time when a great movement of personal witnessing has gripped a large portion of the Christian population.

As followers of Christ we are ALL to be personal soul-winners, and the supreme business of every Christian is to individualize the gospel. Jesus spoke plainly concerning His purpose for us: "as my Father hath sent me, even so send I you" (John 20:21); "Go *ye* therefore, and teach . . ." (Matthew 28:19, 20); "Ye have not chosen me, but I have chosen *you*, and ordained *you*, that *ye* should go and bring forth fruit . . ." (John 15:16). It only remains to determine who He meant by 'you' and 'ye' in these Scriptures.

Every Sunday as we Christians gather in our sanctuaries, we attempt to save the world by evangelizing the church building. The most evangelized space in God's world is the area surrounded by the four walls of our natural structures of lumber, mortar, and stone. There is only one problem! At least 80% of the unconverted people in America do not go to church. Look over your congregation any Sunday. Where are the unsaved? The most of them are lying in bed, eating, reading a paper, watching TV, playing golf, or fishing; out there in the by-ways of our hometown – our Jerusalem.

We have been commanded to be witnesses in Jerusalem. Unless we get a burden for these people and go to them, they may never hear the truth about Jesus Christ. They may meet God never having been introduced to His Son, the [Savior] of the world.

Until now, we have gotten more cooperation from the sinners than the saints because some of them will come to church, but far fewer Christians will go to the homes of the lost. God never said anything to the unconverted about going to church that is as demanding as His greatest single command to Christians: "Go ye . . ."

We should understand that evangelism is not visitation. It is not inviting people to church or Sunday school. It is not handing out tracts. Evangelism does not occur until the lost person is brought to the place of making a decision for Christ and is added to the body of believers. No higher honor could be conferred upon the Christian than to be associated with Jesus in the great work of bringing a lost world to the knowledge of the truth about Him through the Word. It is not only a privilege, but a solemn responsibility. A revival of personal evangelism will be a step in the right direction to witness in our Jerusalem.[10]

(**Author's note:** Rev. Posey, D. Min., is a member of the Eastern Virginia Conference and the Hopewell P. H. Church. Her ministry includes seminars and equipping local church members for personal evangelism.)

LET'S BREAK DOWN DIVIDING WALLS!
Charlene West

One of the most dramatic events of modern history was the opening up of the Berlin Wall. On November 9, 1989, the East German government lifted travel and immigration restrictions, and thousands gathered at the wall which had separated the two Germanys since 1961. By November 15, 7.7 million travel visas had been issued. On November 28, West German Chancellor Kohl proposed a plan for the confederation of the two Germanys. The wall was literally broken down, and Germany became one nation!

There are many forces which divide the people of our planet, but while the systems of this world divide, Jesus unites. He prayed that His people might be one, and the apostle Paul so beautifully tells us about what He did to bring that unity about. With His own body Jesus broke down the wall that separated the Jews and Gentiles and kept them enemies . . ."by means of the cross he united both races into one body and brought them back to God . . . that all of us . . . are able to come in one Spirit into the presence of the Father" (Ephesians 2:14-18; *Today's English Version*).

The New Testament clearly teaches us the necessity to cross these barriers and take the Gospel to all people. Jesus deliberately went into Samaria to evangelize a person in need of Him, and Philip later followed through with a great evangelistic campaign. Peter was definitely commanded to preach the Gospel in a Roman home even though this was not "according to the Law." Philip was sent to Gaza to preach to an Ethiopian; thus God makes it very clear that Blacks are a part of His divine plan. Paul understood the universality of the Gospel and said that God had "made of one blood all nations of men to dwell on all the face of the earth . . . that they should seek the Lord . . . for we are the offspring of God" (Acts 17:26-28).

Many times Christians have gone along with the reigning practices of our dominant culture. Too often they have adopted the opinions, spread the propaganda, and repeated the slogans and ethnic jokes of their communities. Jesus said, "By this shall all men know that ye are my disciples, if ye have love one to another" (John 13:35). The time has come to see the barriers we have put up in the clear light of God's Word. Let's break down the dividing wall that separates us from other members of our Christian family! Here are some things to remember.

1. The blood of Jesus that binds us is stronger than the differences that separate us! In heaven we will sing, "Thou . . . hast redeemed us to God by thy blood out of every kindred, and tongue, and people, and nation" (Revelation 5:9).

2. Pentecost advanced the church on into cultural diversity by allowing the Christians to speak the languages of those around them. There was cultural diversity at Azusa Street. Let's keep it!

3. Let's affirm our unity in Christ. "There is one body, and one Spirit . . . one Lord, one faith, one baptism, one God and Father of all, who is above all, and through all, and in you all" (Ephesians 4:4-6). God excludes no one!

4. Let's preach the Gospel to all people, and then receive all new believers as brothers and sisters regardless of race, nationality, or color. Let's empower them to spiritual leadership in the denomination, conference and local church.

5. Let's repent of the sins spawned by racial prejudice and racism. In so doing, let's see the needs of those who have been denied their political and economic rights, and take actions when we go to the polls to vote.

Billy Graham recently wrote in *Christianity Today*, "Racial and ethnic hostility is the foremost social problem facing our world today. Of all people, Christians should be the most active in reaching out to those of other races, instead of accepting the status quo of division and animosity." God has called us to reverse the trends. Let's break down the walls that divide and truly be one people![11]

HOLMES BIBLE COLLEGE REPORT
Ruth Heath

Truth and holiness, along with all the other Christian principles upon which Holmes Bible College was founded and stands established, are instilled into the heart of each student with all sincerity and sympathetic consideration. The college primarily emphasizes theology and missions, training our young men and women to become laborers in the great harvest of souls over all the earth, both at home and abroad.

The students are given every opportunity to prepare for a life of usefulness in the upbuilding of God's kingdom on earth. The Bible is given pre-eminence, as it should be; an hour of instruction is given first in the morning before literary classes commence. And at the close of the session of classes in the afternoon another hour of Bible instruction is given to all the students. On Monday these two hours of instruction are given to theoretical and practical missions.

Over two-thirds of the ministers licensed or ordained in the Pentecostal Holiness Church today attended Holmes. Much of the progress of our church today results from, and will continue to result greatly from the training so faithfully given to the men and women sent by God to this school, not mentioning those who come from other churches.

After the last war, veterans who had been face to face with the grim realities of life and death in other countries, as well as our own land, came to the Bible College with determination, consecration, zeal, and willingness to put their best effort forth to accept this all-around Christian training, and then spend all their power and energy giving the Gospel to the restless, pleasure-seeking human race. It was necessary for the school, in making preparation to accommodate them, to spend from $15,000 to $20,000. During the previous years a total of 280 veterans has been enrolled. For the coming term we have already enrolled 57, and regret that we do not have housing to accommodate other applicants. We trust, however, that some of them will be able to live in reach of the school and come anyway.

Every Monday morning an hour is given to theoretical missions. The works of great pioneer missionaries, who blazed the trail before our time, are studied from the textbook and serve to inspire the students with active desires to carry on this great work left unfinished only by the death of these great adventurers for Christ. These pioneers, even though they had to pass from the stage of action, give strength to these young Bible students. Holmes Bible College has furnished Africa, India, China, South America, Hawaii, and other foreign countries with capably trained missionaries, along with numerous home missionaries over our nation. Many Christians around the globe testify of the accomplishments of these sacrificing missionaries.

While it was impossible to send missionaries across the ocean, home missions progressed. Recently churches have been established by these trained students; youth leaders furnished who have established or revived youth societies; vacation Bible schools have been introduced into churches never before having them; Sunday School teachers are placing in the hearts of our children the fundamental truths upon which the church of tomorrow will stand. Home missions has indeed blessed our land through students trained at Holmes.

The practical missions class held on Monday afternoon has accomplished worthwhile things for God during the past three years. In 1948, the students through this class sent $700 to Africa to establish a church there. In 1949 these "mission-minded" students raised $1,000 for a church or the Bible School in China to help get the light to those so long in darkness. In 1950, they showed their love for God and zeal for His cause by giving $1,125 to the Lucy Holmes building fund, which structure stands as a monument to the faith Holmes Bible College has exercised during the past few years. The students prayed, and worked, and believed, and God was pleased to reward their efforts to assist in this project, which is really a phase of mission work, for here consecrated souls are prepared to go forth with the full Gospel for all the world. Also, in addition to this, the practical missions class gave the sum of $75.00 this term to India for our faithful missionaries laboring among those benighted people so desperately in need of this Gospel.

The influence of Homes Bible College has surely reached around the world. The works of those who received their training here are bringing forth fruit today, and shall continue to inspire, uplift, encourage, and empower multitudes of people to live for, and wholly serve God. Only eternity shall reveal the complete record of those blessed by the training received here, or the contact with the godly influence of someone who was trained here. America, far and wide, will never cease to feel the influence of such a school as Holmes Bible College, completely dedicated to the service of Lord and Savior, Jesus Christ. Many of the hundreds of young men and women trained for Christian service at Holmes have been unable to pay but very little, if anything, for their tuition and board. The entire faculty, from the president down, serves wholeheartedly without a stipulated salary. The college will on October 5 open the fifty-second term. If you feel that such an institution is worthy of your consideration, your prayers and support will be gratefully appreciated.[12]

CALLED TO ABIDE
Dr. Lydia Figueroa

God spoke to me in 1998: "Abide in Me," He said. I am already doing that! I thought.

"No," He said, "you don't understand; Abide in Me is to be the name of your ministry."

At the time, I had been teaching and holding intercessory prayer meetings in my home for nearly 20 years. With that word, however, I began to study the Gospel of John. For an entire year, I meditated on the book, and by the following year, I had begun to understand what God was saying: He was calling me to plant a church, and its name was to be Abiding in Him IPHC [International Pentecostal Holiness Church].

I accepted Christ as my Savior in 1975. At that moment, my sins were wiped away as He cleansed this broken and wounded 25-year-old Hispanic-American woman. Through His example of washing the disciples' feet, I came to understand the ministry He had for me. My first mandate was to love God and nurture a relationship with Him (abide). Then, out of that relationship, I was to love and serve others.

My call was confirmed by a personal visitation and word from the Lord while I was on a mission trip to Monterrey, Mexico, in 1988. That word, based on 2 Chronicles 20, transformed my life as I discovered that my being a woman in leadership was God's plan, not mine.

At the time of my conversion, I was living in Fayetteville, North Carolina, where I still live after 38 years. I attended Northwood Temple PHC for over 20 years under the leadership of my former pastor and friend (amigo) Dr. John Hedgepeth. Through his love, training, and mentoring, I grew in the knowledge of Jesus Christ and learned to serve the body of Christ. Other strong influences in the process included Faye Hedgepeth, the late Ada Lee Thurman, Roger Barefoot, and others. Their tutelage and exemplary lives helped prepare me to fulfill the calling of a woman pastor and leader in the North Carolina Conference.

Thanks to visionary leaders in the conference who believed God uses women today to make a difference, I obtained my credentials. In 1996, I was ordained as a minister of the gospel of Jesus Christ.

Former Superintendent Elwood Long appointed me as the first woman *i*WIN director for the conference, and I still serve in that role today. That same year, I participated in the EVUSA Church Planters School in Atlanta. I remember looking around the room and thinking, *Wow! I am the only woman in this classroom.* That challenged me, but the job became easier as my classmates welcomed and affirmed me. I believe my success had to do with God's timing and favor. Plus, knowing the call was from God made all the difference in the world.

I have never had to defend my position as a woman in ministry. Instead, I believe I am viewed as a co-laborer with the rest of the body of Christ. Though I have weathered many storms in both my personal life and my ministry, I have felt the hand of God leading me to win many victories. My faith has been tested, and my personal life challenged. Yet, like so many others, I have determined neither to give up nor to waver. I am committed in this until I see Jesus face to face. My testing, trials, and victories have enlarged, developed, matured, and helped me know who His is and who I am in Him.

After the call to plant a church, I immediately began Sunday services in the Delgado home, where we stayed for a year and a half. From there, we rented a warehouse and held services there for two years as the ministry grew.

God had spoken to me years earlier, even before I attended the Church Planters School, about a particular piece of land and a building. Suddenly, there it was: our miracle. With the support of Bishop Chris Thompson and Danny Nelson and the help of Almighty God, we were able to acquire the property that would serve the needs of the Abiding in Him church family. God had it all planned out; all I needed to do was trust Him and obey.

I have been pastoring now for about ten years and am now serving on boards in the North Carolina Conference. I continued to study and participated in many training sessions and classes. In July 2006, I received my doctorate in theology.

As believers and priests, our assignment is clear; we are first called simply to abide in Him. Then we are to work together to see His kingdom come and His will be done here on earth as it is in heaven.[13]

RAHAB'S NAME WAS LISTED WITH THE HEROES OF FAITH
Rev. Ruth Moore

There are many lessons that every Christian woman could learn by studying the life of Rahab after she believes on the true God and changes her way of living. Surely Rahab had come to believe in Israel's God after hearing of how He made the way for them to cross the Red Sea when they came out of Egypt, and of other ways He had helped them win their battles. Also, her testimony unto the two spies proves her faith in the Lord.

Rahab was a willing worker – after having done all she could for the spies, and then asked of them that they would remember her and her relations and spare them in the destruction of Jericho. She did as she had been instructed – she put the line of scarlet thread in the window and began the task of getting her father, mother, and brethren to come into her house. People have always been much the same, and some one must be willing to work and put in many long hours trying to bring them to the Lord. Rahab realized her people would be destroyed if she failed; therefore, she worked tirelessly, not for praise or fame, but to save those she loved.

Again we see in this great woman something else outstanding – her willingness to sacrifice, as she brings her relations into her home to share the comforts of her home, her nice beds and good food. And she seemed to do those things so willingly, in fact, she was so anxious that they come that no doubt she gave them the best and took that which was left for herself. This isn't too much for us to do if it is for the salvation of the soul.

After getting them into her home she must keep them there. If she fails, her work will be in vain. Some of them may complain; they may have grown restless and tired of waiting. Some may have thought they would fare better elsewhere, so we read between the lines and imagine the patience that Rahab must have had to keep them from being destroyed. Surely it takes patience to continue to be interested in the salvation of souls when they don't seem to be interested in themselves. Sometimes they even fail to appreciate your interest.

So dear readers of *The Helping Hand,* let us toil on and have even a greater desire to work harder and be willing to sacrifice and manifest in a greater measure this fruit of the spirit – patience – as we labor to win souls for the Lord. Just as Rahab was rewarded by her life, and those of her father, mother, and brethren being spared, so we too will receive a reward, for our labor is not in vain in the Lord. "And they that be wise shall shine as the brightness of the firmament; and they that turn many to righteousness as the stars for ever and ever." Daniel 12:3[14]

WHAT A GREAT GOD WE SERVE!
Rev. Susan Wells
South Carolina Conference WIN Director

Psalm 77:13 – "Who is so great a God as our God?"

It's hard to believe that this year is almost over. It seems like only yesterday when all we heard about was "Y2K." Now, all of the Y2K books and paraphernalia that were selling like hotcakes a year ago are on the 75 per cent off table.

A lot has taken place during this year of the millennium, and WIN of the South Carolina Conference has been active. We started off the New Year in Jacksonville, Florida, at the zone meeting there. It was in Jacksonville that the vision was cast by Superintendent Fowler for a day of prayer along the eastern seaboard to remove the hindrances to the wave of God's glory.

In June, WIN participated during the 2000 South Carolina camp meeting. District WIN directors opened the evening services with prayer and proclamation, thereby setting a tone of victory that continued through powerful ministry of the Word.

During October 19-21, WIN of the South Carolina Conference held its second annual prayer conference in Columbia, South Carolina, at Forest Drive Baptist Church. Nine states and three countries were represented there. Eddie and Alice Smith of Houston, Texas, were the keynote speakers. They brought fresh insight concerning intercession. Michael Fletcher, pastor of Manna Church in Fayetteville, North Carolina, was a Friday workshop speaker. He spoke on "How to Pastor Intercessors." His word was timely and practical.

Finally, WIN led a day of prayer and fasting on November 4 in Georgetown, South Carolina. The Maryville PHC was the site of the Coastal Prayer Assault. This was the initial step in the fulfilling of Superintendent Fowler's vision for the wave of God's glory covering our state as pastors and intercessors joined together with Conference leadership to remove the hindrances to God's wave of glory.

As we cross the threshold into the next millennium, it is exciting to know that WIN will be a part of God's move in our Conference. Psalm 77:13 asks the question, "Who is so great a God as our God?" The answer is, 'There is no God like ours . . . He is great and greatly to be praised."![15]

(**Author's note:** WIN is a World Intercession Network which was established in November 1982 to concentrate on prayer for IPHC missionaries and the ministries of the church. In 2006, WIN was changed to *i*WIN. The '*i*' stands for the IPHC which is leaning on prayer.)[16]

OUR RESPONSIBILITY TO THE GREAT COMMMISSION
Hazleen Graham

"How then shall they call on him in whom they have not believed? and how shall they believe in him of whom they have not heard? and how shall they hear without a preacher? And how shall they preach, except they be sent? . . . How beautiful are the feet of them that preach the gospel of peace, and bring glad tidings of good things"? (Romans 10:14-15).

There is no sentiment about this Scripture. It is stern, unyielding logic and brings every one of us face to face with our responsibility to the world's ruin or redemption. In fulfilling the great commission, it is our responsibility to reach the **WHOLE WORLD** with the **WHOLE GOSPEL**.

According to A. B. Simpson, founder of the Christian Missionary Alliance, there are three links in the chain of responsibility.

(1) **"How shall they call on him in whom they have not believed?"** Believing is the responsibility of every sinner. God calls upon lost man to believe on the Lord Jesus Christ as [Savior], God cannot save people without their believing on Him. "He that believeth on him is not condemned but he that believeth not is condemned already, because he hath not believed in the name of the only begotten Son of God" [-] John 3:18.

God wants the message of salvation offered to all mankind. Then the responsibility rests with them.

(2) The second link is the human agency. **"How shall they believe in him of whom they have not heard? And how shall they hear without a preacher?"** The agency is the messenger. God has ordained the human agency as the conveyor of the Gospel to mankind. "Now then we are ambassadors for Christ." Christ's first word to His disciples is "go." The call of the heavenly voices is "Whom shall I send, and who will go for us?" - Isaiah 6:8. HE IS WAITING FOR VOLUNTEERS.

(3) The third link brings the responsibility home to everyone of us. **"How shall they preach except they be sent?"** Sending is something that we all can do. Certainly, it is God's business to send a messenger, and the words apostle and missionary just mean "sent ones." Every missionary should be sent by the Holy Spirit. But it is our duty to send them too. As we sacrifice and give to support the endeavors abroad, God will count our work a partnership with them, and we shall share alike in the recompense when the harvest shall be gathered. We may not have been called to GO, but we have certainly been called to SEND.

When a certain Chinese man was asked why he had given up Confucius and Buddha and accepted Jesus Christ instead, he replied: "I was down in a deep pit into which I had fallen; I was sinking in the mire and vainly calling for aid. Suddenly a shadow fell across the pit. Looking up I saw Confucius. I implored him to help me. He proceeded to instruct me in the principles of right living, and told me that if I had only listened to his teaching I would not have been there. My cry was in vain for he was gone and his advice was useless. I needed someone to deliver me from the pit of death.

"Later another shadow fell across the opening and I looked up to see Buddha. I cried out to him, but Buddha folded his arms and said, 'be quiet, be patient, be still. Don't mind your troubles, ignore them; the secret to happiness is to die to self and surrounding[s], to retire to the inward calm of your heart. There you shall find Nirvana, external rest and that will be the end of your existence.' He turned to leave and I knew that Buddha would not save me.

"At that point I was ready to give up hope, when a third shadow fell across my vision. I looked up and saw a man much like myself, with kind and tender countenance. Marks of dried blood were upon his brow. He spoke to me and said, 'My child, I have come to save you. Will you let me help you?' I cried, 'Come, Lord, help me, I perish'! In a moment He leaped down into the pit and put [H]is arms around me. He lifted me up, placed me on the brink and took from me my torn and spattered garments. He washed me and robed me in new raiment, and then [H]e said, 'I have come to save you from your distress, and now if you will follow Me, I will never leave you. I will be your Guide and Friend all the way and will keep you from falling again. The Man's Name was Jesus. I fell at His feet and worshipped Him. "That" said the man, "is why I became a Christian."

The same Jesus who brought you and me out of a horrible pit and the miry clay and set our feet upon a solid rock and established our goings, is longing to do the same for every lost and helpless child of our fallen race. How said, how needless, that we should allow them to perish without ever knowing Him. How can we be so cruel to them and so heartless to Him [?] May the same love that ransomed and redeemed us, compel us to SEND laborers into the harvest field (whole world) to seek and to save that which was lost.

The harvest is GREAT – the harvest is PLENTEOUS – the harvest is (ripe) WHITE. "He that gathereth in summer is a wise son but he that sleepeth in harvest is a son that causeth shame" - Matthew 9:37; Luke 10:2; John 4:35; Proverbs 10:5.[17]

Practical Ways to Support Our Military Heroes
Chaplain Major Christy Sorrow

Operation Iraqi Freedom and other assignments around the world have separated many American troops from family, friends, and all things familiar. Especially during these summer months when temperatures in Iraq can soar to unbelievable heights, how can church leaders best direct their congregations to pray for our military? I would like to suggest prayer on four levels:

1. Political and Military Leaders – Pray for President George W. Bush, Vice President Dick Cheney, Secretary of State Colin Powell, Secretary of Defense Donald Rumsfeld, National Security Advisor Condoleezza Rice, Chairman of the Joint Chiefs of Staff Richard B. Meyers and the Joint Chiefs, Commander in Chief U. S. Central Command General John Abizaid, and other military leaders in the theater of operations.

2. Our Troops – Pray that military personnel will have a keen awareness of God's presence and peace to comfort and guide them. Pray for their physical, emotional, and spiritual strength to sustain them through the intense heat, long hours, fear, and loneliness. Also ask God to renew their sense of purpose to see how their assignments contribute to the cause of freedom.

3. Military Families – Pray especially for those who have deployed loved ones that they too will know God's comfort and peace. Ask God to strengthen them physically, emotionally, and spiritually to care for their children and the responsibilities of home during their loved one's absence. Pray that families will be drawn closer to each other and to God during the separation. Also remember the time of reunion. Pray that families will experience smooth transitions from deployment to post-deployment status.

4. Themselves – Urge your congregations to pray for their own church leaders and members of their congregations to have wisdom and discernment as they watch news coverage to see truth. Ask God to show you creative ways to reach out to members of the military and their families within your own congregation and to show community support when military members or their families are affected by a casualty or tragedy. (I read recently about members of one community who stood along the streets with hands over their hearts as the funeral procession of a fallen soldier drove through town.)

How can church leaders best direct their congregations to action for our military and their families?
1. Pray first.
2. If you know of a deployed military member in the congregation or community, write a personal letter (not a "To Any-Soldier" letter). Letters give them something tangible they can read and reread to sense your support.

3. Use your own gifts and talents to offer (don't wait to be asked) to assist family members in practical ways:
   * Offer free babysitting
   * Prepare a meal or meals
   * Provide lawn care (mow, clip hedges, plant/weed flowers)
   * Clean house
   * Hug the children (If mom is deployed and dad is left behind with the children, another mom's hugs can help temporarily. Read them stories. Brush a daughter's hair. Help match outfits.)
4. Realize that the most effective way any individual can make a difference in our world is through his own sphere of influence; at home, in the neighborhood, in the workplace, to strangers on the street or in the mall. We change our world one person at a time, and it begins when we touch those around us.[18]

(**Author's note:** At the time of the publication of this article, Christy was senior Protestant chaplain at Tinker Air Force Base in Midwest City, Oklahoma. She was then the only female active duty chaplain representing the IPHC.)

A HIDDEN TREAT
Deborah Riley

(**Author's note:** Deborah Riley pastors Family Worship Center, a Pentecostal Holiness Church in Claremore, Oklahoma. She is a member of New Horizons Ministries.)

We hear about abused women in foreign countries who are battered, raped, trafficked, and murdered by intimate partners. Then we think, *But we live in America. We go to church. This doesn't happen to our women!*

Take a reality check! An abused woman may sit on your pew every Sunday; only no one hears her story. She may be suffering in silence, convinced no one would believe her story even if she told it.

Janet[1] was one of them. She was reared in a Christian home, her father a preacher. At age 17, she was allowed to date Rick, a "fine young man." When she became pregnant, marriage was the only acceptable recourse.

A few weeks later, Rick started the first of many adulterous affairs. At home, he ridiculed Janet, undermining her every word and action, contradicting her, and calling her names. Then he belittled her for not knowing what she was talking about. He began restricting her visits to see family and friends and monitoring phone calls.

One Sunday, Janet surrendered her heart to God. Every time she returned home from church, Rick swore and accused her of running out on him, although he was often seen driving by the church to 'check up on her.' Janet lived on a treadmill of fear and defensiveness. She struggled to find ways to show Rick he was twisting her words to say something she did not mean. He threw them back, incriminating her with, 'You've always got to be right, don't you!'

One day Janet invited her sister and her family over for dinner. She gave the guests their favorite pieces of fried chicken, which happened to be Rick's too. Suddenly, he leaped up, yelling at her for giving her "no-good sister" *his* piece of chicken.

They all sat in stunned silence as Janet pleaded, "Honey, they're company."

"They're not *my* company!" He bellowed. Then he stomped out of the room and turned the television up so loud it interrupted their conversation. Janet was humiliated. She never invited anyone into her home again.

Over time, Rick's abuse grew more frequent and severe, with in-your-face screaming and threatening gestures. Then it happened. He balled up his fist and smashed her lip, knocking her front teeth loose. He always blamed her, and she began to believe him. *If I were a better wife, he wouldn't be so angry*, she thought. Needing hope, Janet finally poured out her soul to her pastor, who was also her father. His answer? "Marriage is for life, Honey. You made your bed. Now you have to lie in it."

Abuse comes in many forms – threats, humiliation, coercion, isolation, intimidation, and brute force. The perpetrators gain domination through verbal, emotional, financial, sexual, and physical abuse tactics. Abuse generally is not about anger. It's about control. Any relationship aimed at hurting or eroding a person's self-esteem is abusive, whether physical or not, and it can erupt into violence at any time.

The American Medical Association estimates that over four million women in America are severely assaulted by male partners each year. In a lifetime, one in four women is likely to be abused by a partner.[2] In reported cases of domestic violence, 85 percent of victims are female, and 64 percent are white.[3]

By the time I met Janet, she had "walked on eggshells" for 36 years of marriage. Rick had broken every marriage vow long ago. Only by drawing close to God did she receive courage to stand up to Rick and demand change. She soon realized he might never change because he refused to accept responsibility for his actions.

Through counseling, I helped Janet understand four important things every abused woman should know:
1. Abuse is not your fault.
2. You are not alone.
3. There is help.
4. It is not God's will for you to live in abusive conditions.

Knowledge gave Janet faith that God would show her the way out. And He did. He provided a place and a living for her.

It is difficult for women to leave their abusers. Fear of reprisals, physical exhaustion, emotional trauma, and financial instability are all militating factors.

For several years, I have been involved in counseling hurting women. God has placed a vision in my heart to establish a healing center for abused women in Claremore, Oklahoma. Lydia's House of Restoration is incorporated as a 501(c)3 nonprofit organization, and we have located a serviceable facility for sale that will allow us to house ten women at a time. Our goal is to open Lydia's House as a retreat center where women can get away for a weekend, a vacation, or for several months of healing. Through prayer, counseling, teaching, private Bible study, and hard work, victims of abuse can be transformed into victorious women of God able to return home and help others.

Where is Janet today? She is preaching, counseling, and seeing many other women healed to the glory of God.

*ENDNOTES

[1] The names in this story are changed to protect the innocent. Unfortunately, they also protect the guilty.

[2] Sara Glazer, "Violence Against Women," CQ Researcher, *Congressional Quarterly Inc.*, Vol. 3, No. 8, February 1993, p. 171.

[3] Uniform Crime Reports as cited by M. C. Moewe, "The Hidden Violence: For Richer and For Poorer," Fort *Worth Star-Telegram*, April 5, 1992.[19]

(**Author's note:** These endnotes are as they appear in the article.)

COMMERCIALISM: Digging out of the Tinsel
Renee Ross

In the beginning of the Christmas season many Christian women like myself look forward to digging out the tinsel and other Christmas paraphernalia. There is a peace in a wintry Christmas evening while sitting alone in an easy chair in the quietness of the night, the only light coming from the fireplace and the twinkling lights of a large decorated tree.

However, too often the peace of the moment is short-lived as a mental list of unsurmountable demands of the season are contemplated – community, school, church, and yes, family responsibilities. There are programs, songs and music to learn, costumes to make, caroling, Christmas sacks to be bagged, candy and cookies to make, dinners to plan and cook, and oh, yes, gifts to buy and wrap.

Each Christmas much is often said regarding commercialization and the tinsel of the season. What do I mean by that statement?

World Book dictionary says, commercialism is the method and spirit of commerce. Commerce is buying and selling in large amounts between different places; business, it is trade.

Since primitive men traded sea shells, commercialism has existed in some form. It has become a very dominate characteristic of our age and country and is infecting even our children who cry for the cereal their favorite TV hero eats.

Tinsel figuratively is anything showy but having little value.

We note each year the stores are promoting Christmas sales even earlier and jump from Halloween to Christmas.

As Charles Swindoll has stated "It spooks Santa . . . pumpkins to presents . . . orange and black to red and green."

After all it is business and the highest selling period of the year. Many store managers say the doors of their business could not stay open without the holiday gift purchases.

How do we escape the commercialism of the season? How do we keep our giving from being just commerce, business, or trade? How do we avoid the tinsel, things that are showy but of little value?

It is interesting to me that Thanksgiving comes before Christmas. Is it any wonder that Satan would try to influence us to jump past a time that has been set aside to give thanks for the blessings of God? A time of quiet reflection upon the past and an annual reminder that God has again been ever so faithful. The solid and simple things of life are brought into clear focus, so much so that everything else fades into insignificance.

In Luke 2:8-20 we read the shepherds' encounter with our Lord Jesus at His birth and the wise men's experience with Him in Matthew 2:7-12. When entering His presence the Scripture says they worshipped, glorified and praised Him. The shepherds had begun in fear but left the Christ Child motivated to tell all they had heard and seen as it was told unto them. The wise men started their search for the Messiah deceived by Herod. After entering the house where the baby and Mary, his mother, were and throwing themselves down to worship Him, they left for home truly wise for God had warned them of the deceit and wickedness of Herod. His birth stands as a reminder to us each year that He came to us right in the middle of our need. It is a time of hope and reassurance of His love for those who will press on and worship and praise Him.

Let us return to the manger and behold our Messiah and we too will join the host of heaven singing, "Glory to God in the highest and on earth peace, good will toward men."[20]

(**Author's note:** Renee Ross was elected in August 1989 to serve on the General Women's Ministries Board. She is an ordained minister and serves on the East Oklahoma Conference/New Horizons Women's Ministries Board as president.)

FOCUS ON PRAYER
Mrs. C. F. Isaac

Prayer is speaking to God, in request, confession, or praise. The Bible does not explain the reason for prayer, rather it deals with it as a fact.

It is not necessary to learn a catchy formula or technique for effectual praying. Real prayer far transcends anything mechanical whether it be beads, wheels, beautiful phrases, or the memorized petitions of a stately liturgy.

The Almighty is addressed from the heart; faltering lips are only the vehicle of the soul's yearning. The dumb are not barred from prayer, nor the slow of speech, nor the illiterate.

Prayer at once becomes both the duty and privilege of every believer in Christ; it is the heart line, the royal road to the heavenlies. Through prayer the Word of God is made plain, faith becomes quickened and obedience possible.

Jesus said that men ought to pray and not to faint. Paul urged the Thessalonians to pray without ceasing. Prayer must be constant and continue as long as we live. Just as the destitute widow prolonged her pleas until she was avenged of her adversary, so must we pray until death or the rapture releases us from this duty.

We should not only pray constantly, denoting an attitude of continual contact with God, but also at definite times. This will require setting aside periods of time for prayer. In our fluid society it will not always be possible to observe such set hours as Daniel did or even to pray at morning, noon, and night as David did. But prayer time can be adjusted and faithfully kept even though we might be on the 'swing shift' or a changing schedule.

For the end-time believer special anointing in prayer has been made available. This is one of the more important aspects of the Pentecostal experience. Pentecost connects one with that power in prayer enjoyed by the early church. With Paul, Spirit-filled believers can say, "I pray with the Spirit and with the understanding also."

This praying in the Holy Spirit can lead to a fruitful field of soul-winning through intercession. A Christian in England tells how she spent an entire morning under a heavy burden, praying in the Holy Ghost, speaking in a language of heaven. At the close of her prayer it was revealed to her that the Spirit had been pleading, through her, for her unsaved loved ones. Within that month all of her family was brought to a saving knowledge of Christ.

June Carter, one of our own missionaries, stayed on her knees, praying in the Spirit, until a wayward young man was smitten by heavy conviction and brought that very day to Christ. Many such prayer warriors are needed to intercede for lost souls.

Unprecedented opportunities for intercession through prayer will be presenting themselves to the women of our church during the month of April. It is not without design that an emphasis on prayer has been placed on the W. A. Calendar in the same month that the church is launching a Simultaneous Revival program. Women are urged to take their place along with those men who "lift up holy hands without wrath and doubting," to pray God's blessings on the church and the lost.

God wishes to work through us in the exercise of prayer to bring to pass His purposes on earth. "Thy will be done on earth" is breathed in the closet of prayer and brought forth on the harvest fields of the world."[21]

---

[1] Blanche King, *The Pentecostal Message*, pp. 116-124.
[2] Mary Ford, *The Pentecostal Message, Number Two*, pp. 107-113.
[3] Eulah Taylor, *The Advocate*, April 3, 1952, pp. 5-6, 14-15; April 10, 1952, pp. 12-13.
[4] Beulah Taylor, *The Advocate*, September 11, 1952, p. 9.
[5] Ella Muncy, *The Advocate*, December 1985, pp. 10-11.
[6] Violet Curlee, *The Advocate*, April 1994, pp. 8-9.
[7] Dessie McCurley, *The Advocate*, March 6 & 13, 1919, pp. 4-5.
[8] Rita Wrenn, *The Advocate*, January 11, 1980, p. 13.
[9] Ruth Johnson, *The Advocate*, August 1994, pp. 4-5.
[10] Jeraldine Posey, *The Advocate*, April 1994, pp. 4-5.
[11] Charlene West, *Evangelism USA*, April 1996, p. 7.
[12] Ruth Heath, *The Advocate*, September 7, 1950, pp. 5-6.
[13] Dr. Lydia Figueroa, *IPHC Experience*, May 2009, pp. 10-11.
[14] Ruth Moore, *The Helping Hand*, January 1954, pp. 12-13.
[15] Susan Wells, *The Challenge*, Winter 2000, p. 5.
[16] www.iphc.org., Ministries and Divisions, *i*WIN.
[17] Hazeleen Graham, *The Challenge*, Summer 1989, pp. 6-7.
[18] Chaplain Christy Sorrow, *Issachar File*, August 2003, p. 4.
[19] Deborah Riley, *IPHC Experience*, September 2004, pp. 10-11.
[20] Renee Ross, *The Helping Hand*, November-December 1990, p. 7.
[21] Mrs. C. F. Isaac, *The Helping Hand*, April 1962, pp. 3, 7.

CHAPTER 11

God Has Spoken

"And afterward, I will pour out my Spirit on all people. Your sons and daughters will prophesy . . . Even on my servants, both men and women, I will pour out of my Spirit in those days" – Joel 2:28-29-NIV.

God spoke in centuries past through the prophet Joel to give these words about the infilling of the Holy Spirit. His promise was that this would occur "afterward . . . in those days." Primarily, this prophecy was for Israel in the day of its restoration after the devastating plague of locusts with a severe drought that had desolated the land. The prophet calls upon the nation to repent of their sins and ask God to spare the nation and its land. God hears, and the country is blessed with abundant harvest.[1] This incident is also the basis for a vision of the future and the ultimate restoration both in the tribulation and the reign of Messiah which follows it.[2] However, the Day of Pentecost saw another fulfillment of the prophecy as Peter indicates in his sermon on that occasion. In defense of his fellow believers who had been accused of drinking too much wine (Acts 2:13), he says, *"These men are not drunk, as you suppose . . . No, this is what was spoken by the prophet Joel"* – Acts. 2:15a, 16-NIV.

Peter's affirmation is that God had spoken in another age, and He had kept His word by sending the Promise of the Father, the third person of the Godhead, in the century in which he lived. They were experiencing, to a further extent, the blessings God promised through Joel. Not only would the Lord shower Judah's fields with water, He also would fill their souls with spiritual rain at a later time.

"The fulfillment of Joel's prophecy that was manifested in the initial outpouring of the Spirit on the Day of Pentecost stretched into the first century and broke in periodic intervals during the Middle Ages and the Reformation until He was poured out again in its latter rain fullness near the close of the Nineteenth Century."[3] This blessing is to be poured out regardless of sex, age, or social status, as is clearly stated in Colossians 3:11, *"Here there is no Greek or Jew, circumcised or uncircumcised, barbarian,*

Scythian, slave or free, but Christ is all, and is in all"-NIV. The gift of the Spirit is wide enough to encompass all who believe, regardless.

Men and women spilled out of that upper room empowered by God to share jointly in the responsibility of spreading the "Good News" about the crucified, risen, and glorified Son of God. Jesus' "Go" was not limited to the male gender.

This book is an attempt to spotlight women who have heard and answered the call of God to preach. He spoke to them in various ways to get their attention and response, but often others tried to get in the way and thwart God's plan because they were opposed to women preachers. They could not and will not find any scriptural injunction forbidding women to fill pulpits. Their objections are based simply on prejudice, opinion, and personal preference. Those folk have elevated themselves to positions that cause them to feel they know more about this than God knows. He spoke (called) in days gone by, He speaks (calls) now, and will continue to speak (call) in the future as long as there is a need to spread the Word.

The early women ministers were truly pioneers and suffered hardship in blazing a gospel trial in homes, school houses, brush arbors, churches, hospitals, and on street corners. Not only did they face opposition because they were women, the ones who ministered in the late nineteenth and early twentieth century faced those who were unwilling to accept the holiness movement.

They suffered fear for their lives when shots were fired; when individuals threatened them with hanging and bodily harm in various other ways; when stones and rotten vegetables were thrown at them; when they were whipped, spit upon, drenched with slop water, egged, and slandered. Yet, they continued to preach because they were willing to sacrifice anything, even their lives, because of their love for Jesus.

The majority of the first women preachers had little education, but their school of learning was found in the Bible. They read it to find out what God had for them, so what they knew was based on the truths of God's Word. The Holy Spirit was their teacher; He led them into the revelation of the deeper experiences (sanctification and the baptism of the Holy Spirit) sometimes even before they heard others preach about it. They could not go wrong so long as they depended on God's Spirit. Their heart's desire was to share these wondrous blessings with others who needed to receive them.

These ladies dug thousands out of the pit of sin as they preached in out-of-the way places or in churches. Their pulpits were anywhere there was a sinner to be reached or a Christian to be spurred on. No place was too rugged for them. They were never sorry for the sacrifices they made or the gross indignities they suffered.

While on the home front, these dear ones were also wives and mothers often bearing and rearing a large family (as many as eleven children) and working alongside their husbands to run a farm. They milked cows, raised chickens, picked cotton, drove the tractor, and fed the livestock.

Because of the efforts of these forerunners, life has been a bit easier for women preachers in the latter part of the twentieth century and into the present one. That is not to say that they have not been refused opportunities to fill pulpits and been told they should not speak out in church services. They have suffered hurt, though perhaps not physically like those first pathfinders.

In more recent years, the ladies have gone into jails/prisons, nursing homes, hospice care units, and hospitals ministering in ways the earlier preachers could not have. Ways and means have changed; technology at our disposal has advanced; but the message is the same: Jesus saves! Millions still hear the "joyful sound" because women are willing to carry the tidings of salvation to the lost and encouragement to the redeemed.

Some have chosen rather unconventional ways to reach others, but even if they are chainsaw artists, bikers, street painters, counselors, teachers, pastors, or evangelists, they, no doubt, know what God expects from them and make every effort to minister.

The majority of those who responded to the survey used to solicit information for this book state that they have experienced difficulty because they are lady ministers and that fact has been the greatest hindrance to what they are trying to do for the Lord. This criticism has come for men and women alike. A few respondents indicate that they have not detected any reluctance on the part of anyone, male or female, to accept them.

The earliest lady minister of record is Berta Maxwell whose name appears on the roll for the Eighth Annual Convention of the North Carolina Conference, November 20, 1907. She joined the conference six years earlier in 1901. Sketchy information about Sister Maxwell is included in Chapter 7.

The Pentecostal Holiness Church formed in 1907 in Falcon, North Carolina listed two women among the eight original ordained ministers. In addition, a goodly number of other women served in evangelistic and ministerial capacities.[4] In 1911, the names of three women are listed in the minutes of the Twelfth Annual Convention of the North Carolina Conference: Mrs. F. M. Britton, Annie Cotton, and Berta Maxwell. The records for the Thirteenth Annual Convention, held on November 19-21, 1912, show there were five lady preachers: Mrs. F. M. Britton, Annie Cotton, Dovie Dunn, Berta Maxwell, and Beadie Noble. As the years passed, more and more women were moving up into the ranks of licensed and ordained ministers in their respective conferences, especially after the consolidation of the Pentecostal Holiness Church with the Fire Baptized Holiness Church. Until the time of the merger, the history of the two organizations was separate.

Dr. Vinson Synan in his book *The Holiness-Pentecostal Movement in the United States* addresses the subject of women clergy in the Pentecostal Holiness Church. "Another Pentecostal practice that varied from the norm of other churches was that of allowing women to preach. The holiness movement had long allowed women to preach, basing its action on the prophecy in Joel 2:28 . . . the pentecostals by the middle of the twentieth century probably had more women preachers than any other branch of Christianity."

He states that the Pentecostal Holiness Church had 473 women ministers out of a total of 2,638 in 1966.[5] This figure indicates that almost 18 percent of the preachers were female. Of course, over time that number has increased steadily. Perhaps because it has been easier for more women to answer God's call, the conferences have been more willing to allow them to pastor and evangelize, and the people in the congregations have been more tolerant.

Look again at these women whose names appear on the pages of this book. Really look at them as more than names on a page. See them as real people who at one time in the past or in the present have taken on the responsibilities of a minister of the gospel. See them as soldiers of the cross. See them as trail blazers. See them on an equal level with men who have the same calling. Release them to operate in the gifts given them by the omniscient God who knows all things. His wisdom is above ours. Often he has called the most unlikely people to do His work. Get behind these women, let them know you love and respect them, encourage them in the Lord, and let these handmaids speak.

---

[1] H. T. Sell, *Bible Study by Books*, p. 126.
[2] Charles Lee Feinberg, *Joel, Amos, and Obadiah the Major Messages of the Minor Prophets*, p. 27.
[3] H. P. Robinson, *Focus on Doctrine*, p. 38.
[4] Dr. Harold Hunter, Centennial Notes, July 20, 2010, www.IPHC.org
[5] Dr. Vinson Synan, p. 188. (Footnote in his book, *The Pentecostal Holiness Advocate*, July 11, 1918, p. 6.)

Bibliography

Beacham, Paul F., D.D., *Questions and Answers on the Scriptures and Related Subjects*, The Publishing House, Pentecostal Holiness Church, Franklin Spring, Georgia, 1950, pp. 527-528.

Campbell, Joseph E., Th.D., *The Pentecostal Holiness Church 1898-1948*, The Publishing House, Pentecostal Holiness Church, Franklin Springs, Georgia, 1951, pp. 233-234, 332-333. 336-337.

Feinberg, Charles Lee, *Joel, Amos, and Obadiah, the Major Messages of the Minor Prophets*, American Board of Missions to the Jews, Inc., New York, 1948, p. 27.

Ford, Rev. Mary, "Obedience," *The Pentecostal Message Number Two*, The Publishing House, Pentecostal Holiness Church, Franklin Springs, Georgia, 1953, pp. 107-113.

Hunter, Dr. Harold, "Centennial Notes," (www.IPHC.org).

King, Blanche, "God's Calling – His Enabling," *The Pentecostal Message*, The Publishing House, Pentecostal Holiness Church, Franklin Spring, Georgia, 1950, pp. 116-124.

King, J. H., *Yet Speaketh*, The Publishing House, Pentecostal Holiness Church, Franklin Spring, Georgia, 1949; Foreword by Mrs. Blanche Leon King.

Laird, Charlton, *Webster's New World Thesaurus*, The World Publishing Company, New York, 1971, p. 669.

Malcolm, Kari, *Women at the Crossroads*, Intervarsity Press, Downes Grove, Illinois, 1982, pp. 97-98.

Marsh, Mandana, "Minister and Teacher Pens Devotional Book," *The Hopewell News*, February 8, 2005. Copyright 2005. Reprinted with permission.

Paul, Harold, *From Printer's Devil to Bishop*, Advocate Press, Franklin Springs, Georgia, pp. 131-136.

Pharr, Jim, "Woman Minister is Active," *The Fayetteville Observer*, September 23, 1977. Copyright 1977. Reprinted with permission.

Robinson, H. P., *Focus on Doctrine*, Advocate Press, Franklin Springs, Georgia, [no publication date], p. 38.

Sell, H. T., *Bible Study by Books*, Fleming H. Revell Company, New York, 1926, p. 126.

Synan, Dr. Vinson, *The Holiness-Pentecostal Movement in the United States*, William B. Eerdmans Publishing Company, Grand Rapids, Michigan, 1971, p. 188. (Footnote in his book, *The Pentecostal Holiness Advocate*, July 11, 1918, p. 6.)

Vincent, Marvin, R., D.D., "The Epistle to the Romans," *Word Studies in the New Testament*, William B. Eerdmans Publish Company, Grand Rapids, Michigan, 1989, p. 2.

Wuest, Kenneth S, "Philippians in the Greek New Testament," *Word Studies in the Greek New Testament*, Vol. II, William B. Eerdmans Publishing Company, Grand Rapids, Michigan, 1966, p. 108.

THE PENTECOSTAL HOLINESS CHURCH YEAR BOOK, Advocate Press, Franklin Springs, Georgia:

1925
1932
1933
1947
1952
1971

Periodicals

The Advocate, Advocate Press, Franklin Springs, Georgia:

Advertisement for Greta Campbell Trio record "Lead Me Saviour," January 1969, p. 5.

Barnett, J. L., "Fourth Quarterly Conference of the Franklin Springs District of the Annual Conference of Georgia," October 11, 1919, p. 4.

Brown, Betty, "Twenty-Five Experiences in Yadkinvill," October 31, 1964.

Brown, Rev. Marvin, "The Advocate Salutes Martha Roberta Rose," May 13, 1979, p. 11.

Carter, Rev. W. W., "Late Flowers," November 30, 1950, pp. 4-5.

Casey, Mrs. Lorene, "Pastor Resigns at Okmulgee, Oklahoma," August 3, 1957, p. 8.

Curlee, Violet, "Song of the Shepherd," April 1994, pp. 8-9.

Dillard, Gertrude Blake, "Seventy-eight Years of Christian Service, August 11, 1973, p. 7.

------"First Woman Superintendent Appointed," June 1984, p. 15.

Fletcher, Lorene, "Old Fashion Brush Arbor Revival," November 13, 1969.

------"From Sister Goff," November 17, 1952.

Garner, Rev. Lelan, "Revival at Greenwood Church," April 12, 1969.

------"Georgia Conference Minutes," February 5, 1920, p. 14.

Hayes, Rev. R. B., "Women Preaching," July 11, 1918, p. 6.

Heath, Ruth, "Holmes Bible College Report," September 7, 1950, pp. 5-6.

Inman, Rev. Elsie, "Southern California, 'This is God's House,'" May 14, 1953, p. 17.

Johnson, Ruth, "Caring For a Flock of Suffering Sheep," August 1994, pp. 4-5.

King, Blanche Leon, "Among the Women," October 5, 1950, p. 10.

------, "Among the Women," January 11, 1951, p. 9.

Liles, Rev. Henrietta, "Work in San Benito," December 4, 1952.

Massey, Rev. Ray, "Greta Campbell Trio Conducts Revival at Langley," June 30, 1973.

McCurley, Mrs. Dessie, "Inspiring Thoughts From the Prophets," March 6, 13, 1919.

------"1978 King Memorial Lectures," September 10, 1978, p. 20.

------"Minutes of the Anderson District of the Upper South Carolina Conference," May 13, 1920, p. 6.

------"Minutes of the Second Quarterly Conference of the Griffin District of the Georgia Conference," May 20, 1920, pp. 2-3.

------"Minutes of the Second Quarterly Conference of the Mountain Park District, Oklahoma," March 25, 1920, p. 6.

------"Minutes of the Second Quarterly Conference of the Oklahoma District," March 4, 1920, p. 20.

------"Minutes of the Third Quarterly Conference of the Wagoner District, Oklahoma Conference," June 3, 1920, p. 4.

------"Minutes of the Fourth General Conference of the Pentecostal Holiness Church," May 1921.

Morgan, N. T., "First Quarterly Conference of the Oklahoma District," November 27 and December 4, 1919, p. 6.

------"Quarterly Conference," July 13, 1919, p. 7.

Morris, Rev. Eddie, "A Mother's Day Tribute to," May 14, 1978, pp. 9, 15.

Muncy, Ella, "Hidden Treasures," December 1985.

------"Oildale Church Reports," March 3, 1955.

Peyton, Rev. C. J., "Revival Continues in Pulaski," February 28, 1952.

Posey, Jeraldine, ". . . In Jerusalem . . . My Hometown," April 1994, pp. 4-5.

------"Rev. and Mrs. L. B. Edge Observe Thirty-five Years in the Ministry," August, 25, 1955, p. 2.

------"Revival Schedule for Pearl Benz," November 16, 1950.

------"Report of Stationing Committee, North Carolina Conference," December 18, 1919, p. 6.

Shealy, Lois, "Revival in Batesburg," October 2, 1952.

Smith, Alfred, "Twenty-Seven Experiences in Braggs Revival," October 31, 1964.

Smith, Arthur, "First Quarterly Conference of the Wagoner District, Oklahoma," November 20, 1919, p. 14.

Sorrow, Christy, "Conversation with a Female Chaplain," May 1996, pp. 12-13.

Taylor, Beulah, "Christian Freedom vs. Pagan License," April 10, 1952, p. 9.

Taylor, Eulah, "The Will of God Your Sanctification," April 3 & 10, 1952, pp. 5-6, 12-15.

------, "Thirty Experiences in Del City, Oklahoma Revival," March 3, 1955.

------, "Turner Conducts Revival in Carthage, North Carolina," March 17, 1955.

Waters, Mrs. Maxine, "Revival at Roanoke Rapids," May 24, 1969.

Williams, Rev. Arthur, "Old Time Revival," January 10, 1952.

York, Thurnace, "My Grandmother, Dollie York, Was a P. H. Pioneer," November 6, 1958, p. 12.

The Challenge, The South Carolina Conference of the IPHC, Inc., Lake City, South Carolina:

------, "Cana of Galilee Church," Spring/Summer, 2010.

------, "Celebrating Faithfulness," Summer 2005, back page.

Coker, Rev. Leona, "The Potter's House," Spring 1992, p. 9.

------, "Evangelists Linda Faber and Shelby Jeffcoat Available," Winter 1973, p. 13.

------, "Fires of Revival and Evangelism at Lancaster First Church," Spring 1989.

------"Full time Evangelists," December 1961.

Graham, "Our Responsibility to the Great Commission," Summer 1989, pp. 6-7.

------, "Hispanic Church News," Fall 2006, p. 18.

Kreigbaum, Ann, "Christian Academy," Winter 2002.

------, "Lula Mae Putnam," Winter 1970, p. 5; Winter 1971, p. 3; Spring 1972, pp. 6, 9; Spring 1978, p. 7; Summer 1982, p. 8; Summer 1993.

------, "Margie Tanner," Winter 2005, p. 4.

------, "A Passion for God," Spring 2000.

------, "Reverend Natalie Carnes Honored," Spring 1970, p. 4.

------, "Revival at Wagener, South Carolina," Spring 2000.

Sanders, Rev. Kristen, "Spotlight on Children's Ministry," Fall 2008.

Strickland, Janice, "I Am a Woman," Fall 1994.

------, "Thelma Player Honored," Fall 2007.

------, "Tribute to Rev. Nita Alexander," Summer 1980, pp. 3-4.

Wells, "What A Great God We Serve," Winter 2000.

------"Women Evangelists," Winter 1970.

The Co-Worker, Western North Carolina Conference, Browns Summit, North Carolina:

------, "Report of Revivals" (Conducted by Rev. Effie Roberson), 1954, pp. 3-4, 6.

The Evangel, North Carolina Conference, Falcon, North Carolina.

------, "Deborah Williams," February 1992, p. 4.

Huggins, Mrs. I. M., "Sermon of the Month," April 1969, p. 5.

Lundy, Dr. Ray, "In Memory," July 1995, p. 3.

Jarvis, Rev. Viola B., "Lowland and Hobucken Have Great Revivals," March 1951.

Thomas, Mrs. Moses, "Abbotsburg Reporting Best Revival in Church History," May 1949.

------"Youth Camp Speakers," June 1969.

Obituaries: January 1964, April & July 1969, August 1975, October 1977, July 1991, January 1993, January/February 1994, December 2002, July & November 2003, February 2006.

Evangelism USA, LifeSprings Resources, Franklin Springs, Georgia.

------, "Prayer and Prophetic Evangelism," November/December 1997, p. 4.

------ "Riley, Deborah Williams," Spring 2001, back page.

West, Charlene, "Intercultural Ministries," August/September 1997, p. 6.

------, "Let's Break Down Dividing Walls," April 1996, p. 7.

Whipple, Debbie, "Taking Control Of The Air, Before Sending In The Ground Troops," January/February 1999, p. 2.

The Experience, LifeSprings, Franklin Springs, Georgia.

Figueroa, Lydia, "Called to Abide," May 2009, pp. 10-11.

------, "Meet Charlene West," January 2004, p. 11.

Riley, Deborah, "A Hidden Heart," September 2004, pp. 10-11.

Stewart, Jewell, (Article about Mrs. Lila Isaac), September 2006, p. 9.

------, "Tarpley Commissioned as Second Female PH Air Force Chaplain," September 2005, p. 16.

Vaughan, Patsy, "Out-of-the-Box Thinking for Women Ministers," October 2008, pp. 20-21.

Whipple, Debbie, "Don't Treat Me Like I'm Dying," March 2006, pp. 6-7.

The Helping Hand, Advocate Press, Franklin Springs, Georgia.

Cohn, Mrs. J. R., "Our President," November 1953, pp. 10-11.

------, "The First General Vice-President," September 1961, p. 12.

Flowers, Alfreda, "General W. A. President, Mrs. Lila Isaac," July 1977, p. 5

------, "General Vice-President," September 1961, p. 13.

Goodman, Nelle, "Julie," July/August 1986, p. 5.

Hoag, Rev. Mary, "Truxall Auxiliary," June 1954, p. 10.

Isaac, Mrs. C. F., "Focus on Prayer," April 1962, pp. 3, 7.

Kamleiter, Mark and Judy, "Women in our Heritage," March 1977, pp. 4-5.

King, Blanche L., "Conference President in Fatal Accident," January 1961, p. 6.

McGraw, Ann, "The Hands of a Shepherdess," November/December 1995, p. 13.

Moore, Doris, "My Friend . . . My Spiritual Mother," May/June 1986, p. 3.

Moore, Ruth, "Rahab's Name was Listed With the Heroes of Faith," January 1954, pp. 12-13.

------, "Our W. A. Officials," October 1961, p. 4.

Robinson, Agnes, "A Great Lady," August 1, 1977, p. 10.

------, "Women Can Make a Difference in Their Worlds," May/June 1986, pp. 4-5.

Rohde, Shirley Spengler, "Woman's Touch," January/February, 1988, pp. 6-7.

Ross, Renee, "Digging out of the Tinsel," November/December 1990, p. 7.

Russell, Mrs. J. L., Sr., "Women in our Heritage," April 1977, pp, 3-4.

Thurman, Mrs. Carl, "Thoughts From the President," December 1954, pp. 7-8.

Tripp, Lois, "Winter . . . then Spring – Summer . . . Sunset," May/June 1986, p. 3.

------, "WOMEN – Liberated to Minister," January/February 1988, p. 3.

Issachar File, LifeSprings Resources, Franklin Springs, Georgia.

Leggett, Bishop James, "Affirming Women in Ministry," March 1999, p. 2.

Ridings, Dean, "Some Leaders are Born Women," March 1999, pp. 1, 3-4.

Sorrow, Christy, "Practical Ways to Support Our Military Heroes," August 2003, p. 4.

Spencer, Shirley, "A Woman with a Mandate from God," March 4, 1999, p. 4.

Virginia Conference News – Appalachian Conference Messenger, Virginia/Appalachian Conference, Dublin, Virginia.

------, "Available for Revivals, Women's Meetings," March 1998, p. 3.

------, "The Cericolas Ready to Serve," January 2005.

------, "Elizabeth Lynne Gilliam," August 2001, p. 3.

------, "Greenville First in Spiritual Quest," March 1995.

------, "International Evangelist Available," May 1995, p. 5.

Jones, Mrs. W. B., "Mrs. Campbell in Revival at Bethel," February 1956.

------, "Lee McKenzie and Vickie Viars," 1998.

Long, Rev. A. M. "Salem [Virginia] Enjoys Another Good Revival," June 1996.

Moss, Bernard, "Mrs. Campbell in Richmond" [Virginia], December 1955.

------, "Mrs. Campbell Conducts Revival at Redland, N. C.," November 1955.

------, "Mrs. Campbell Conducts Revival with the St. John P. H. Church," March 1956.

Myers, Wanda, "Women's Ministries," October 2004, p. 6.

------, "New Church in Staunton [Virginia] Organized," December 1991, p. 7.

------, "New Sanctuary in Tazwell" [Virginia], September 1996, p. 2.

------, "Rev. Kathy Sandlin and Sharon Hartman," 2000.

------, "Rev. Kathy Sandlin to Speak at June 3 WM Convention," May 2005, p. 5.

------, "Rev. Vela Sizemore," January 2001.

------, "Roderfield Honors Pastor," January 2006, back page.

Story, Mrs. D. J., "Sister Campbell at White Sulphur," 1954.

------, "Tazwell Church Experiences Miracles," July 2002, p. 8.

Todd, Rev. O. N., Jr., "Mrs. Campbell in Birmingham" [Alabama], December 1955.

Miscellaneous

"Deborah's Daughters Newsletters," August 2006, December 2006, August 2007, January 2009, August 2009, January 2010.

Hubbard, Oris, e-mails received from him dated August 5 & 6, 2010.

Knowles, Pauline, personal information in respondent form and biographical sketch.

Knowles, Rita, letter to the author.

Marshburn, Dr. Janice, e-mail to the author dated February 4, 2010.

Waddell, Rev. Dr. Maxine, Chair, Board of Directors, AJAMM Ministries International, Inc., e-mail dated February 10, 2011.

Whitfield, Bishop Jim, letter to the author, April 22, 2010.

Acknowledgement

A work of this magnitude cannot be done without the assistance of a number of people who are very important to obtaining information and verifying the accuracy of that material.

First, I thank my daughter, Joye Slife, librarian at Emmanuel College, for making the archives there available to me. She put up with my harassment on many occasions to find something for me or cover my tracks when I had failed to obtain all the necessary information. She patiently dealt with me when she had other things to keep her occupied and also put us to bed and fed her dad and me on our visits there to look for gems. Joye has been a valuable research assistant.

Second, I thank my husband, Frank, who has been my right hand in research and has accompanied me on the trips I have taken to look for material. He also has put up with disrupted routines and my preoccupation with working on the manuscript.

Third, I thank my daughter, Pam, who has edited and proofed the book. It is a humbling experience to have one of your children "check your work." I needed another eye on the manuscript to detect those abominable typos, since spell-check does not catch them all.

Fourth, my grandson Reuben Slife also read part of the manuscript and made some good suggestions for improving the writing.

Special thanks also go the Rev. Larry Jones, Archivist in the South Carolina Conference; Mrs. Betty Thompson, Archivists in the North Carolina Conference; Shirley Spencer, Executive Editor of Publications of the IPHC; Marilyn Hudson, Director of Library Services at Southwestern Christian University; Dr. Kristen Welch, Assistant Professor of English at Longwood University; Dr. Janice Marshburn, Director of Deborah's Daughters and Women's Ministries in the North Carolina Conference; Bishop Dayton Birt, Redemption Ministries Conference; and Bonnie Conrad, Executive Assistant to the Bishop, Redemption Ministries Conference. All of these folk made a positive contribution in helping me gather information by opening their archives to me or pointing me in the right direction to make another contact.

May God smile on you.

About the Author

Dr. Posey's ministry unofficially started before she was twenty years old as a student at Holmes Bible College in Greenville, South Carolina from October 1949 to May 1952. Officially, her ministry began when she was licensed in the Eastern Virginia Conference (Redemption Ministries) of the International Pentecostal Holiness Church (IPHC) the same year she graduated from Holmes. Later, she was the first woman minister to be ordained by that conference, where she served two churches as interim pastor.

After graduating from Holmes, the president, Dr. Paul F. Beacham, invited her back to teach, and she was on the faculty a year and a half. She left Holmes to marry Francis Posey, who also had been a student and faculty member at the school until he was drafted into the Army during the Korean Conflict. They were missionaries in Lusaka, Zambia (Northern Rhodesia) with Rev. and Mrs. John Guthrie.

She earned a bachelor of theology degree at Holmes Bible, a bachelor of science and a master of arts degree in English from Virginia Commonwealth University in Richmond, Virginia, and a doctor of ministry degree from Bethany Theological Seminary located in Dothan, Alabama.

Dr. Posey's happiest times are when she is studying, preaching or teaching. That has been her passion for a number of years and has proven to be that which has kept her in a relationship with God. She feels that one cannot get any closer to Him than to see His nature, character, and attributes unfold as you apply yourself to study and ministry.

She also enjoys writing and has published two books: *Gleanings for Private Devotion* and *God Is . . . In The Psalms*.

She and her husband have four children, six grandchildren, and a great granddaughter. Their oldest daughter, Pam Parsons, is an in-house employment lawyer for a Fortune 500 company in Charlotte, North Carolina; the youngest daughter, Joye Slife, is librarian at Emmanuel College in Franklin Springs, Georgia and also has been librarian at Holmes Bible College; the oldest son, Kevin, is a contractor in Midlothian, Virginia; the youngest son, Todd, an alumnus of Emmanuel College and Virginia State University, is a Licensed Professional Counselor and a Licensed Clinical Addictions Specialist. He is Program Director for the Fletcher Center in Danville, Virginia. He is also an ordained minister in the Cornerstone Conference of the IPHC.

Made in the USA
Middletown, DE
20 December 2015